Zenescope Entertainment Presents:

Grimm Fairy Tales

Volume 10

D1059783

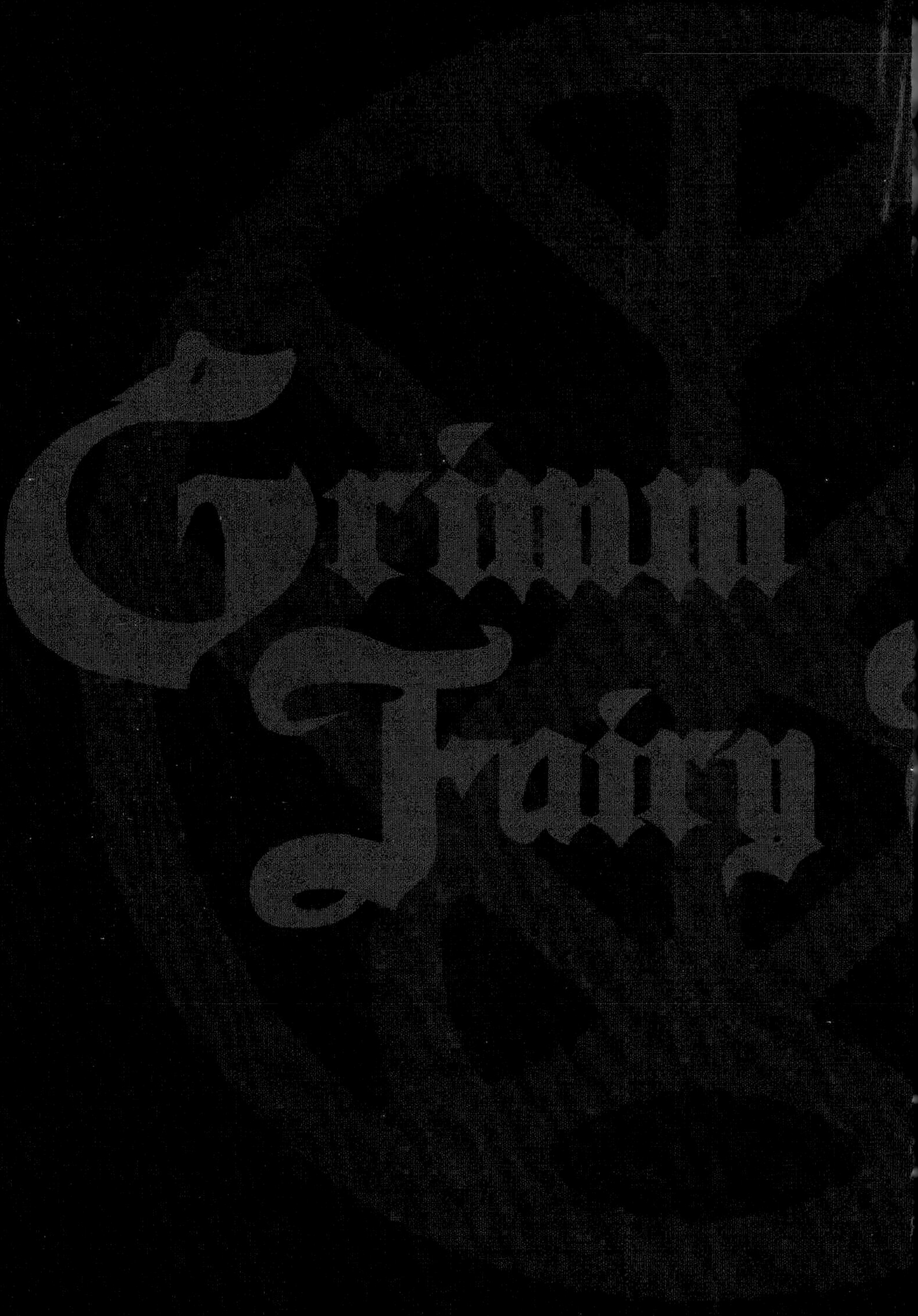
Grimm
Fairy

GRIMM FAIRY TALES

CREATED AND STORY BY
JOE BRUSHA
RALPH TEDESCO

TRADE DESIGN BY
CHRISTOPHER COTE

TRADE EDITED BY
RALPH TEDESCO

THIS VOLUME REPRINTS THE
COMIC SERIES GRIMM FAIRY TALES
ISSUES #57-62 AND THE DREAM
EATER SAGA ISSUE #0 PUBLISHED BY
ZENESCOPE ENTERTAINMENT

WWW.ZENESCOPE.COM

FIRST EDITION, SEPTEMBER 2011
ISBN: 978-0-9817550-4-5

WWW.ZENESCOPE.COM
ZENESCOPE ENTERTAINMENT, INC.

JOE BRUSHA - PRESIDENT
RALPH TEDESCO - V.P./ EDITOR-IN-CHIEF
ANTHONY SPAY- ART DIRECTOR
RAVEN GREGORY - EXECUTIVE EDITOR
CHRISTOPHER COTE - PRODUCTION MANAGER

Zenescope Entertainment presents:

Grimm Fairy Tales™ Volume 10

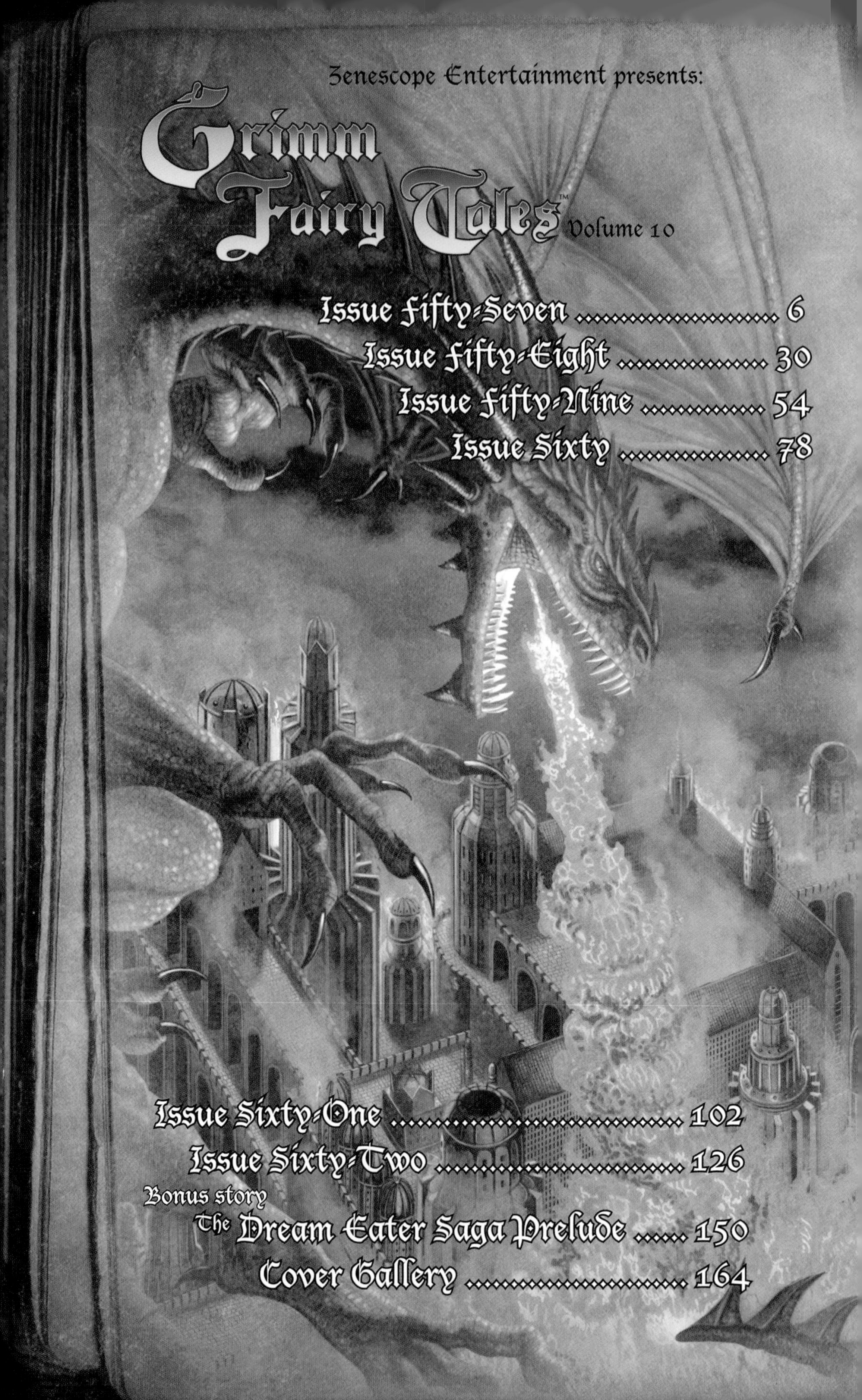

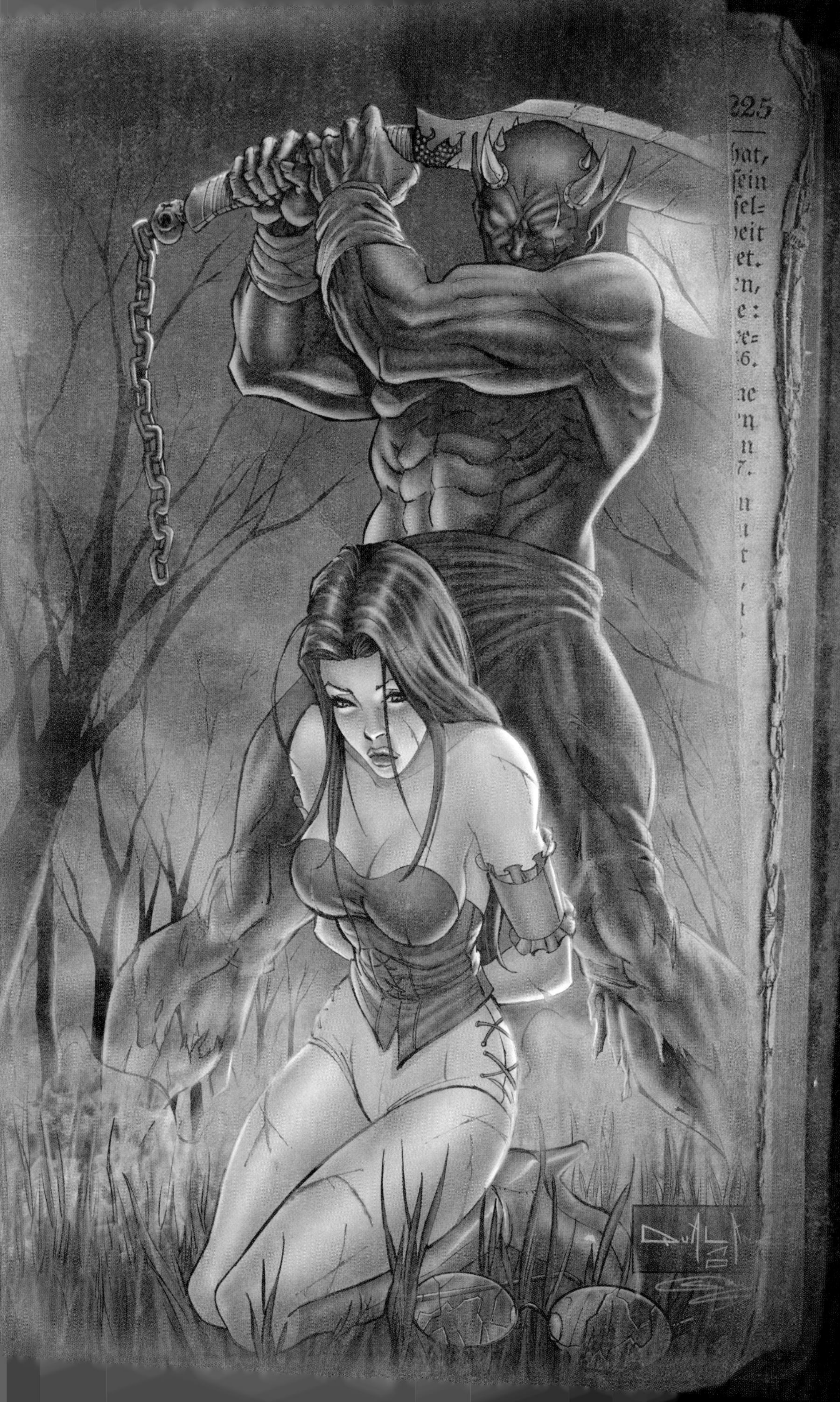

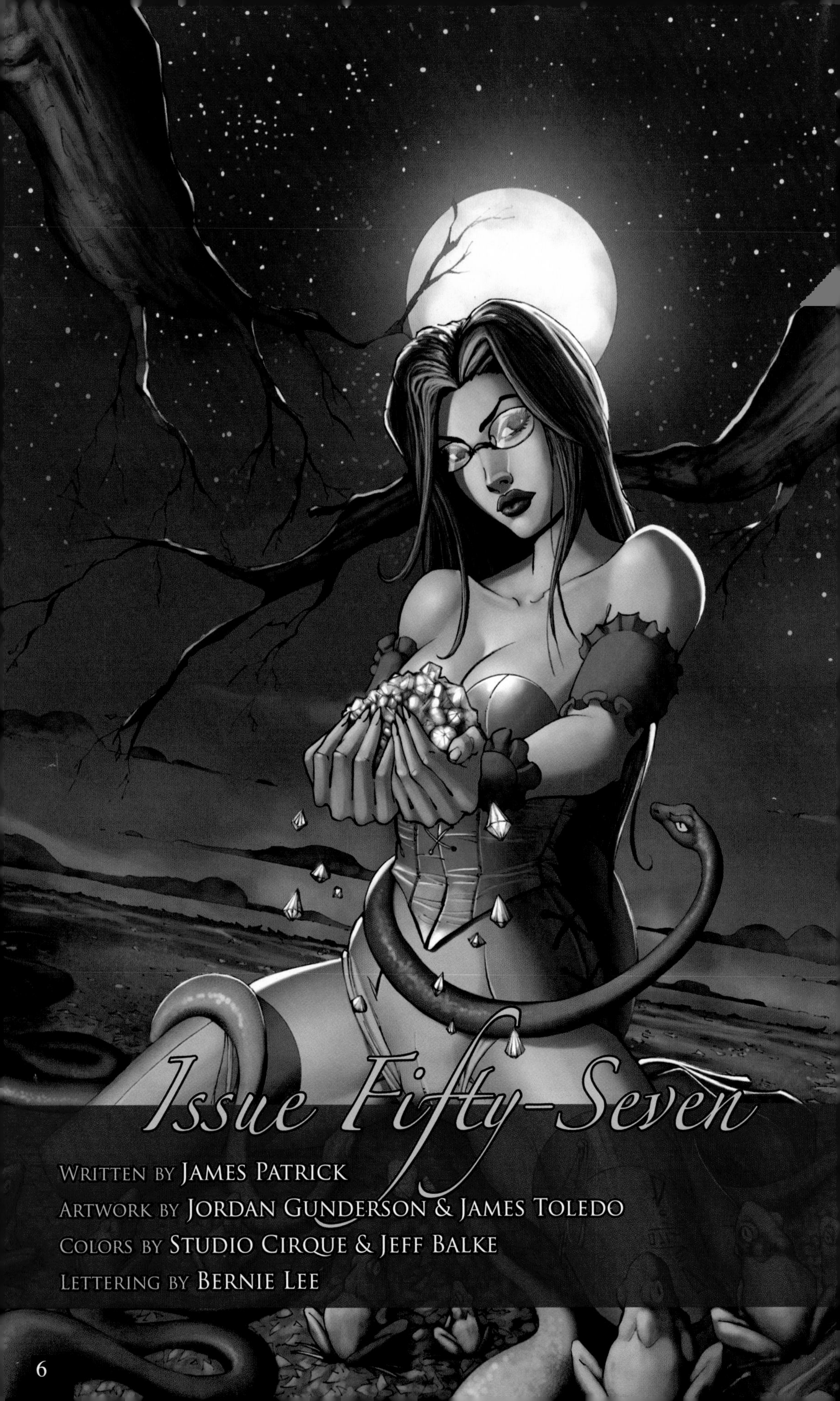

Issue Fifty-Seven

WRITTEN BY JAMES PATRICK
ARTWORK BY JORDAN GUNDERSON & JAMES TOLEDO
COLORS BY STUDIO CIRQUE & JEFF BALKE
LETTERING BY BERNIE LEE

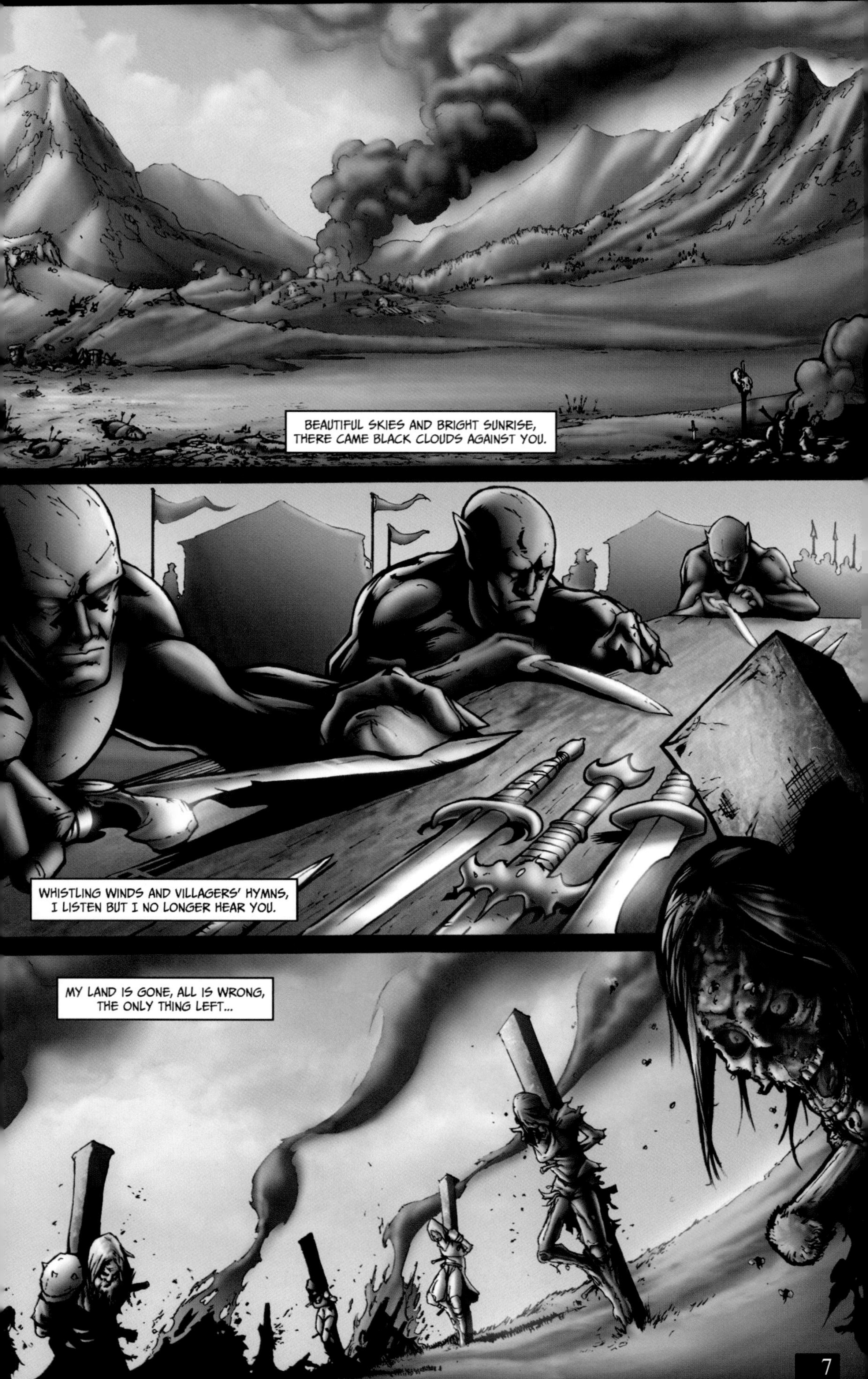
BEAUTIFUL SKIES AND BRIGHT SUNRISE, THERE CAME BLACK CLOUDS AGAINST YOU.
WHISTLING WINDS AND VILLAGERS' HYMNS, I LISTEN BUT I NO LONGER HEAR YOU.
MY LAND IS GONE, ALL IS WRONG, THE ONLY THING LEFT...

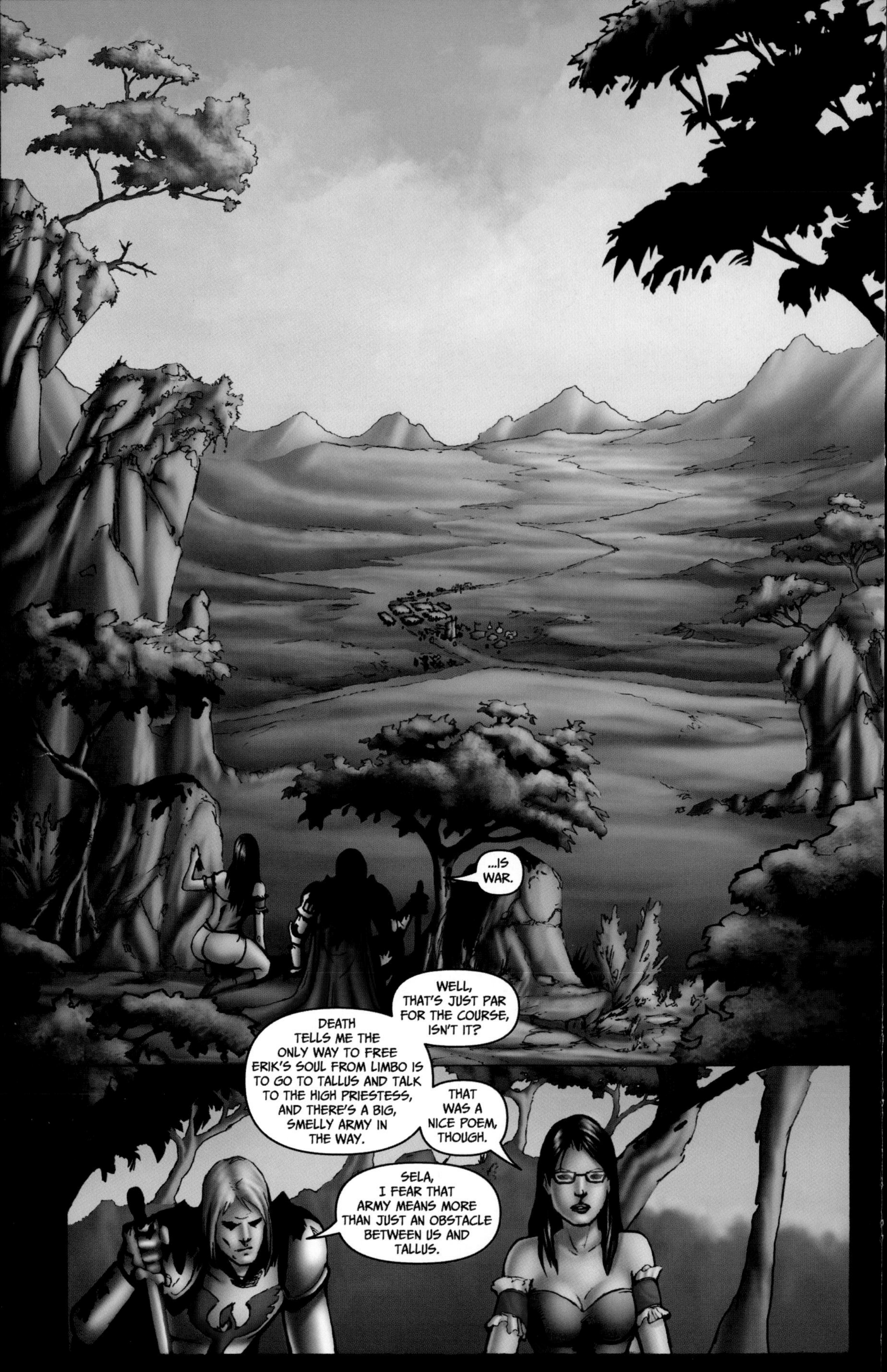
...IS WAR.
WELL, THAT'S JUST PAR FOR THE COURSE, ISN'T IT?
DEATH TELLS ME THE ONLY WAY TO FREE ERIK'S SOUL FROM LIMBO IS TO GO TO TALLUS AND TALK TO THE HIGH PRIESTESS, AND THERE'S A BIG, SMELLY ARMY IN THE WAY.
THAT WAS A NICE POEM, THOUGH.
SELA, I FEAR THAT ARMY MEANS MORE THAN JUST AN OBSTACLE BETWEEN US AND TALLUS.

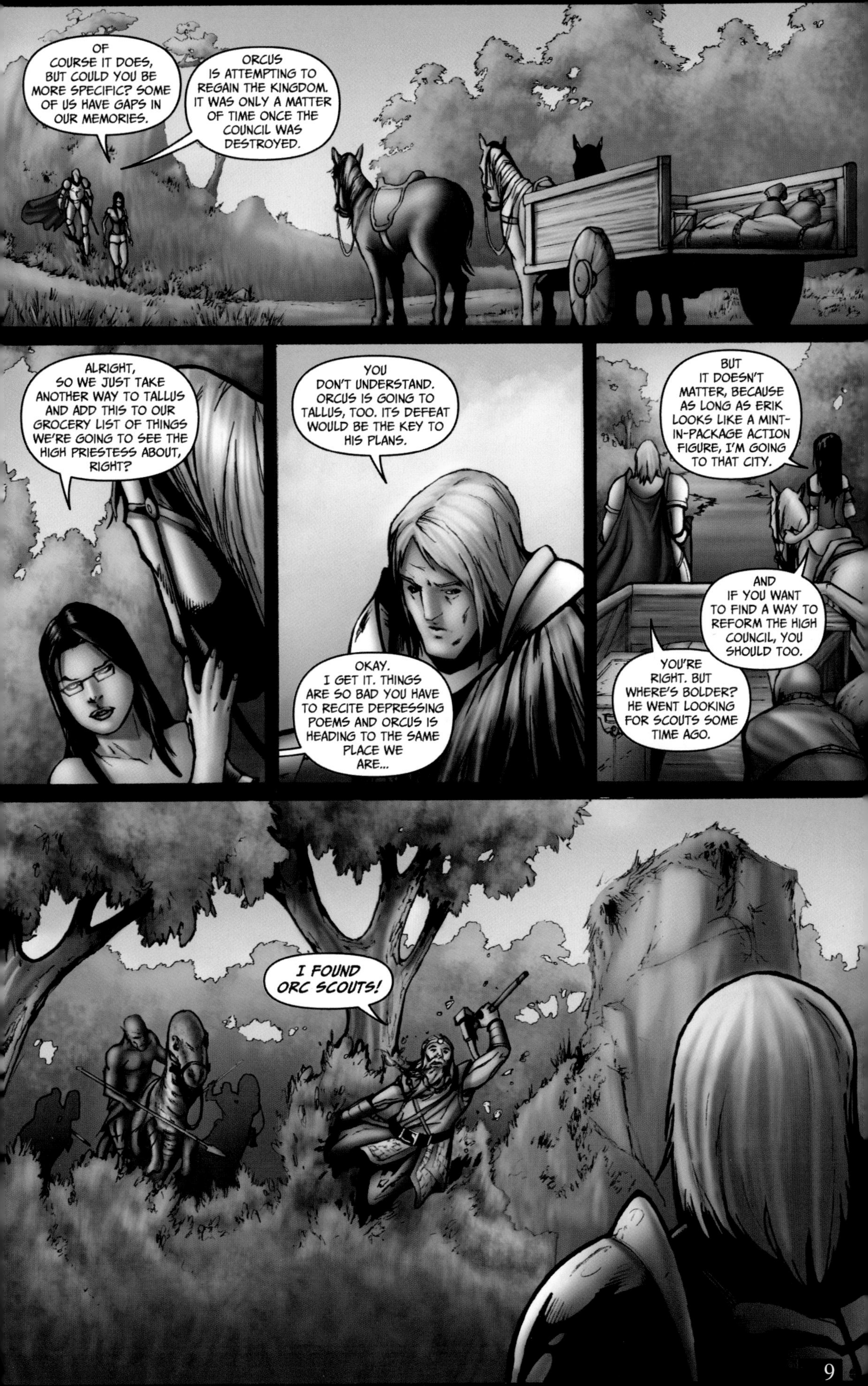
OF COURSE IT DOES, BUT COULD YOU BE MORE SPECIFIC? SOME OF US HAVE GAPS IN OUR MEMORIES.
ORCUS IS ATTEMPTING TO REGAIN THE KINGDOM. IT WAS ONLY A MATTER OF TIME ONCE THE COUNCIL WAS DESTROYED.
ALRIGHT, SO WE JUST TAKE ANOTHER WAY TO TALLUS AND ADD THIS TO OUR GROCERY LIST OF THINGS WE'RE GOING TO SEE THE HIGH PRIESTESS ABOUT, RIGHT?
YOU DON'T UNDERSTAND. ORCUS IS GOING TO TALLUS, TOO. ITS DEFEAT WOULD BE THE KEY TO HIS PLANS.
OKAY. I GET IT. THINGS ARE SO BAD YOU HAVE TO RECITE DEPRESSING POEMS AND ORCUS IS HEADING TO THE SAME PLACE WE ARE...
BUT IT DOESN'T MATTER, BECAUSE AS LONG AS ERIK LOOKS LIKE A MINT-IN-PACKAGE ACTION FIGURE, I'M GOING TO THAT CITY.
AND IF YOU WANT TO FIND A WAY TO REFORM THE HIGH COUNCIL, YOU SHOULD TOO.
YOU'RE RIGHT. BUT WHERE'S BOLDER? HE WENT LOOKING FOR SCOUTS SOME TIME AGO.
I FOUND ORC SCOUTS!

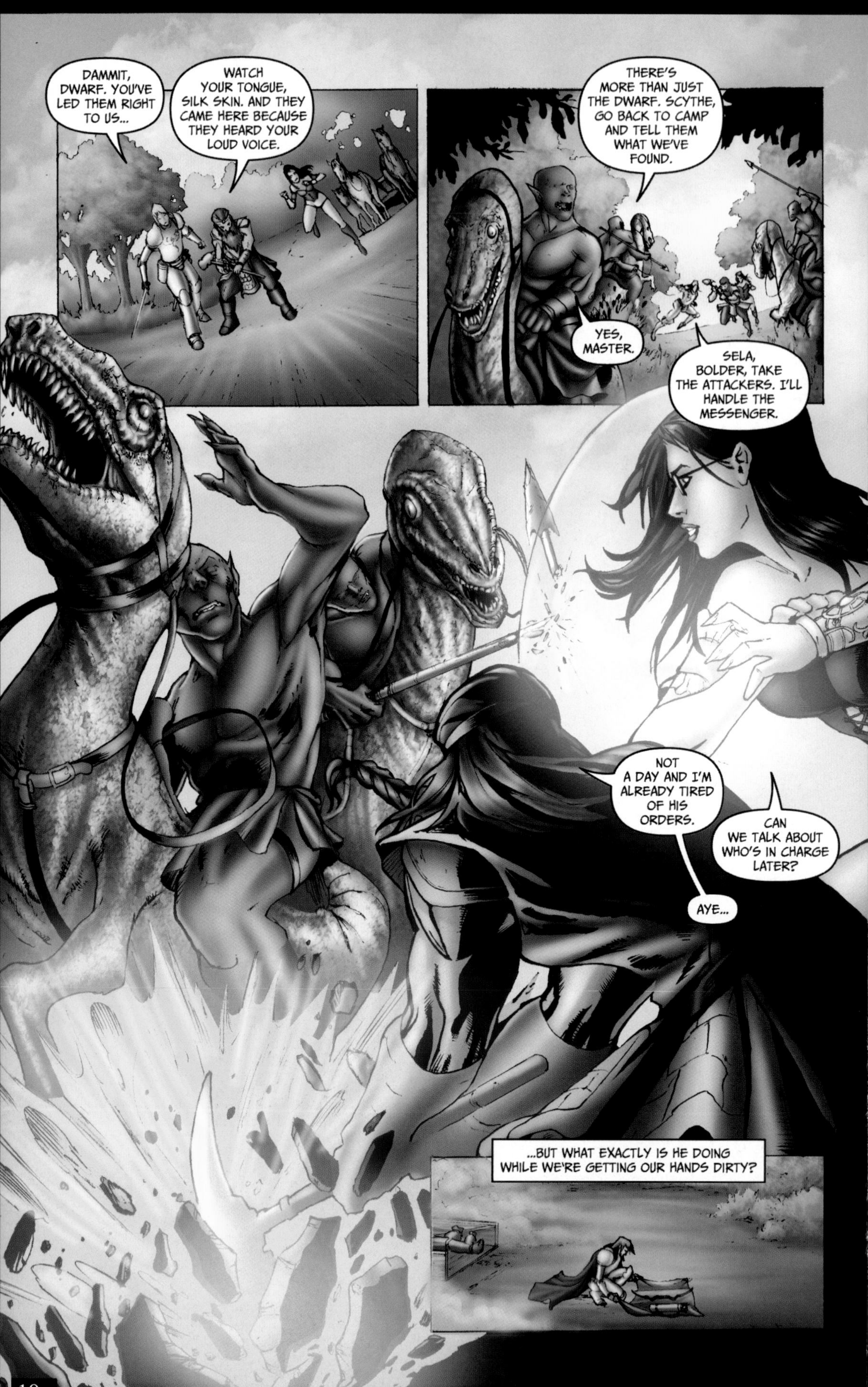

DAMMIT, DWARF. YOU'VE LED THEM RIGHT TO US...
WATCH YOUR TONGUE, SILK SKIN. AND THEY CAME HERE BECAUSE THEY HEARD YOUR LOUD VOICE.
THERE'S MORE THAN JUST THE DWARF. SCYTHE, GO BACK TO CAMP AND TELL THEM WHAT WE'VE FOUND.
YES, MASTER.
SELA, BOLDER, TAKE THE ATTACKERS. I'LL HANDLE THE MESSENGER.
NOT A DAY AND I'M ALREADY TIRED OF HIS ORDERS.
CAN WE TALK ABOUT WHO'S IN CHARGE LATER?
AYE...
...BUT WHAT EXACTLY IS HE DOING WHILE WE'RE GETTING OUR HANDS DIRTY?

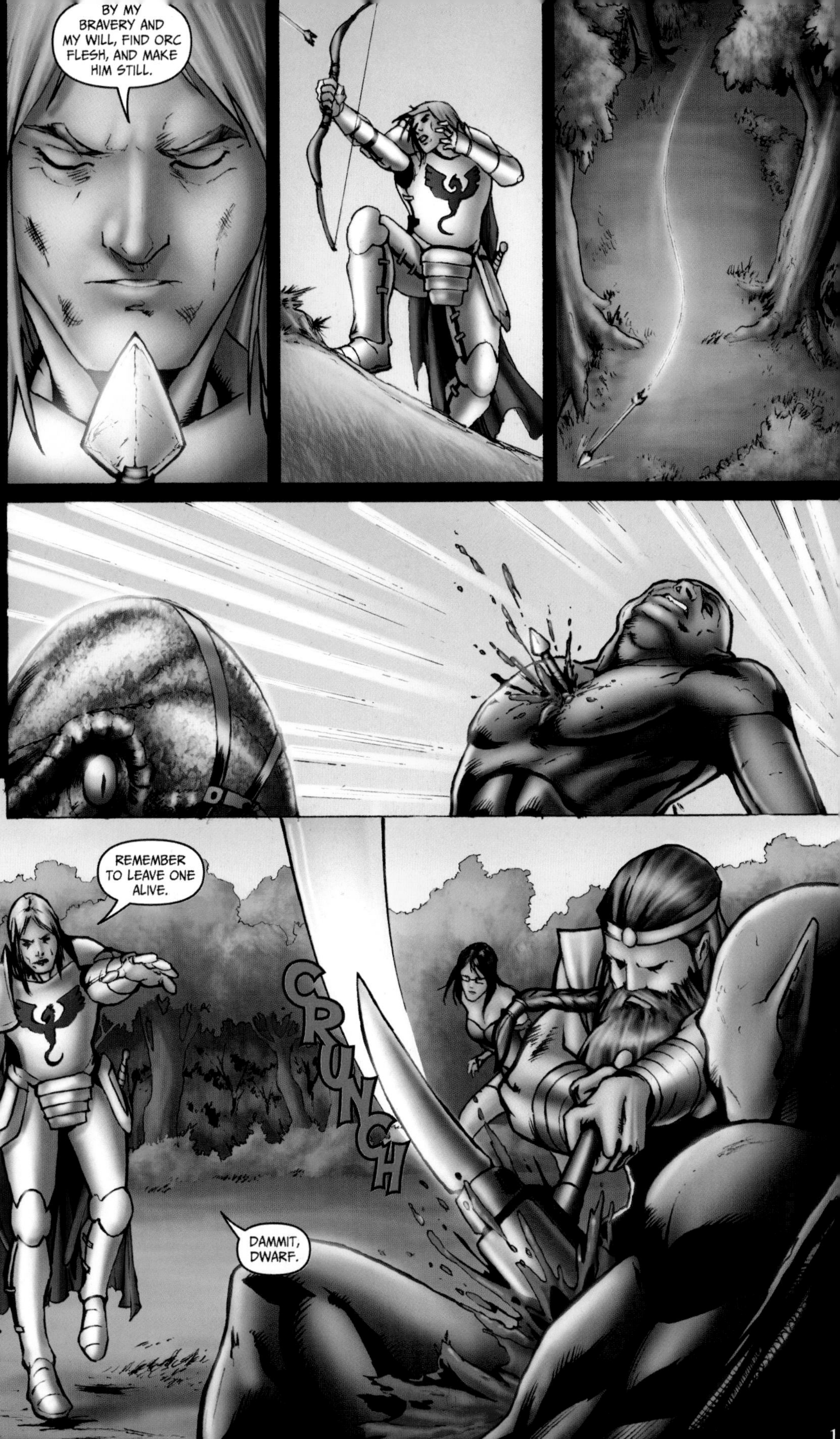
BY MY BRAVERY AND MY WILL, FIND ORC FLESH, AND MAKE HIM STILL.
REMEMBER TO LEAVE ONE ALIVE.
CRUNCH
DAMMIT, DWARF.

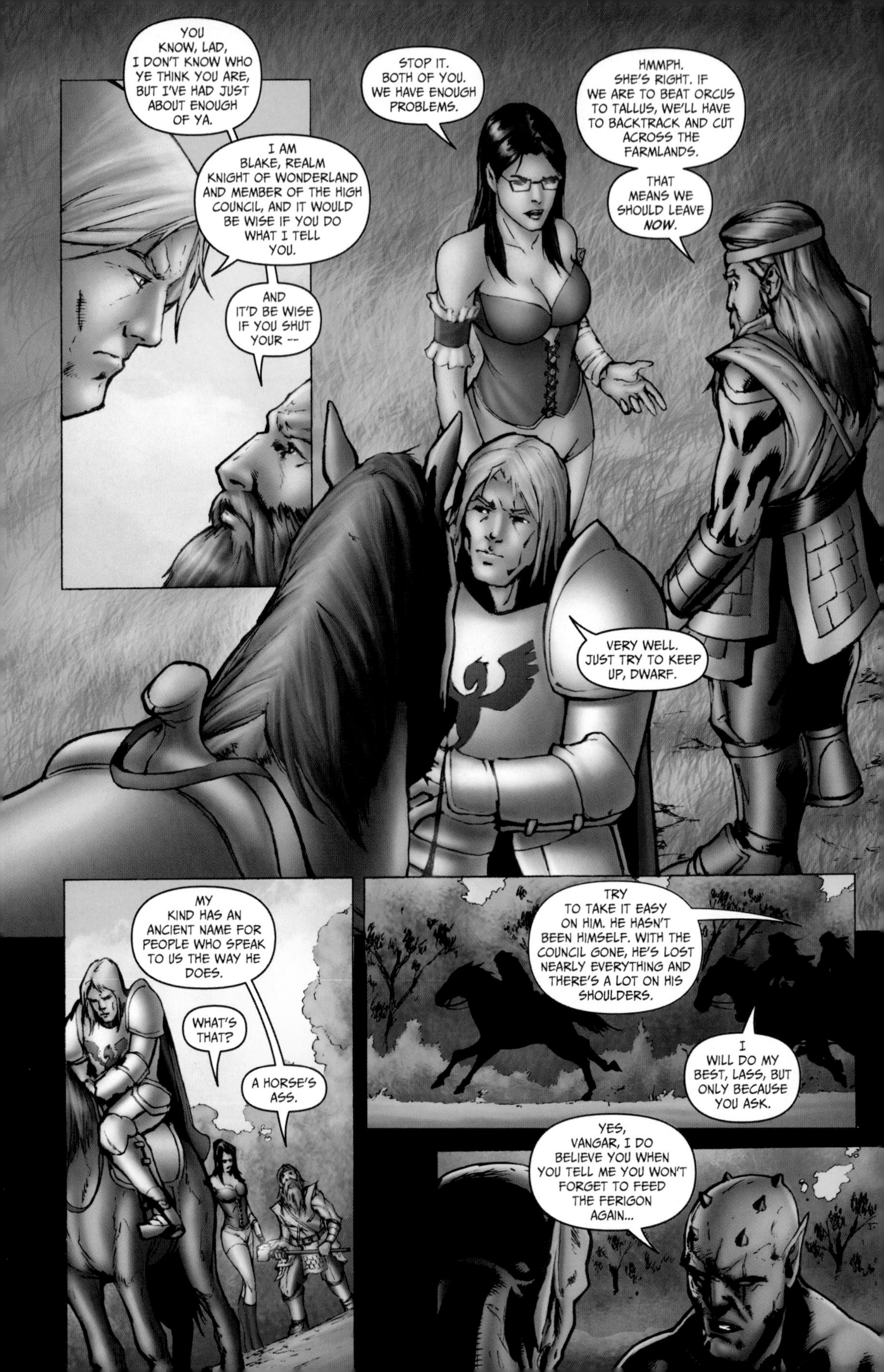
YOU KNOW, LAD, I DON'T KNOW WHO YE THINK YOU ARE, BUT I'VE HAD JUST ABOUT ENOUGH OF YA.
I AM BLAKE, REALM KNIGHT OF WONDERLAND AND MEMBER OF THE HIGH COUNCIL, AND IT WOULD BE WISE IF YOU DO WHAT I TELL YOU.
AND IT'D BE WISE IF YOU SHUT YOUR --
STOP IT. BOTH OF YOU. WE HAVE ENOUGH PROBLEMS.
HMMPH. SHE'S RIGHT. IF WE ARE TO BEAT ORCUS TO TALLUS, WE'LL HAVE TO BACKTRACK AND CUT ACROSS THE FARMLANDS.
THAT MEANS WE SHOULD LEAVE ***NOW***.
VERY WELL. JUST TRY TO KEEP UP, DWARF.
MY KIND HAS AN ANCIENT NAME FOR PEOPLE WHO SPEAK TO US THE WAY HE DOES.
WHAT'S THAT?
A HORSE'S ASS.
TRY TO TAKE IT EASY ON HIM. HE HASN'T BEEN HIMSELF. WITH THE COUNCIL GONE, HE'S LOST NEARLY EVERYTHING AND THERE'S A LOT ON HIS SHOULDERS.
I WILL DO MY BEST, LASS, BUT ONLY BECAUSE YOU ASK.
YES, VANGAR, I DO BELIEVE YOU WHEN YOU TELL ME YOU WON'T FORGET TO FEED THE FERIGON AGAIN...

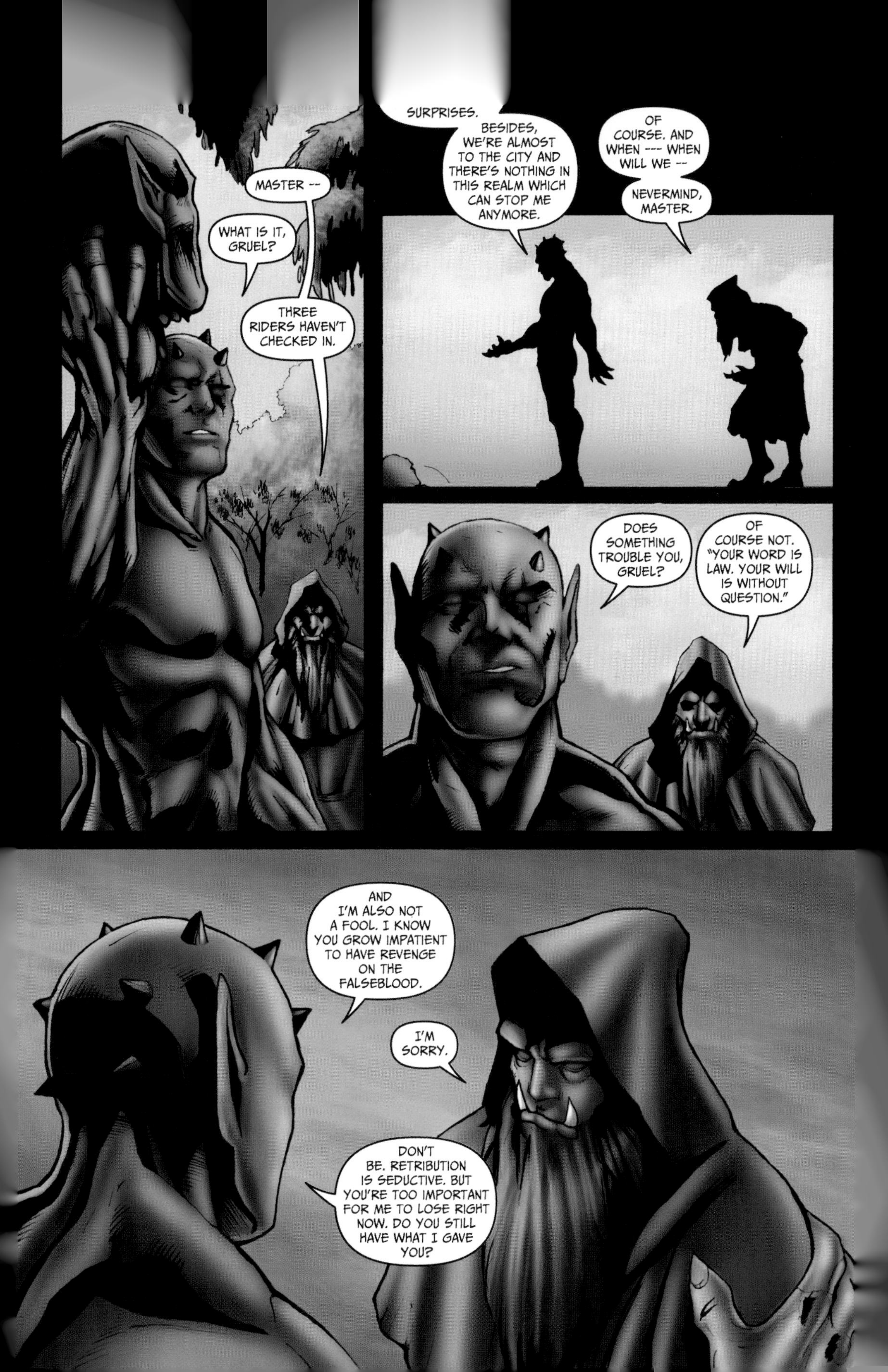
MASTER --
WHAT IS IT, GRUEL?
THREE RIDERS HAVEN'T CHECKED IN.
SURPRISES.
BESIDES, WE'RE ALMOST TO THE CITY AND THERE'S NOTHING IN THIS REALM WHICH CAN STOP ME ANYMORE.
OF COURSE. AND WHEN --- WHEN WILL WE --
NEVERMIND, MASTER.
DOES SOMETHING TROUBLE YOU, GRUEL?
OF COURSE NOT. "YOUR WORD IS LAW. YOUR WILL IS WITHOUT QUESTION."
AND I'M ALSO NOT A FOOL. I KNOW YOU GROW IMPATIENT TO HAVE REVENGE ON THE FALSEBLOOD.
I'M SORRY.
DON'T BE. RETRIBUTION IS SEDUCTIVE. BUT YOU'RE TOO IMPORTANT FOR ME TO LOSE RIGHT NOW. DO YOU STILL HAVE WHAT I GAVE YOU?

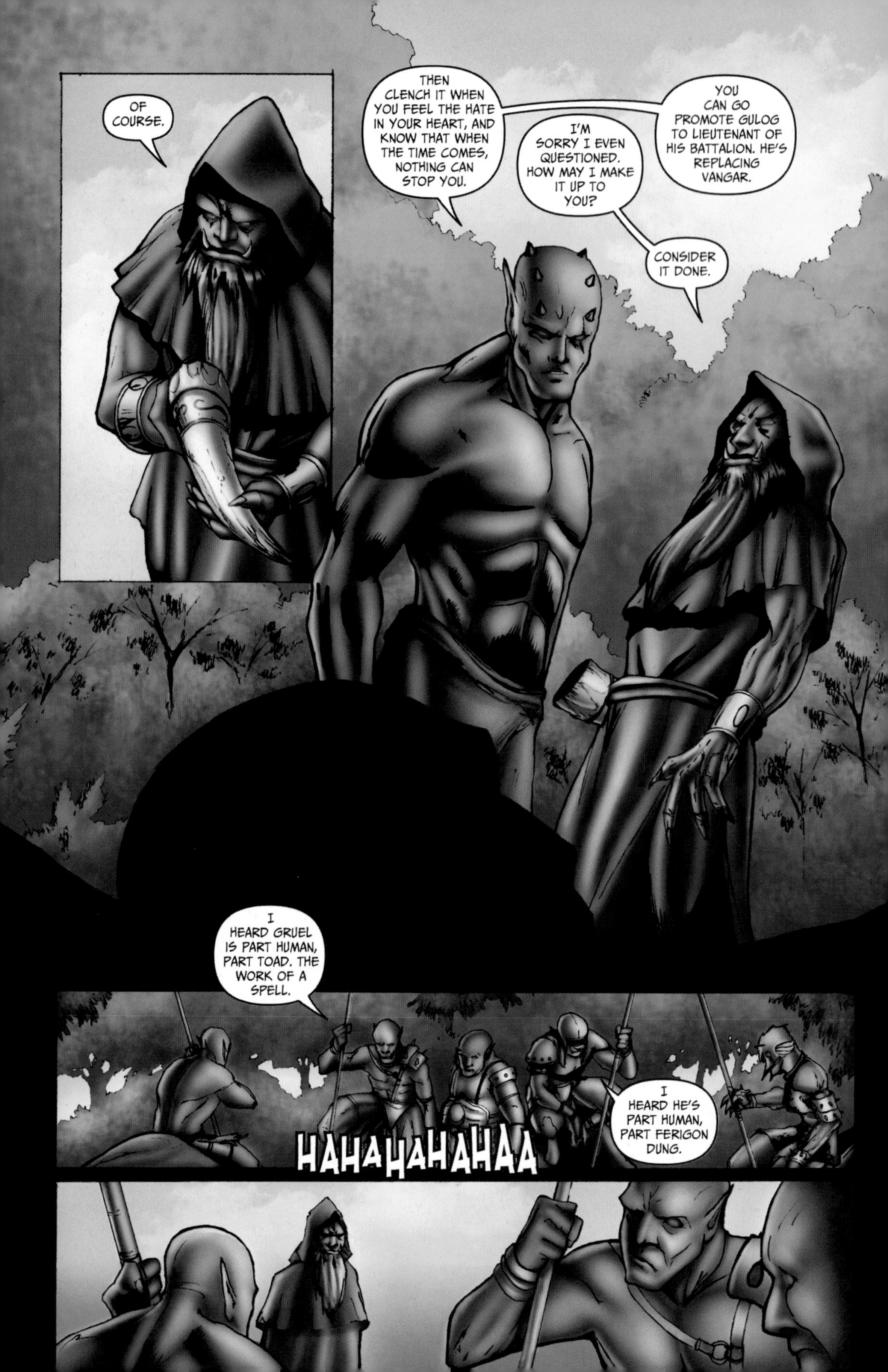
OF COURSE.
THEN CLENCH IT WHEN YOU FEEL THE HATE IN YOUR HEART, AND KNOW THAT WHEN THE TIME COMES, NOTHING CAN STOP YOU.
I'M SORRY I EVEN QUESTIONED. HOW MAY I MAKE IT UP TO YOU?
YOU CAN GO PROMOTE GULOG TO LIEUTENANT OF HIS BATTALION. HE'S REPLACING VANGAR.
CONSIDER IT DONE.
I HEARD GRUEL IS PART HUMAN, PART TOAD. THE WORK OF A SPELL.
I HEARD HE'S PART HUMAN, PART FERIGON DUNG.
HAHAHAHAHAA

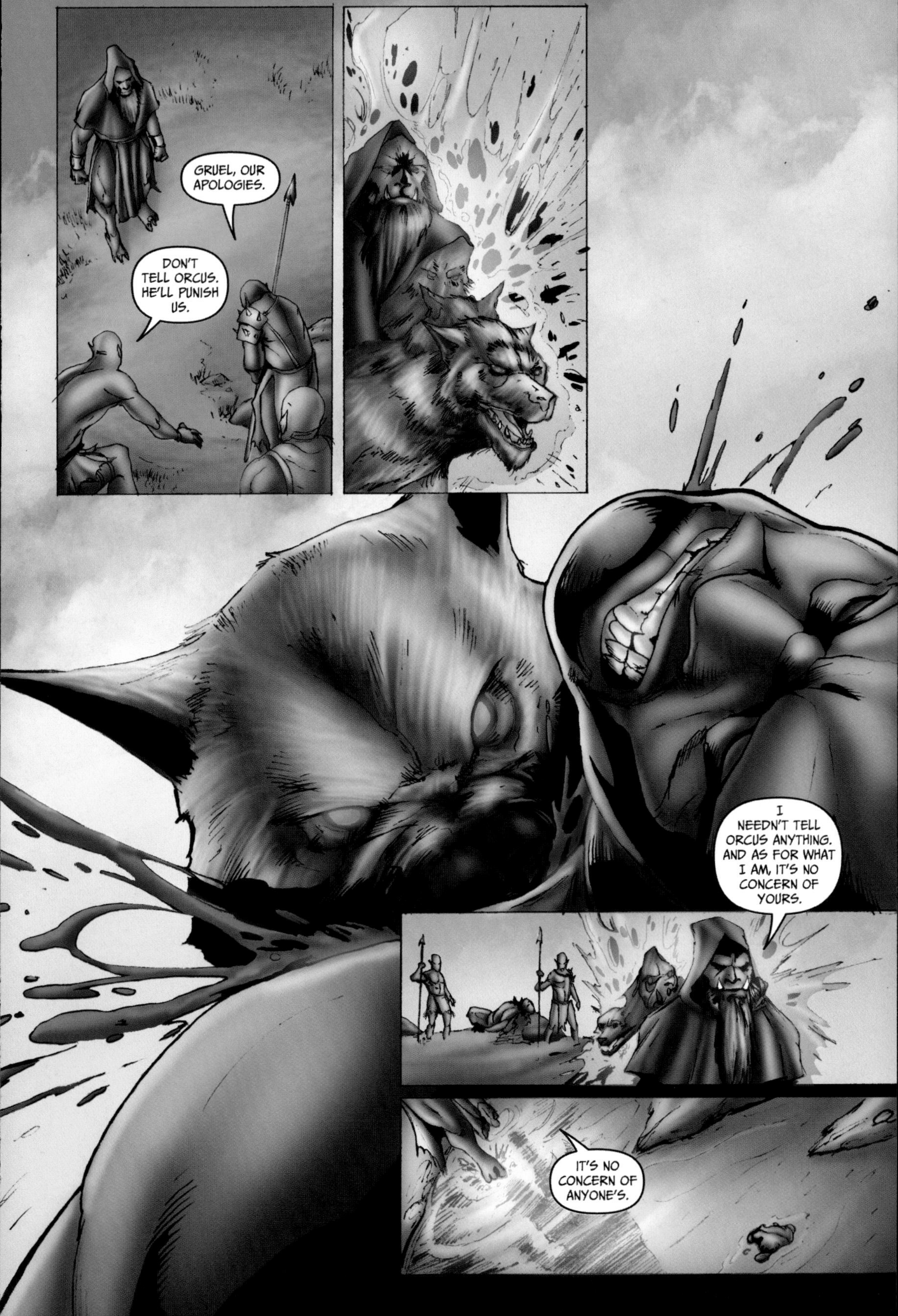
GRUEL, OUR APOLOGIES.
DON'T TELL ORCUS. HE'LL PUNISH US.
I NEEDN'T TELL ORCUS ANYTHING. AND AS FOR WHAT I AM, IT'S NO CONCERN OF YOURS.
IT'S NO CONCERN OF ANYONE'S.

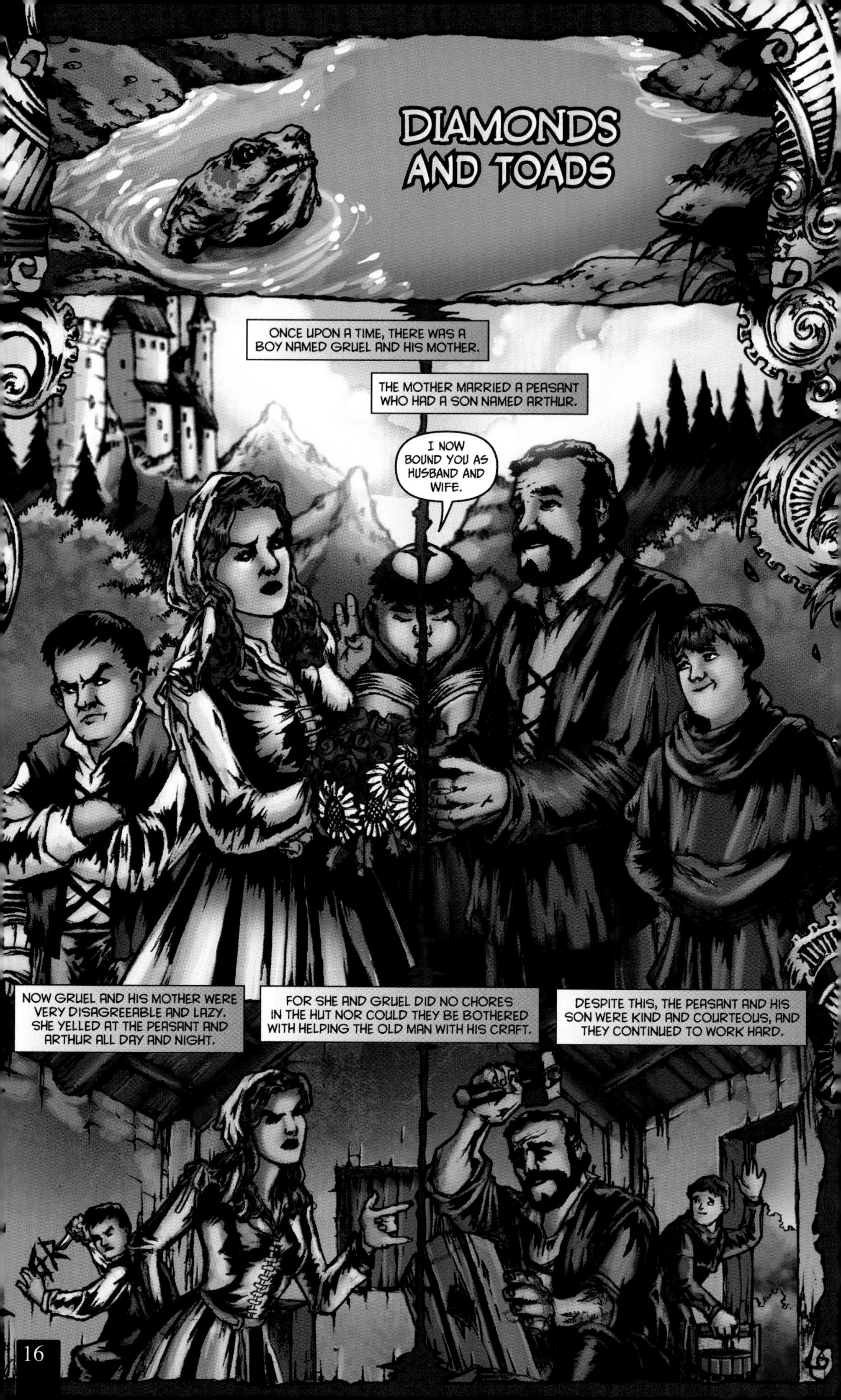
DIAMONDS AND TOADS
ONCE UPON A TIME, THERE WAS A BOY NAMED GRUEL AND HIS MOTHER.
THE MOTHER MARRIED A PEASANT WHO HAD A SON NAMED ARTHUR.
I NOW BOUND YOU AS HUSBAND AND WIFE.
NOW GRUEL AND HIS MOTHER WERE VERY DISAGREEABLE AND LAZY. SHE YELLED AT THE PEASANT AND ARTHUR ALL DAY AND NIGHT.
FOR SHE AND GRUEL DID NO CHORES IN THE HUT NOR COULD THEY BE BOTHERED WITH HELPING THE OLD MAN WITH HIS CRAFT.
DESPITE THIS, THE PEASANT AND HIS SON WERE KIND AND COURTEOUS, AND THEY CONTINUED TO WORK HARD.

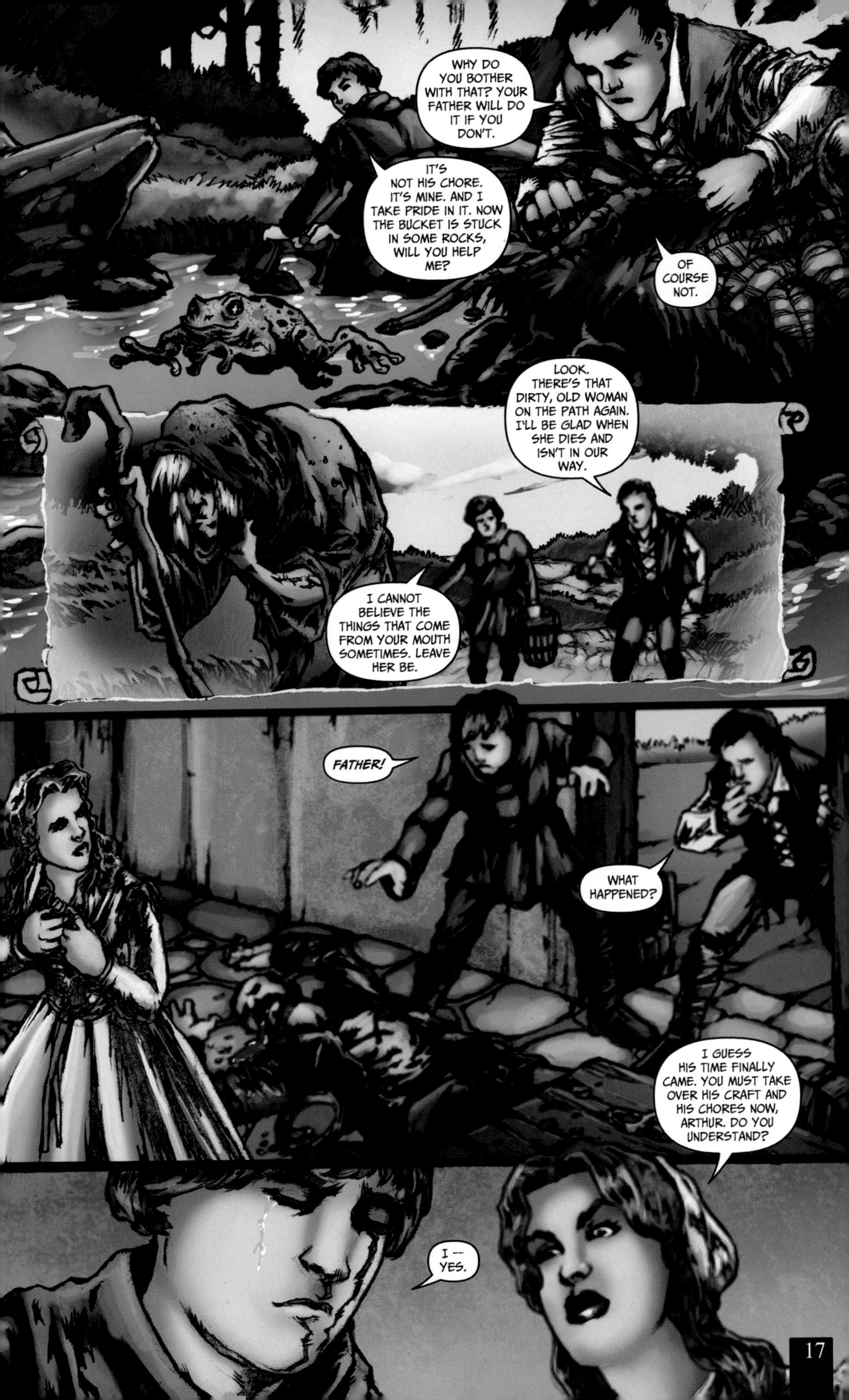
WHY DO YOU BOTHER WITH THAT? YOUR FATHER WILL DO IT IF YOU DON'T.
IT'S NOT HIS CHORE. IT'S MINE. AND I TAKE PRIDE IN IT. NOW THE BUCKET IS STUCK IN SOME ROCKS, WILL YOU HELP ME?
OF COURSE NOT.
LOOK. THERE'S THAT DIRTY, OLD WOMAN ON THE PATH AGAIN. I'LL BE GLAD WHEN SHE DIES AND ISN'T IN OUR WAY.
I CANNOT BELIEVE THE THINGS THAT COME FROM YOUR MOUTH SOMETIMES. LEAVE HER BE.
FATHER!
WHAT HAPPENED?
I GUESS HIS TIME FINALLY CAME. YOU MUST TAKE OVER HIS CRAFT AND HIS CHORES NOW, ARTHUR. DO YOU UNDERSTAND?
I -- YES.

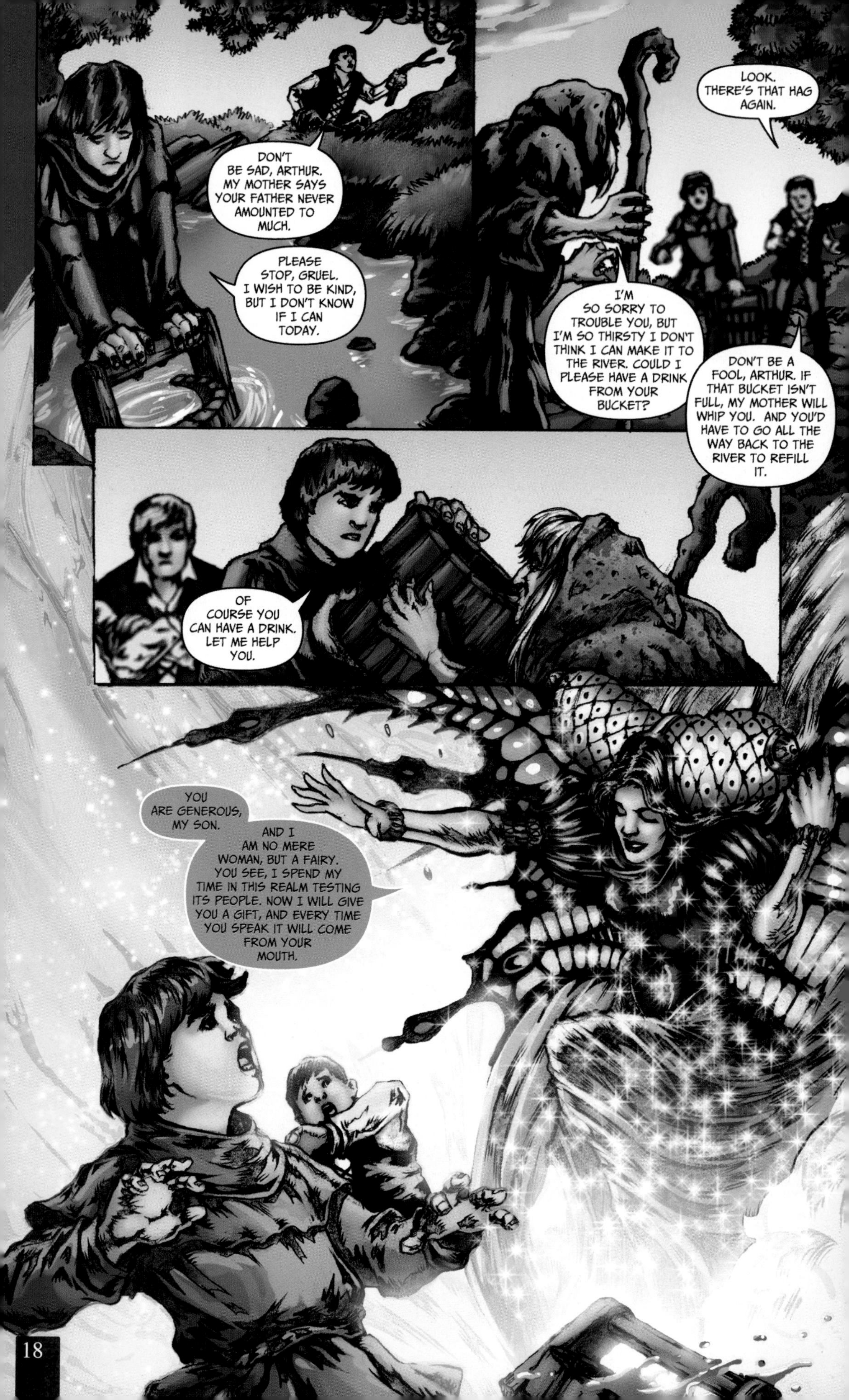
DON'T BE SAD, ARTHUR. MY MOTHER SAYS YOUR FATHER NEVER AMOUNTED TO MUCH.
PLEASE STOP, GRUEL. I WISH TO BE KIND, BUT I DON'T KNOW IF I CAN TODAY.
LOOK. THERE'S THAT HAG AGAIN.
I'M SO SORRY TO TROUBLE YOU, BUT I'M SO THIRSTY I DON'T THINK I CAN MAKE IT TO THE RIVER. COULD I PLEASE HAVE A DRINK FROM YOUR BUCKET?
DON'T BE A FOOL, ARTHUR. IF THAT BUCKET ISN'T FULL, MY MOTHER WILL WHIP YOU. AND YOU'D HAVE TO GO ALL THE WAY BACK TO THE RIVER TO REFILL IT.
OF COURSE YOU CAN HAVE A DRINK. LET ME HELP YOU.
YOU ARE GENEROUS, MY SON.
AND I AM NO MERE WOMAN, BUT A FAIRY. YOU SEE, I SPEND MY TIME IN THIS REALM TESTING ITS PEOPLE. NOW I WILL GIVE YOU A GIFT, AND EVERY TIME YOU SPEAK IT WILL COME FROM YOUR MOUTH.

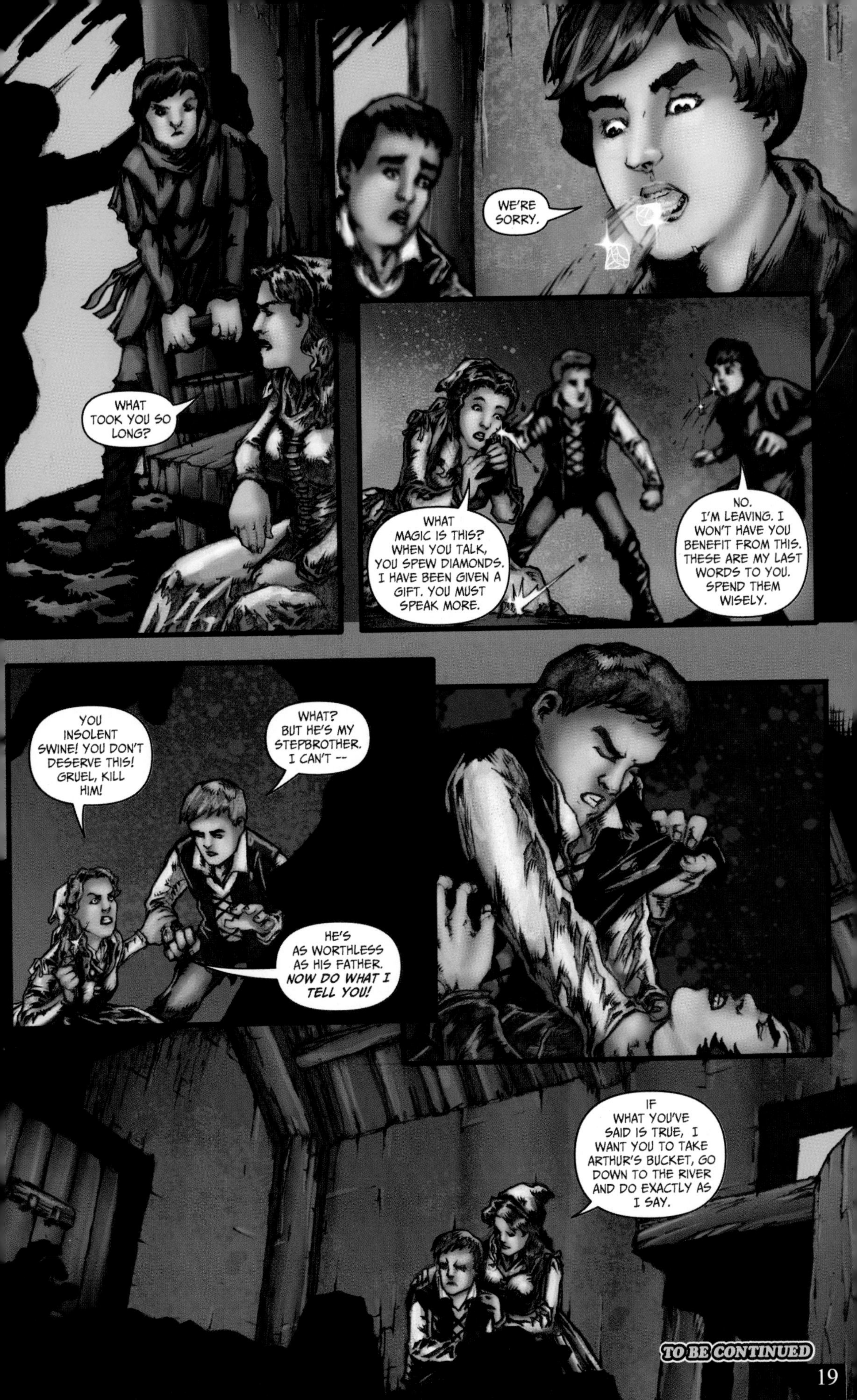
WE'RE SORRY.
WHAT TOOK YOU SO LONG?
WHAT MAGIC IS THIS? WHEN YOU TALK, YOU SPEW DIAMONDS. I HAVE BEEN GIVEN A GIFT. YOU MUST SPEAK MORE.
NO. I'M LEAVING. I WON'T HAVE YOU BENEFIT FROM THIS. THESE ARE MY LAST WORDS TO YOU. SPEND THEM WISELY.
YOU INSOLENT SWINE! YOU DON'T DESERVE THIS! GRUEL, KILL HIM!
WHAT? BUT HE'S MY STEPBROTHER. I CAN'T --
HE'S AS WORTHLESS AS HIS FATHER. NOW DO WHAT I TELL YOU!
IF WHAT YOU'VE SAID IS TRUE, I WANT YOU TO TAKE ARTHUR'S BUCKET, GO DOWN TO THE RIVER AND DO EXACTLY AS I SAY.
TO BE CONTINUED

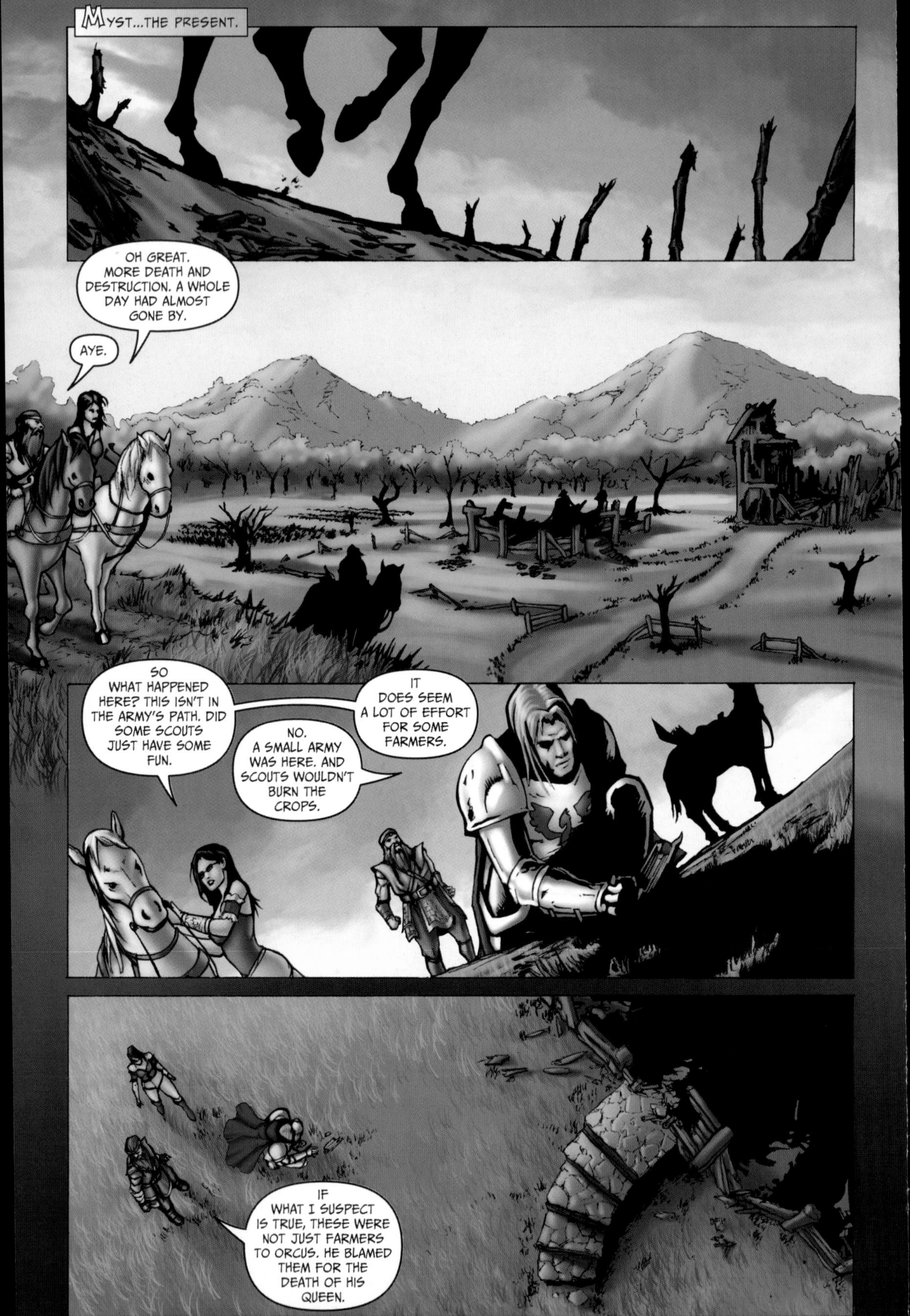
MYST...THE PRESENT.
OH GREAT. MORE DEATH AND DESTRUCTION. A WHOLE DAY HAD ALMOST GONE BY.
AYE.
SO WHAT HAPPENED HERE? THIS ISN'T IN THE ARMY'S PATH. DID SOME SCOUTS JUST HAVE SOME FUN.
NO. A SMALL ARMY WAS HERE. AND SCOUTS WOULDN'T BURN THE CROPS.
IT DOES SEEM A LOT OF EFFORT FOR SOME FARMERS.
IF WHAT I SUSPECT IS TRUE, THESE WERE NOT JUST FARMERS TO ORCUS. HE BLAMED THEM FOR THE DEATH OF HIS QUEEN.

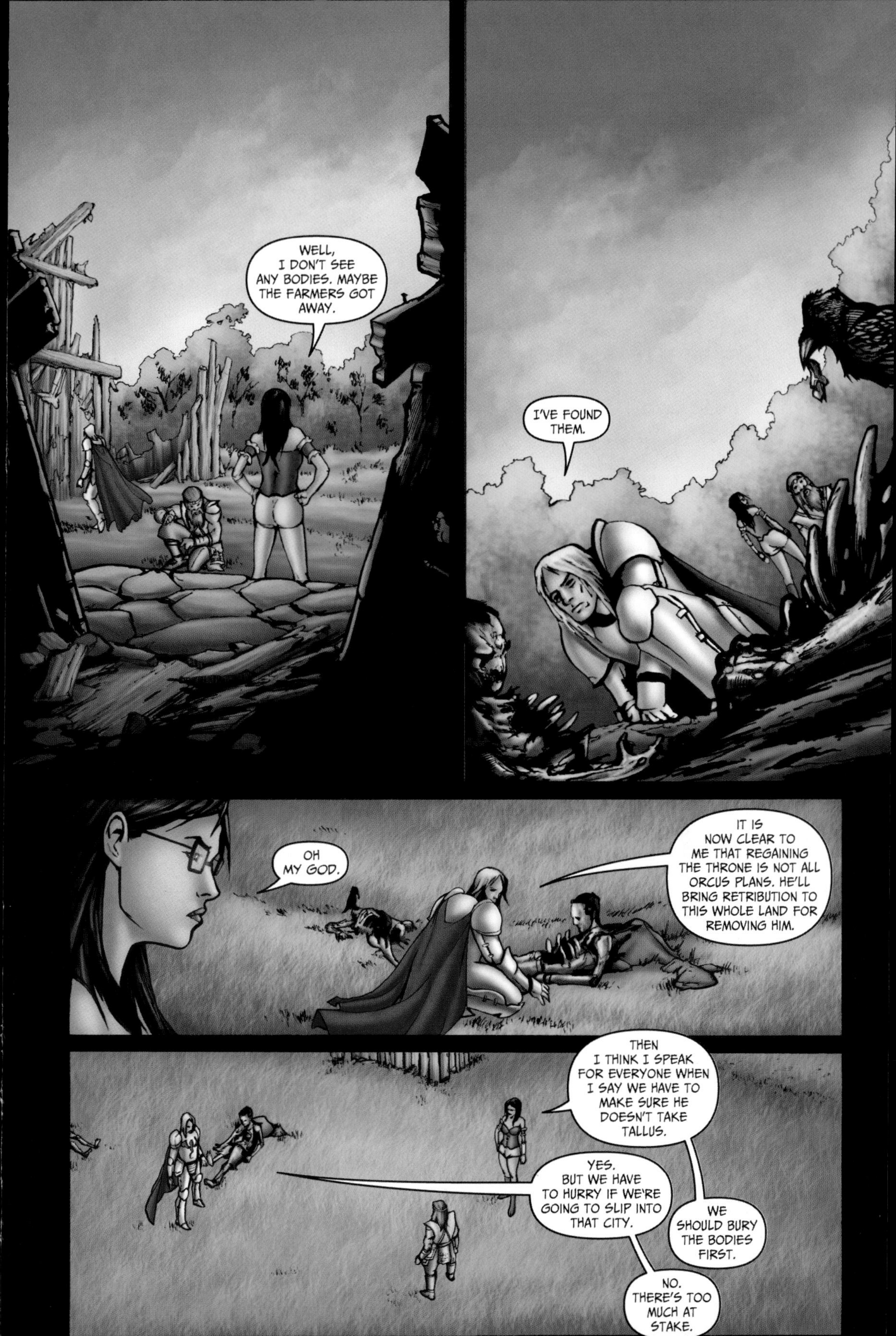
WELL, I DON'T SEE ANY BODIES. MAYBE THE FARMERS GOT AWAY.
I'VE FOUND THEM.
OH MY GOD.
IT IS NOW CLEAR TO ME THAT REGAINING THE THRONE IS NOT ALL ORCUS PLANS. HE'LL BRING RETRIBUTION TO THIS WHOLE LAND FOR REMOVING HIM.
THEN I THINK I SPEAK FOR EVERYONE WHEN I SAY WE HAVE TO MAKE SURE HE DOESN'T TAKE TALLUS.
YES. BUT WE HAVE TO HURRY IF WE'RE GOING TO SLIP INTO THAT CITY.
WE SHOULD BURY THE BODIES FIRST.
NO. THERE'S TOO MUCH AT STAKE.

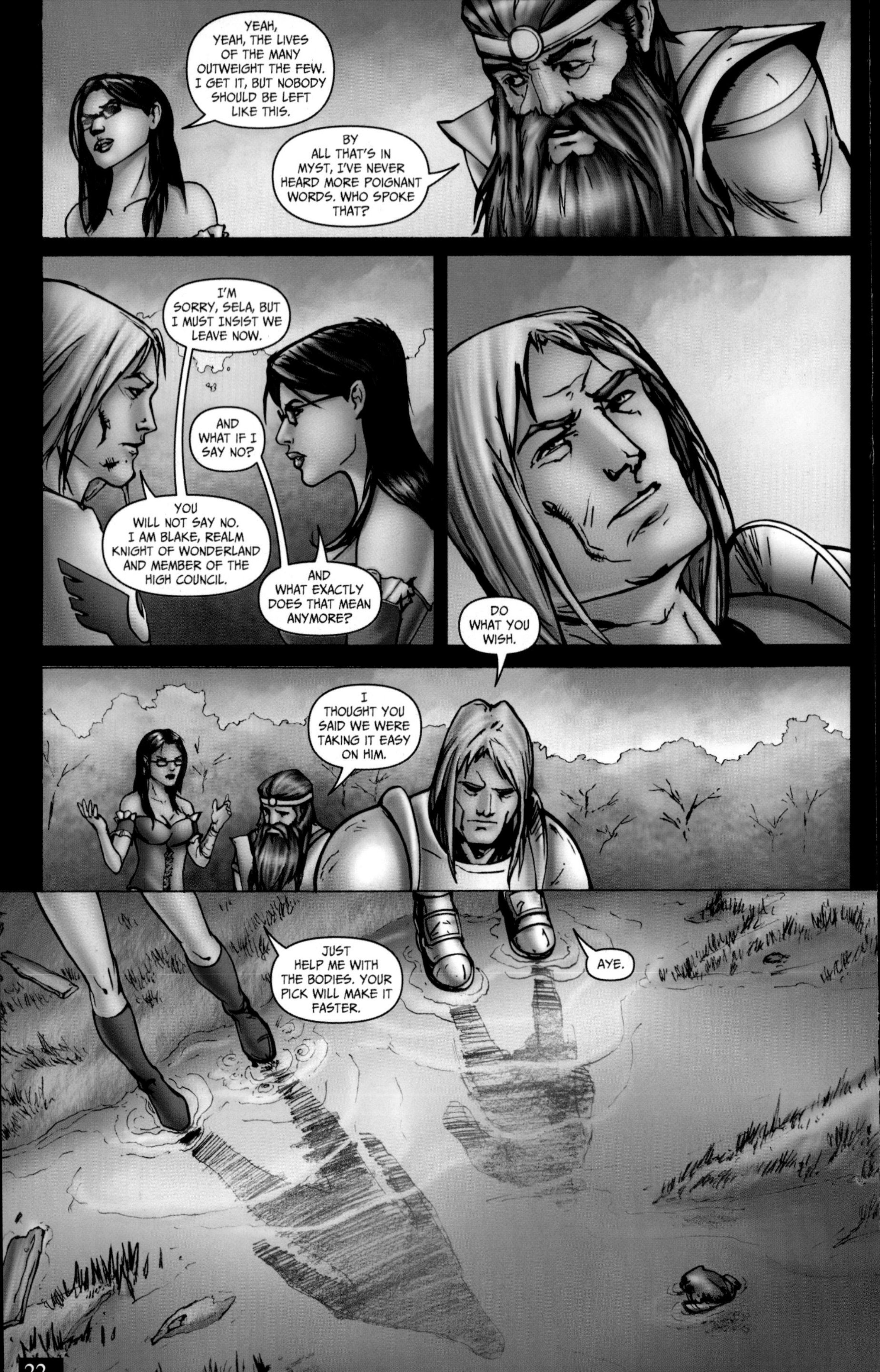
YEAH, YEAH, THE LIVES OF THE MANY OUTWEIGHT THE FEW. I GET IT, BUT NOBODY SHOULD BE LEFT LIKE THIS.
BY ALL THAT'S IN MYST, I'VE NEVER HEARD MORE POIGNANT WORDS. WHO SPOKE THAT?
I'M SORRY, SELA, BUT I MUST INSIST WE LEAVE NOW.
AND WHAT IF I SAY NO?
YOU WILL NOT SAY NO. I AM BLAKE, REALM KNIGHT OF WONDERLAND AND MEMBER OF THE HIGH COUNCIL.
AND WHAT EXACTLY DOES THAT MEAN ANYMORE?
DO WHAT YOU WISH.
I THOUGHT YOU SAID WE WERE TAKING IT EASY ON HIM.
JUST HELP ME WITH THE BODIES. YOUR PICK WILL MAKE IT FASTER.
AYE.

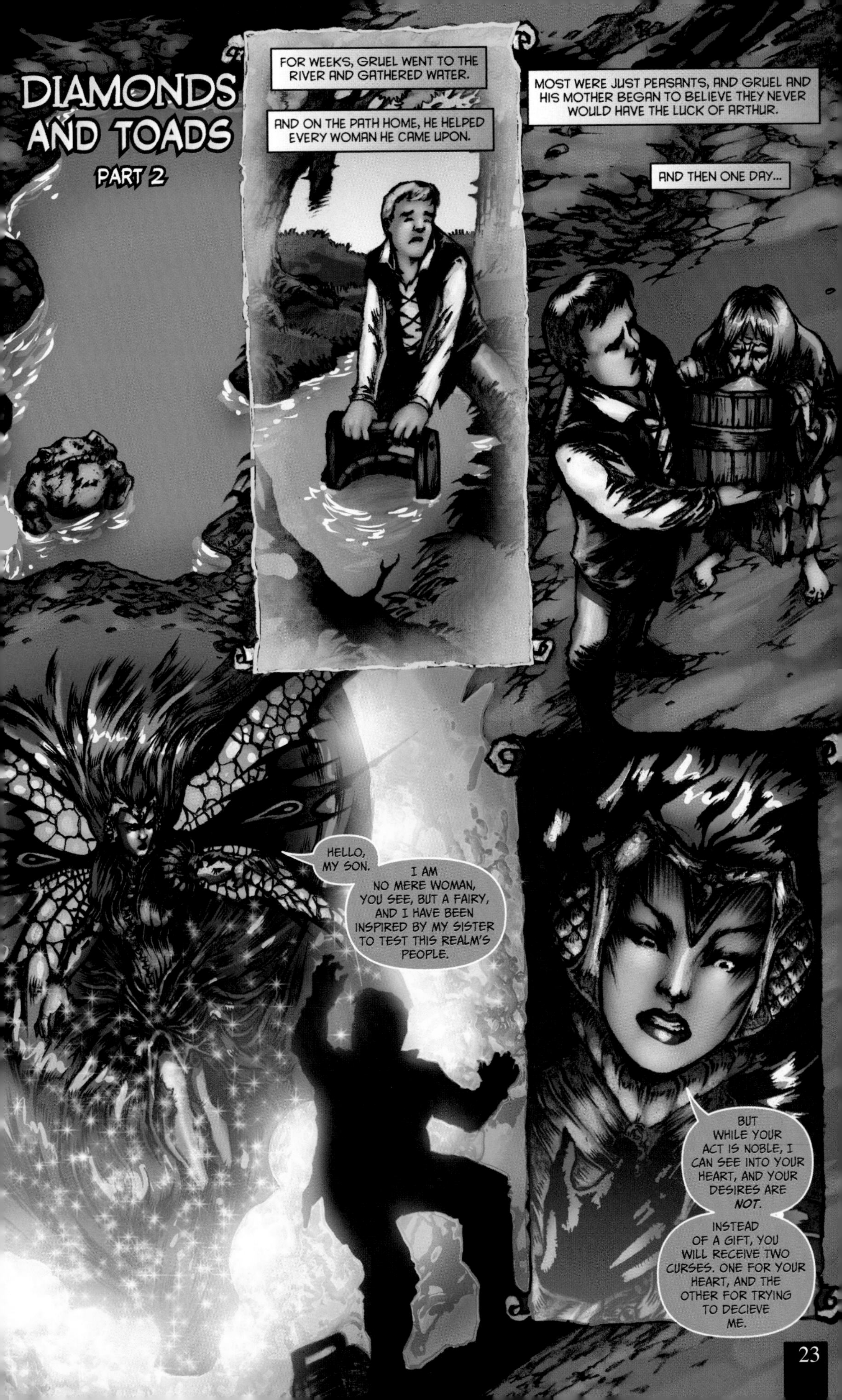
DIAMONDS AND TOADS
PART 2
FOR WEEKS, GRUEL WENT TO THE RIVER AND GATHERED WATER.
AND ON THE PATH HOME, HE HELPED EVERY WOMAN HE CAME UPON.
MOST WERE JUST PEASANTS, AND GRUEL AND HIS MOTHER BEGAN TO BELIEVE THEY NEVER WOULD HAVE THE LUCK OF ARTHUR.
AND THEN ONE DAY...
HELLO, MY SON.
I AM NO MERE WOMAN, YOU SEE, BUT A FAIRY, AND I HAVE BEEN INSPIRED BY MY SISTER TO TEST THIS REALM'S PEOPLE.
BUT WHILE YOUR ACT IS NOBLE, I CAN SEE INTO YOUR HEART, AND YOUR DESIRES ARE *NOT*.
INSTEAD OF A GIFT, YOU WILL RECEIVE TWO CURSES. ONE FOR YOUR HEART, AND THE OTHER FOR TRYING TO DECIEVE ME.

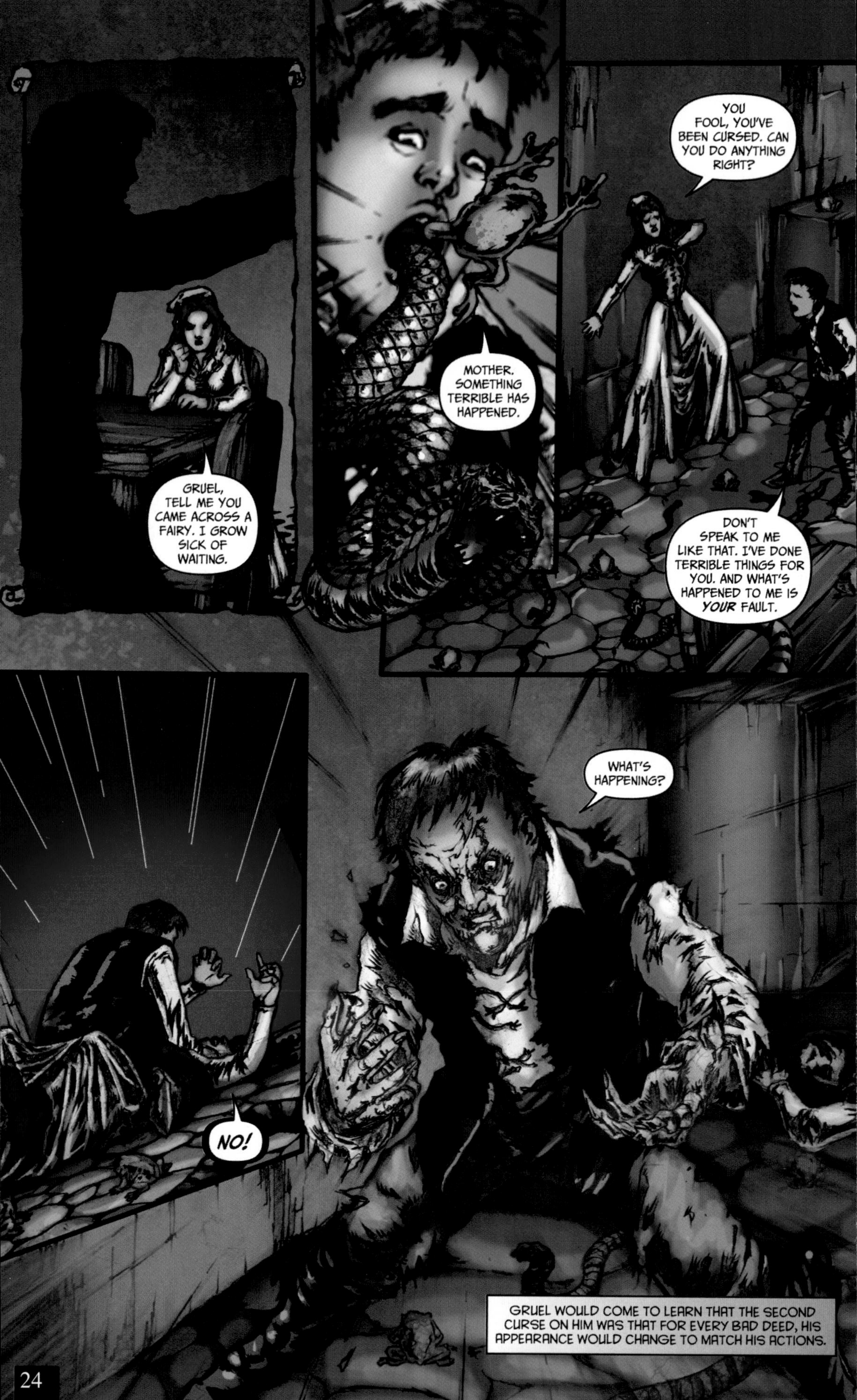
GRUEL, TELL ME YOU CAME ACROSS A FAIRY. I GROW SICK OF WAITING.
MOTHER. SOMETHING TERRIBLE HAS HAPPENED.
YOU FOOL, YOU'VE BEEN CURSED. CAN YOU DO ANYTHING RIGHT?
DON'T SPEAK TO ME LIKE THAT. I'VE DONE TERRIBLE THINGS FOR YOU. AND WHAT'S HAPPENED TO ME IS *YOUR* FAULT.
NO!
WHAT'S HAPPENING?
GRUEL WOULD COME TO LEARN THAT THE SECOND CURSE ON HIM WAS THAT FOR EVERY BAD DEED, HIS APPEARANCE WOULD CHANGE TO MATCH HIS ACTIONS.

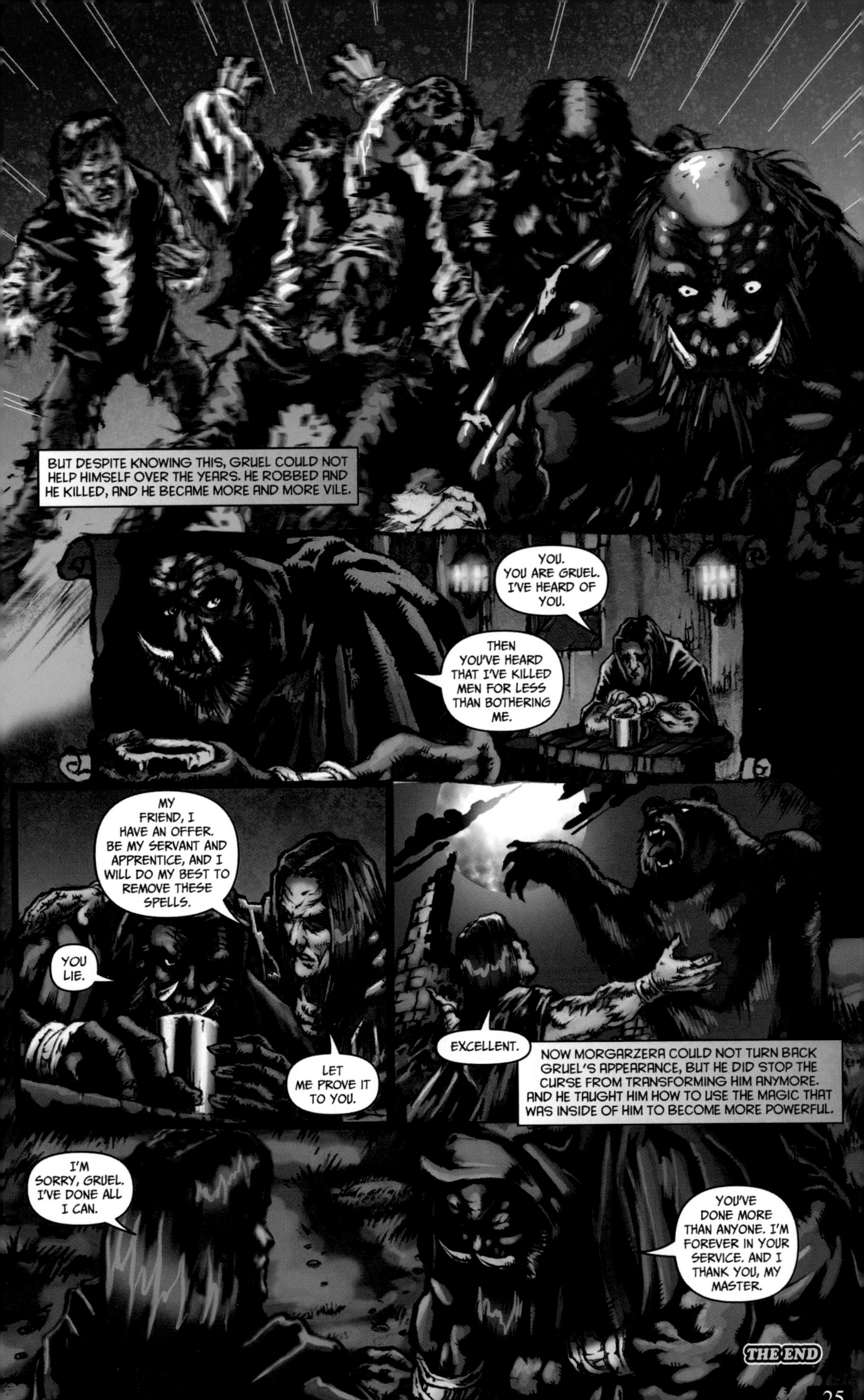

BUT DESPITE KNOWING THIS, GRUEL COULD NOT HELP HIMSELF OVER THE YEARS. HE ROBBED AND HE KILLED, AND HE BECAME MORE AND MORE VILE.
YOU. YOU ARE GRUEL. I'VE HEARD OF YOU.
THEN YOU'VE HEARD THAT I'VE KILLED MEN FOR LESS THAN BOTHERING ME.
MY FRIEND, I HAVE AN OFFER. BE MY SERVANT AND APPRENTICE, AND I WILL DO MY BEST TO REMOVE THESE SPELLS.
YOU LIE.
LET ME PROVE IT TO YOU.
EXCELLENT.
NOW MORGARZERA COULD NOT TURN BACK GRUEL'S APPEARANCE, BUT HE DID STOP THE CURSE FROM TRANSFORMING HIM ANYMORE. AND HE TAUGHT HIM HOW TO USE THE MAGIC THAT WAS INSIDE OF HIM TO BECOME MORE POWERFUL.
I'M SORRY, GRUEL. I'VE DONE ALL I CAN.
YOU'VE DONE MORE THAN ANYONE. I'M FOREVER IN YOUR SERVICE. AND I THANK YOU, MY MASTER.
THE END

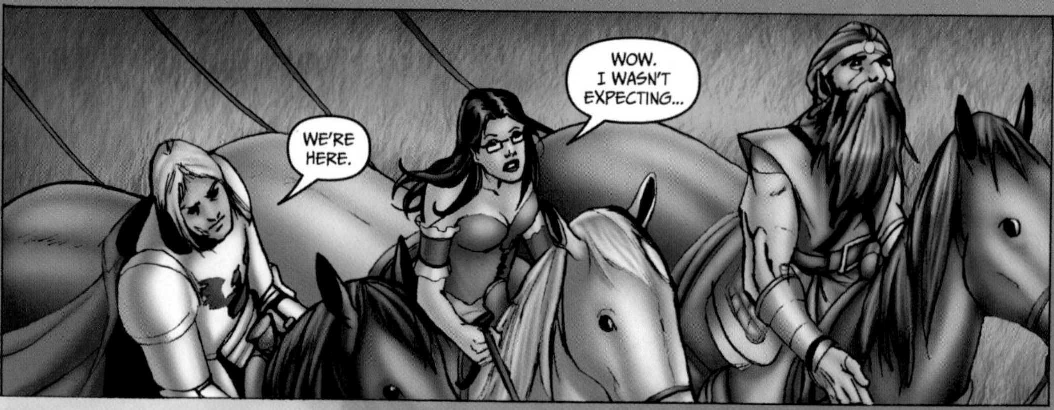
WE'RE HERE.
WOW. I WASN'T EXPECTING...

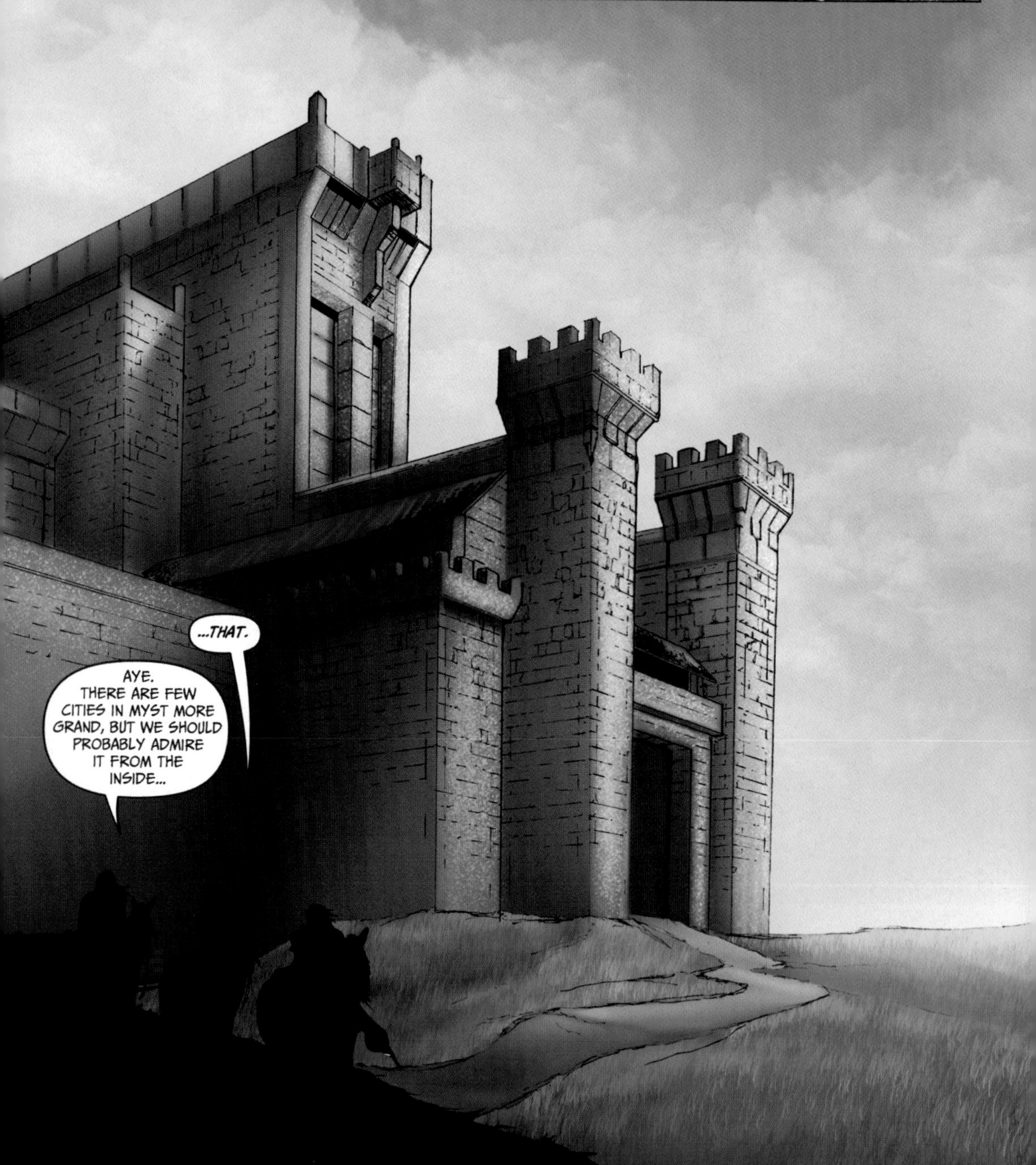
...THAT.
AYE. THERE ARE FEW CITIES IN MYST MORE GRAND, BUT WE SHOULD PROBABLY ADMIRE IT FROM THE INSIDE...

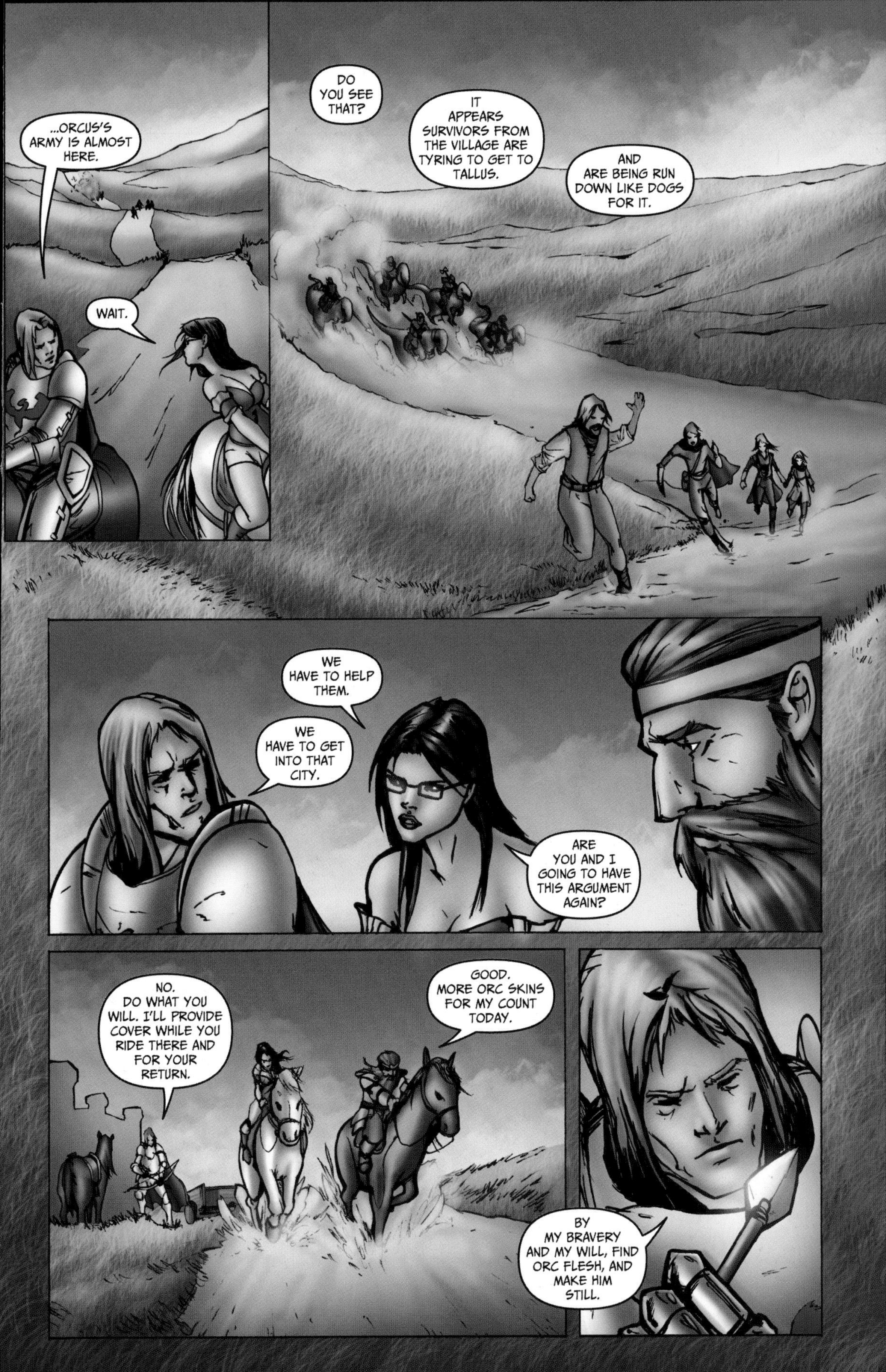
...ORCUS'S ARMY IS ALMOST HERE.
WAIT.
DO YOU SEE THAT?
IT APPEARS SURVIVORS FROM THE VILLAGE ARE TYRING TO GET TO TALLUS.
AND ARE BEING RUN DOWN LIKE DOGS FOR IT.
WE HAVE TO HELP THEM.
WE HAVE TO GET INTO THAT CITY.
ARE YOU AND I GOING TO HAVE THIS ARGUMENT AGAIN?
NO. DO WHAT YOU WILL. I'LL PROVIDE COVER WHILE YOU RIDE THERE AND FOR YOUR RETURN.
GOOD. MORE ORC SKINS FOR MY COUNT TODAY.
BY MY BRAVERY AND MY WILL, FIND ORC FLESH, AND MAKE HIM STILL.

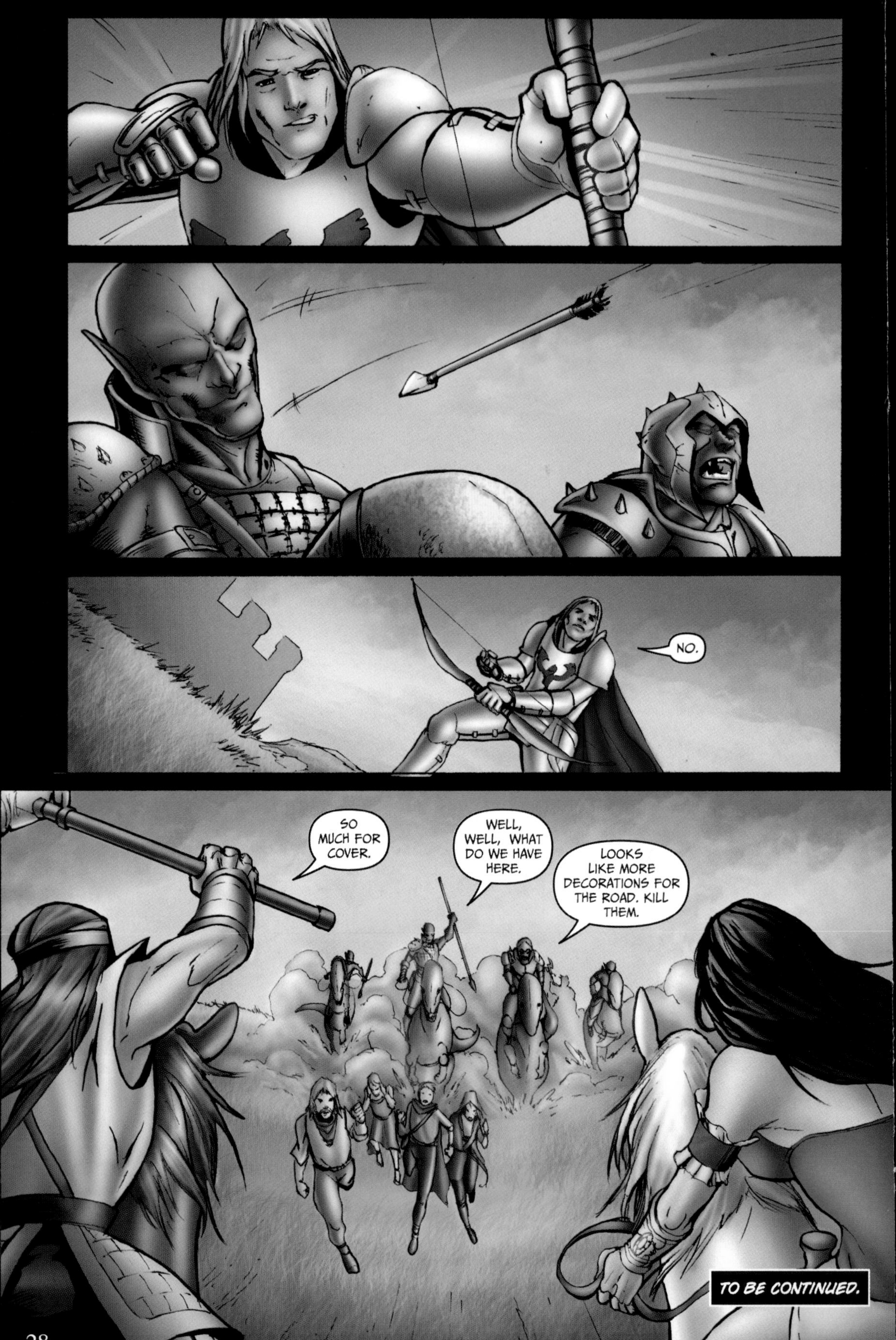
NO.
SO MUCH FOR COVER.
WELL, WELL, WHAT DO WE HAVE HERE.
LOOKS LIKE MORE DECORATIONS FOR THE ROAD. KILL THEM.
TO BE CONTINUED.

Grimm Fairy Tales

Volume 10

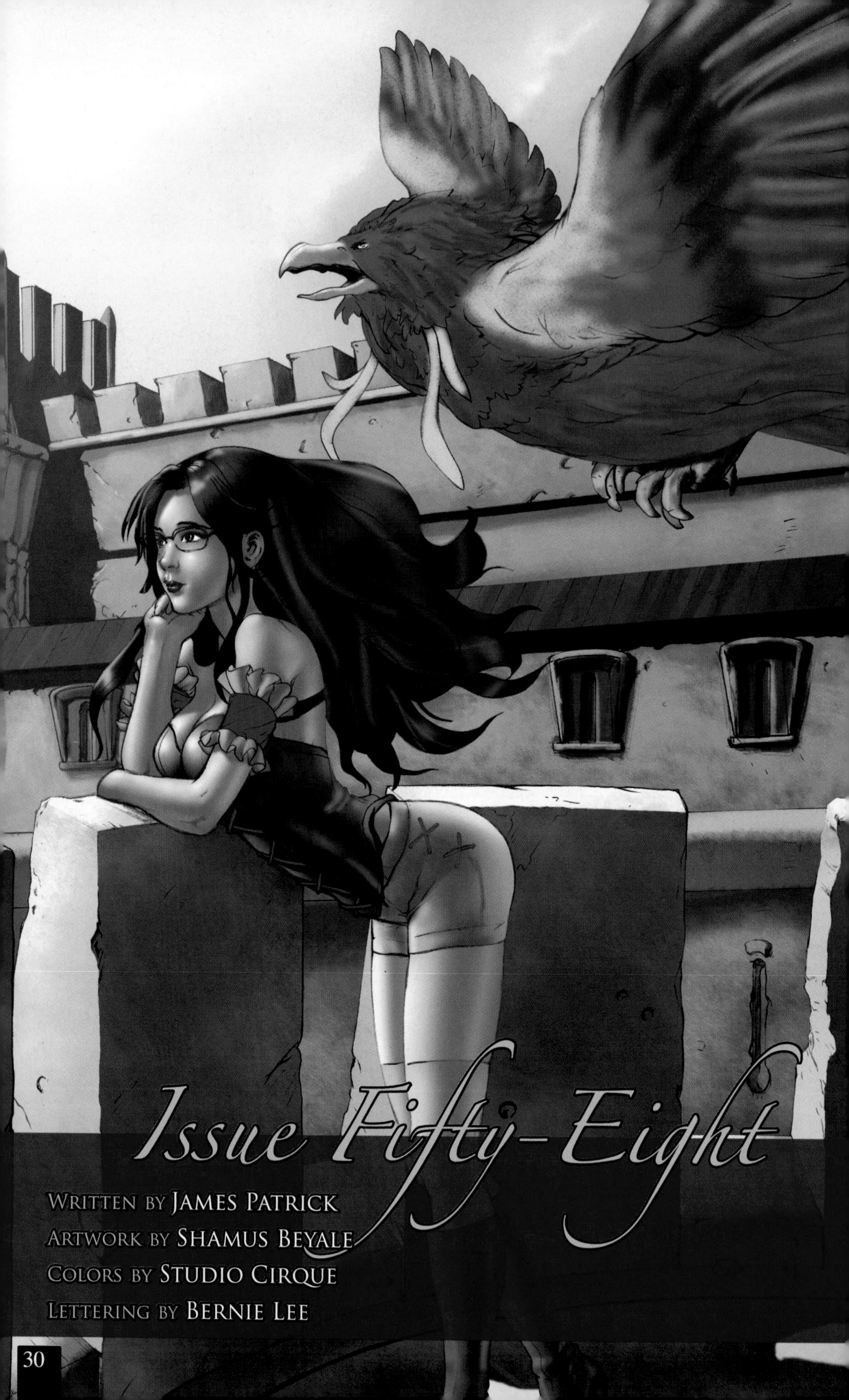

Issue Fifty-Eight

Written by James Patrick
Artwork by Shamus Beyale
Colors by Studio Cirque
Lettering by Bernie Lee

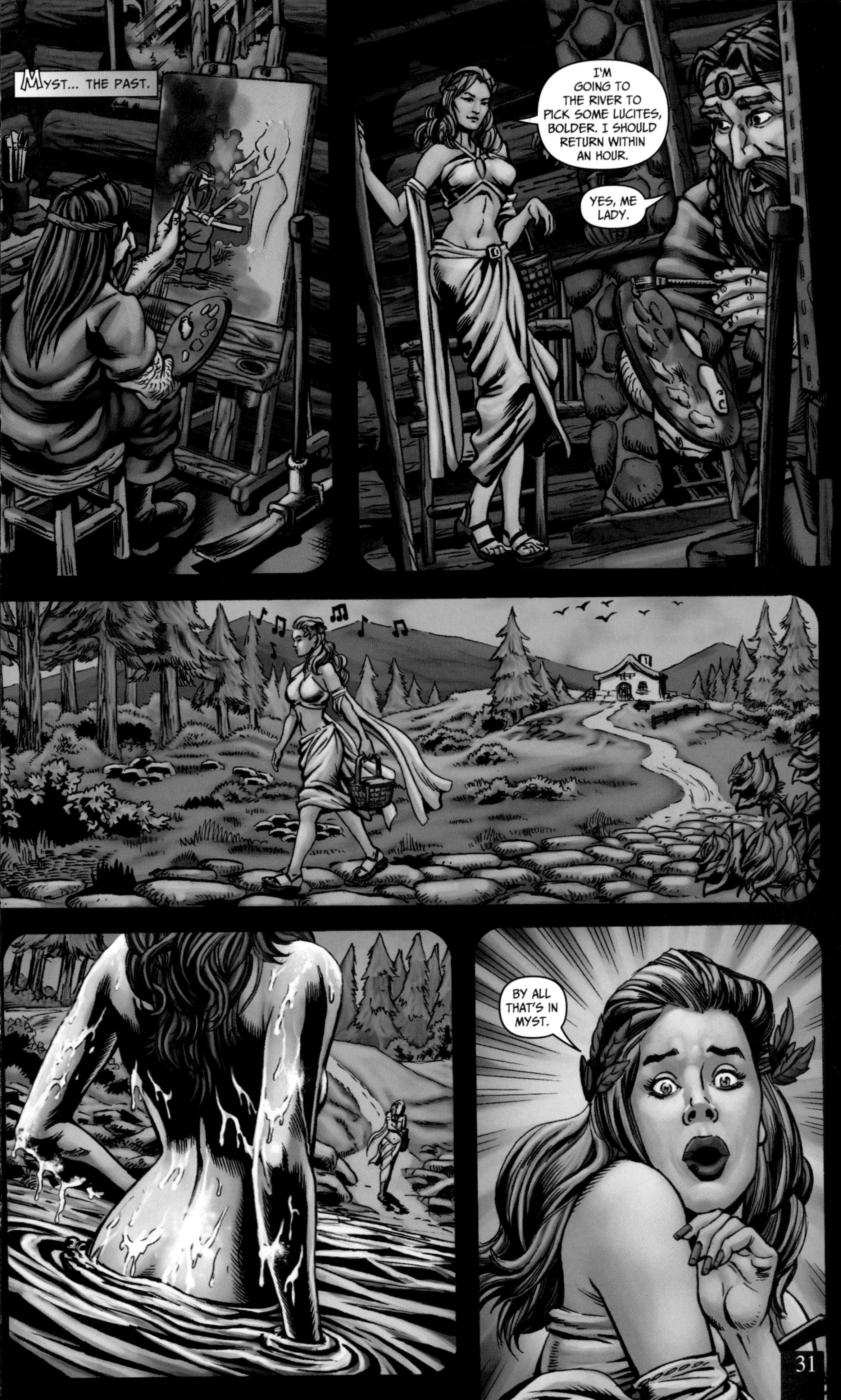
MYST... THE PAST.
I'M GOING TO THE RIVER TO PICK SOME LUCITES, BOLDER. I SHOULD RETURN WITHIN AN HOUR.
YES, ME LADY.
BY ALL THAT'S IN MYST.

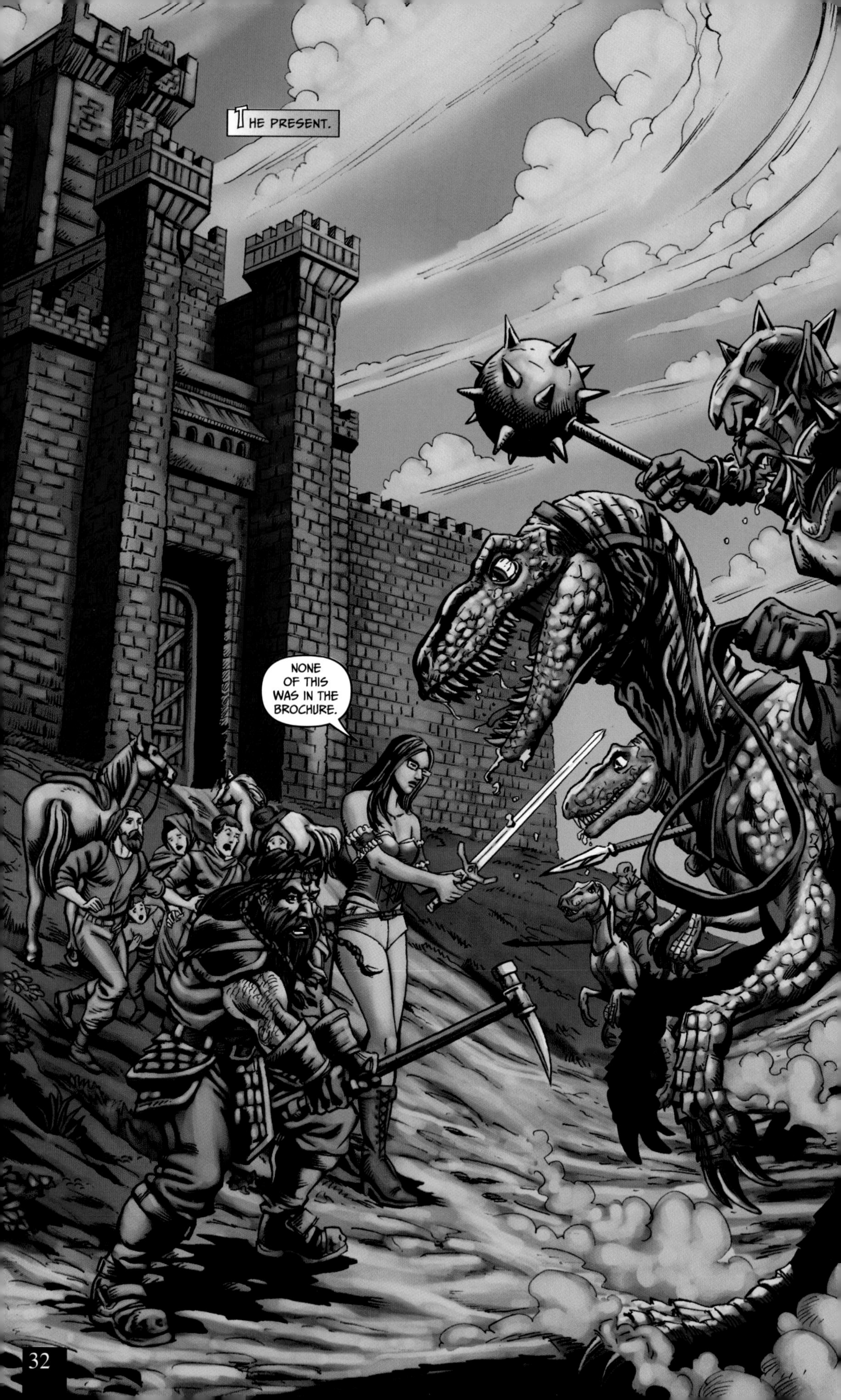
THE PRESENT.
NONE OF THIS WAS IN THE BROCHURE.

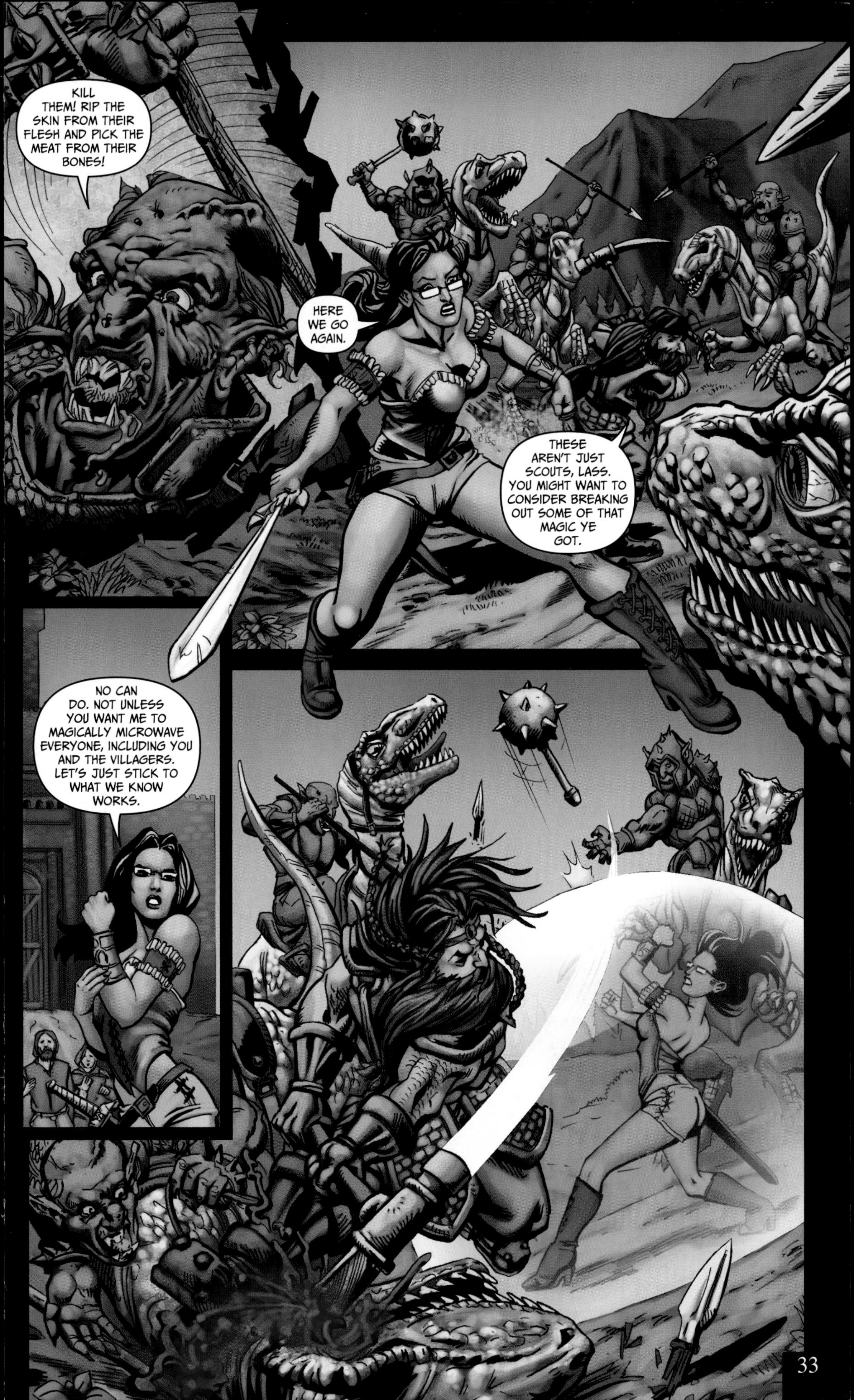
KILL THEM! RIP THE SKIN FROM THEIR FLESH AND PICK THE MEAT FROM THEIR BONES!
HERE WE GO AGAIN.
THESE AREN'T JUST SCOUTS, LASS. YOU MIGHT WANT TO CONSIDER BREAKING OUT SOME OF THAT MAGIC YE GOT.
NO CAN DO. NOT UNLESS YOU WANT ME TO MAGICALLY MICROWAVE EVERYONE, INCLUDING YOU AND THE VILLAGERS. LET'S JUST STICK TO WHAT WE KNOW WORKS.

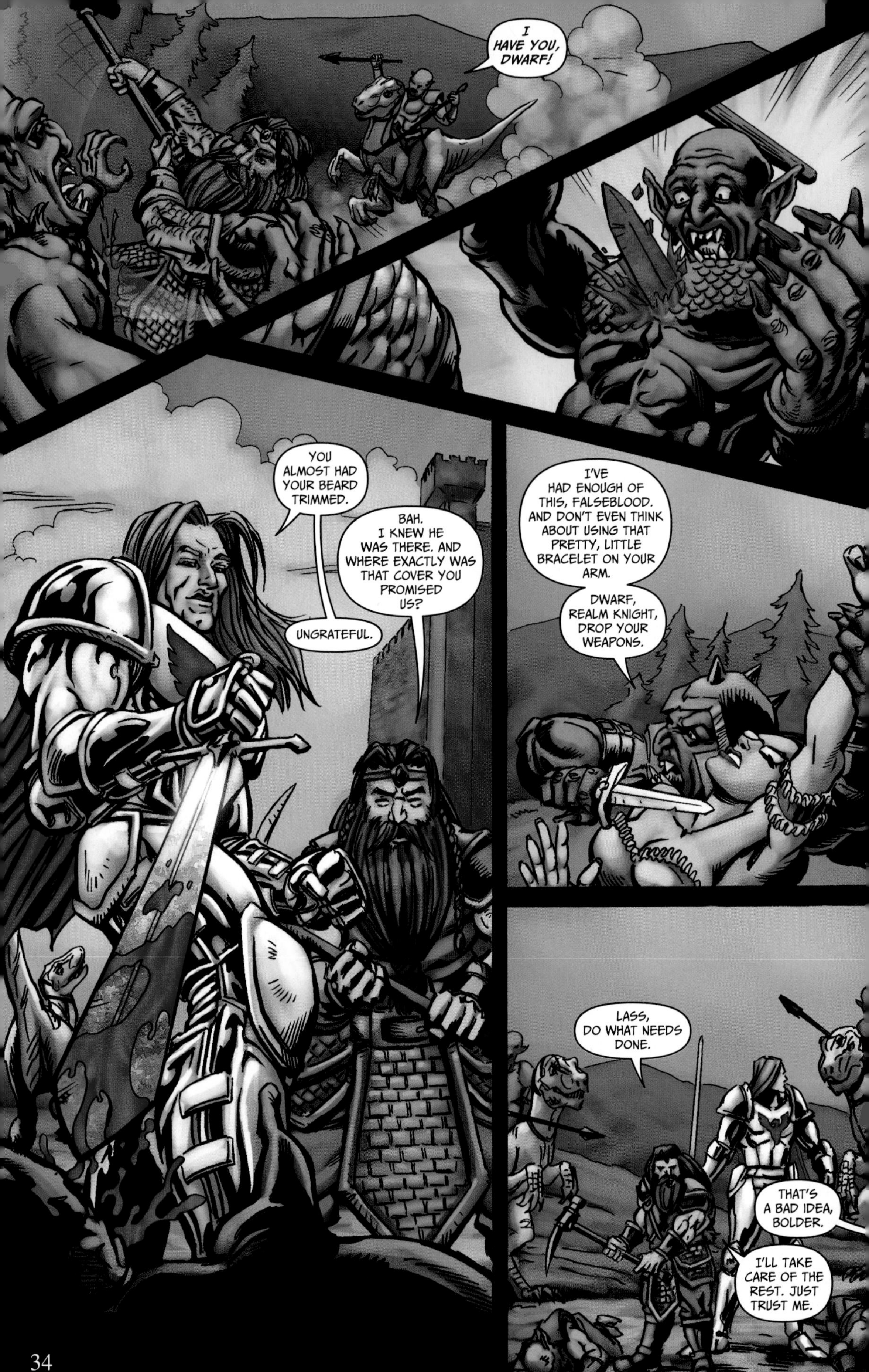
I HAVE YOU, DWARF!
YOU ALMOST HAD YOUR BEARD TRIMMED.
UNGRATEFUL.
BAH. I KNEW HE WAS THERE. AND WHERE EXACTLY WAS THAT COVER YOU PROMISED US?
I'VE HAD ENOUGH OF THIS, FALSEBLOOD. AND DON'T EVEN THINK ABOUT USING THAT PRETTY, LITTLE BRACELET ON YOUR ARM.
DWARF, REALM KNIGHT, DROP YOUR WEAPONS.
LASS, DO WHAT NEEDS DONE.
THAT'S A BAD IDEA, BOLDER.
I'LL TAKE CARE OF THE REST. JUST TRUST ME.

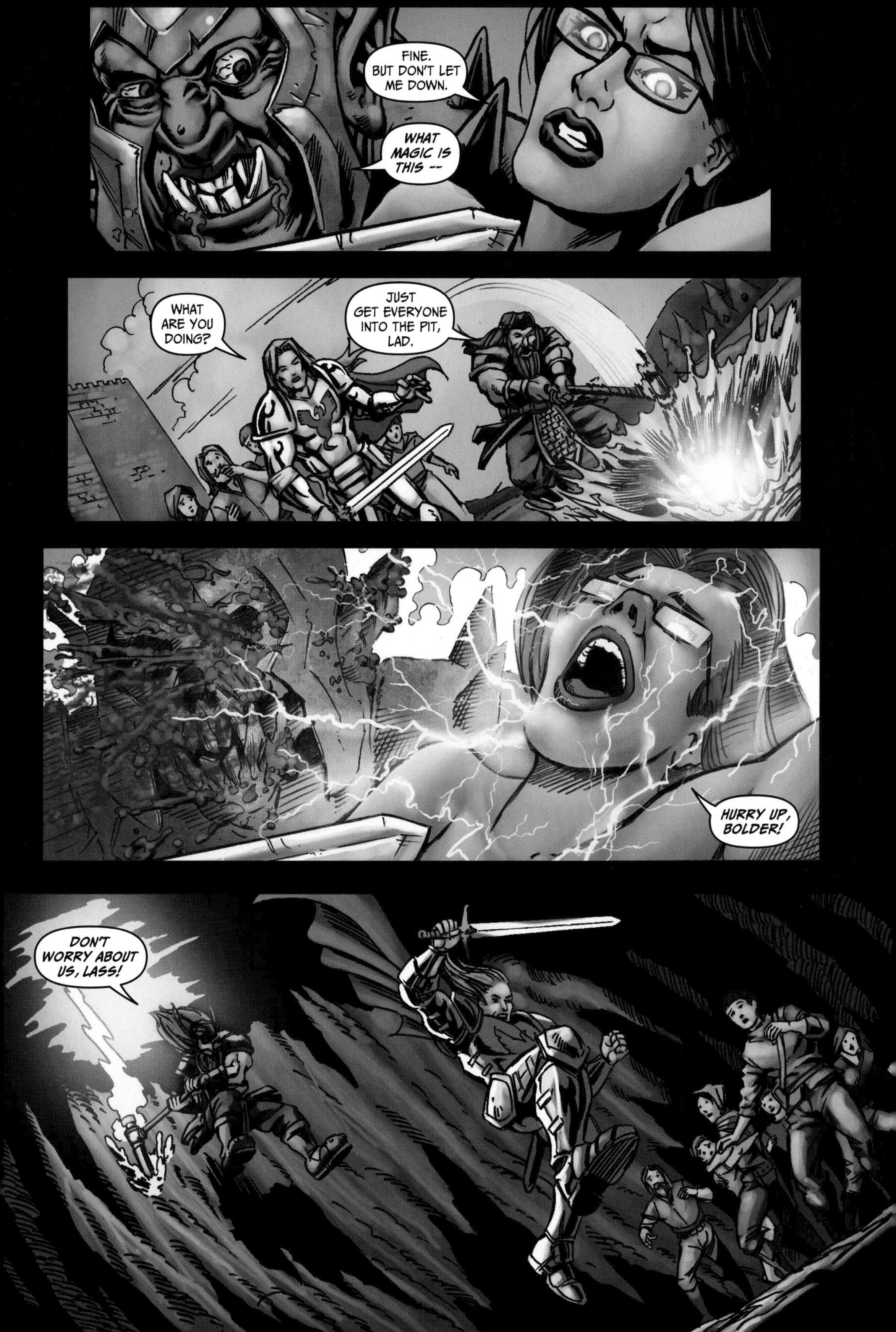
FINE. BUT DON'T LET ME DOWN.
WHAT MAGIC IS THIS --
WHAT ARE YOU DOING?
JUST GET EVERYONE INTO THE PIT, LAD.
HURRY UP, BOLDER!
DON'T WORRY ABOUT US, LASS!

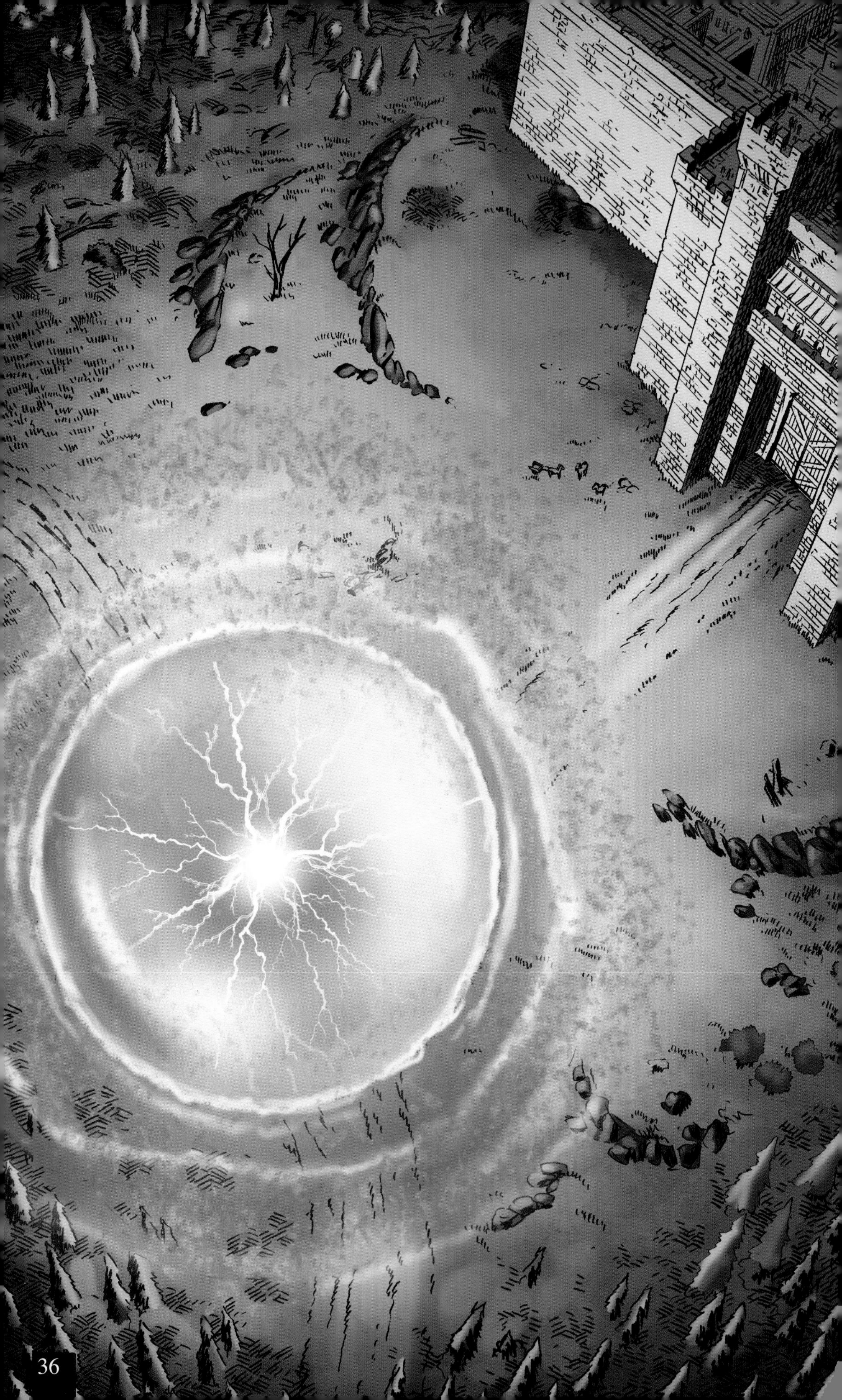

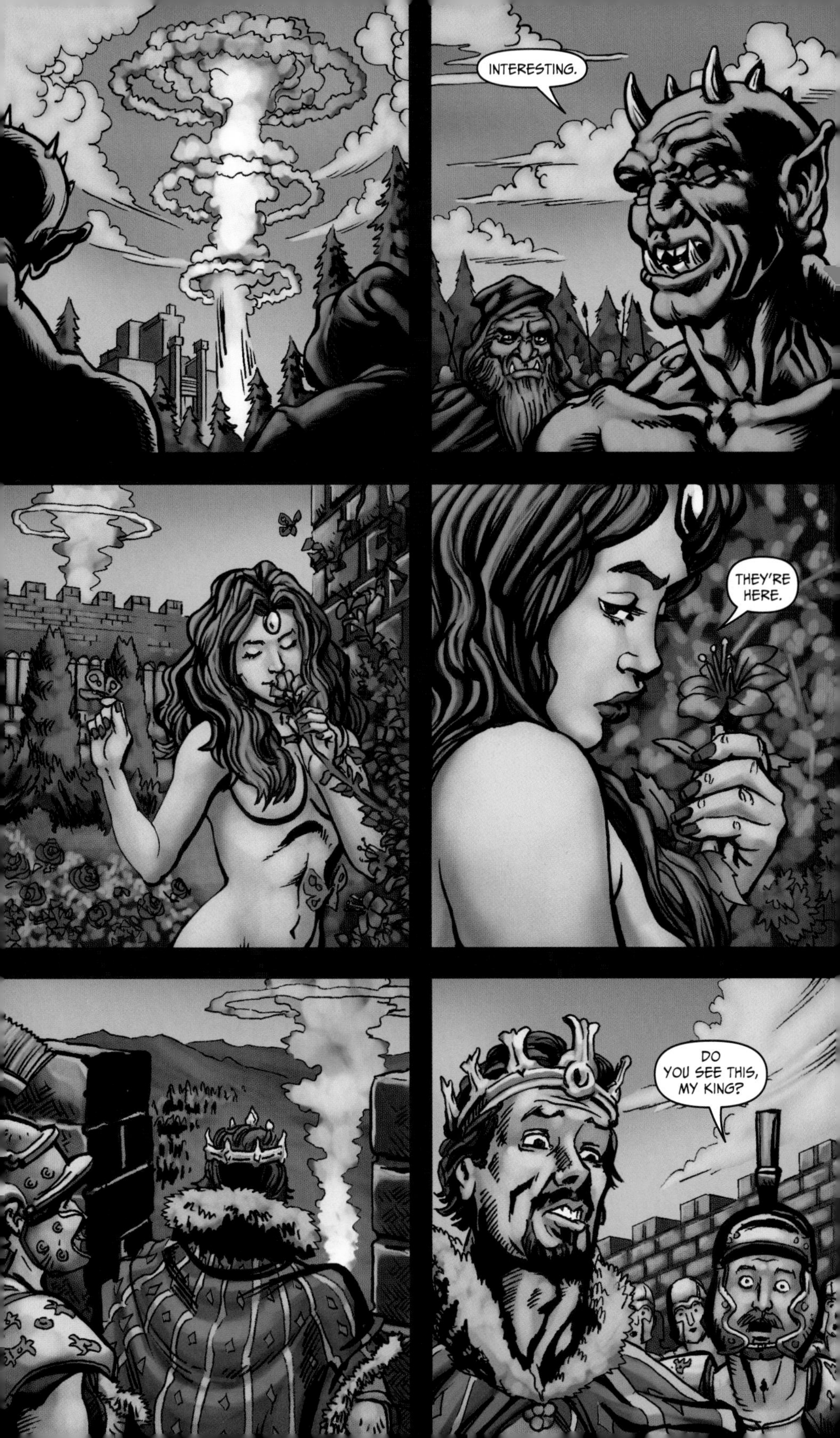
INTERESTING.
THEY'RE HERE.
DO YOU SEE THIS, MY KING?

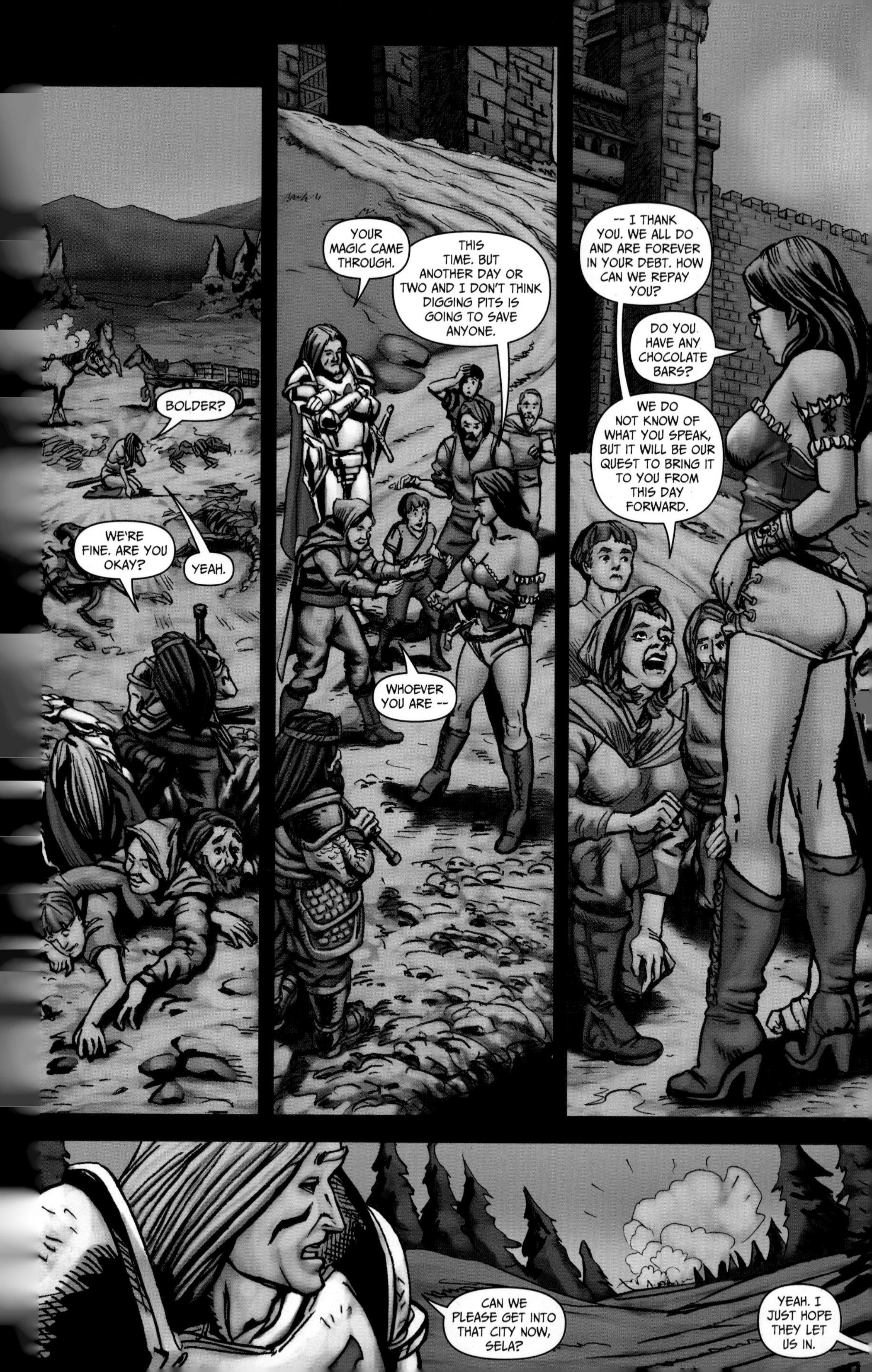
BOLDER?
WE'RE FINE. ARE YOU OKAY?
YEAH.
YOUR MAGIC CAME THROUGH.
THIS TIME. BUT ANOTHER DAY OR TWO AND I DON'T THINK DIGGING PITS IS GOING TO SAVE ANYONE.
WHOEVER YOU ARE --
-- I THANK YOU. WE ALL DO AND ARE FOREVER IN YOUR DEBT. HOW CAN WE REPAY YOU?
DO YOU HAVE ANY CHOCOLATE BARS?
WE DO NOT KNOW OF WHAT YOU SPEAK, BUT IT WILL BE OUR QUEST TO BRING IT TO YOU FROM THIS DAY FORWARD.
CAN WE PLEASE GET INTO THAT CITY NOW, SELA?
YEAH. I JUST HOPE THEY LET US IN.

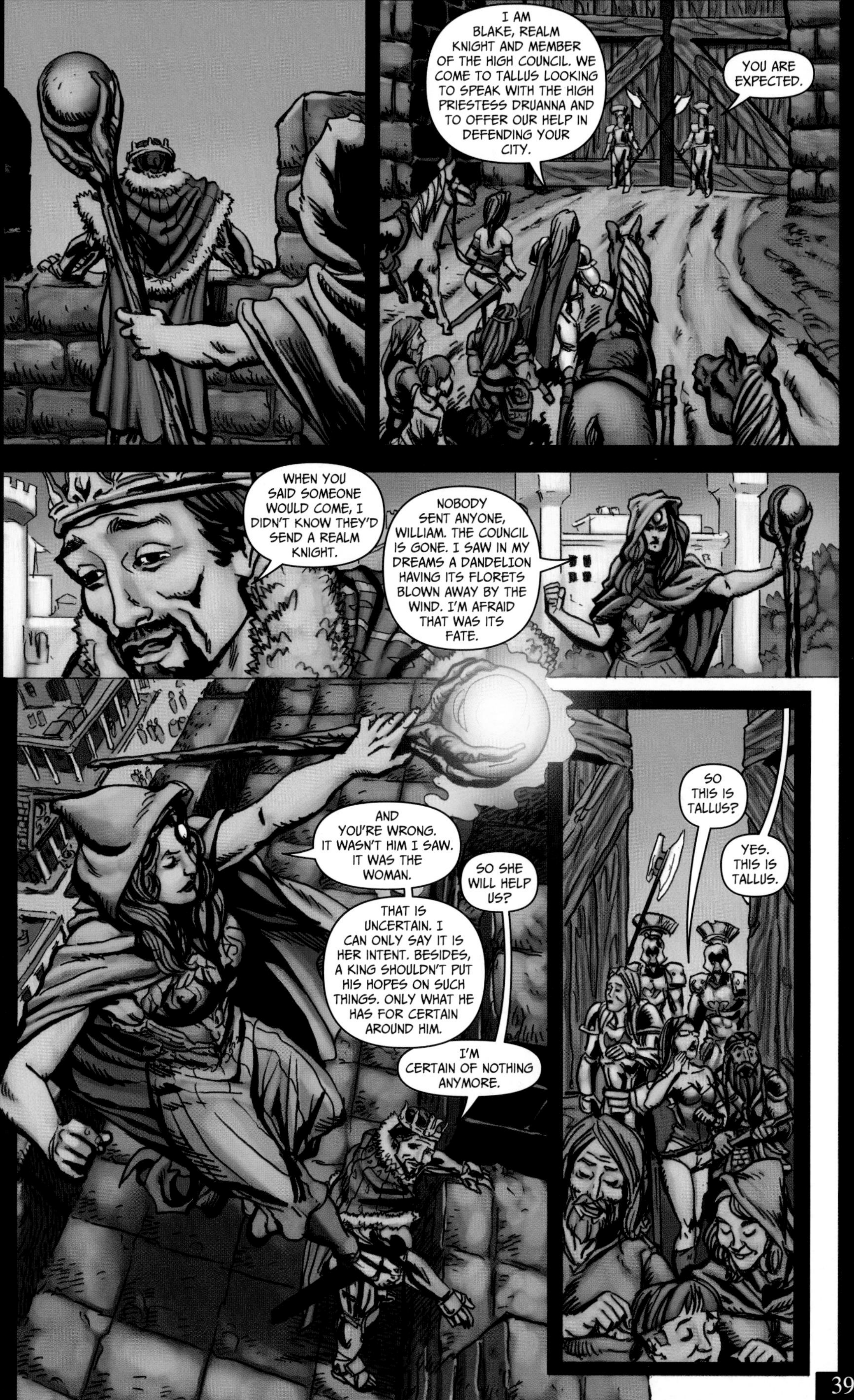
I AM BLAKE, REALM KNIGHT AND MEMBER OF THE HIGH COUNCIL. WE COME TO TALLUS LOOKING TO SPEAK WITH THE HIGH PRIESTESS DRUANNA AND TO OFFER OUR HELP IN DEFENDING YOUR CITY.
YOU ARE EXPECTED.
WHEN YOU SAID SOMEONE WOULD COME, I DIDN'T KNOW THEY'D SEND A REALM KNIGHT.
NOBODY SENT ANYONE, WILLIAM. THE COUNCIL IS GONE. I SAW IN MY DREAMS A DANDELION HAVING ITS FLORETS BLOWN AWAY BY THE WIND. I'M AFRAID THAT WAS ITS FATE.
AND YOU'RE WRONG. IT WASN'T HIM I SAW. IT WAS THE WOMAN.
SO SHE WILL HELP US?
THAT IS UNCERTAIN. I CAN ONLY SAY IT IS HER INTENT. BESIDES, A KING SHOULDN'T PUT HIS HOPES ON SUCH THINGS. ONLY WHAT HE HAS FOR CERTAIN AROUND HIM.
I'M CERTAIN OF NOTHING ANYMORE.
SO THIS IS TALLUS?
YES. THIS IS TALLUS.

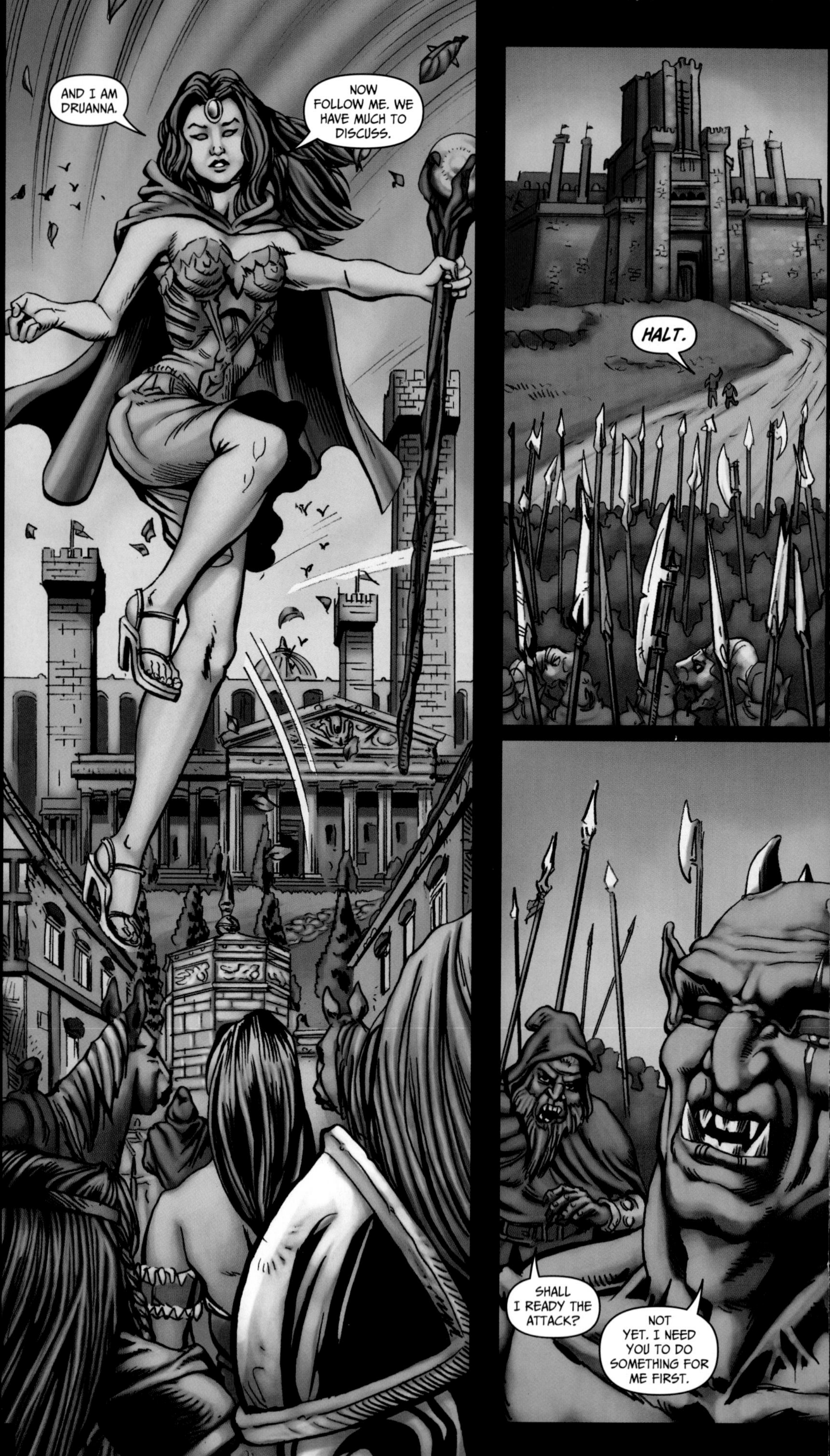
AND I AM DRUANNA.
NOW FOLLOW ME. WE HAVE MUCH TO DISCUSS.
HALT.
SHALL I READY THE ATTACK?
NOT YET. I NEED YOU TO DO SOMETHING FOR ME FIRST.

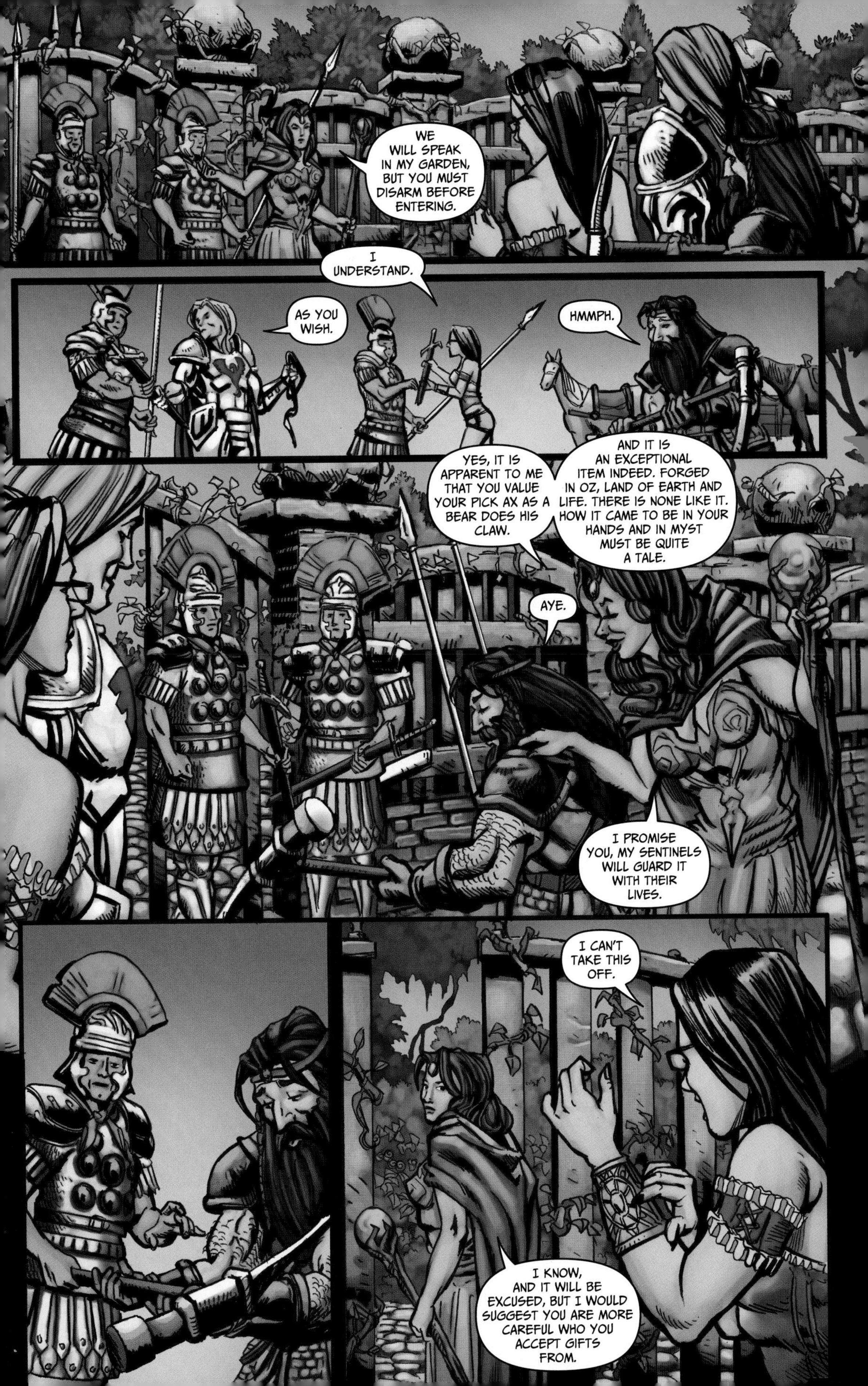
WE WILL SPEAK IN MY GARDEN, BUT YOU MUST DISARM BEFORE ENTERING.
I UNDERSTAND.
AS YOU WISH.
HMMPH.
YES, IT IS APPARENT TO ME THAT YOU VALUE YOUR PICK AX AS A BEAR DOES HIS CLAW.
AND IT IS AN EXCEPTIONAL ITEM INDEED. FORGED IN OZ, LAND OF EARTH AND LIFE. THERE IS NONE LIKE IT. HOW IT CAME TO BE IN YOUR HANDS AND IN MYST MUST BE QUITE A TALE.
AYE.
I PROMISE YOU, MY SENTINELS WILL GUARD IT WITH THEIR LIVES.
I CAN'T TAKE THIS OFF.
I KNOW, AND IT WILL BE EXCUSED, BUT I WOULD SUGGEST YOU ARE MORE CAREFUL WHO YOU ACCEPT GIFTS FROM.

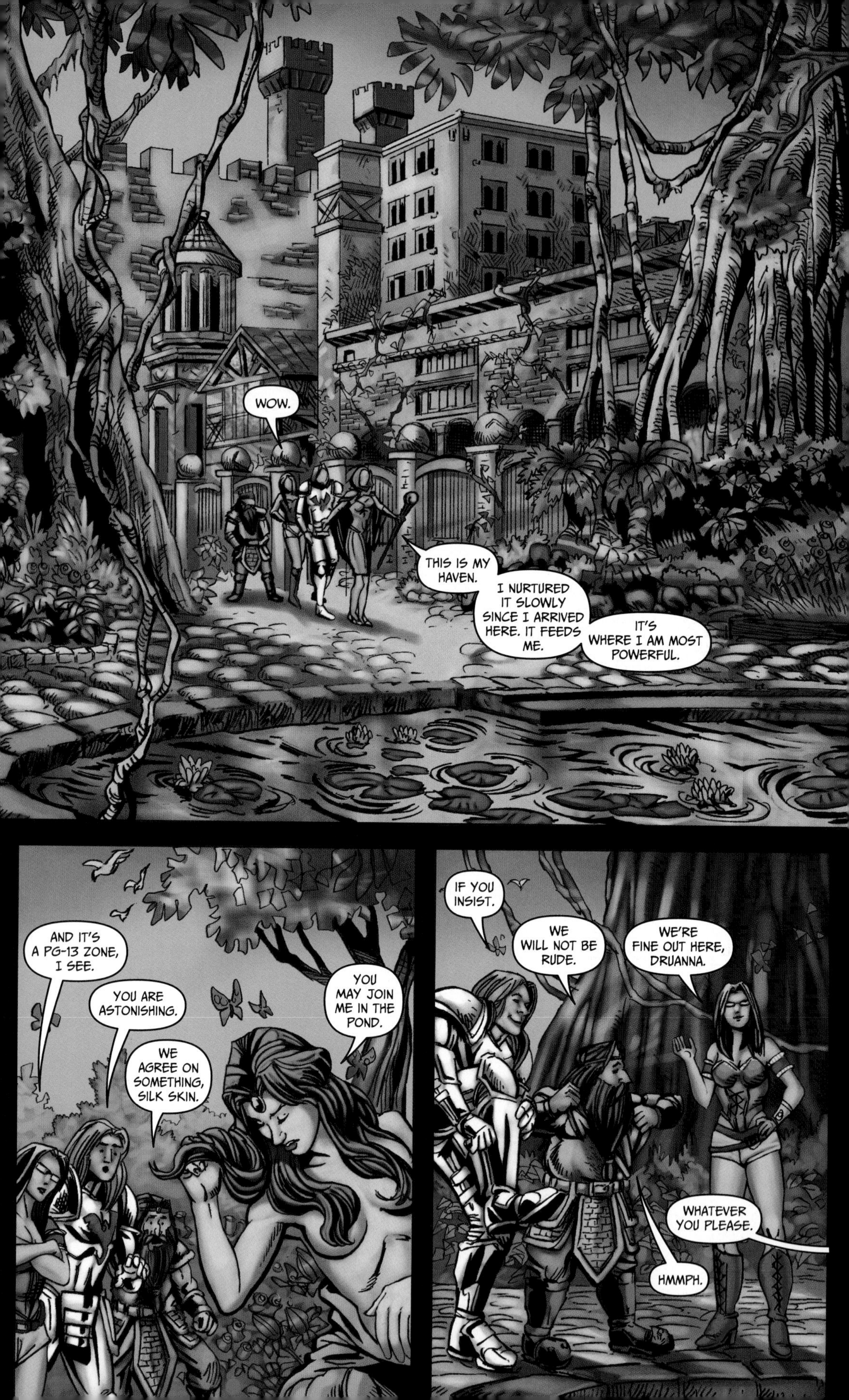
WOW.
THIS IS MY HAVEN.
I NURTURED IT SLOWLY SINCE I ARRIVED HERE. IT FEEDS ME.
IT'S WHERE I AM MOST POWERFUL.
AND IT'S A PG-13 ZONE, I SEE.
YOU ARE ASTONISHING.
WE AGREE ON SOMETHING, SILK SKIN.
YOU MAY JOIN ME IN THE POND.
IF YOU INSIST.
WE WILL NOT BE RUDE.
WE'RE FINE OUT HERE, DRUANNA.
WHATEVER YOU PLEASE.
HMMPH.

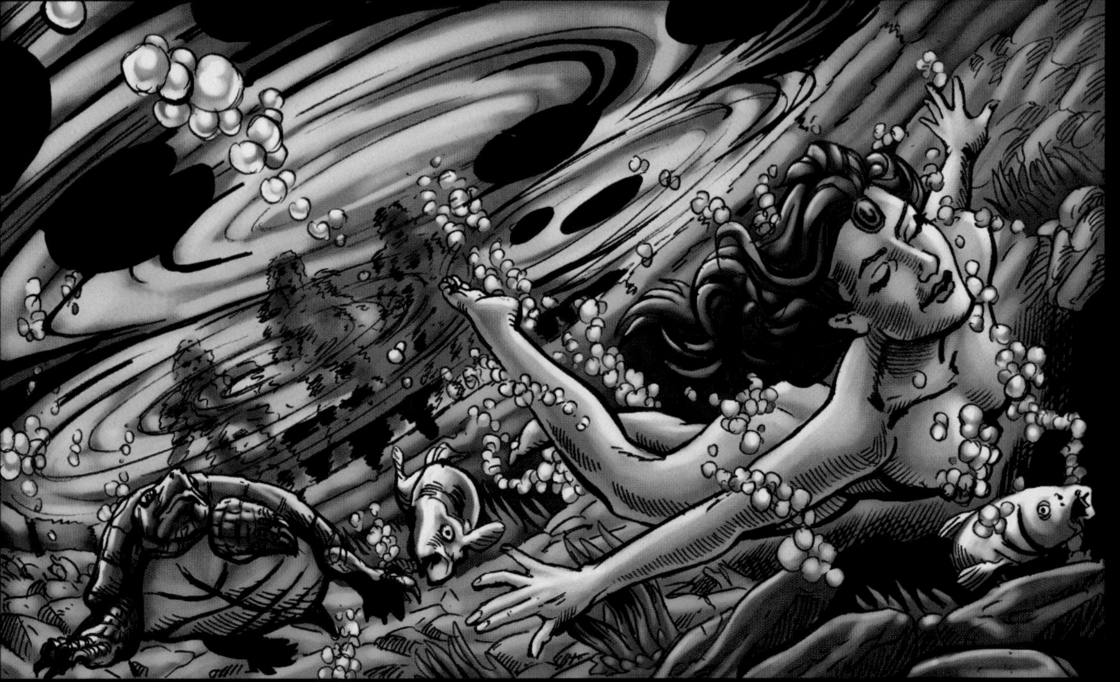

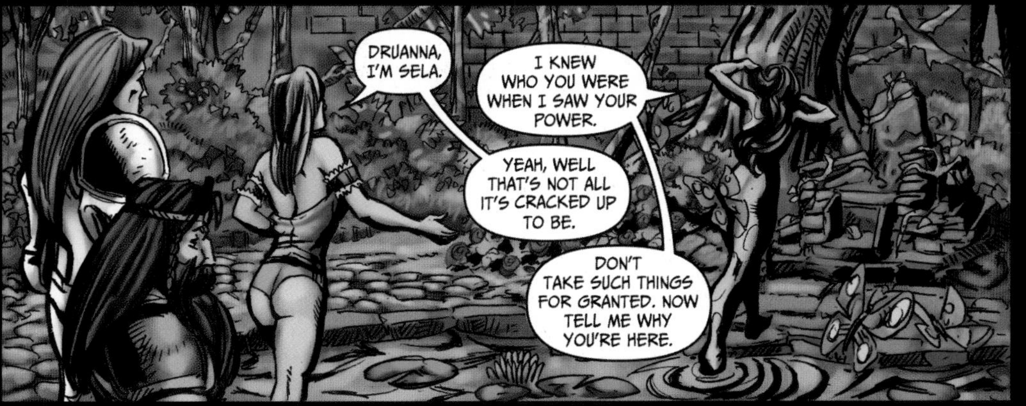
DRUANNA, I'M SELA.
I KNEW WHO YOU WERE WHEN I SAW YOUR POWER.
YEAH, WELL THAT'S NOT ALL IT'S CRACKED UP TO BE.
DON'T TAKE SUCH THINGS FOR GRANTED. NOW TELL ME WHY YOU'RE HERE.

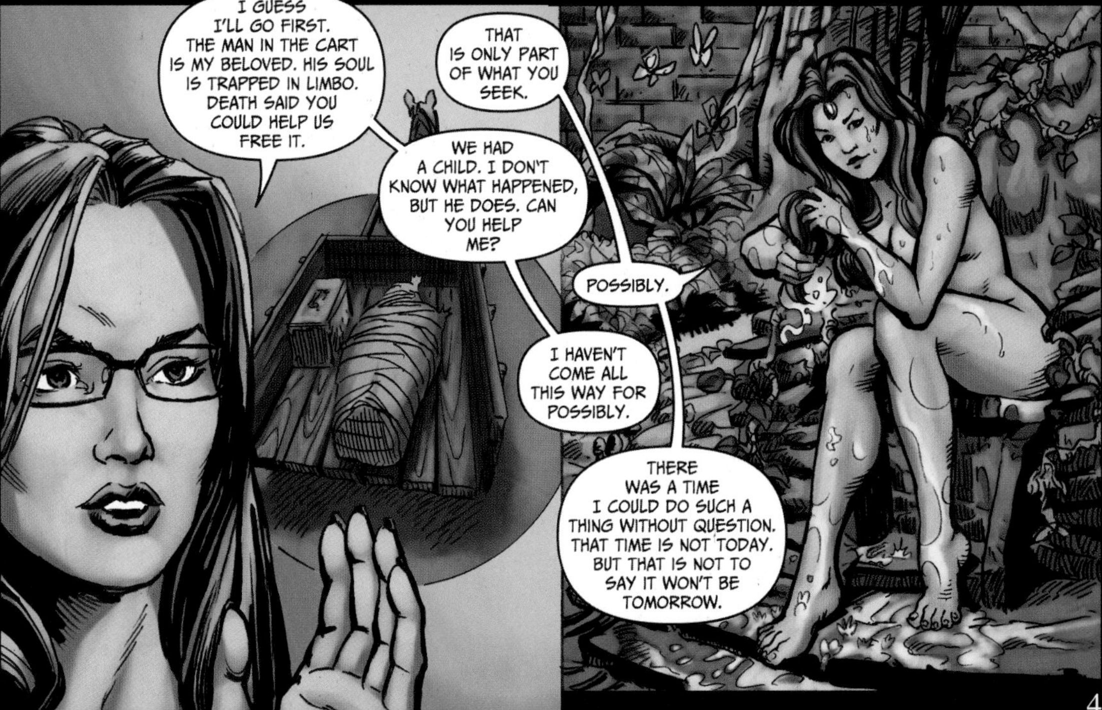
I GUESS I'LL GO FIRST. THE MAN IN THE CART IS MY BELOVED. HIS SOUL IS TRAPPED IN LIMBO. DEATH SAID YOU COULD HELP US FREE IT.
THAT IS ONLY PART OF WHAT YOU SEEK.
WE HAD A CHILD. I DON'T KNOW WHAT HAPPENED, BUT HE DOES. CAN YOU HELP ME?
POSSIBLY.
I HAVEN'T COME ALL THIS WAY FOR POSSIBLY.
THERE WAS A TIME I COULD DO SUCH A THING WITHOUT QUESTION. THAT TIME IS NOT TODAY. BUT THAT IS NOT TO SAY IT WON'T BE TOMORROW.

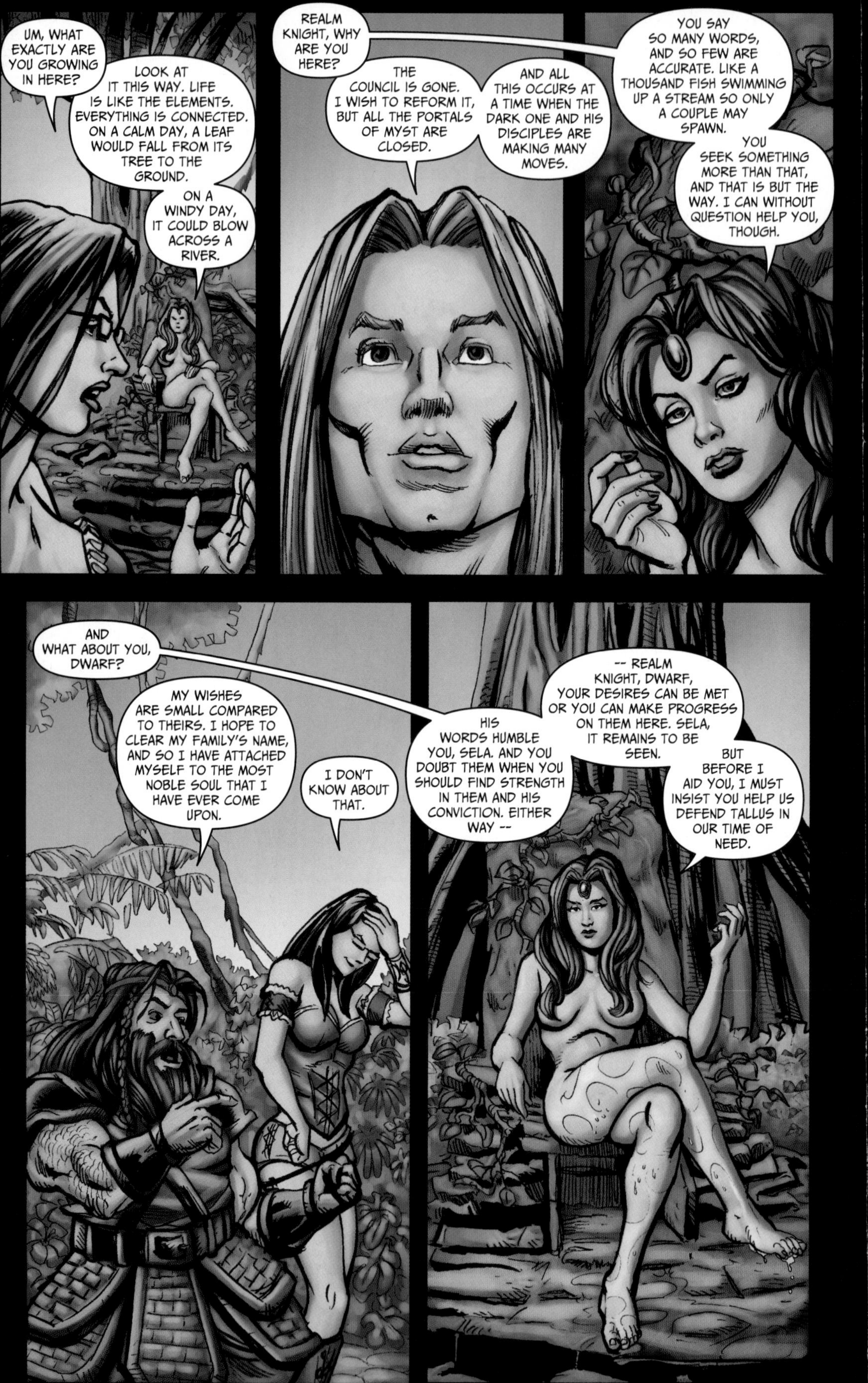
UM, WHAT EXACTLY ARE YOU GROWING IN HERE?
LOOK AT IT THIS WAY. LIFE IS LIKE THE ELEMENTS. EVERYTHING IS CONNECTED. ON A CALM DAY, A LEAF WOULD FALL FROM ITS TREE TO THE GROUND.
ON A WINDY DAY, IT COULD BLOW ACROSS A RIVER.
REALM KNIGHT, WHY ARE YOU HERE?
THE COUNCIL IS GONE. I WISH TO REFORM IT, BUT ALL THE PORTALS OF MYST ARE CLOSED.
AND ALL THIS OCCURS AT A TIME WHEN THE DARK ONE AND HIS DISCIPLES ARE MAKING MANY MOVES.
YOU SAY SO MANY WORDS, AND SO FEW ARE ACCURATE. LIKE A THOUSAND FISH SWIMMING UP A STREAM SO ONLY A COUPLE MAY SPAWN.
YOU SEEK SOMETHING MORE THAN THAT, AND THAT IS BUT THE WAY. I CAN WITHOUT QUESTION HELP YOU, THOUGH.
AND WHAT ABOUT YOU, DWARF?
MY WISHES ARE SMALL COMPARED TO THEIRS. I HOPE TO CLEAR MY FAMILY'S NAME, AND SO I HAVE ATTACHED MYSELF TO THE MOST NOBLE SOUL THAT I HAVE EVER COME UPON.
I DON'T KNOW ABOUT THAT.
HIS WORDS HUMBLE YOU, SELA. AND YOU DOUBT THEM WHEN YOU SHOULD FIND STRENGTH IN THEM AND HIS CONVICTION. EITHER WAY --
-- REALM KNIGHT, DWARF, YOUR DESIRES CAN BE MET OR YOU CAN MAKE PROGRESS ON THEM HERE. SELA, IT REMAINS TO BE SEEN.
BUT BEFORE I AID YOU, I MUST INSIST YOU HELP US DEFEND TALLUS IN OUR TIME OF NEED.

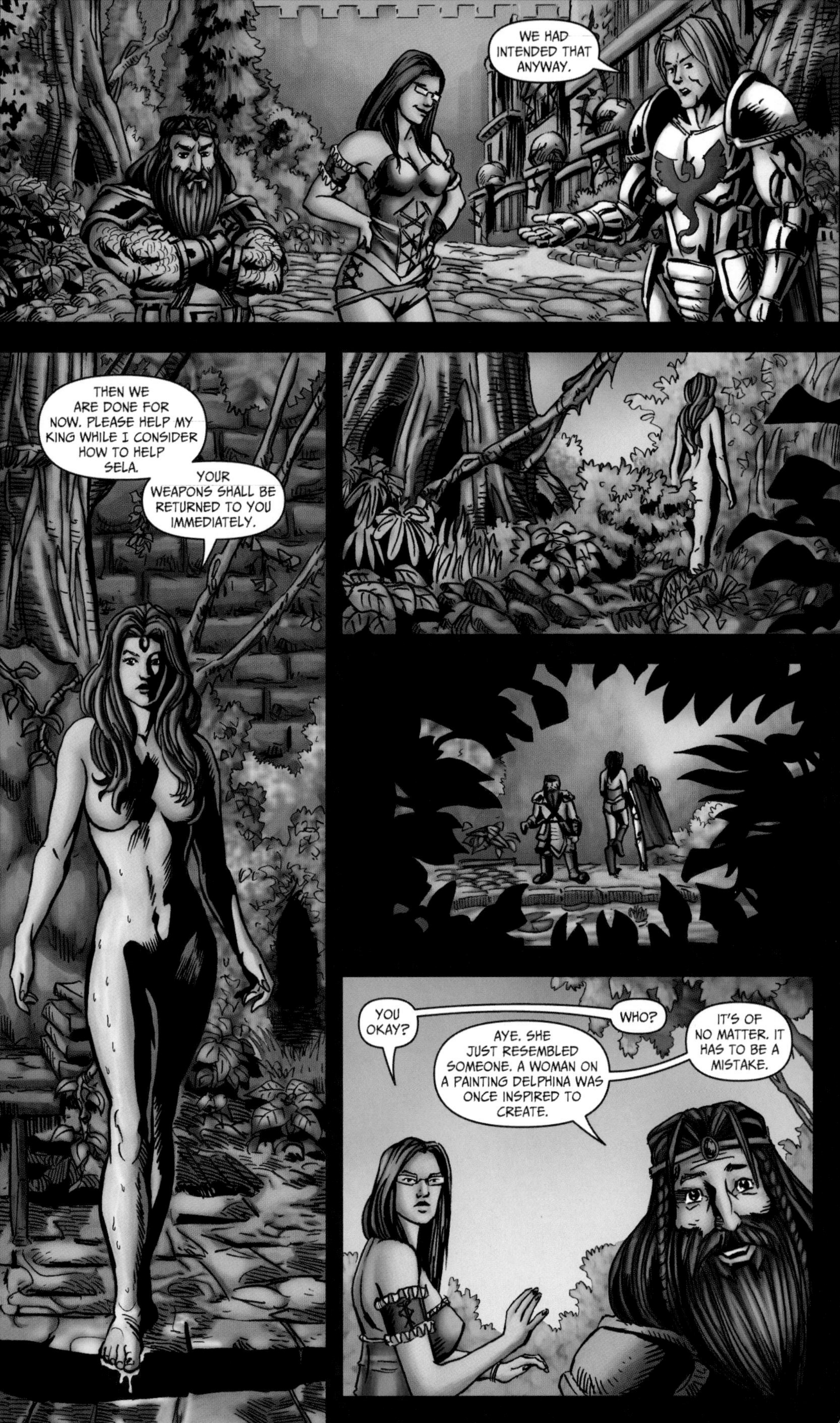
WE HAD INTENDED THAT ANYWAY.
THEN WE ARE DONE FOR NOW. PLEASE HELP MY KING WHILE I CONSIDER HOW TO HELP SELA.
YOUR WEAPONS SHALL BE RETURNED TO YOU IMMEDIATELY.
YOU OKAY?
AYE. SHE JUST RESEMBLED SOMEONE. A WOMAN ON A PAINTING DELPHINA WAS ONCE INSPIRED TO CREATE.
WHO?
IT'S OF NO MATTER. IT HAS TO BE A MISTAKE.

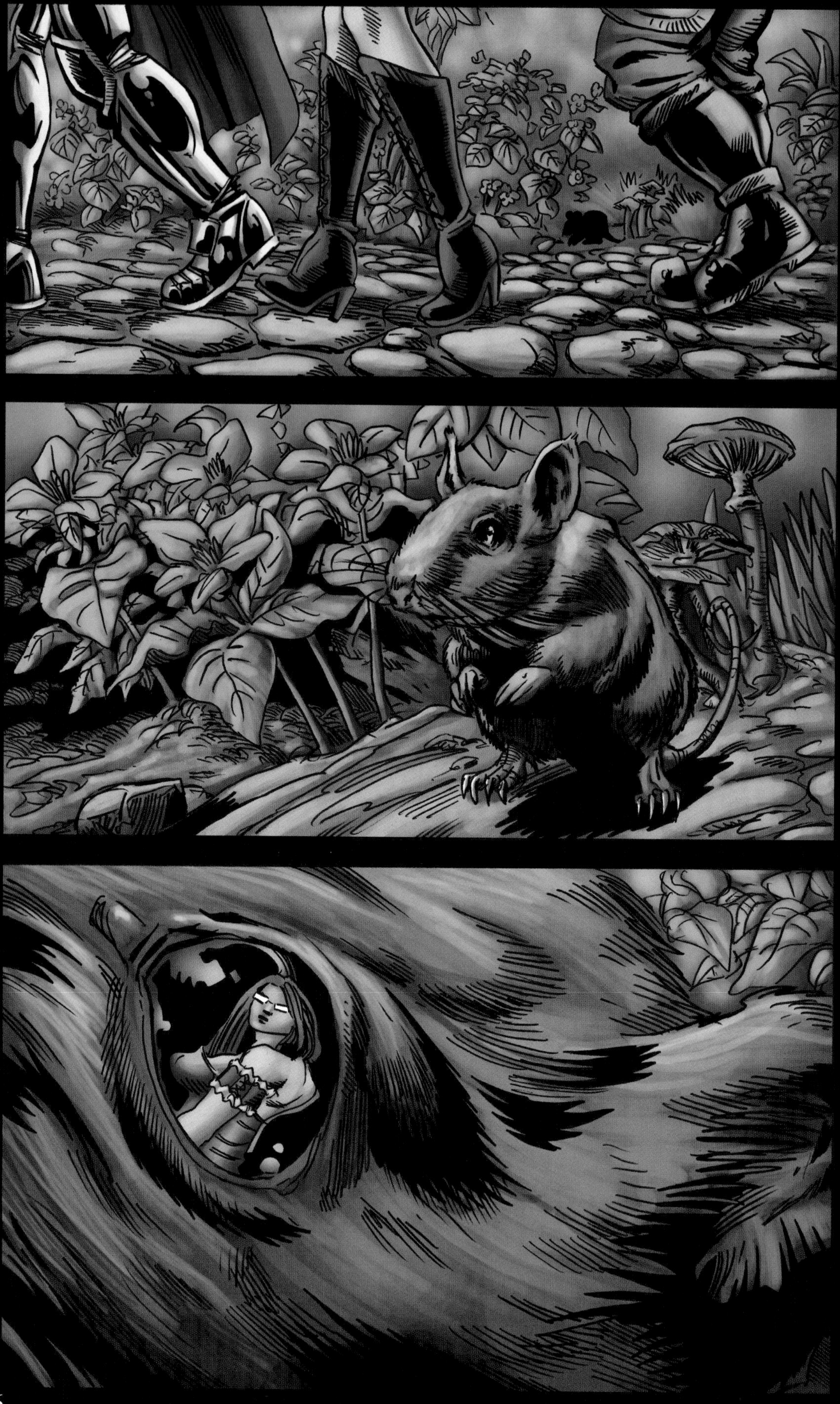

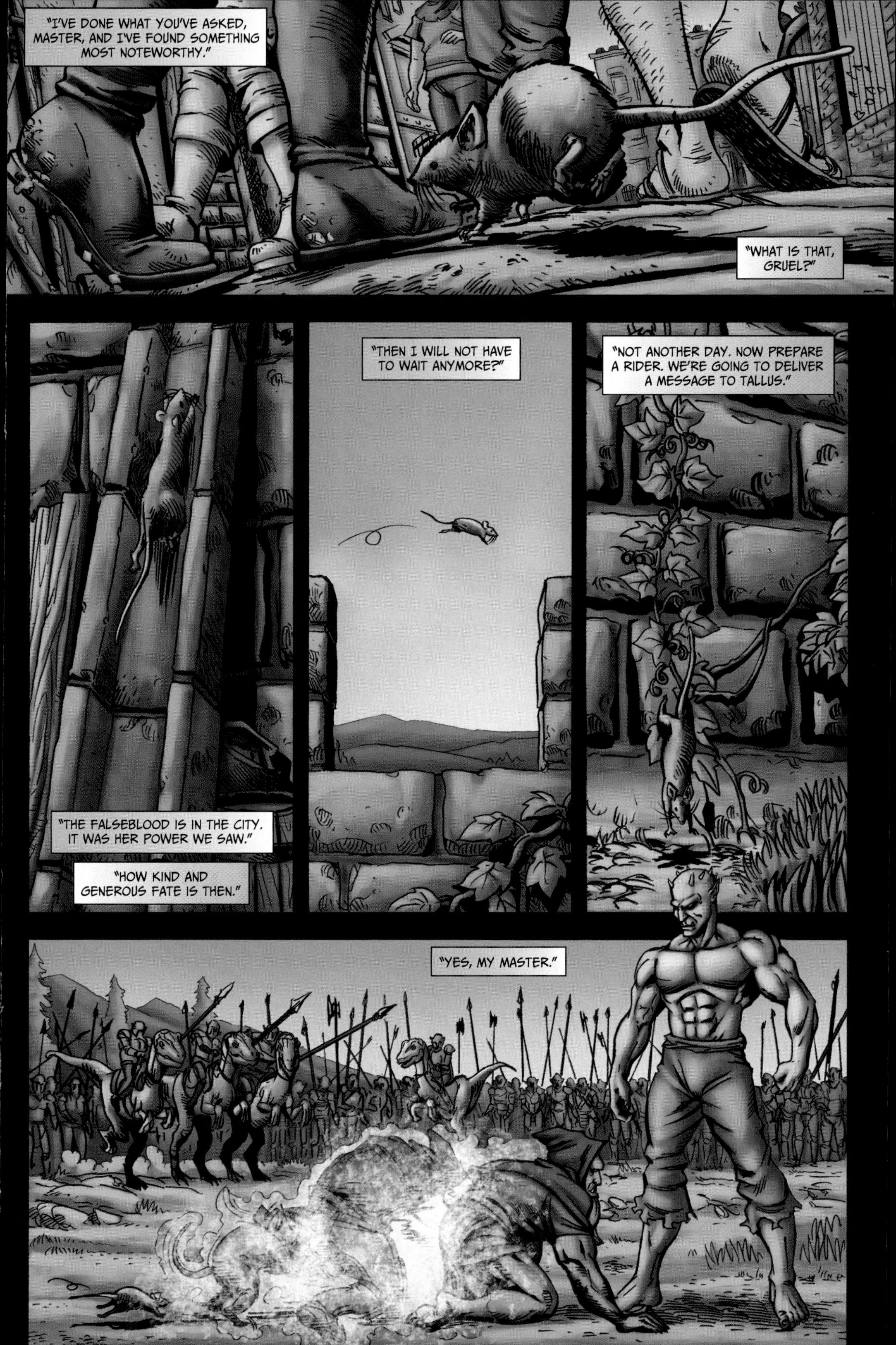
"I'VE DONE WHAT YOU'VE ASKED, MASTER, AND I'VE FOUND SOMETHING MOST NOTEWORTHY."
"WHAT IS THAT, GRUEL?"
"THE FALSEBLOOD IS IN THE CITY. IT WAS HER POWER WE SAW."
"HOW KIND AND GENEROUS FATE IS THEN."
"THEN I WILL NOT HAVE TO WAIT ANYMORE?"
"NOT ANOTHER DAY. NOW PREPARE A RIDER. WE'RE GOING TO DELIVER A MESSAGE TO TALLUS."
"YES, MY MASTER."

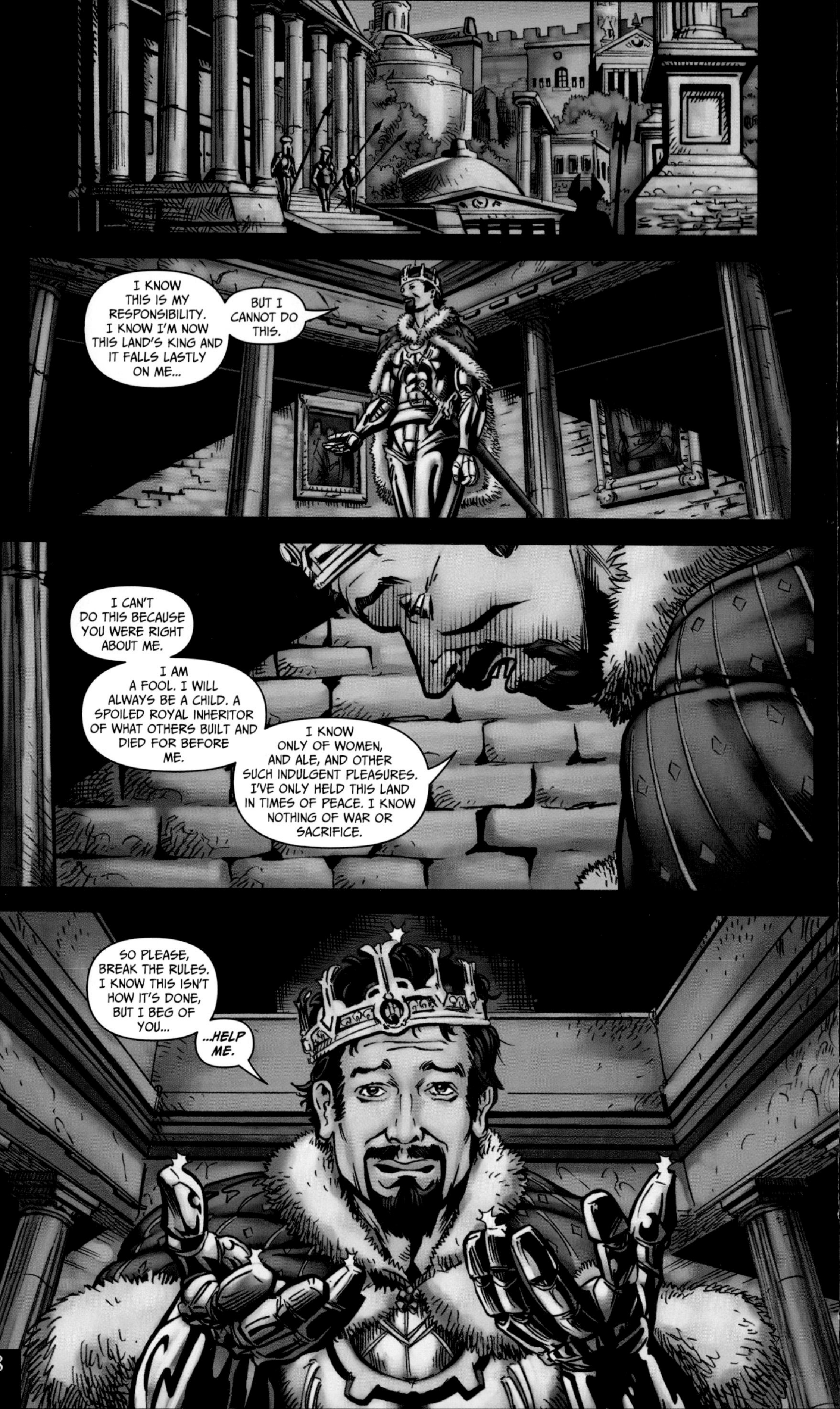
I KNOW THIS IS MY RESPONSIBILITY. I KNOW I'M NOW THIS LAND'S KING AND IT FALLS LASTLY ON ME...
BUT I CANNOT DO THIS.
I CAN'T DO THIS BECAUSE YOU WERE RIGHT ABOUT ME.
I AM A FOOL. I WILL ALWAYS BE A CHILD. A SPOILED ROYAL INHERITOR OF WHAT OTHERS BUILT AND DIED FOR BEFORE ME.
I KNOW ONLY OF WOMEN, AND ALE, AND OTHER SUCH INDULGENT PLEASURES. I'VE ONLY HELD THIS LAND IN TIMES OF PEACE. I KNOW NOTHING OF WAR OR SACRIFICE.
SO PLEASE, BREAK THE RULES. I KNOW THIS ISN'T HOW IT'S DONE, BUT I BEG OF YOU...
...HELP ME.

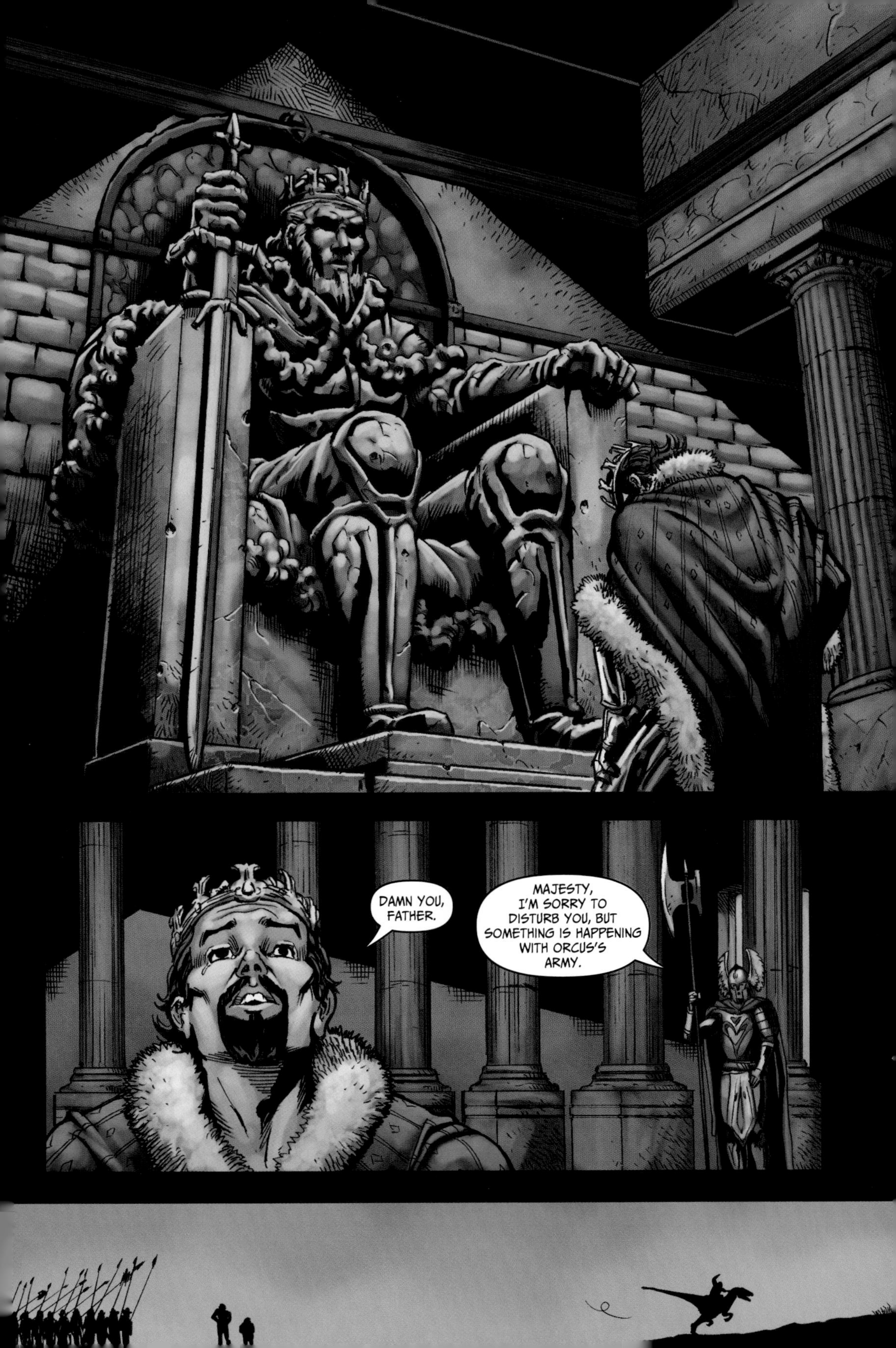
DAMN YOU, FATHER.
MAJESTY, I'M SORRY TO DISTURB YOU, BUT SOMETHING IS HAPPENING WITH ORCUS'S ARMY.

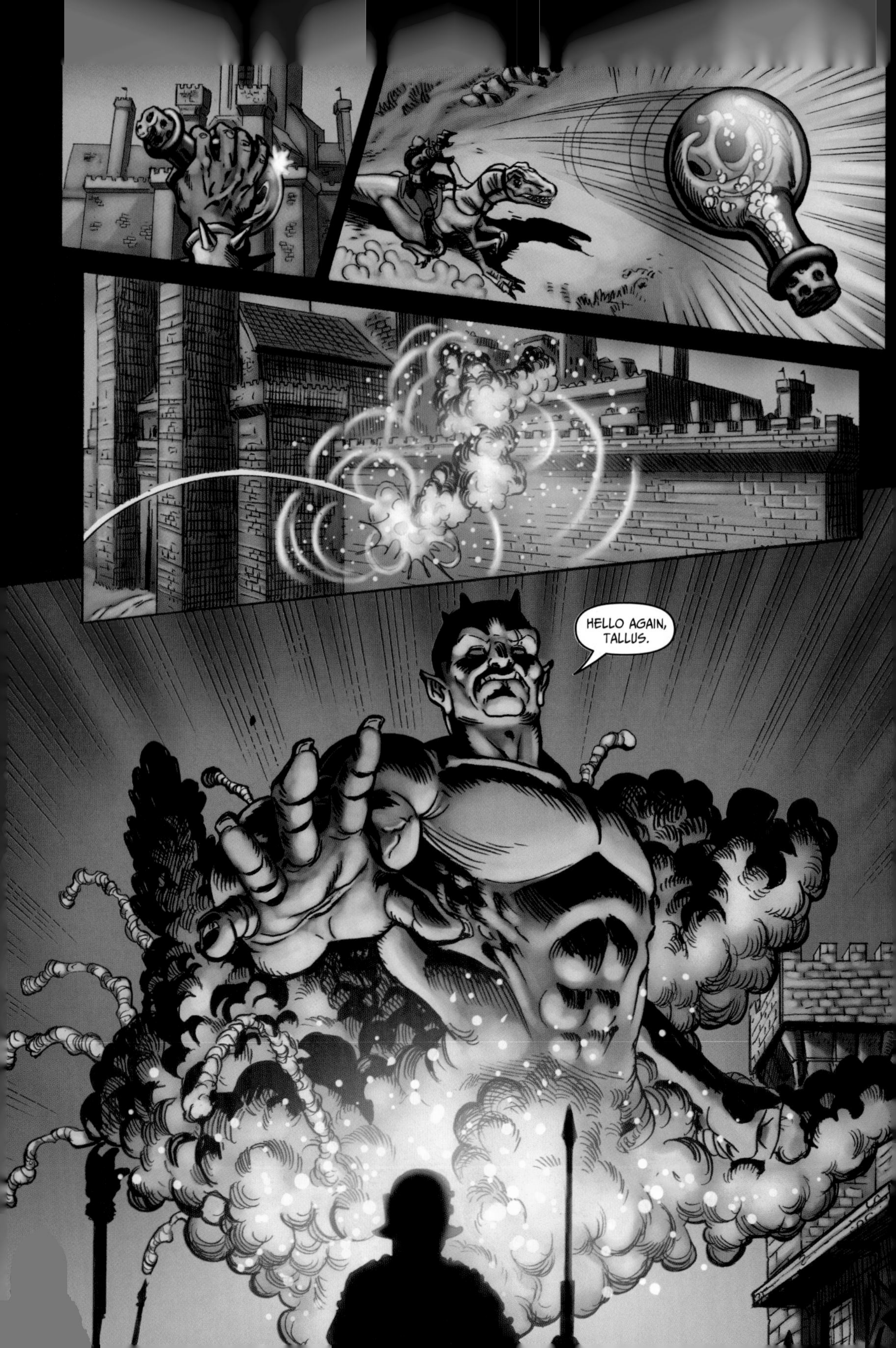
HELLO AGAIN,
TALLUS.

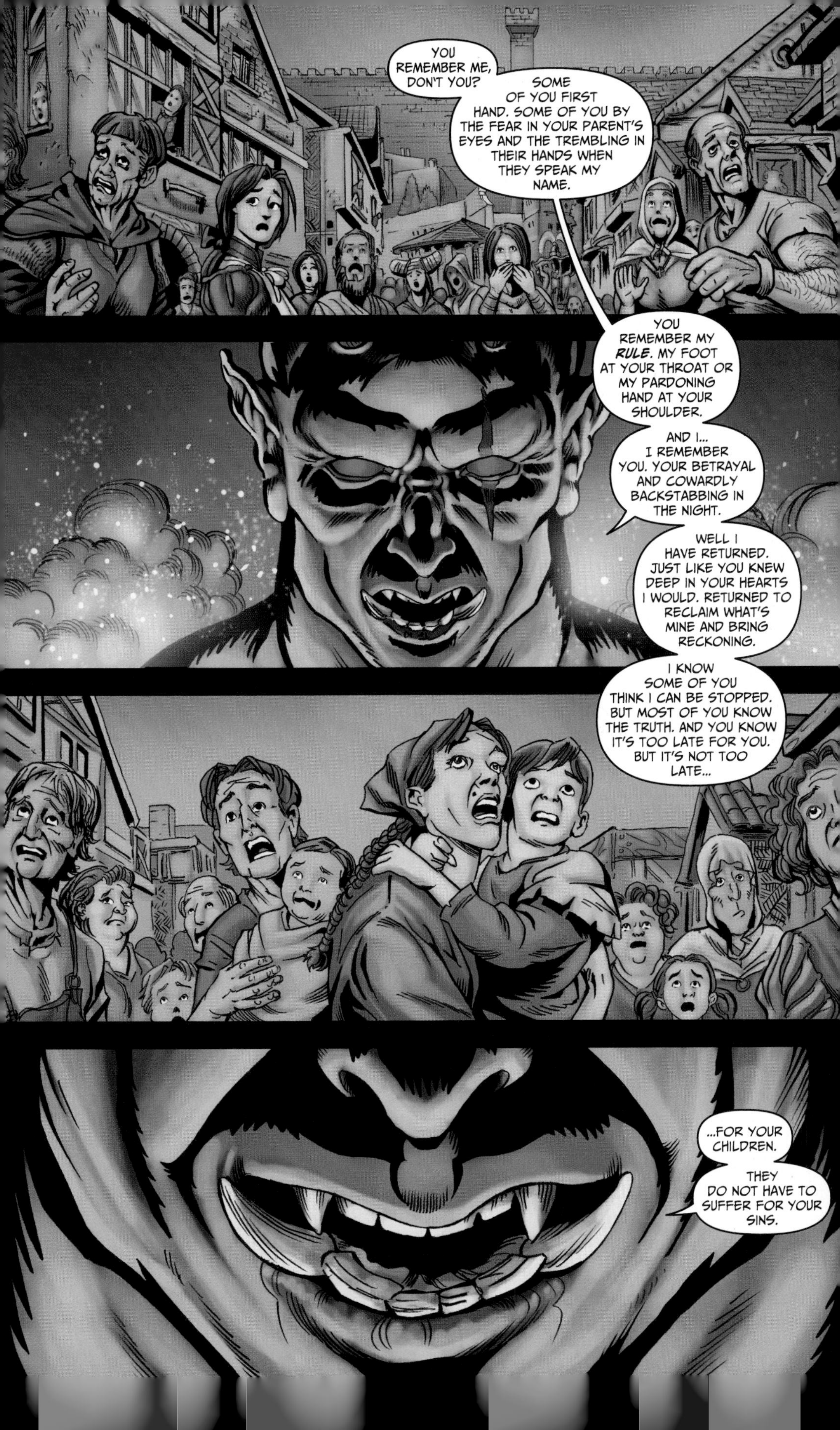
YOU REMEMBER ME, DON'T YOU?
SOME OF YOU FIRST HAND. SOME OF YOU BY THE FEAR IN YOUR PARENT'S EYES AND THE TREMBLING IN THEIR HANDS WHEN THEY SPEAK MY NAME.
YOU REMEMBER MY *RULE*. MY FOOT AT YOUR THROAT OR MY PARDONING HAND AT YOUR SHOULDER.
AND I... I REMEMBER YOU. YOUR BETRAYAL AND COWARDLY BACKSTABBING IN THE NIGHT.
WELL I HAVE RETURNED. JUST LIKE YOU KNEW DEEP IN YOUR HEARTS I WOULD. RETURNED TO RECLAIM WHAT'S MINE AND BRING RECKONING.
I KNOW SOME OF YOU THINK I CAN BE STOPPED. BUT MOST OF YOU KNOW THE TRUTH. AND YOU KNOW IT'S TOO LATE FOR YOU. BUT IT'S NOT TOO LATE...
...FOR YOUR CHILDREN.
THEY DO NOT HAVE TO SUFFER FOR YOUR SINS.

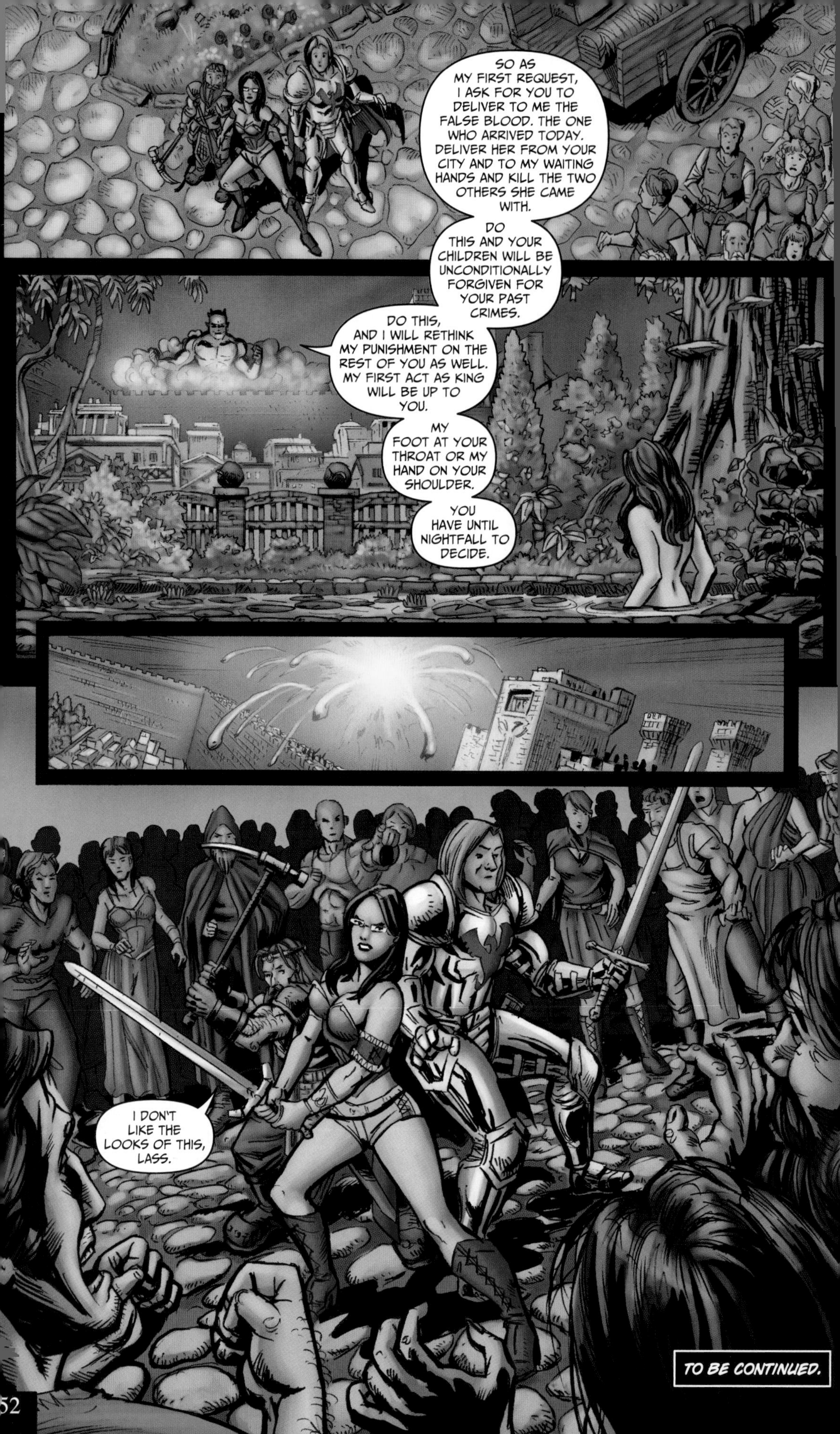

SO AS MY FIRST REQUEST, I ASK FOR YOU TO DELIVER TO ME THE FALSE BLOOD. THE ONE WHO ARRIVED TODAY. DELIVER HER FROM YOUR CITY AND TO MY WAITING HANDS AND KILL THE TWO OTHERS SHE CAME WITH.
DO THIS AND YOUR CHILDREN WILL BE UNCONDITIONALLY FORGIVEN FOR YOUR PAST CRIMES.
DO THIS, AND I WILL RETHINK MY PUNISHMENT ON THE REST OF YOU AS WELL. MY FIRST ACT AS KING WILL BE UP TO YOU.
MY FOOT AT YOUR THROAT OR MY HAND ON YOUR SHOULDER.
YOU HAVE UNTIL NIGHTFALL TO DECIDE.
I DON'T LIKE THE LOOKS OF THIS, LASS.
TO BE CONTINUED.

Grimm Fairy Tales

Volume 10

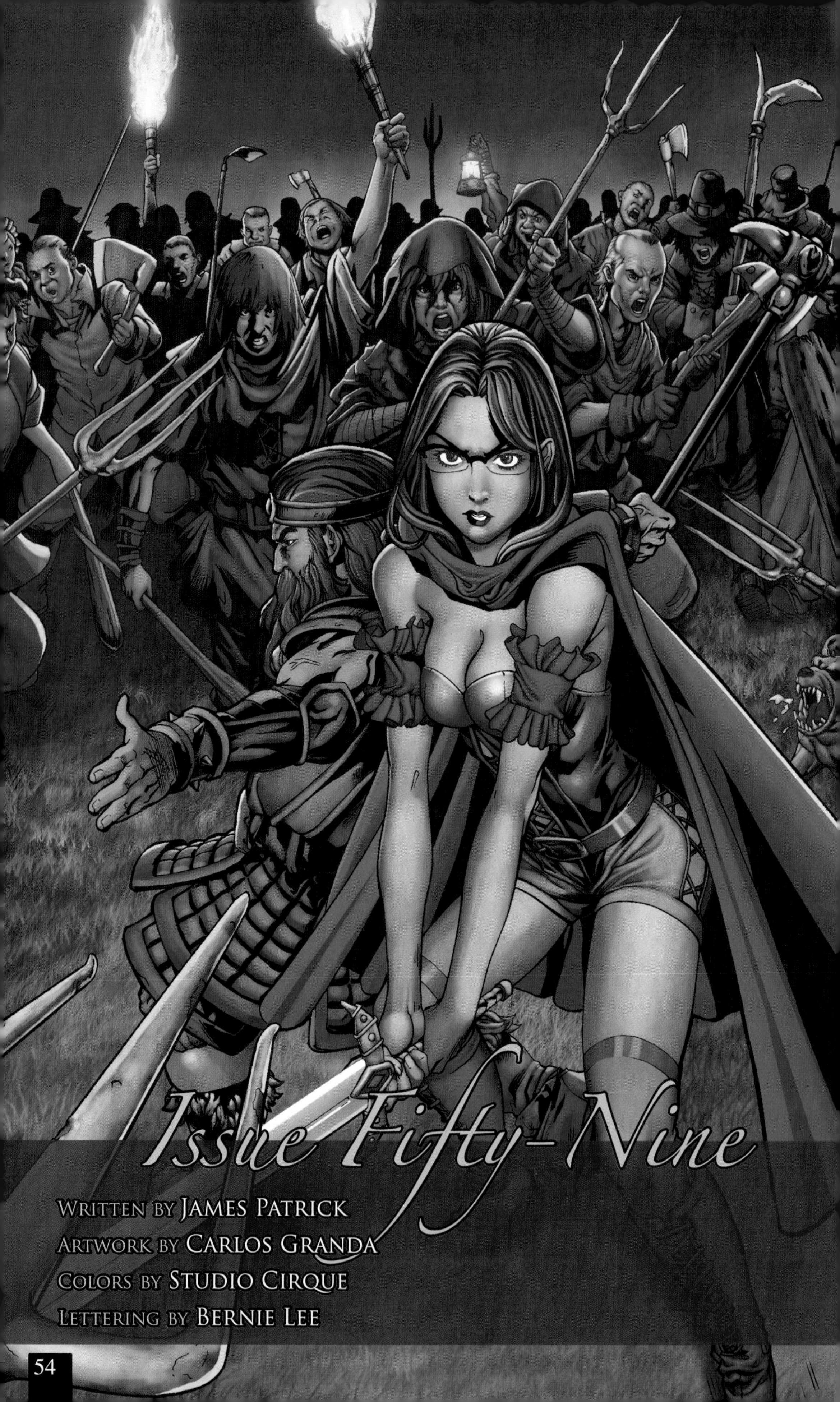

Issue Fifty-Nine

Written by James Patrick
Artwork by Carlos Granda
Colors by Studio Cirque
Lettering by Bernie Lee

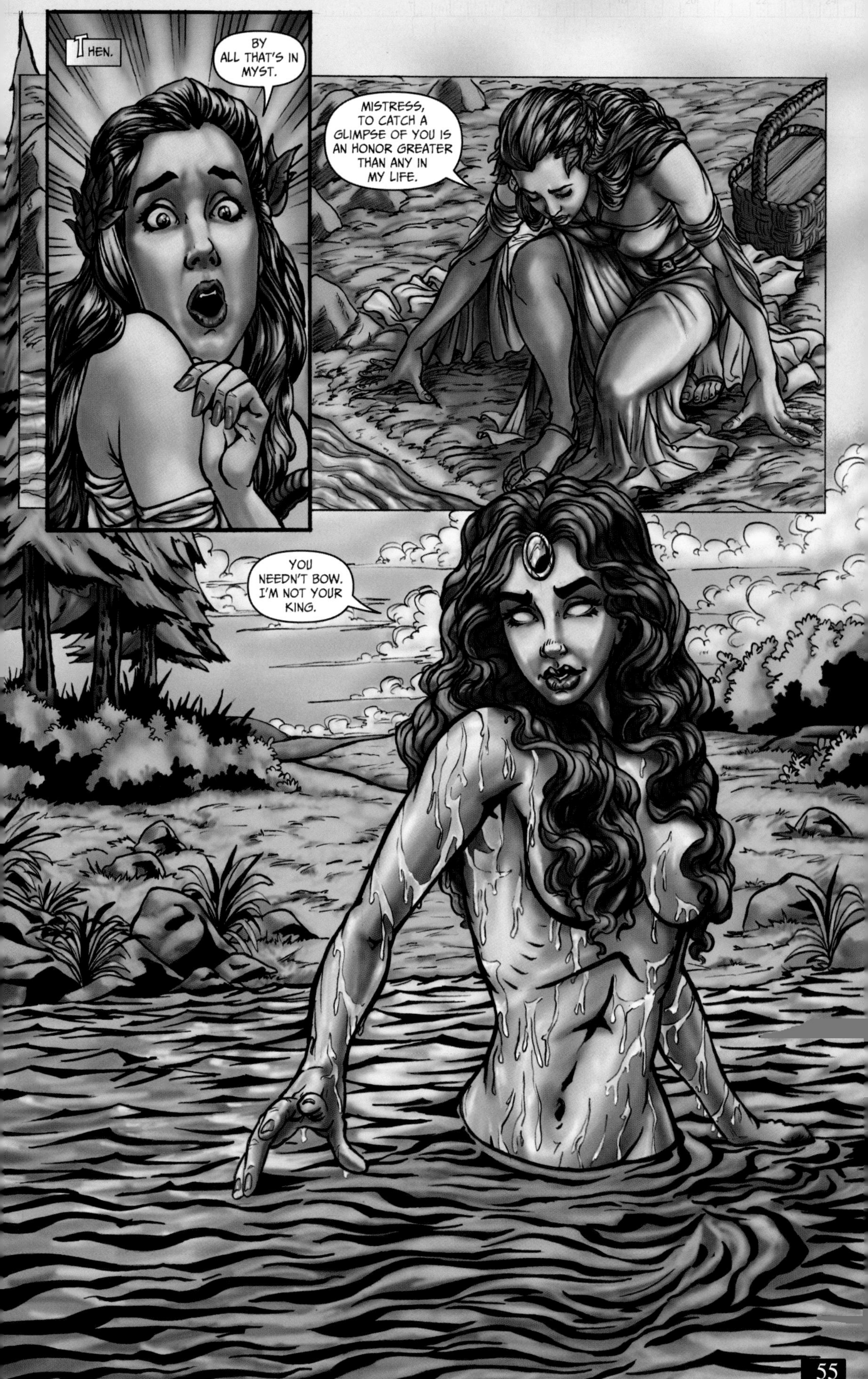
THEN.
BY ALL THAT'S IN MYST.
MISTRESS, TO CATCH A GLIMPSE OF YOU IS AN HONOR GREATER THAN ANY IN MY LIFE.
YOU NEEDN'T BOW. I'M NOT YOUR KING.

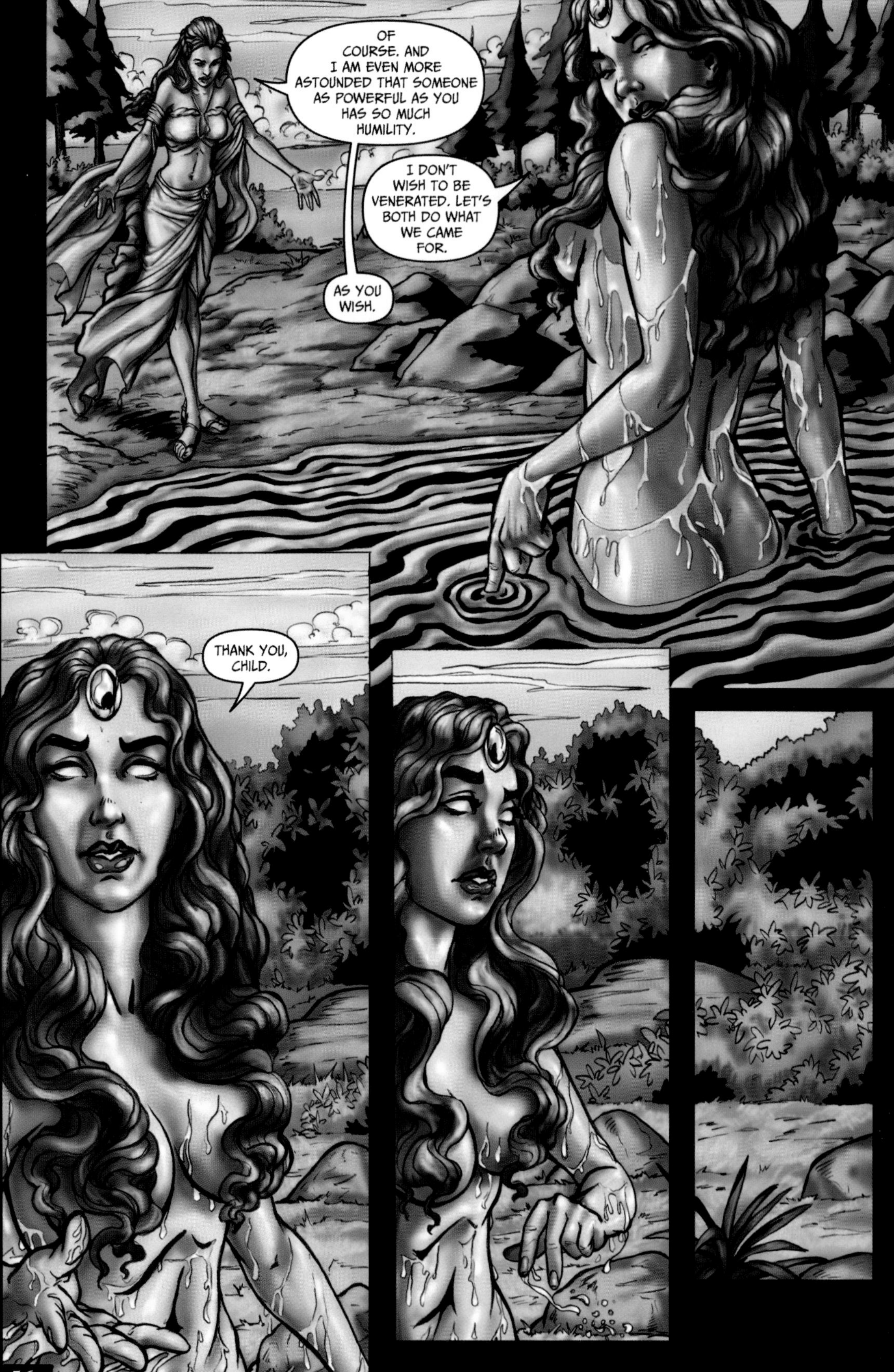
OF COURSE. AND I AM EVEN MORE ASTOUNDED THAT SOMEONE AS POWERFUL AS YOU HAS SO MUCH HUMILITY.
I DON'T WISH TO BE VENERATED. LET'S BOTH DO WHAT WE CAME FOR.
AS YOU WISH.
THANK YOU, CHILD.

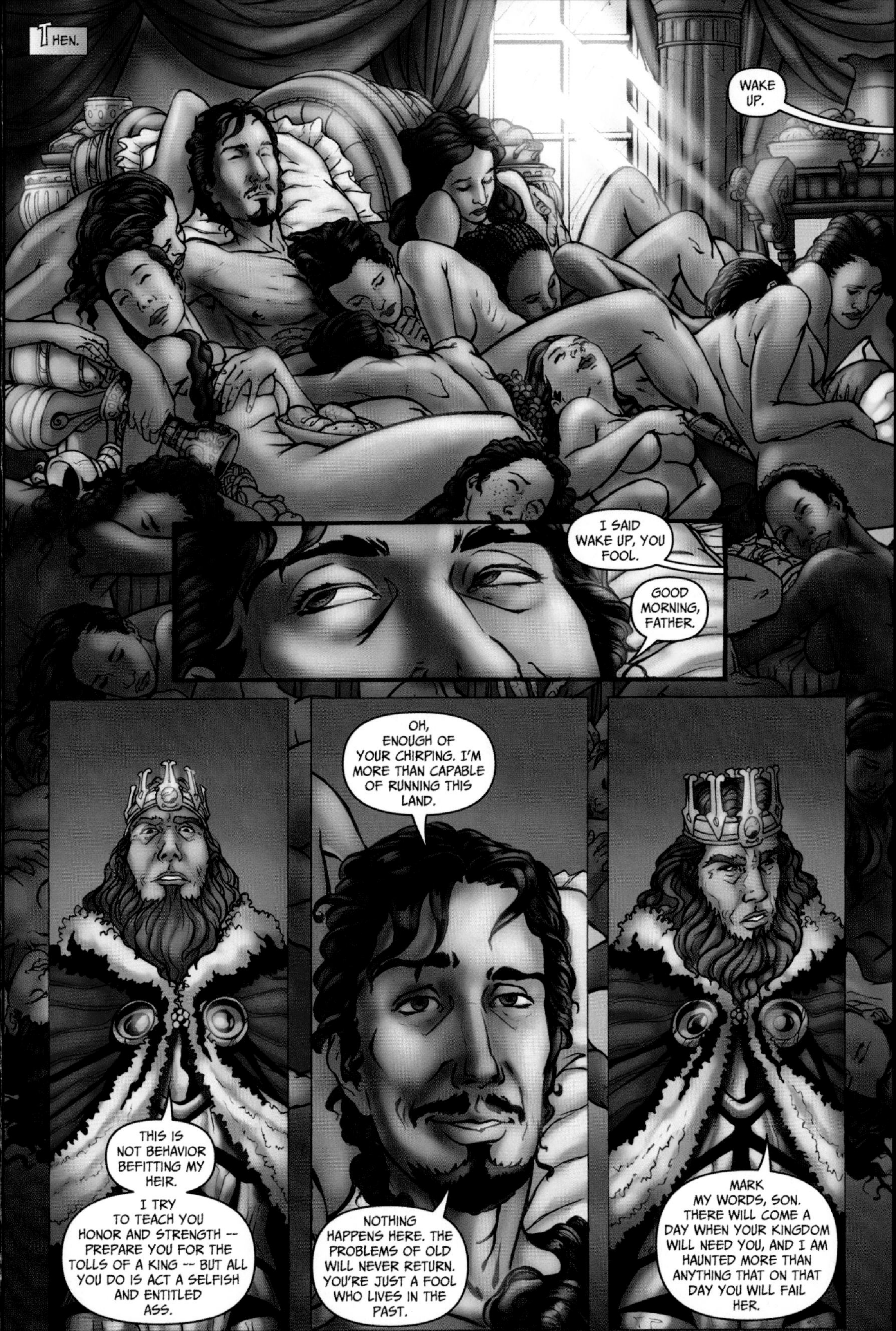
THEN.
WAKE UP.
I SAID WAKE UP, YOU FOOL.
GOOD MORNING, FATHER.
OH, ENOUGH OF YOUR CHIRPING. I'M MORE THAN CAPABLE OF RUNNING THIS LAND.
THIS IS NOT BEHAVIOR BEFITTING MY HEIR.
I TRY TO TEACH YOU HONOR AND STRENGTH -- PREPARE YOU FOR THE TOLLS OF A KING -- BUT ALL YOU DO IS ACT A SELFISH AND ENTITLED ASS.
NOTHING HAPPENS HERE. THE PROBLEMS OF OLD WILL NEVER RETURN. YOU'RE JUST A FOOL WHO LIVES IN THE PAST.
MARK MY WORDS, SON. THERE WILL COME A DAY WHEN YOUR KINGDOM WILL NEED YOU, AND I AM HAUNTED MORE THAN ANYTHING THAT ON THAT DAY YOU WILL FAIL HER.

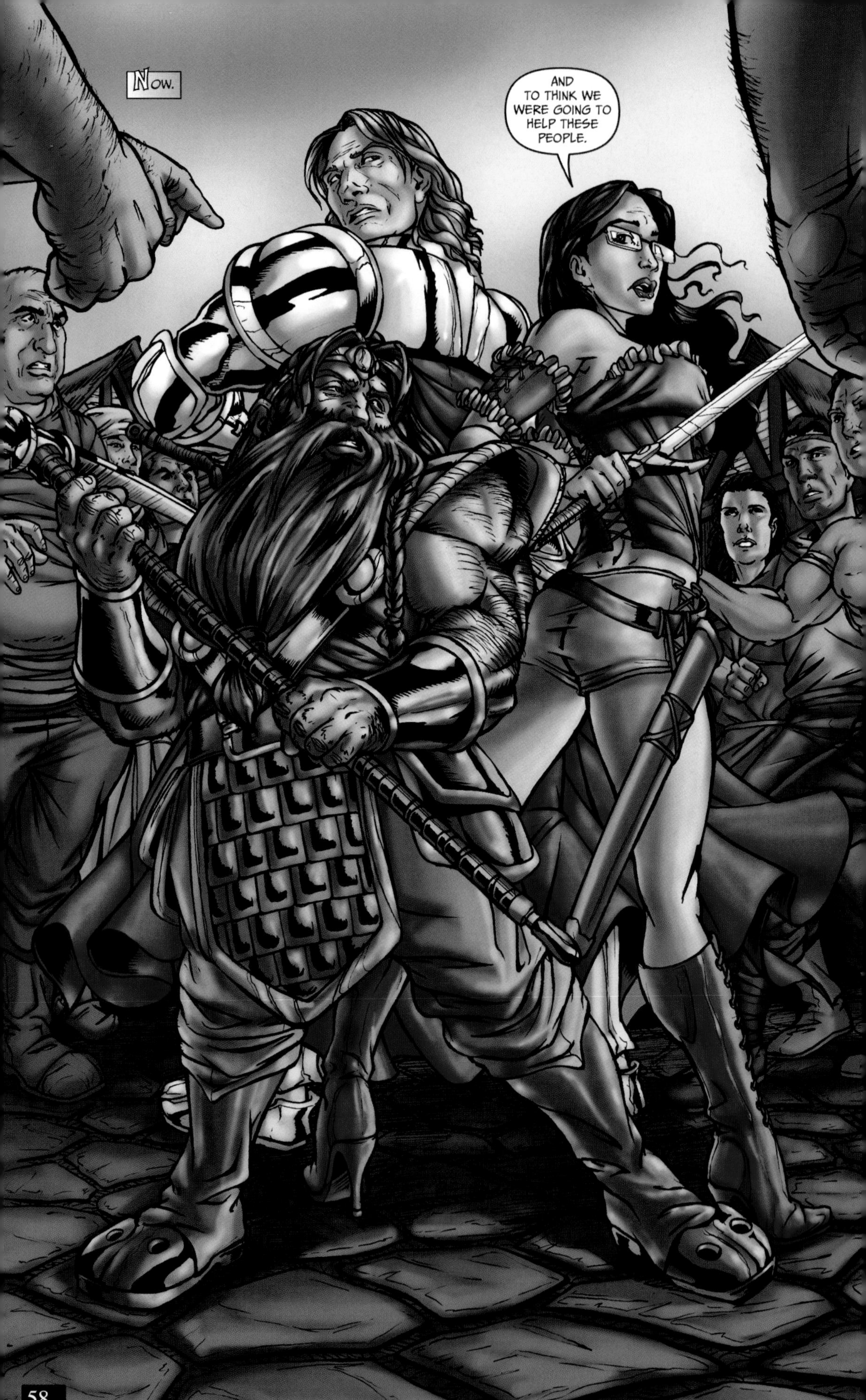
Now.
AND TO THINK WE WERE GOING TO HELP THESE PEOPLE.

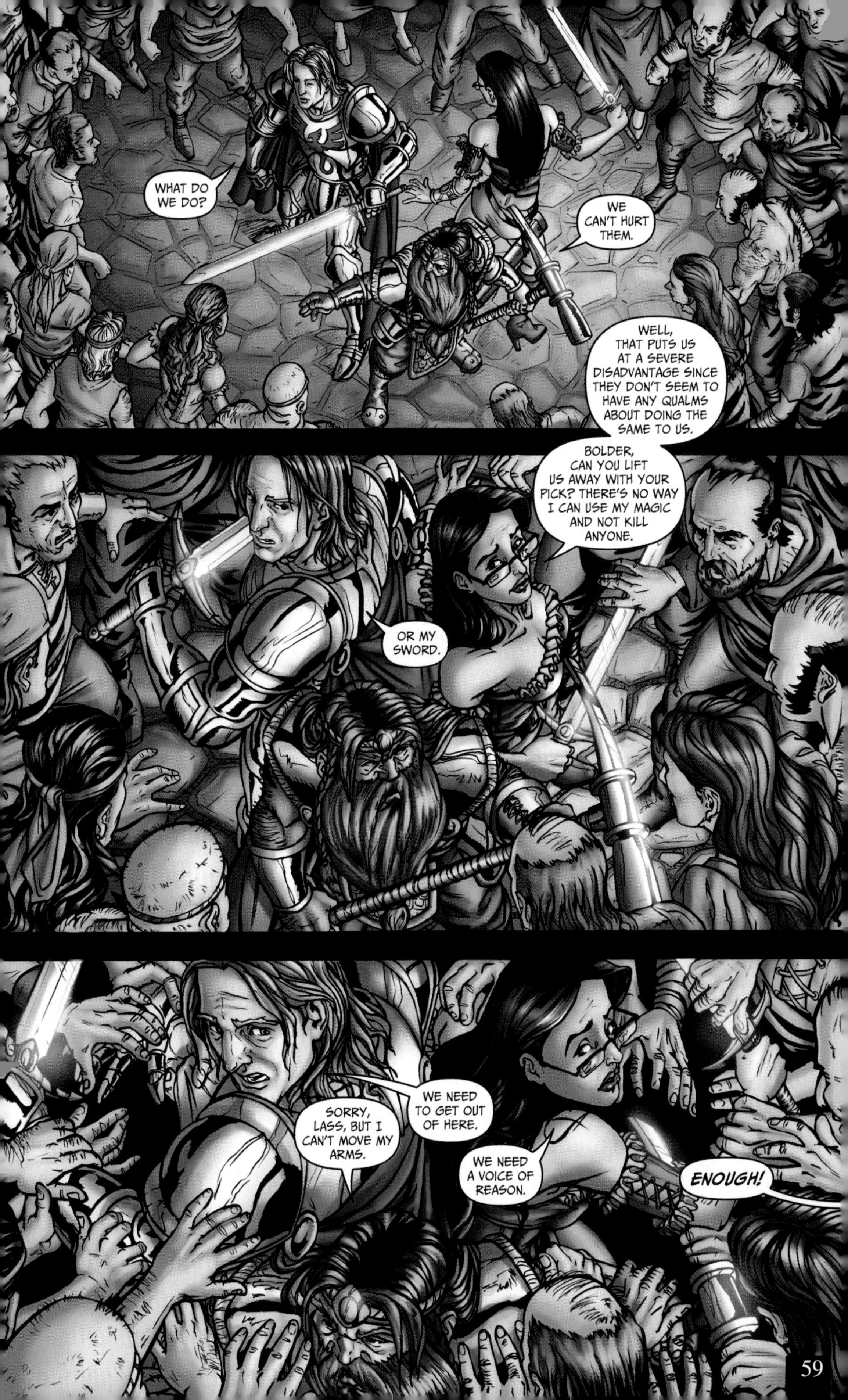
WHAT DO WE DO?
WE CAN'T HURT THEM.
WELL, THAT PUTS US AT A SEVERE DISADVANTAGE SINCE THEY DON'T SEEM TO HAVE ANY QUALMS ABOUT DOING THE SAME TO US.
BOLDER, CAN YOU LIFT US AWAY WITH YOUR PICK? THERE'S NO WAY I CAN USE MY MAGIC AND NOT KILL ANYONE.
OR MY SWORD.
WE NEED TO GET OUT OF HERE.
SORRY, LASS, BUT I CAN'T MOVE MY ARMS.
WE NEED A VOICE OF REASON.
ENOUGH!

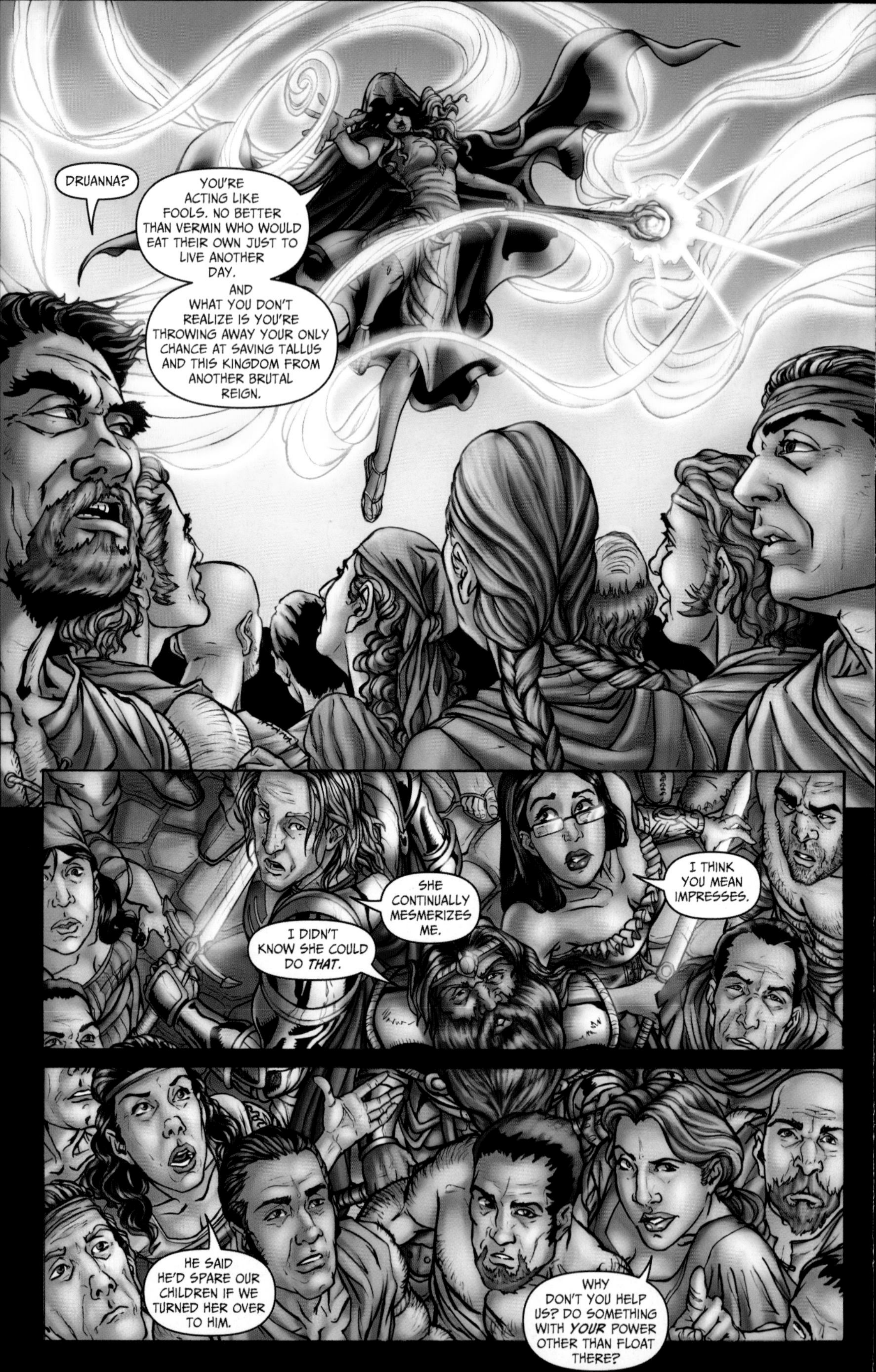

DRUANNA?
YOU'RE ACTING LIKE FOOLS. NO BETTER THAN VERMIN WHO WOULD EAT THEIR OWN JUST TO LIVE ANOTHER DAY.
AND WHAT YOU DON'T REALIZE IS YOU'RE THROWING AWAY YOUR ONLY CHANCE AT SAVING TALLUS AND THIS KINGDOM FROM ANOTHER BRUTAL REIGN.
SHE CONTINUALLY MESMERIZES ME.
I DIDN'T KNOW SHE COULD DO *THAT*.
I THINK YOU MEAN IMPRESSES.
HE SAID HE'D SPARE OUR CHILDREN IF WE TURNED HER OVER TO HIM.
WHY DON'T YOU HELP US? DO SOMETHING WITH ***YOUR*** POWER OTHER THAN FLOAT THERE?

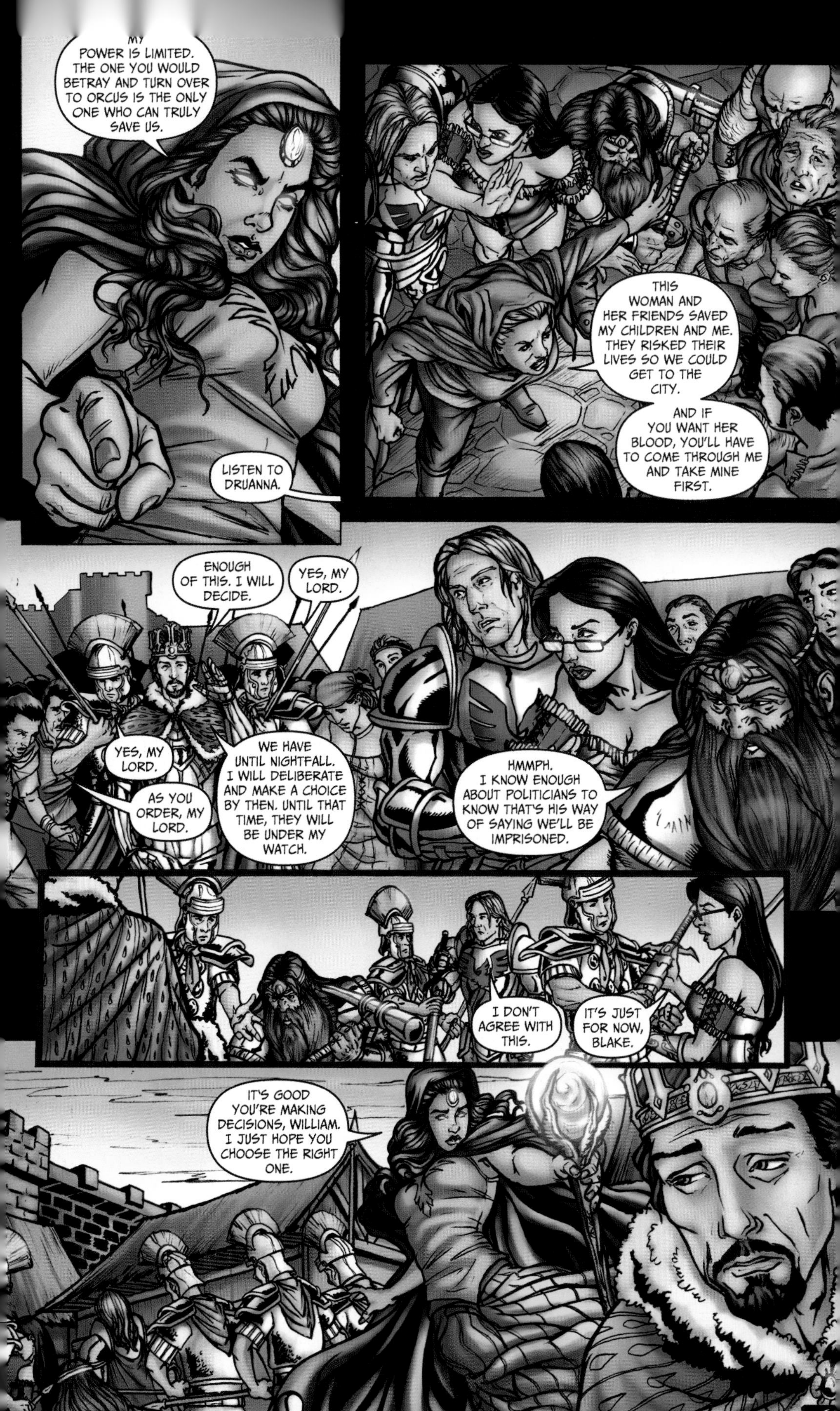

MY POWER IS LIMITED. THE ONE YOU WOULD BETRAY AND TURN OVER TO ORCUS IS THE ONLY ONE WHO CAN TRULY SAVE US.
LISTEN TO DRUANNA.
THIS WOMAN AND HER FRIENDS SAVED MY CHILDREN AND ME. THEY RISKED THEIR LIVES SO WE COULD GET TO THE CITY.
AND IF YOU WANT HER BLOOD, YOU'LL HAVE TO COME THROUGH ME AND TAKE MINE FIRST.
ENOUGH OF THIS. I WILL DECIDE.
YES, MY LORD.
YES, MY LORD.
AS YOU ORDER, MY LORD.
WE HAVE UNTIL NIGHTFALL. I WILL DELIBERATE AND MAKE A CHOICE BY THEN. UNTIL THAT TIME, THEY WILL BE UNDER MY WATCH.
HMMPH. I KNOW ENOUGH ABOUT POLITICIANS TO KNOW THAT'S HIS WAY OF SAYING WE'LL BE IMPRISONED.
I DON'T AGREE WITH THIS.
IT'S JUST FOR NOW, BLAKE.
IT'S GOOD YOU'RE MAKING DECISIONS, WILLIAM. I JUST HOPE YOU CHOOSE THE RIGHT ONE.

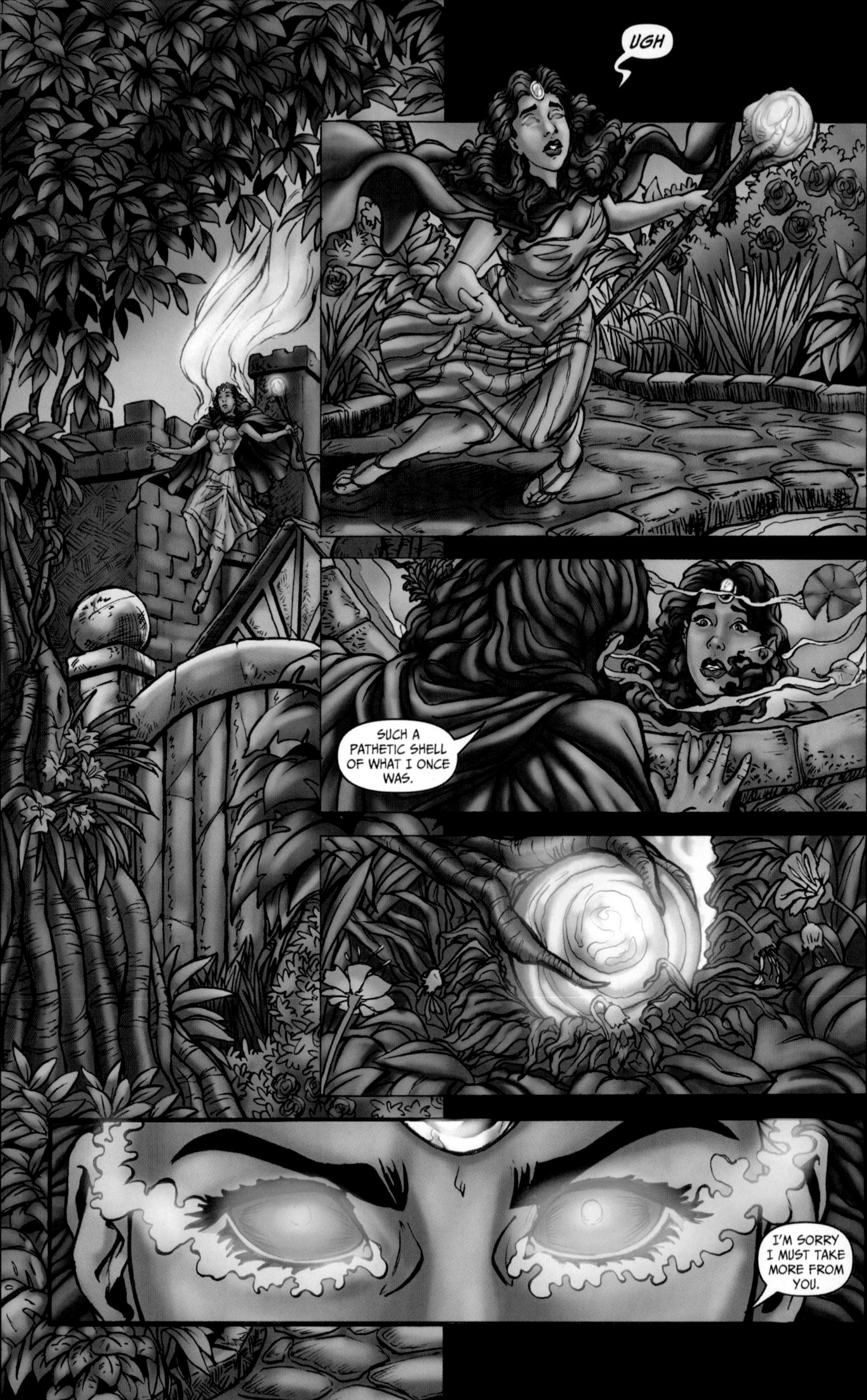
UGH
SUCH A PATHETIC SHELL OF WHAT I ONCE WAS.
I'M SORRY I MUST TAKE MORE FROM YOU.

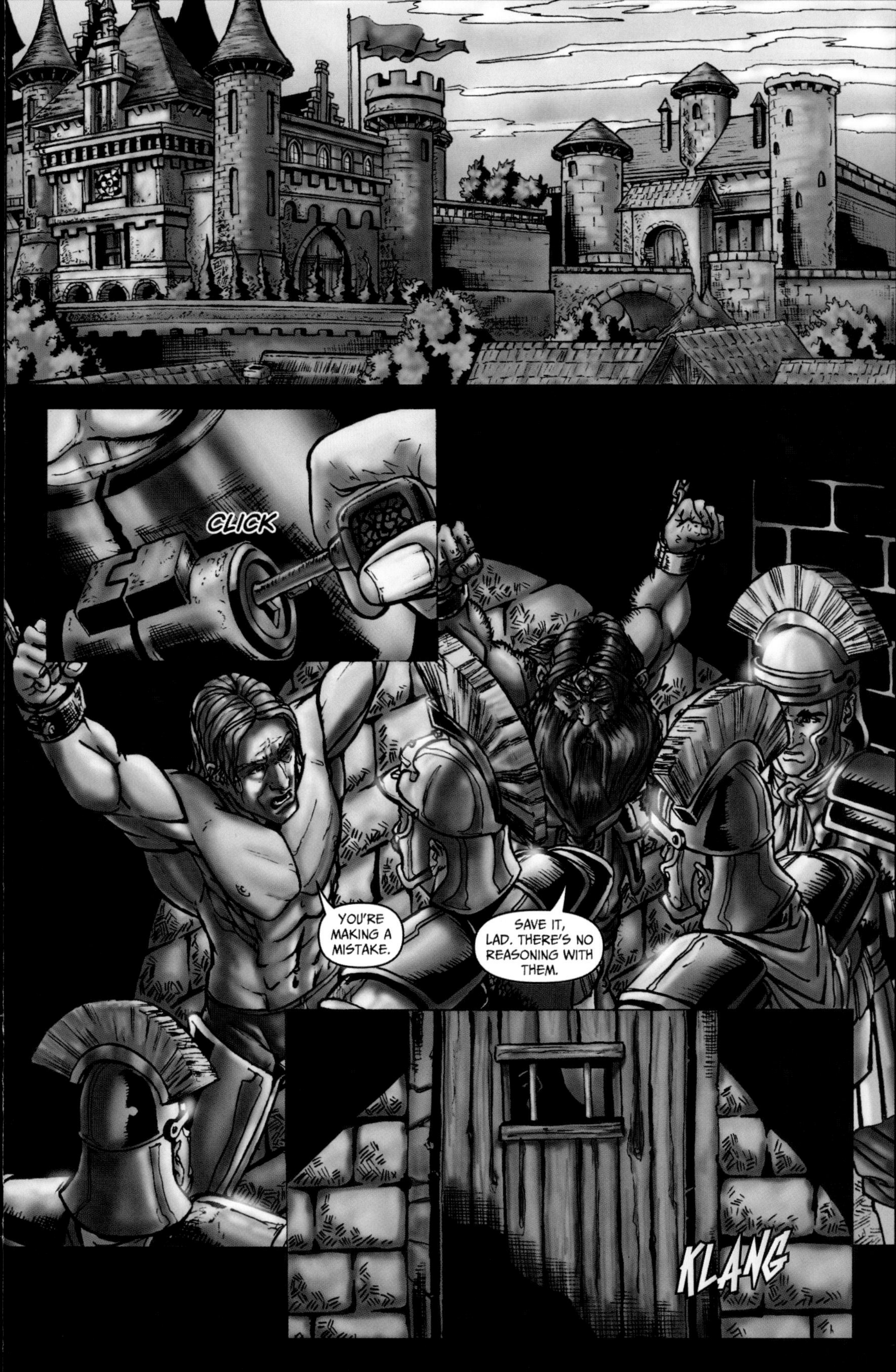
CLICK
YOU'RE MAKING A MISTAKE.
SAVE IT, LAD. THERE'S NO REASONING WITH THEM.
KLANG

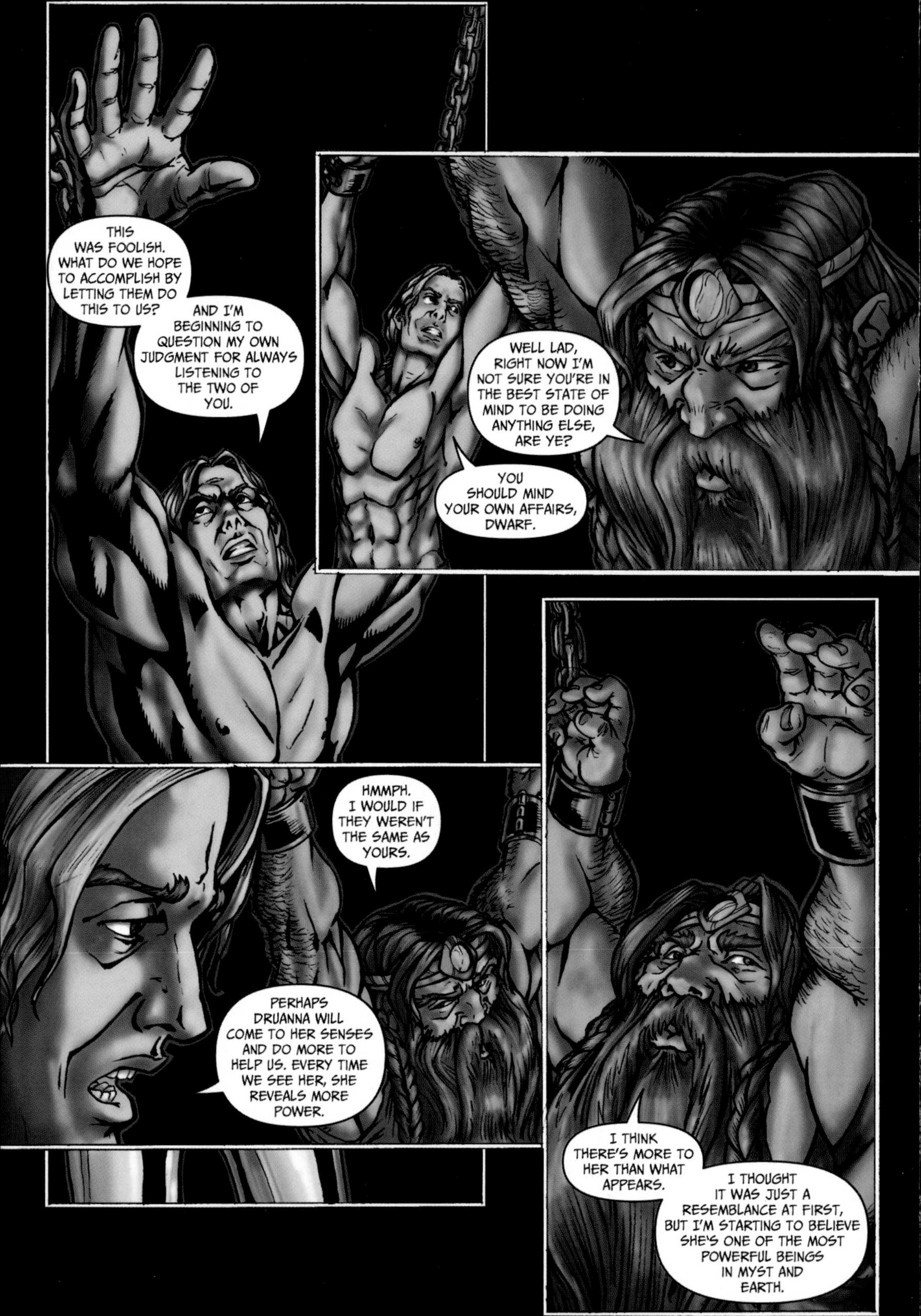
THIS WAS FOOLISH. WHAT DO WE HOPE TO ACCOMPLISH BY LETTING THEM DO THIS TO US?
AND I'M BEGINNING TO QUESTION MY OWN JUDGMENT FOR ALWAYS LISTENING TO THE TWO OF YOU.
WELL LAD, RIGHT NOW I'M NOT SURE YOU'RE IN THE BEST STATE OF MIND TO BE DOING ANYTHING ELSE, ARE YE?
YOU SHOULD MIND YOUR OWN AFFAIRS, DWARF.
HMMPH. I WOULD IF THEY WEREN'T THE SAME AS YOURS.
PERHAPS DRUANNA WILL COME TO HER SENSES AND DO MORE TO HELP US. EVERY TIME WE SEE HER, SHE REVEALS MORE POWER.
I THINK THERE'S MORE TO HER THAN WHAT APPEARS.
I THOUGHT IT WAS JUST A RESEMBLANCE AT FIRST, BUT I'M STARTING TO BELIEVE SHE'S ONE OF THE MOST POWERFUL BEINGS IN MYST AND EARTH.

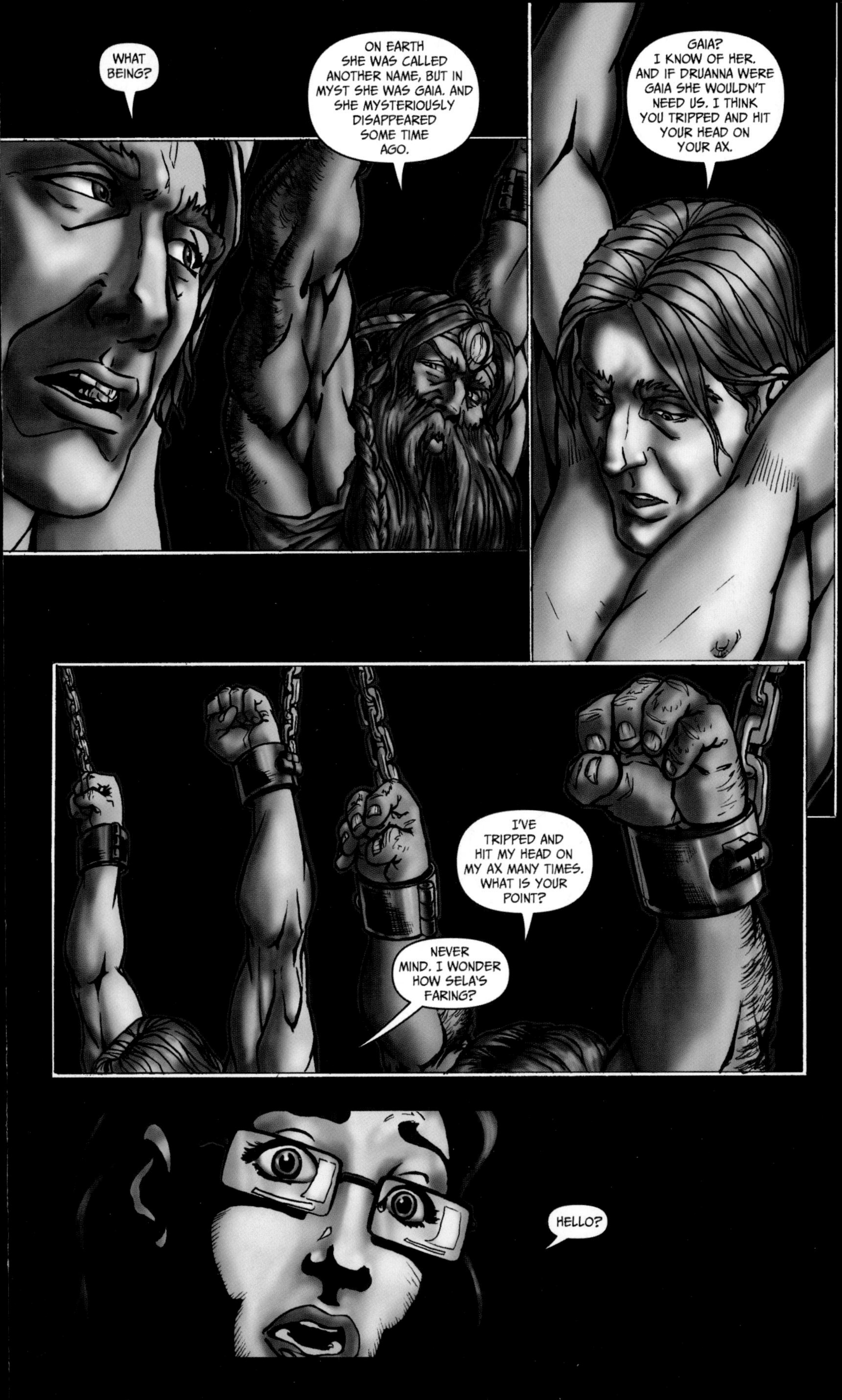
WHAT BEING?
ON EARTH SHE WAS CALLED ANOTHER NAME, BUT IN MYST SHE WAS GAIA. AND SHE MYSTERIOUSLY DISAPPEARED SOME TIME AGO.
GAIA? I KNOW OF HER. AND IF DRUANNA WERE GAIA SHE WOULDN'T NEED US. I THINK YOU TRIPPED AND HIT YOUR HEAD ON YOUR AX.
I'VE TRIPPED AND HIT MY HEAD ON MY AX MANY TIMES. WHAT IS YOUR POINT?
NEVER MIND. I WONDER HOW SELA'S FARING?
HELLO?

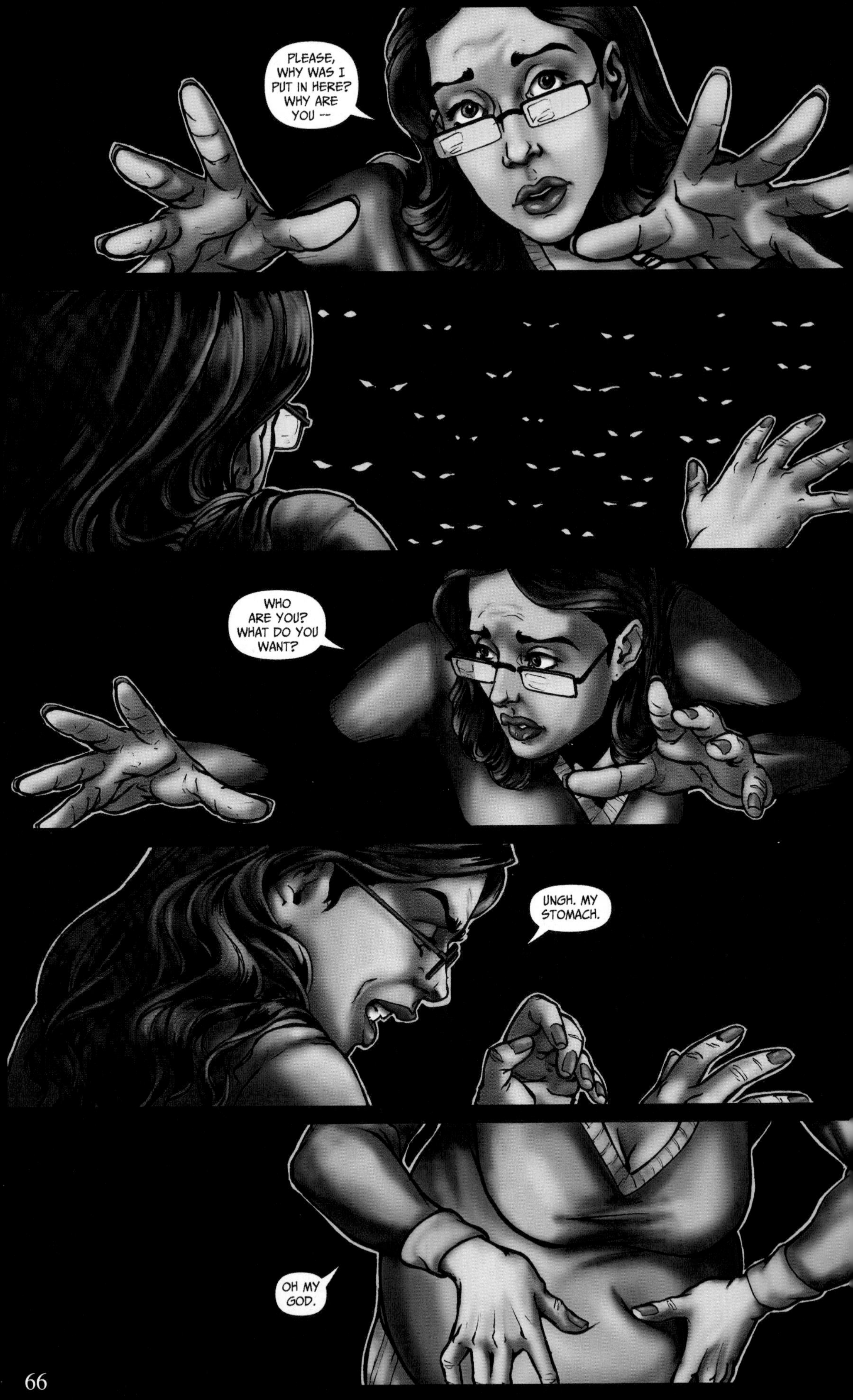
PLEASE, WHY WAS I PUT IN HERE? WHY ARE YOU --
WHO ARE YOU? WHAT DO YOU WANT?
UNGH. MY STOMACH.
OH MY GOD.

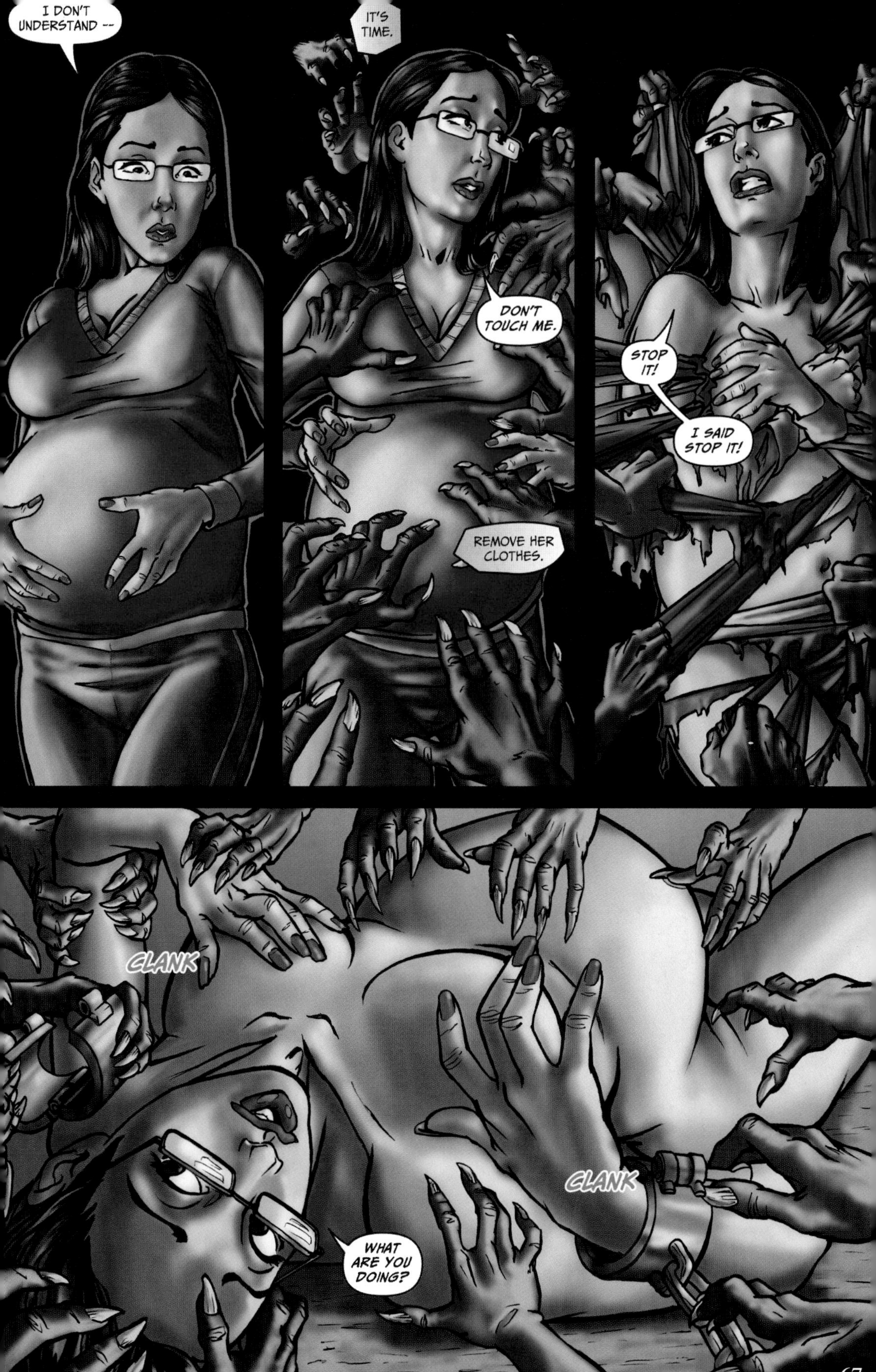
I DON'T UNDERSTAND --
IT'S TIME.
DON'T TOUCH ME.
REMOVE HER CLOTHES.
STOP IT!
I SAID STOP IT!
CLANK
CLANK
WHAT ARE YOU DOING?

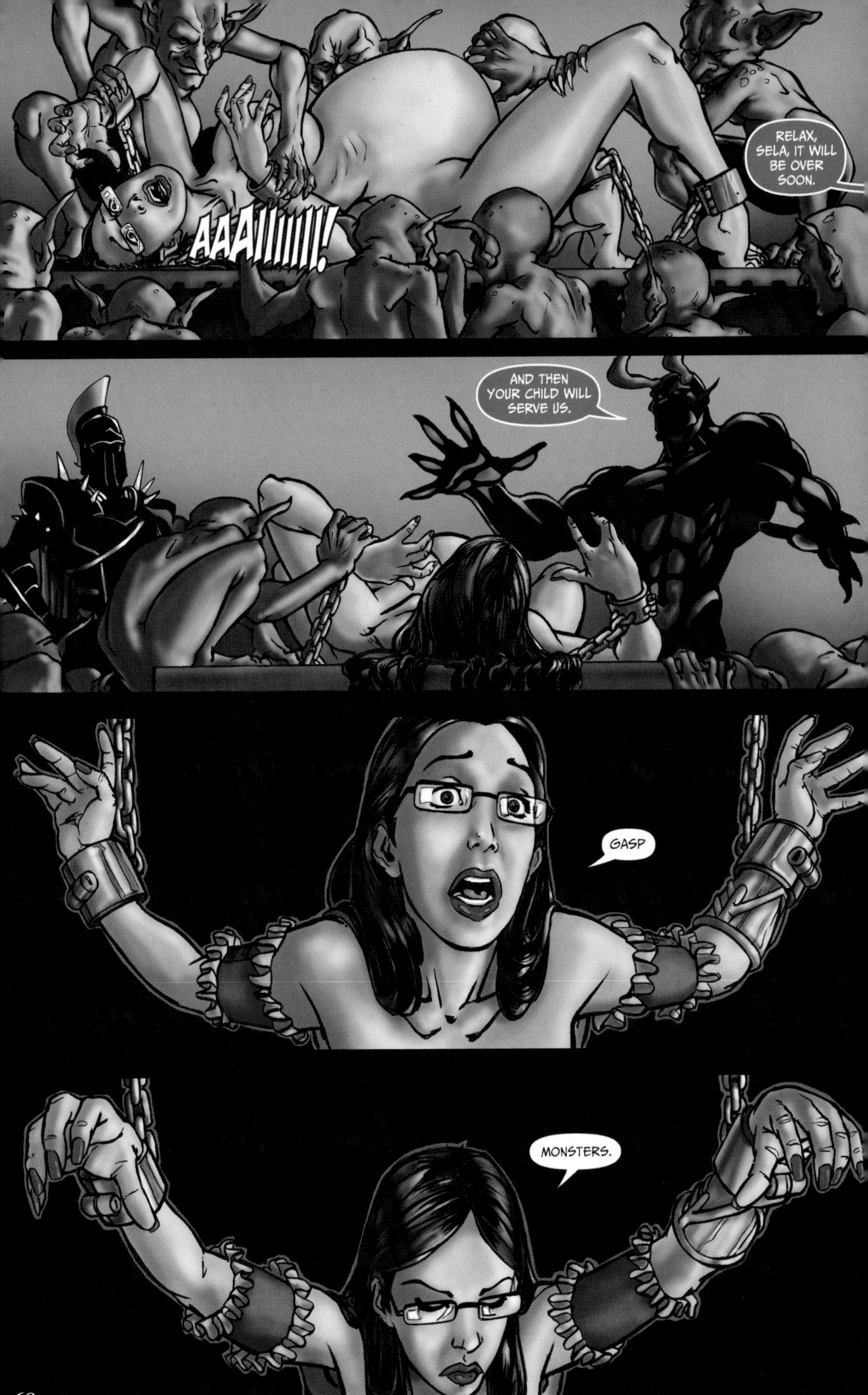
AAAIIIIIII!
RELAX, SELA, IT WILL BE OVER SOON.
AND THEN YOUR CHILD WILL SERVE US.
GASP
MONSTERS.

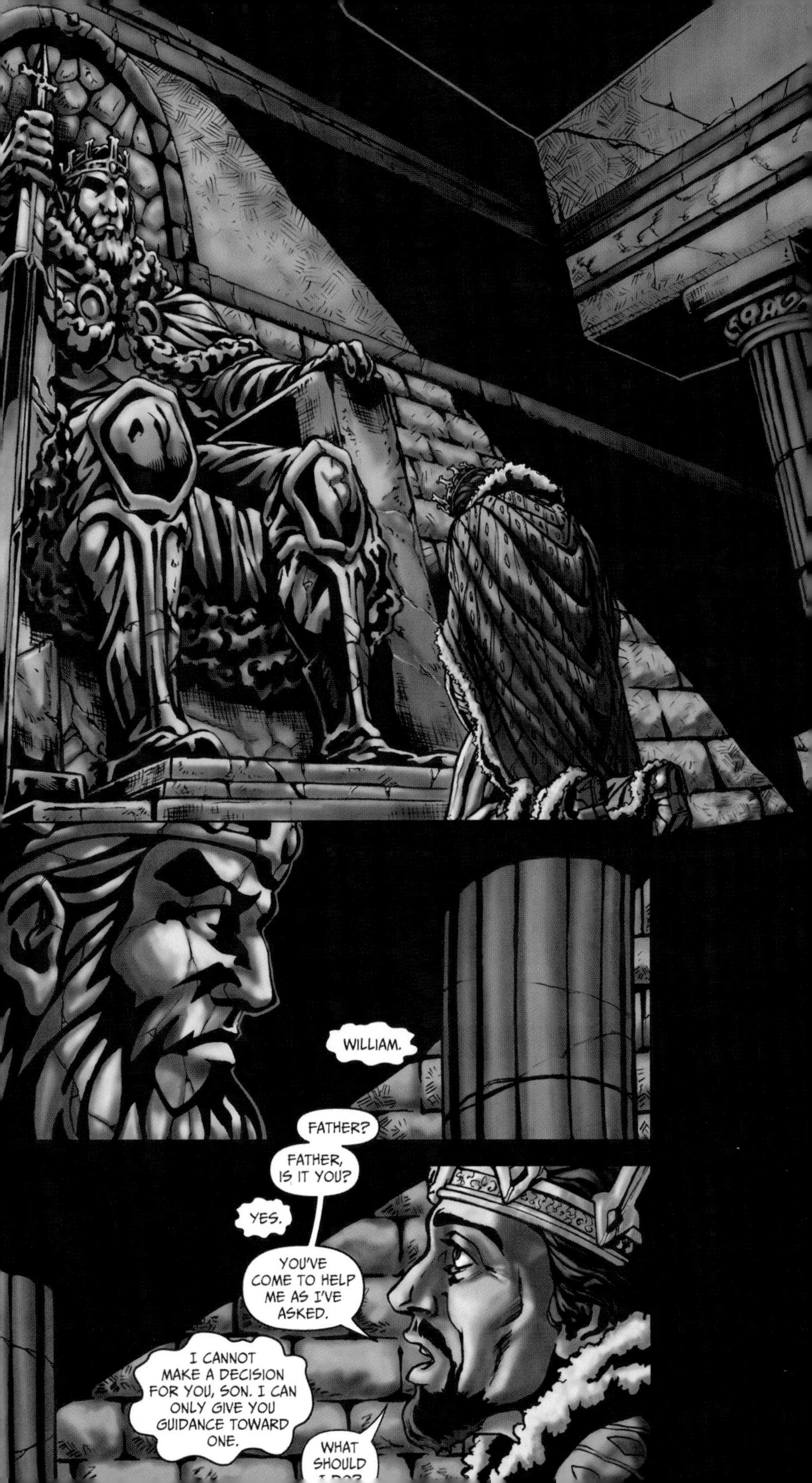
WILLIAM.
FATHER?
FATHER, IS IT YOU?
YES.
YOU'VE COME TO HELP ME AS I'VE ASKED.
I CANNOT MAKE A DECISION FOR YOU, SON. I CAN ONLY GIVE YOU GUIDANCE TOWARD ONE.
WHAT SHOULD

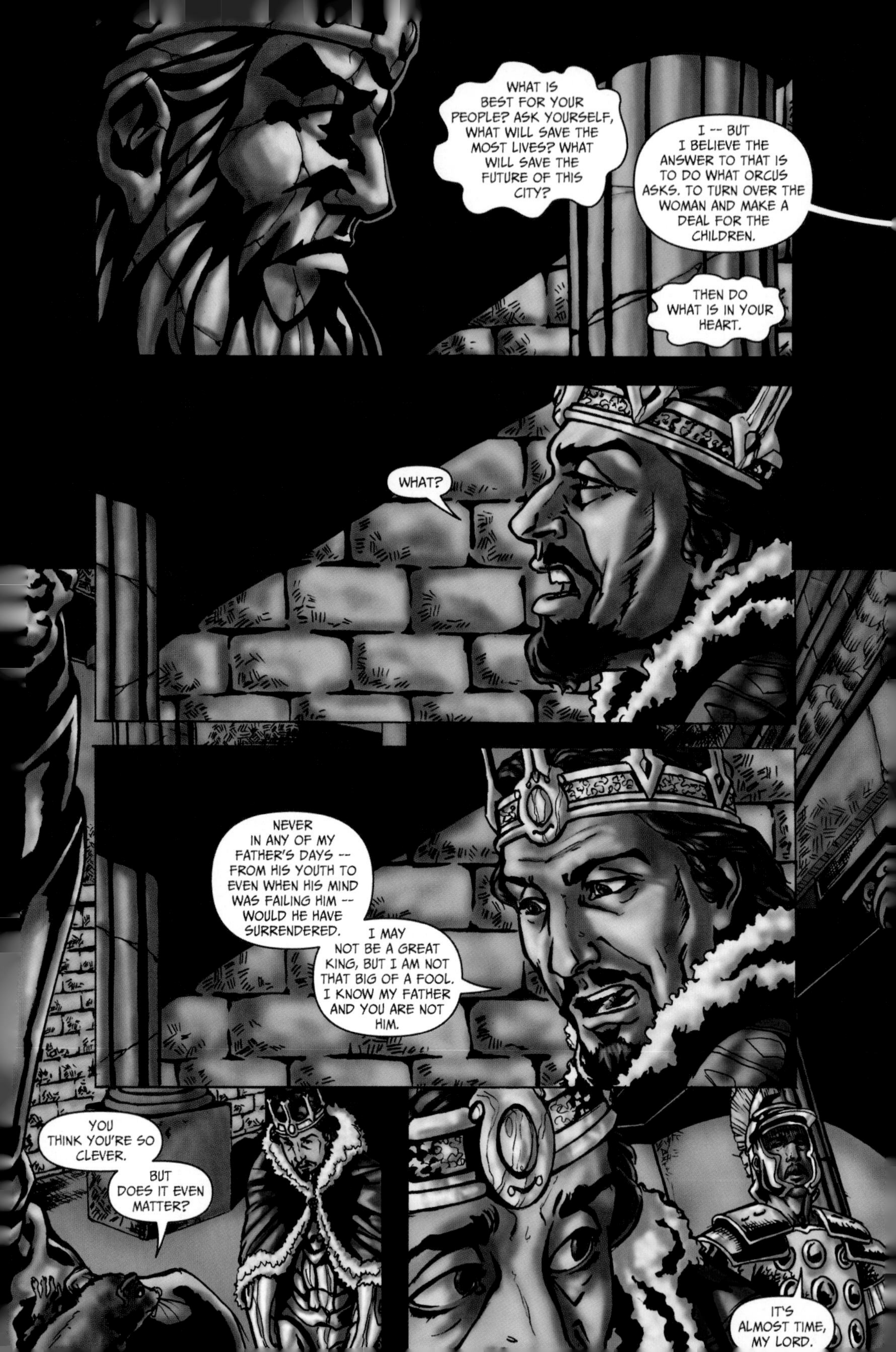
WHAT IS BEST FOR YOUR PEOPLE? ASK YOURSELF, WHAT WILL SAVE THE MOST LIVES? WHAT WILL SAVE THE FUTURE OF THIS CITY?
I -- BUT I BELIEVE THE ANSWER TO THAT IS TO DO WHAT ORCUS ASKS. TO TURN OVER THE WOMAN AND MAKE A DEAL FOR THE CHILDREN.
THEN DO WHAT IS IN YOUR HEART.
WHAT?
NEVER IN ANY OF MY FATHER'S DAYS -- FROM HIS YOUTH TO EVEN WHEN HIS MIND WAS FAILING HIM -- WOULD HE HAVE SURRENDERED.
I MAY NOT BE A GREAT KING, BUT I AM NOT THAT BIG OF A FOOL. I KNOW MY FATHER AND YOU ARE NOT HIM.
YOU THINK YOU'RE SO CLEVER.
BUT DOES IT EVEN MATTER?
IT'S ALMOST TIME, MY LORD.

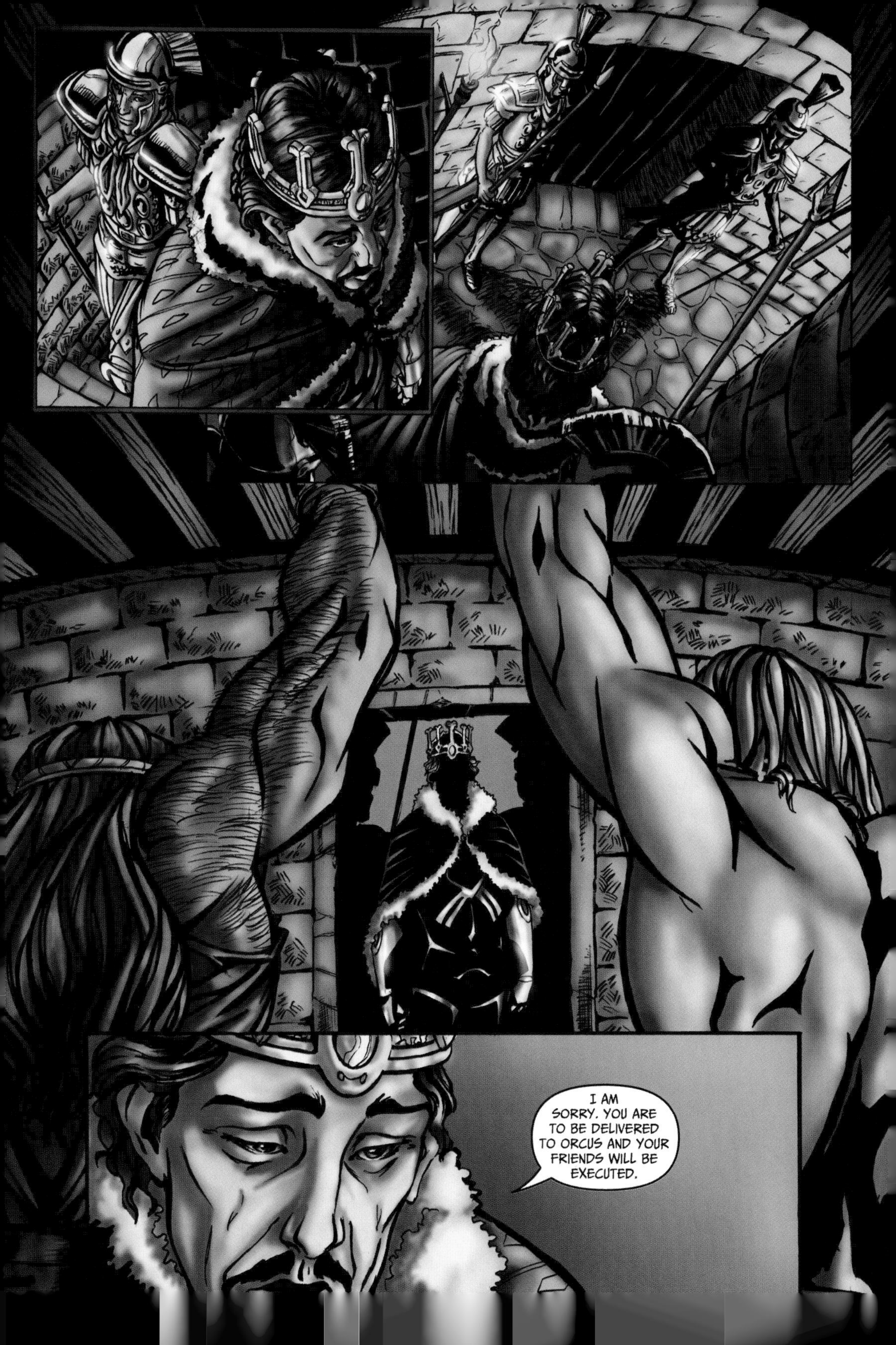
I AM SORRY. YOU ARE TO BE DELIVERED TO ORCUS AND YOUR FRIENDS WILL BE EXECUTED.

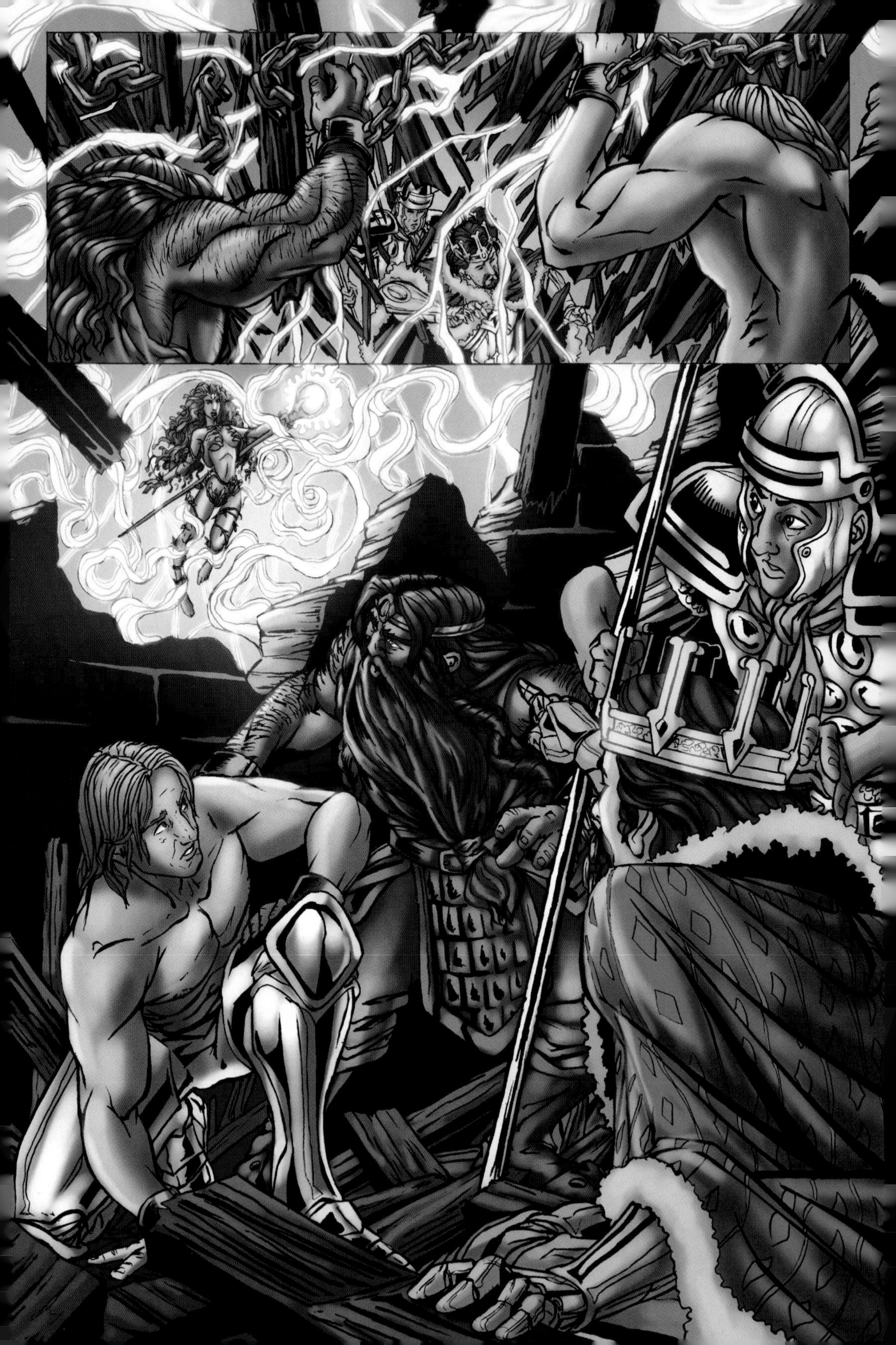

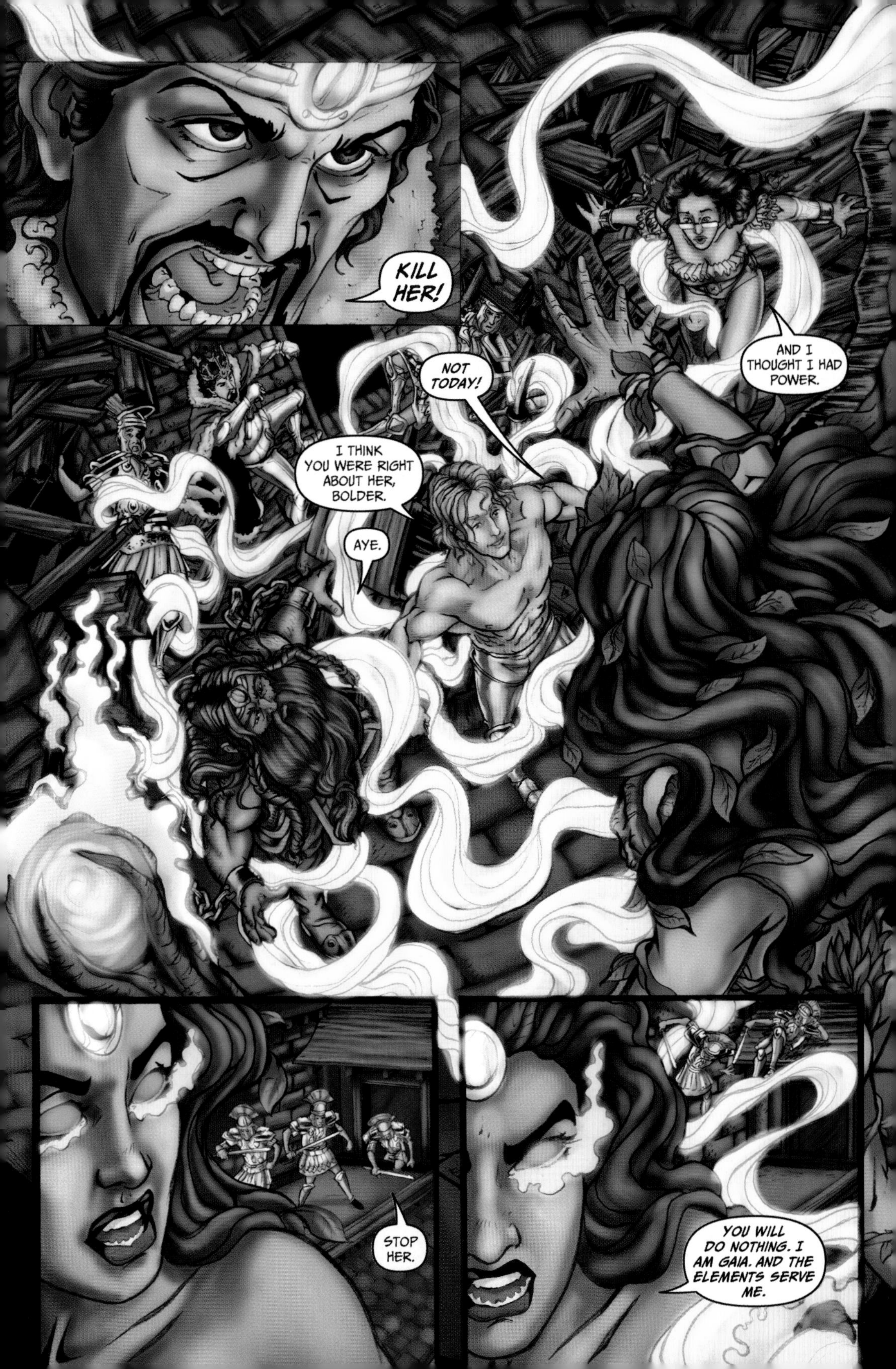
KILL HER!
AND I THOUGHT I HAD POWER.
NOT TODAY!
I THINK YOU WERE RIGHT ABOUT HER, BOLDER.
AYE.
STOP HER.
YOU WILL DO NOTHING. I AM GAIA. AND THE ELEMENTS SERVE ME.

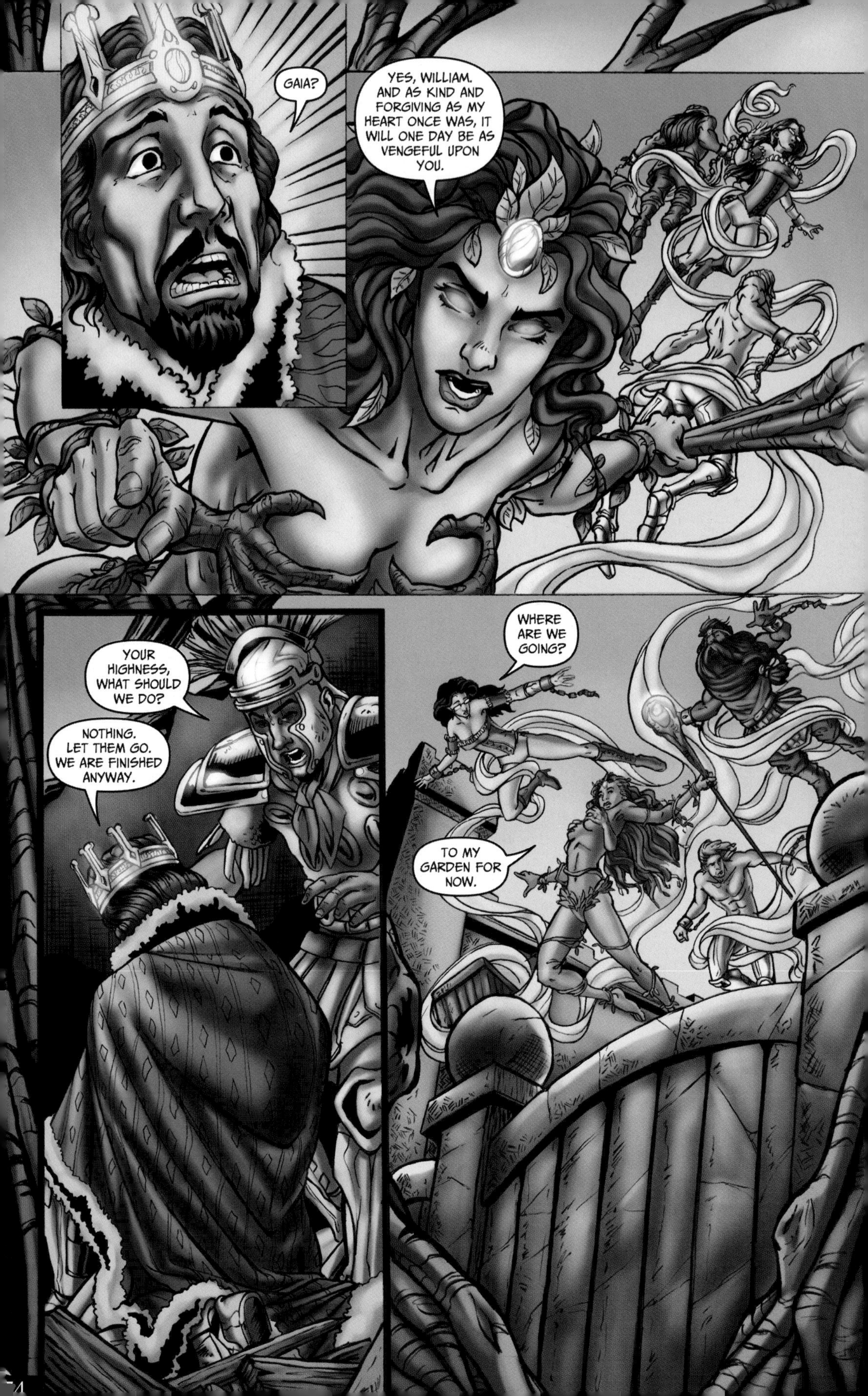
GAIA?
YES, WILLIAM. AND AS KIND AND FORGIVING AS MY HEART ONCE WAS, IT WILL ONE DAY BE AS VENGEFUL UPON YOU.
YOUR HIGHNESS, WHAT SHOULD WE DO?
NOTHING. LET THEM GO. WE ARE FINISHED ANYWAY.
WHERE ARE WE GOING?
TO MY GARDEN FOR NOW.

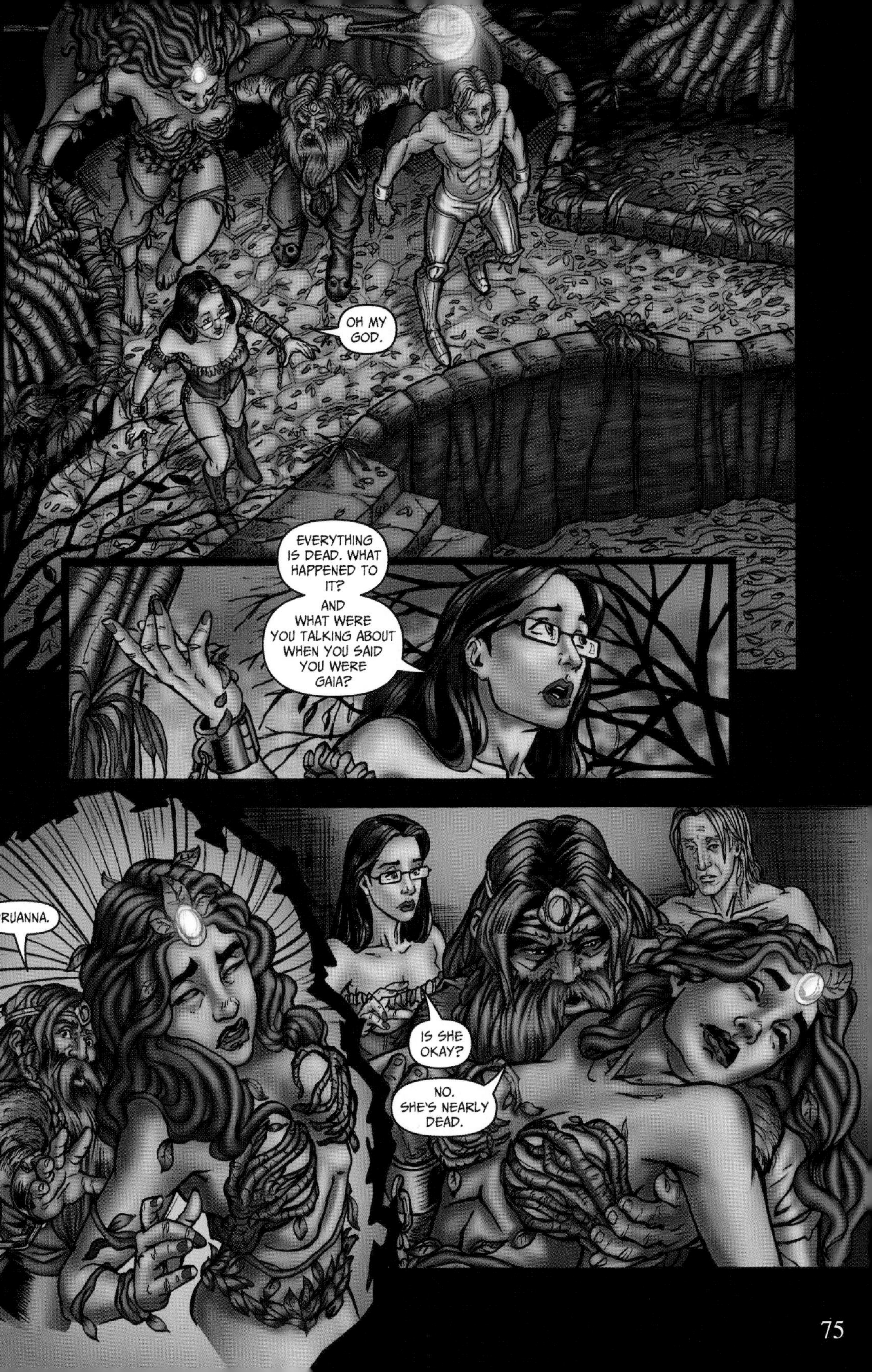
OH MY GOD.
EVERYTHING IS DEAD. WHAT HAPPENED TO IT?
AND WHAT WERE YOU TALKING ABOUT WHEN YOU SAID YOU WERE GAIA?
DRUANNA.
IS SHE OKAY?
NO. SHE'S NEARLY DEAD.

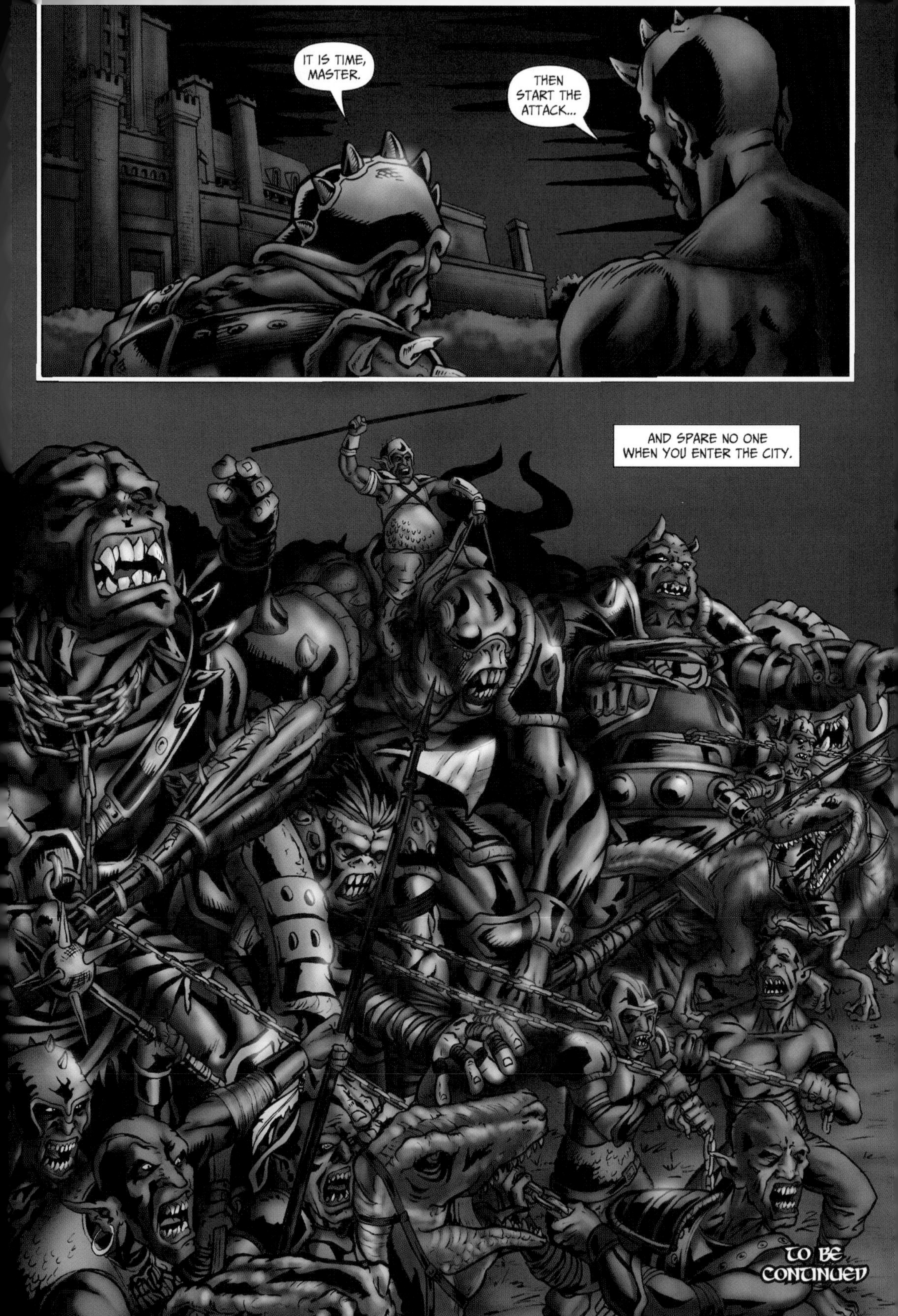
IT IS TIME, MASTER.
THEN START THE ATTACK...
AND SPARE NO ONE WHEN YOU ENTER THE CITY.
TO BE CONTINUED

Grimm Fairy Tales

Volume 10

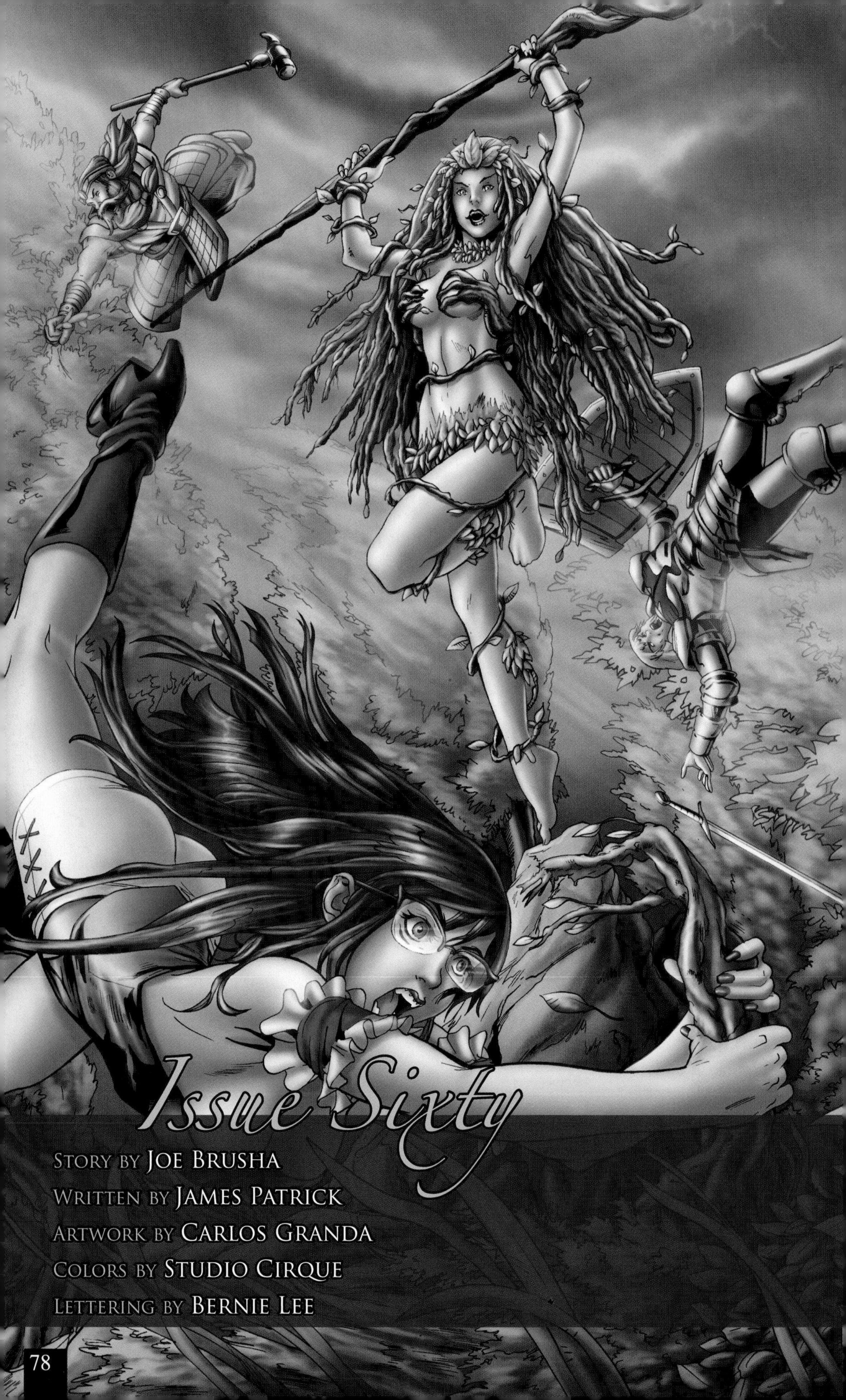

Issue Sixty

Story by Joe Brusha
Written by James Patrick
Artwork by Carlos Granda
Colors by Studio Cirque
Lettering by Bernie Lee

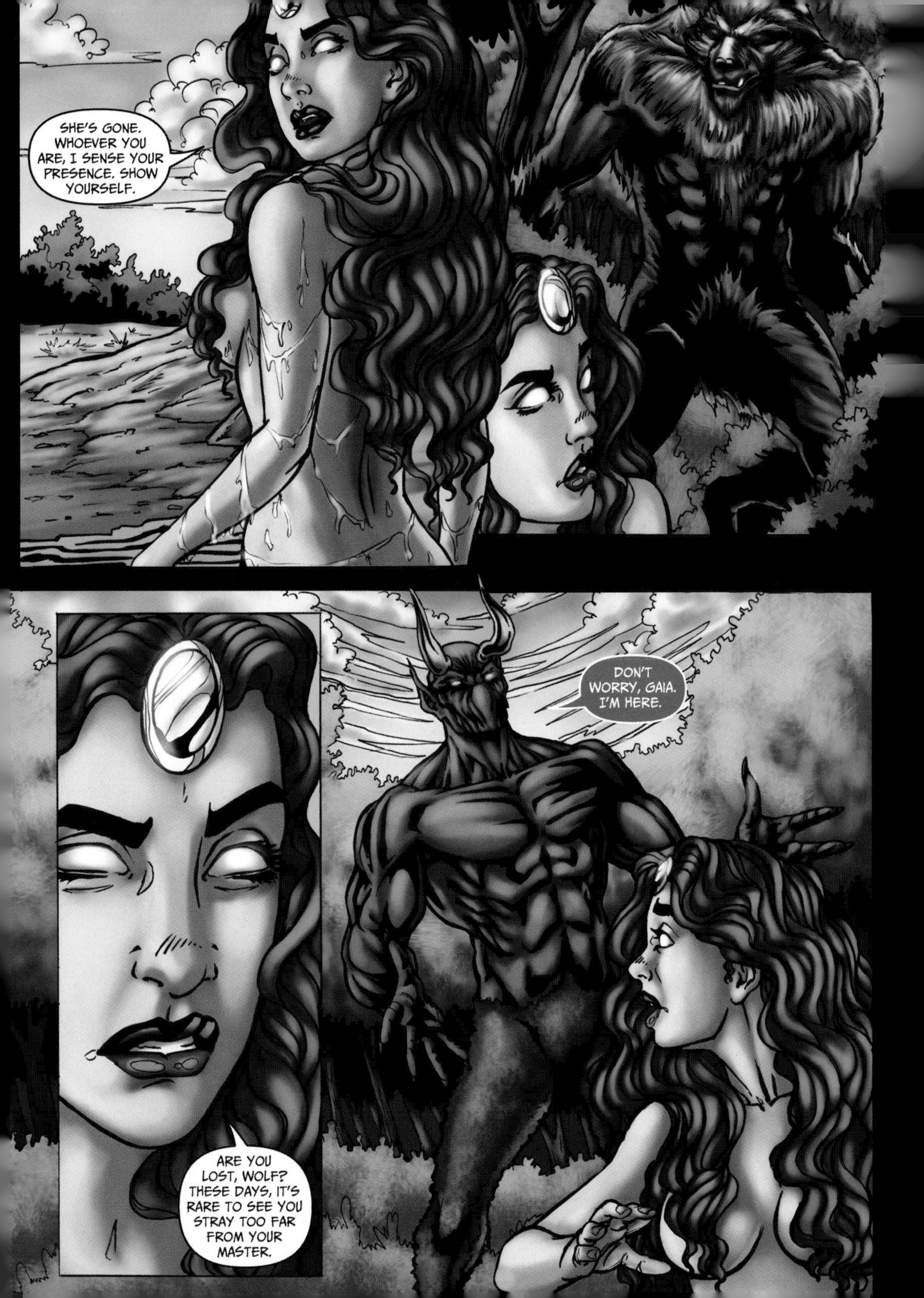
SHE'S GONE. WHOEVER YOU ARE, I SENSE YOUR PRESENCE. SHOW YOURSELF.
DON'T WORRY, GAIA. I'M HERE.
ARE YOU LOST, WOLF? THESE DAYS, IT'S RARE TO SEE YOU STRAY TOO FAR FROM YOUR MASTER.

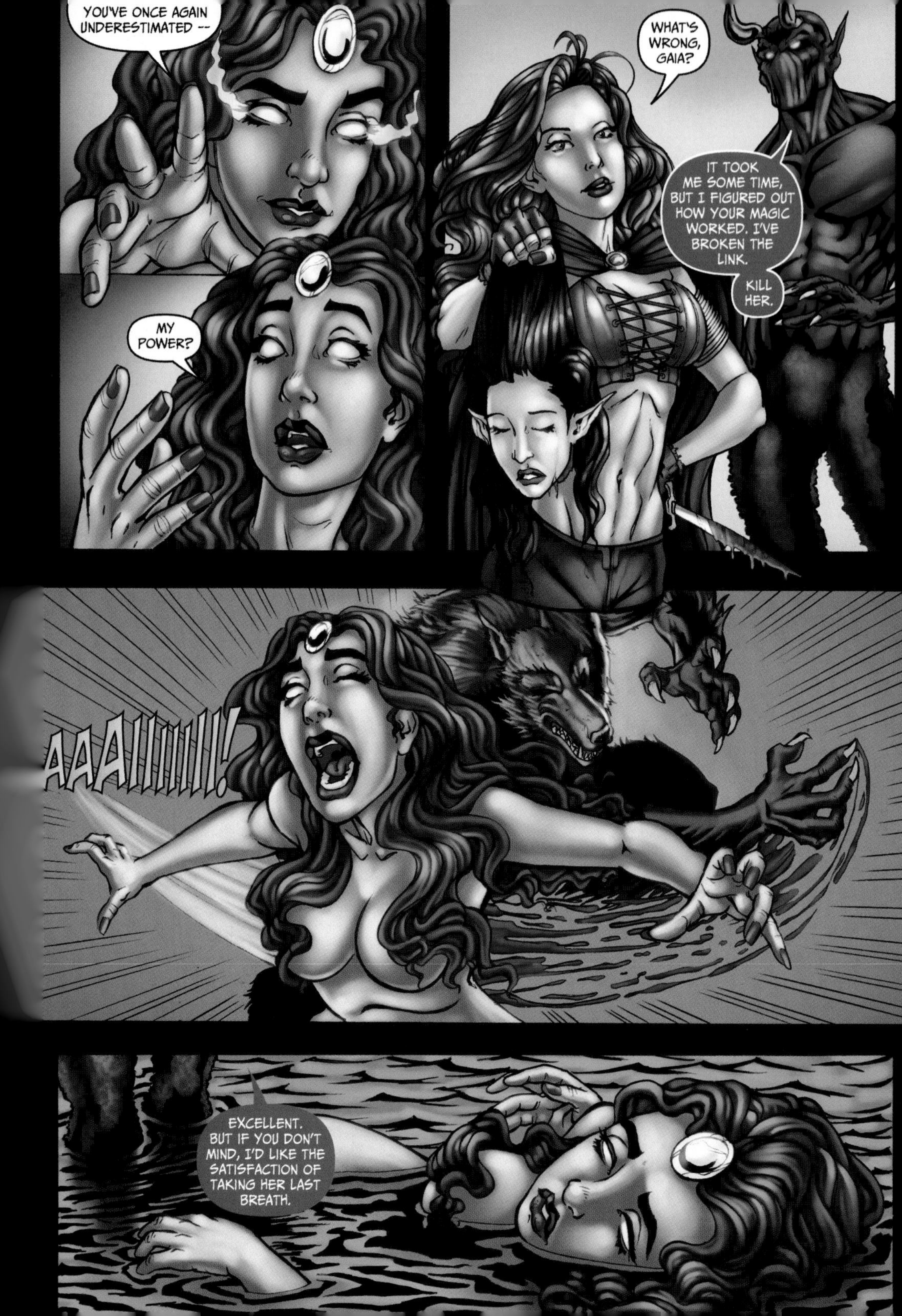
YOU'VE ONCE AGAIN UNDERESTIMATED --
MY POWER?
WHAT'S WRONG, GAIA?
IT TOOK ME SOME TIME, BUT I FIGURED OUT HOW YOUR MAGIC WORKED. I'VE BROKEN THE LINK.
KILL HER.
AAAIIIIIII!
EXCELLENT. BUT IF YOU DON'T MIND, I'D LIKE THE SATISFACTION OF TAKING HER LAST BREATH.

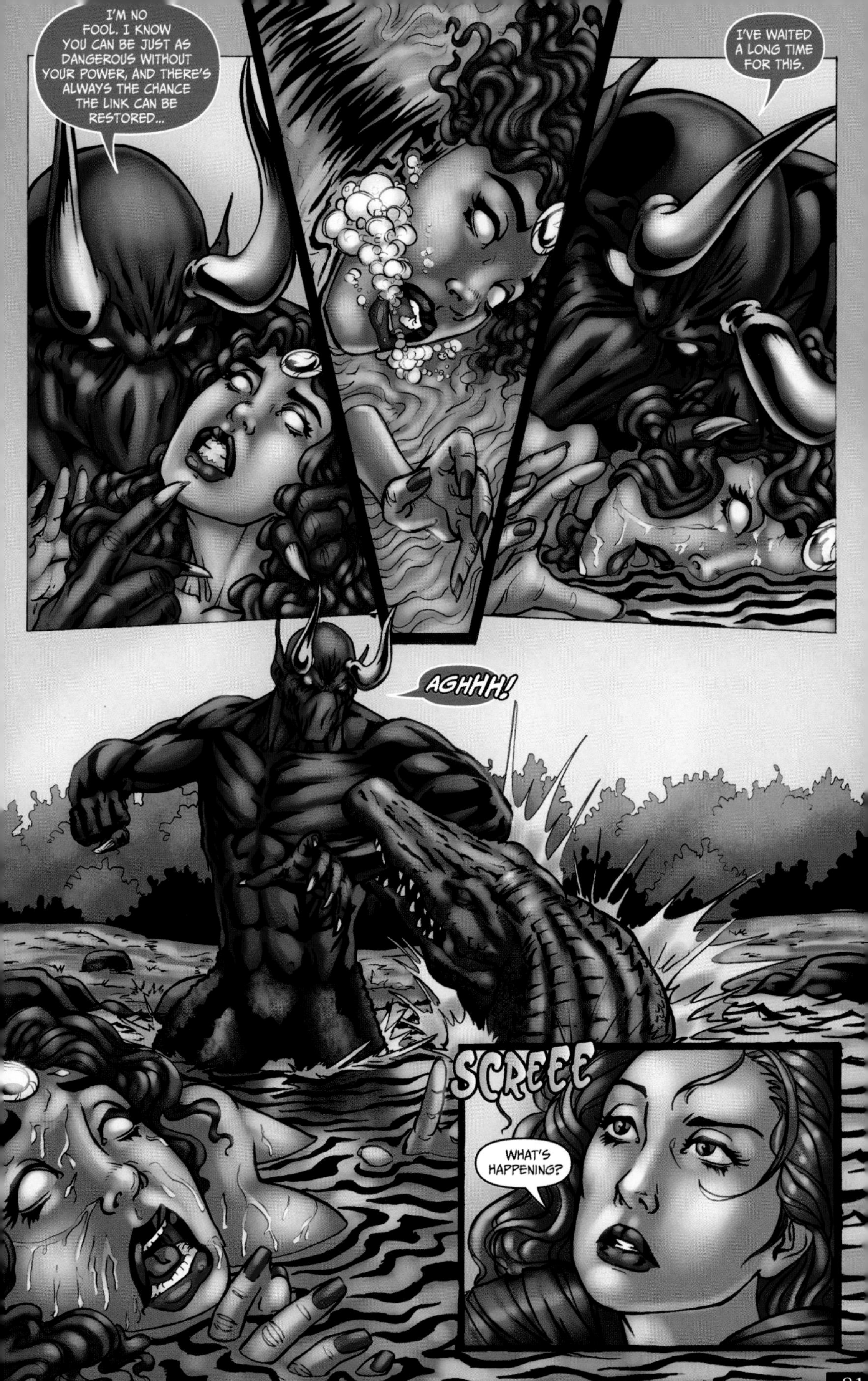
I'M NO FOOL. I KNOW YOU CAN BE JUST AS DANGEROUS WITHOUT YOUR POWER, AND THERE'S ALWAYS THE CHANCE THE LINK CAN BE RESTORED...
I'VE WAITED A LONG TIME FOR THIS.
AGHHH!
SCREEE
WHAT'S HAPPENING?

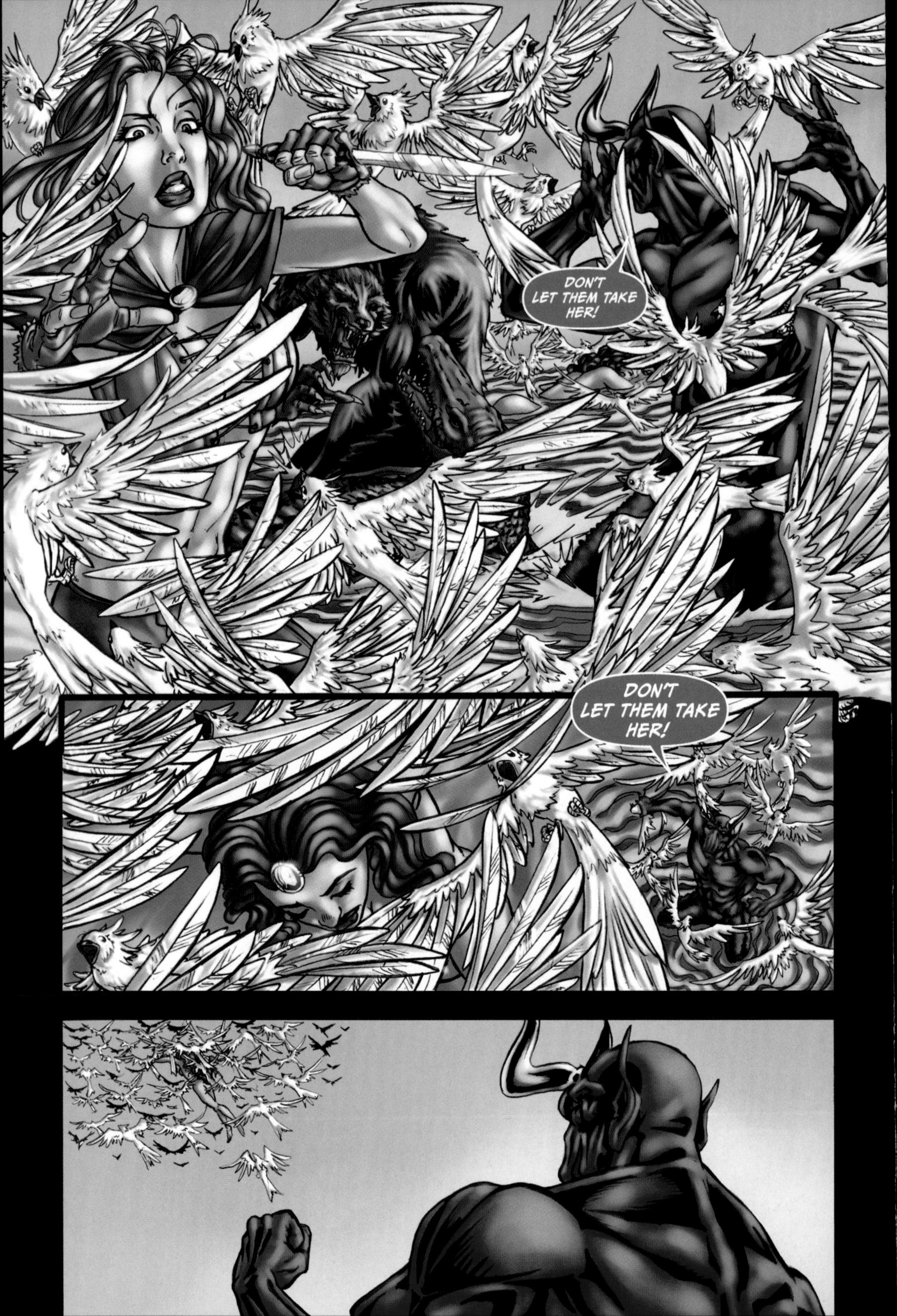
DON'T LET THEM TAKE HER!
DON'T LET THEM TAKE HER!

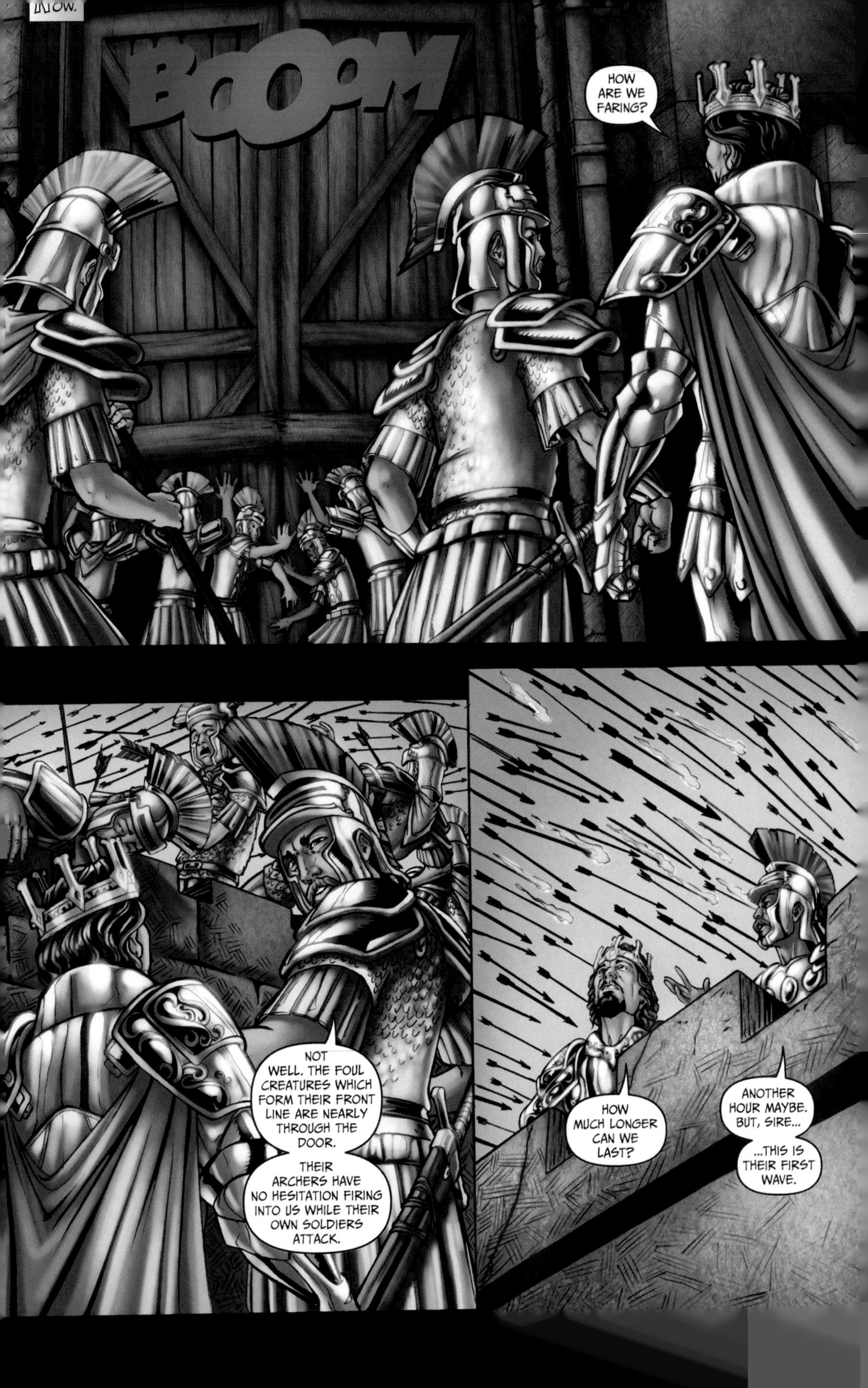
NOW.
BOOOM
HOW ARE WE FARING?
NOT WELL. THE FOUL CREATURES WHICH FORM THEIR FRONT LINE ARE NEARLY THROUGH THE DOOR.
THEIR ARCHERS HAVE NO HESITATION FIRING INTO US WHILE THEIR OWN SOLDIERS ATTACK.
HOW MUCH LONGER CAN WE LAST?
ANOTHER HOUR MAYBE. BUT, SIRE...
...THIS IS THEIR FIRST WAVE.

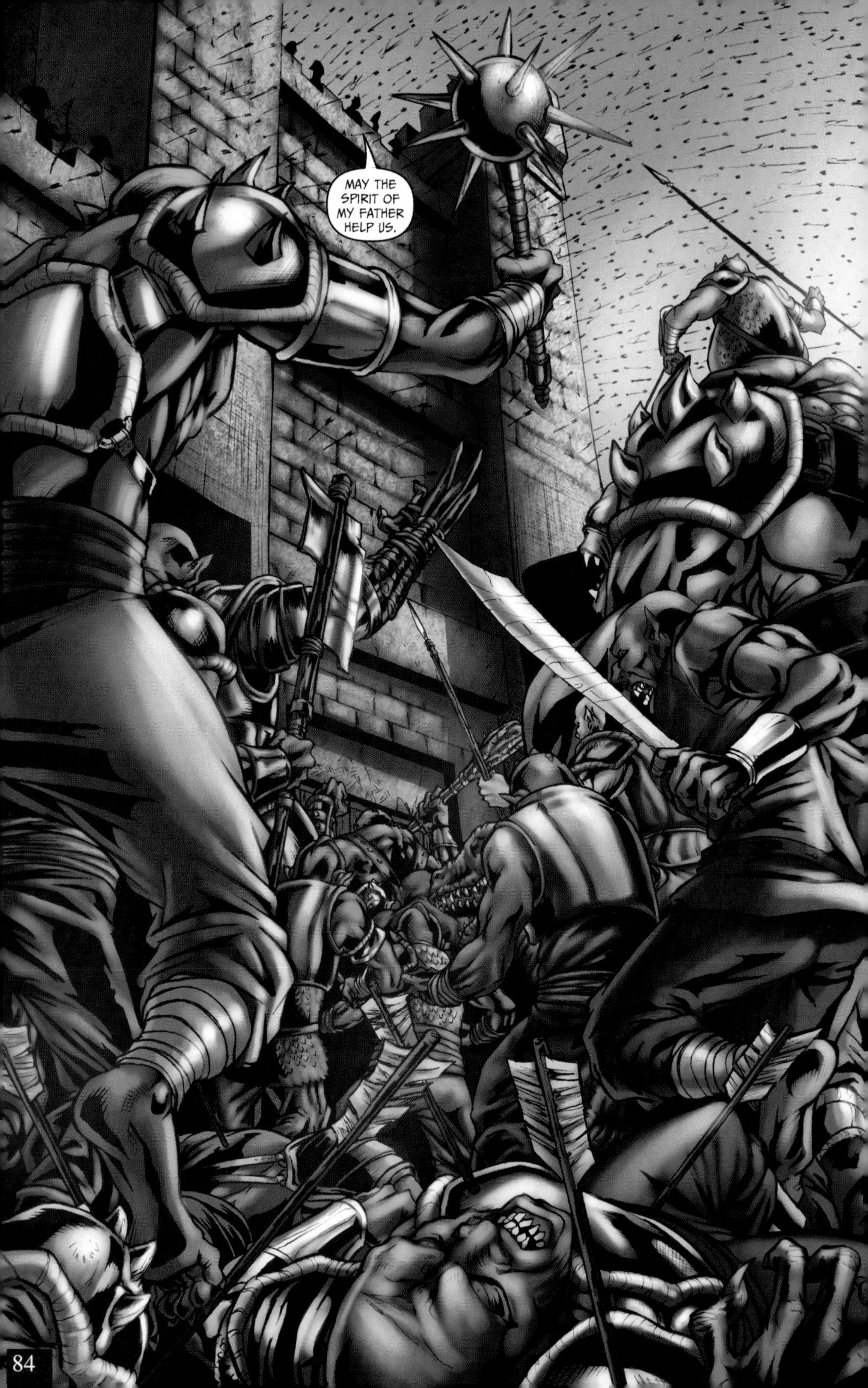
MAY THE SPIRIT OF MY FATHER HELP US.

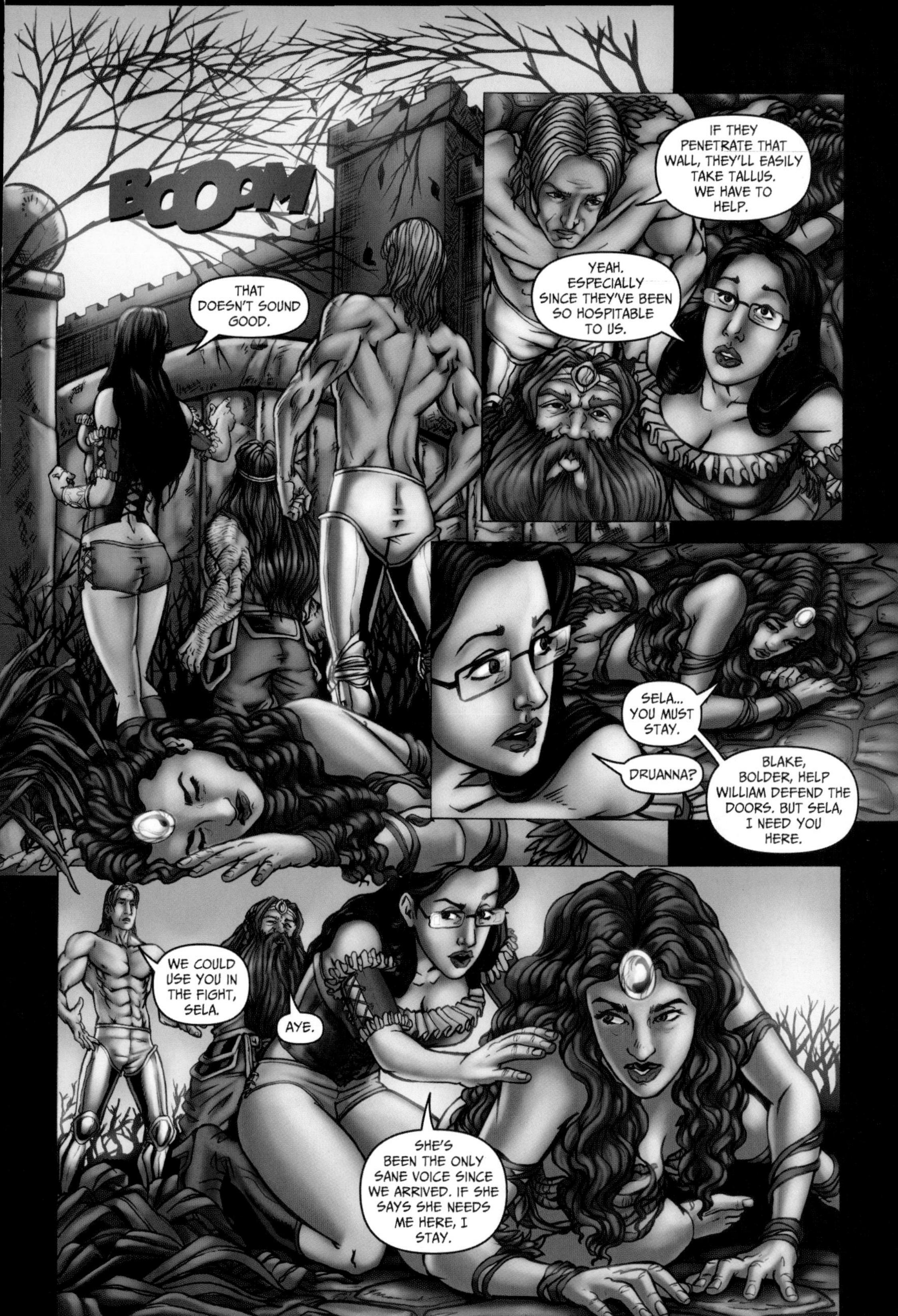
BOOOM
THAT DOESN'T SOUND GOOD.
IF THEY PENETRATE THAT WALL, THEY'LL EASILY TAKE TALLUS. WE HAVE TO HELP.
YEAH. ESPECIALLY SINCE THEY'VE BEEN SO HOSPITABLE TO US.
SELA... YOU MUST STAY.
DRUANNA?
BLAKE, BOLDER, HELP WILLIAM DEFEND THE DOORS. BUT SELA, I NEED YOU HERE.
WE COULD USE YOU IN THE FIGHT, SELA.
AYE.
SHE'S BEEN THE ONLY SANE VOICE SINCE WE ARRIVED. IF SHE SAYS SHE NEEDS ME HERE, I STAY.

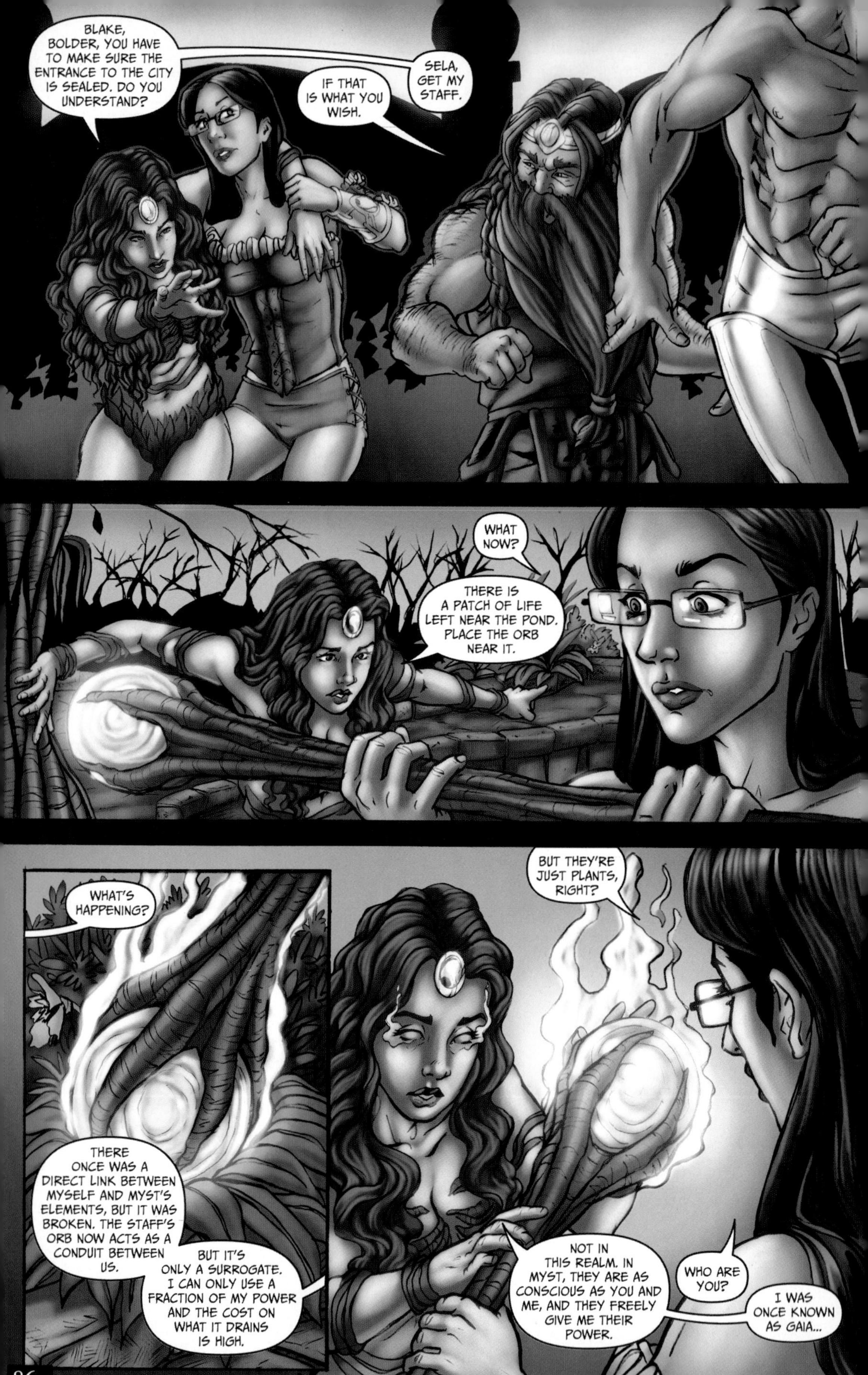
BLAKE, BOLDER, YOU HAVE TO MAKE SURE THE ENTRANCE TO THE CITY IS SEALED. DO YOU UNDERSTAND?
IF THAT IS WHAT YOU WISH.
SELA, GET MY STAFF.
WHAT NOW?
THERE IS A PATCH OF LIFE LEFT NEAR THE POND. PLACE THE ORB NEAR IT.
WHAT'S HAPPENING?
THERE ONCE WAS A DIRECT LINK BETWEEN MYSELF AND MYST'S ELEMENTS, BUT IT WAS BROKEN. THE STAFF'S ORB NOW ACTS AS A CONDUIT BETWEEN US.
BUT IT'S ONLY A SURROGATE. I CAN ONLY USE A FRACTION OF MY POWER AND THE COST ON WHAT IT DRAINS IS HIGH.
BUT THEY'RE JUST PLANTS, RIGHT?
NOT IN THIS REALM. IN MYST, THEY ARE AS CONSCIOUS AS YOU AND ME, AND THEY FREELY GIVE ME THEIR POWER.
WHO ARE YOU?
I WAS ONCE KNOWN AS GAIA...

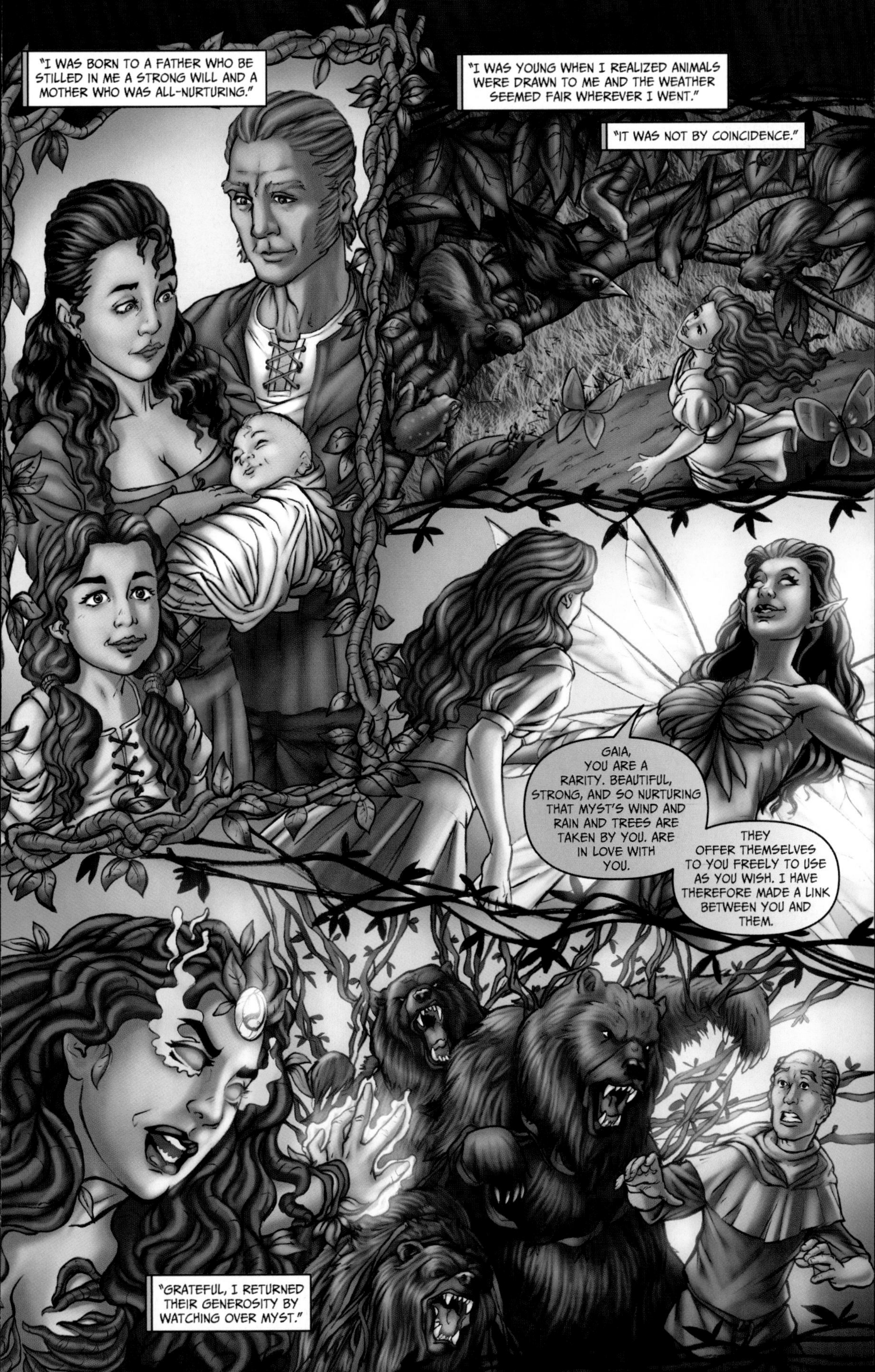
"I WAS BORN TO A FATHER WHO BE STILLED IN ME A STRONG WILL AND A MOTHER WHO WAS ALL-NURTURING."
"I WAS YOUNG WHEN I REALIZED ANIMALS WERE DRAWN TO ME AND THE WEATHER SEEMED FAIR WHEREVER I WENT."
"IT WAS NOT BY COINCIDENCE."
GAIA, YOU ARE A RARITY. BEAUTIFUL, STRONG, AND SO NURTURING THAT MYST'S WIND AND RAIN AND TREES ARE TAKEN BY YOU. ARE IN LOVE WITH YOU.
THEY OFFER THEMSELVES TO YOU FREELY TO USE AS YOU WISH. I HAVE THEREFORE MADE A LINK BETWEEN YOU AND THEM.
"GRATEFUL, I RETURNED THEIR GENEROSITY BY WATCHING OVER MYST."

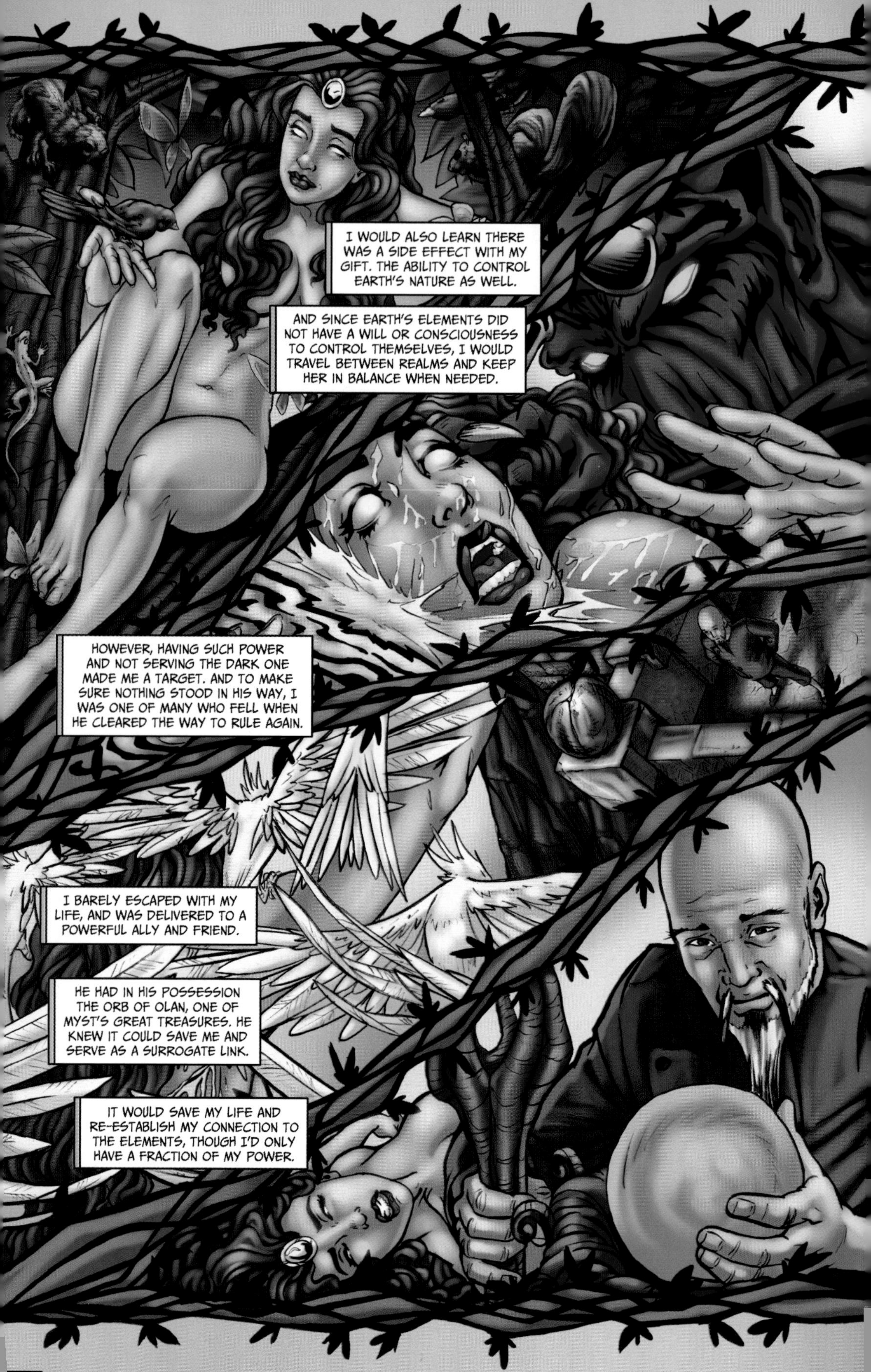
I WOULD ALSO LEARN THERE WAS A SIDE EFFECT WITH MY GIFT. THE ABILITY TO CONTROL EARTH'S NATURE AS WELL.
AND SINCE EARTH'S ELEMENTS DID NOT HAVE A WILL OR CONSCIOUSNESS TO CONTROL THEMSELVES, I WOULD TRAVEL BETWEEN REALMS AND KEEP HER IN BALANCE WHEN NEEDED.
HOWEVER, HAVING SUCH POWER AND NOT SERVING THE DARK ONE MADE ME A TARGET. AND TO MAKE SURE NOTHING STOOD IN HIS WAY, I WAS ONE OF MANY WHO FELL WHEN HE CLEARED THE WAY TO RULE AGAIN.
I BARELY ESCAPED WITH MY LIFE, AND WAS DELIVERED TO A POWERFUL ALLY AND FRIEND.
HE HAD IN HIS POSSESSION THE ORB OF OLAN, ONE OF MYST'S GREAT TREASURES. HE KNEW IT COULD SAVE ME AND SERVE AS A SURROGATE LINK.
IT WOULD SAVE MY LIFE AND RE-ESTABLISH MY CONNECTION TO THE ELEMENTS, THOUGH I'D ONLY HAVE A FRACTION OF MY POWER.

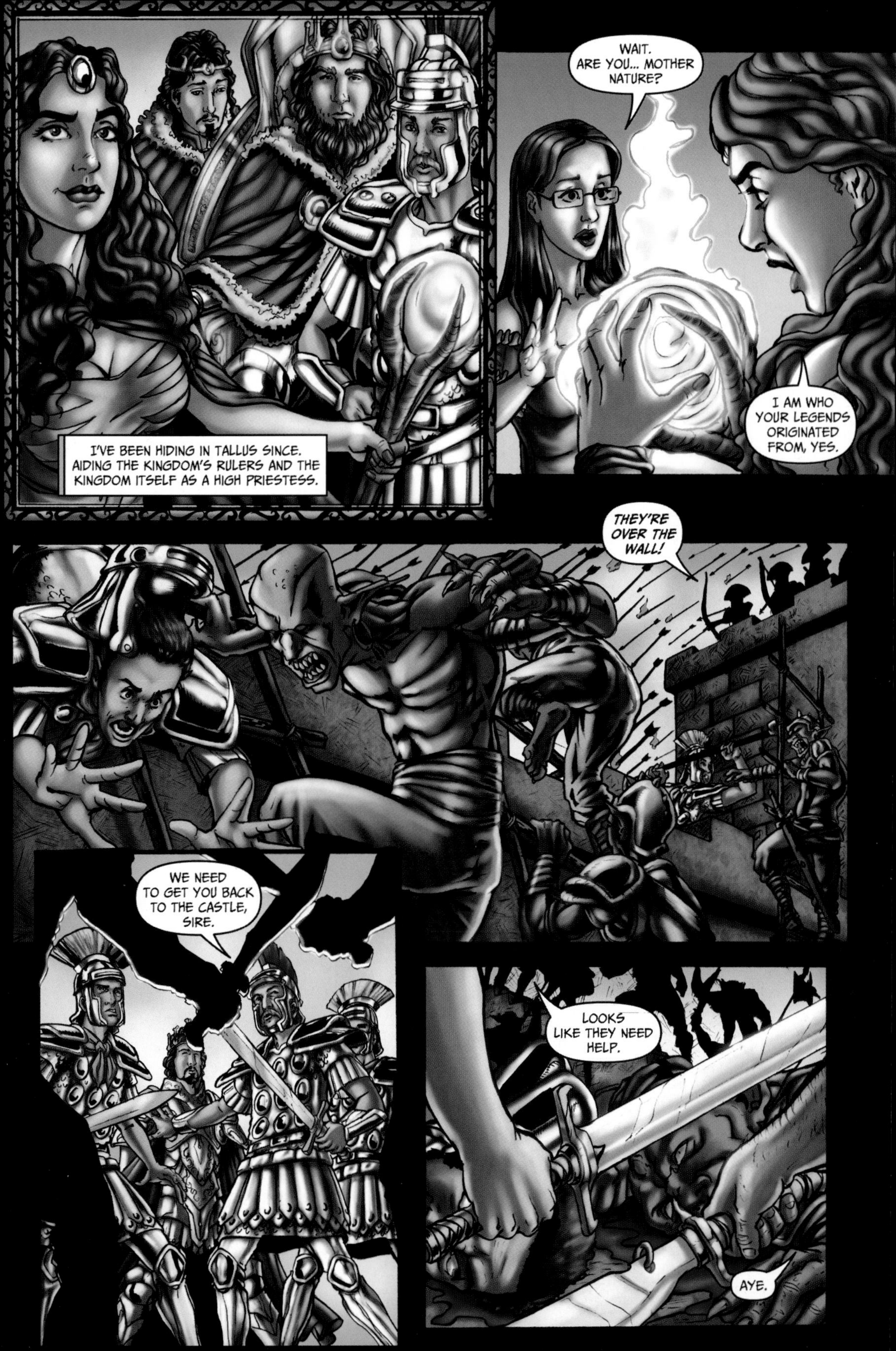

I'VE BEEN HIDING IN TALLUS SINCE. AIDING THE KINGDOM'S RULERS AND THE KINGDOM ITSELF AS A HIGH PRIESTESS.
WAIT. ARE YOU... MOTHER NATURE?
I AM WHO YOUR LEGENDS ORIGINATED FROM, YES.
THEY'RE OVER THE WALL!
WE NEED TO GET YOU BACK TO THE CASTLE, SIRE.
LOOKS LIKE THEY NEED HELP.
AYE.

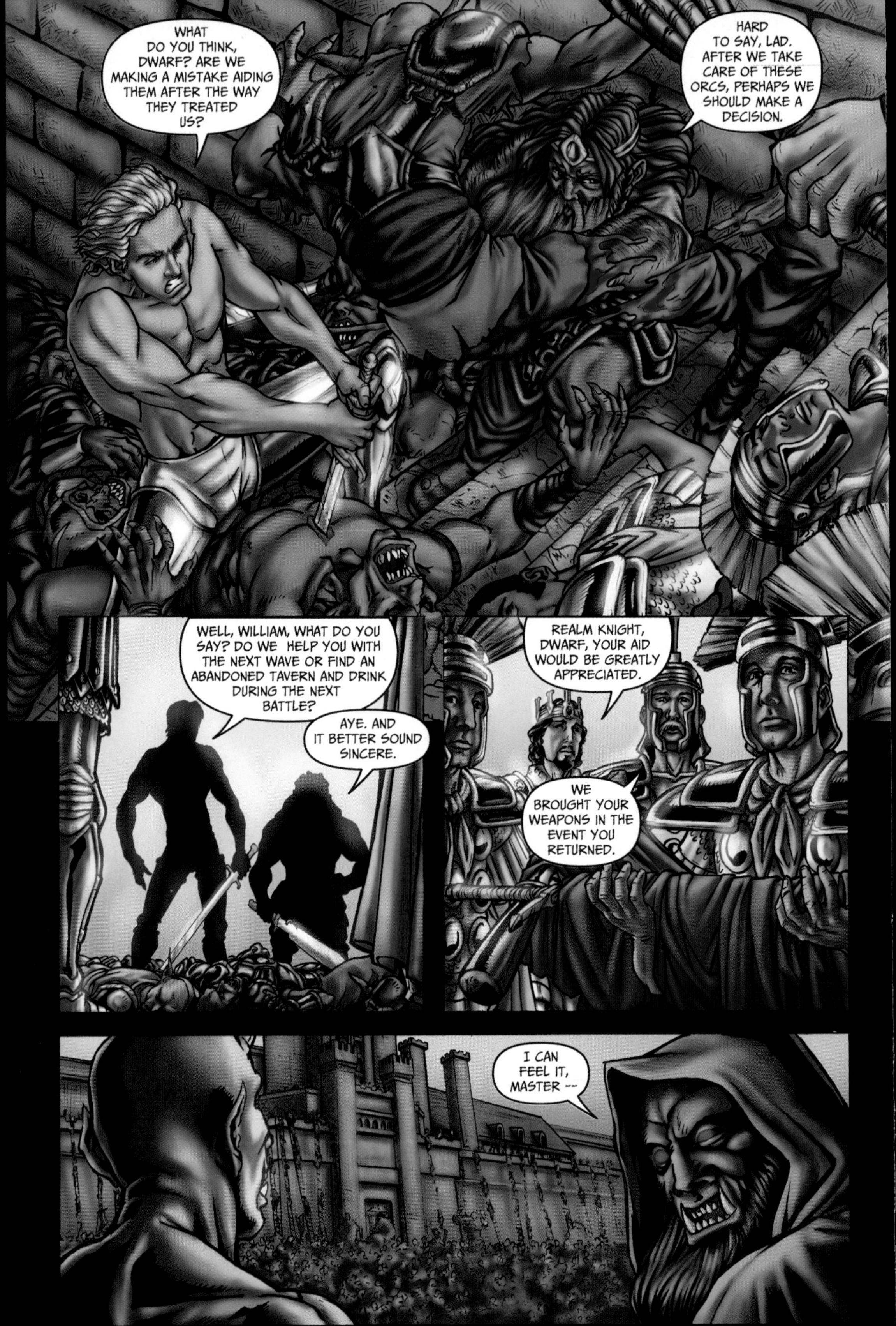
WHAT DO YOU THINK, DWARF? ARE WE MAKING A MISTAKE AIDING THEM AFTER THE WAY THEY TREATED US?
HARD TO SAY, LAD. AFTER WE TAKE CARE OF THESE ORCS, PERHAPS WE SHOULD MAKE A DECISION.
WELL, WILLIAM, WHAT DO YOU SAY? DO WE HELP YOU WITH THE NEXT WAVE OR FIND AN ABANDONED TAVERN AND DRINK DURING THE NEXT BATTLE?
AYE. AND IT BETTER SOUND SINCERE.
REALM KNIGHT, DWARF, YOUR AID WOULD BE GREATLY APPRECIATED.
WE BROUGHT YOUR WEAPONS IN THE EVENT YOU RETURNED.
I CAN FEEL IT, MASTER --

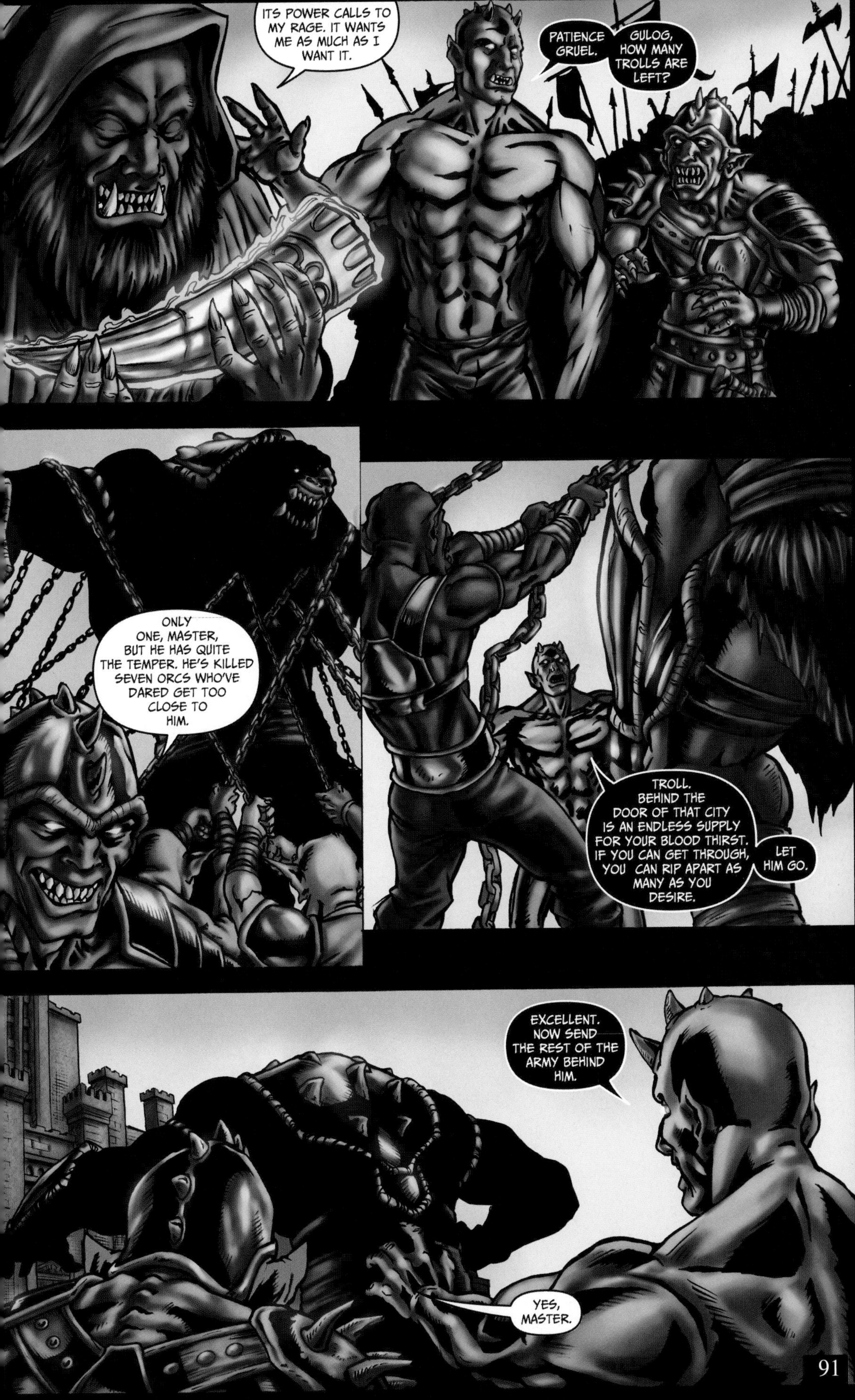

ITS POWER CALLS TO MY RAGE. IT WANTS ME AS MUCH AS I WANT IT.
PATIENCE GRUEL.
GULOG, HOW MANY TROLLS ARE LEFT?
ONLY ONE, MASTER, BUT HE HAS QUITE THE TEMPER. HE'S KILLED SEVEN ORCS WHO'VE DARED GET TOO CLOSE TO HIM.
TROLL. BEHIND THE DOOR OF THAT CITY IS AN ENDLESS SUPPLY FOR YOUR BLOOD THIRST. IF YOU CAN GET THROUGH, YOU CAN RIP APART AS MANY AS YOU DESIRE.
LET HIM GO.
EXCELLENT. NOW SEND THE REST OF THE ARMY BEHIND HIM.
YES, MASTER.

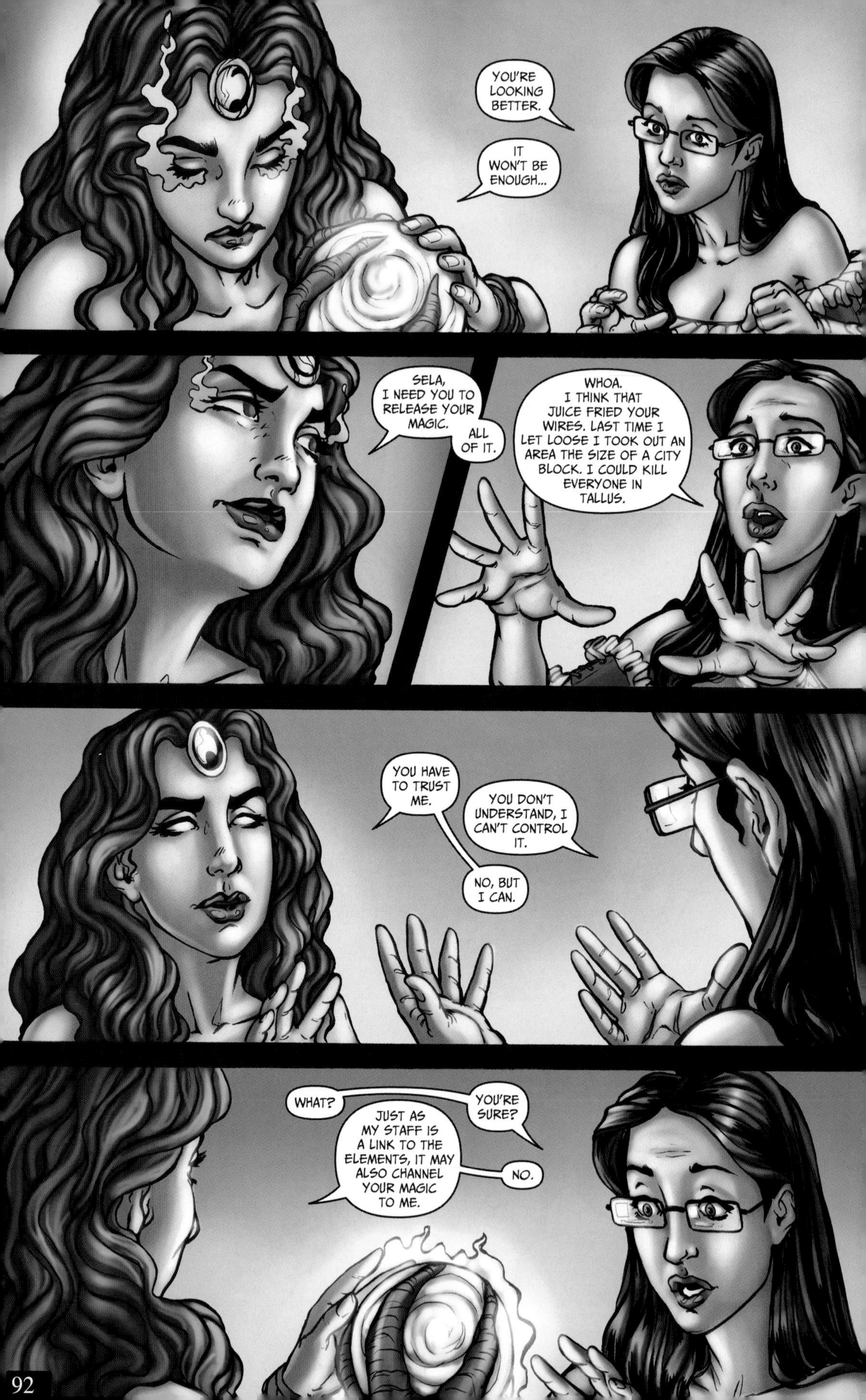

YOU'RE LOOKING BETTER.
IT WON'T BE ENOUGH...
SELA, I NEED YOU TO RELEASE YOUR MAGIC.
ALL OF IT.
WHOA. I THINK THAT JUICE FRIED YOUR WIRES. LAST TIME I LET LOOSE I TOOK OUT AN AREA THE SIZE OF A CITY BLOCK. I COULD KILL EVERYONE IN TALLUS.
YOU HAVE TO TRUST ME.
YOU DON'T UNDERSTAND, I CAN'T CONTROL IT.
NO, BUT I CAN.
WHAT?
YOU'RE SURE?
JUST AS MY STAFF IS A LINK TO THE ELEMENTS, IT MAY ALSO CHANNEL YOUR MAGIC TO ME.
NO.

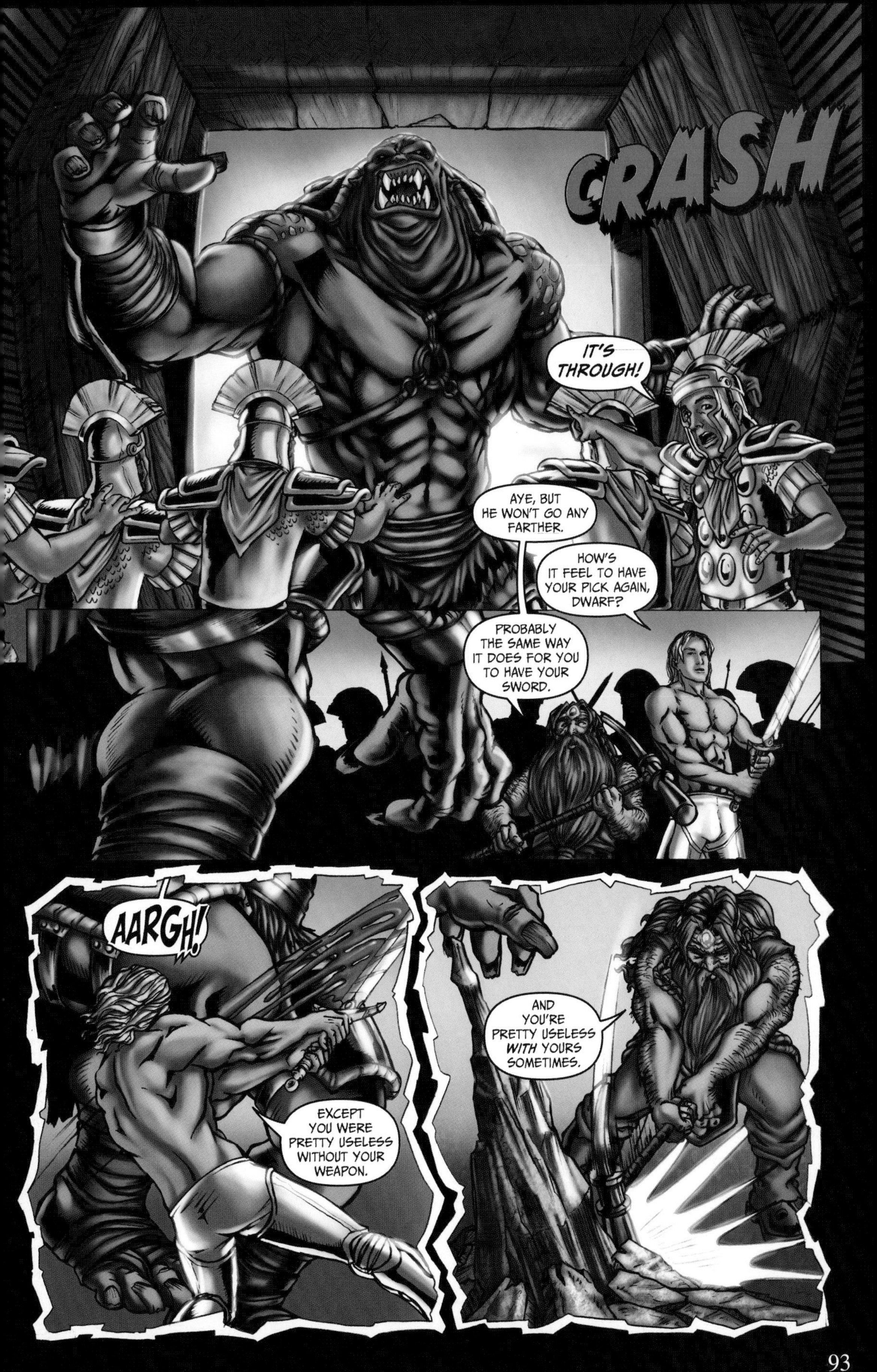

CRASH
IT'S THROUGH!
AYE, BUT HE WON'T GO ANY FARTHER.
HOW'S IT FEEL TO HAVE YOUR PICK AGAIN, DWARF?
PROBABLY THE SAME WAY IT DOES FOR YOU TO HAVE YOUR SWORD.
AARGH!
EXCEPT YOU WERE PRETTY USELESS WITHOUT YOUR WEAPON.
AND YOU'RE PRETTY USELESS *WITH* YOURS SOMETIMES.

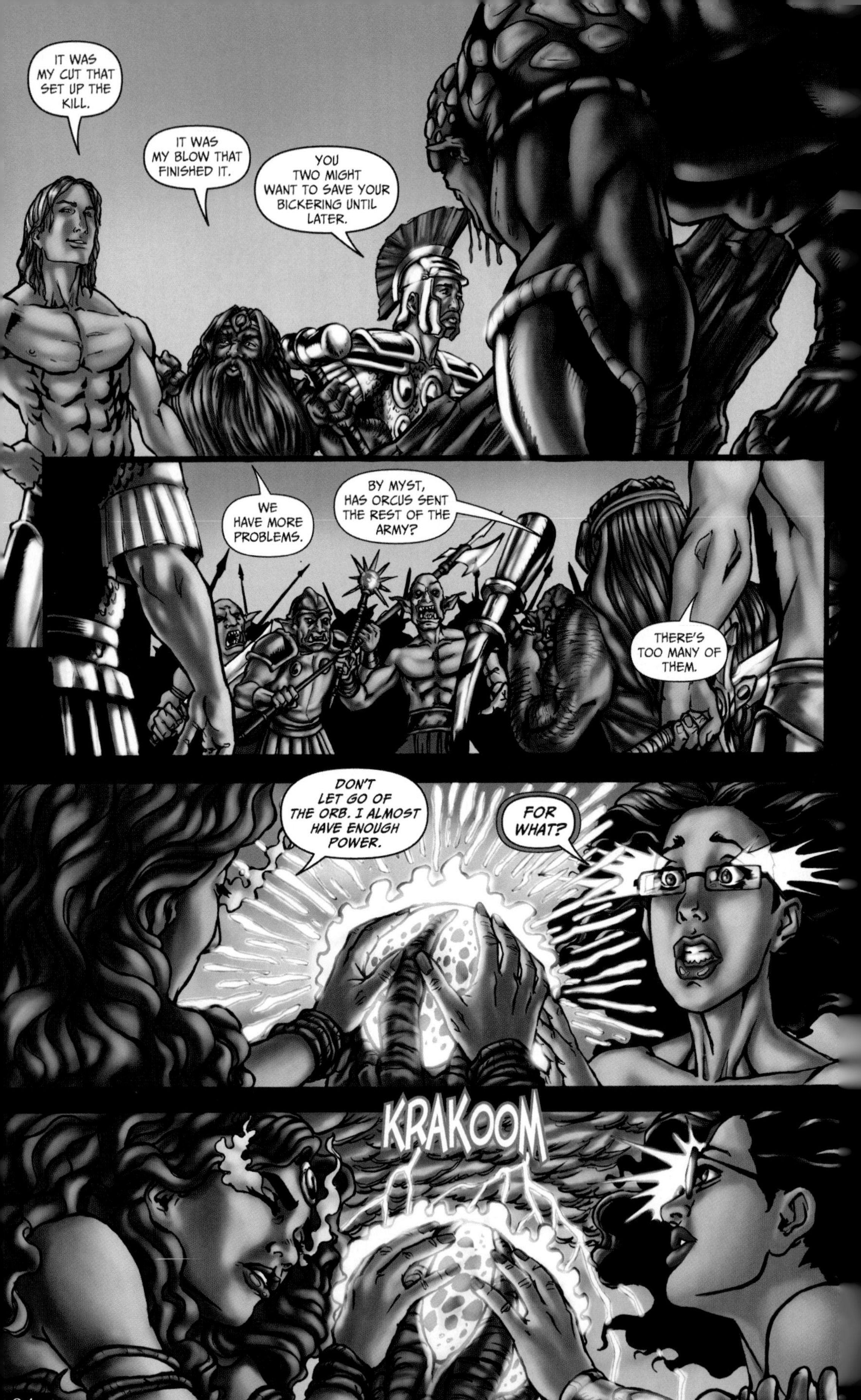
IT WAS MY CUT THAT SET UP THE KILL.
IT WAS MY BLOW THAT FINISHED IT.
YOU TWO MIGHT WANT TO SAVE YOUR BICKERING UNTIL LATER.
WE HAVE MORE PROBLEMS.
BY MYST, HAS ORCUS SENT THE REST OF THE ARMY?
THERE'S TOO MANY OF THEM.
DON'T LET GO OF THE ORB. I ALMOST HAVE ENOUGH POWER.
FOR WHAT?
KRAKOOM

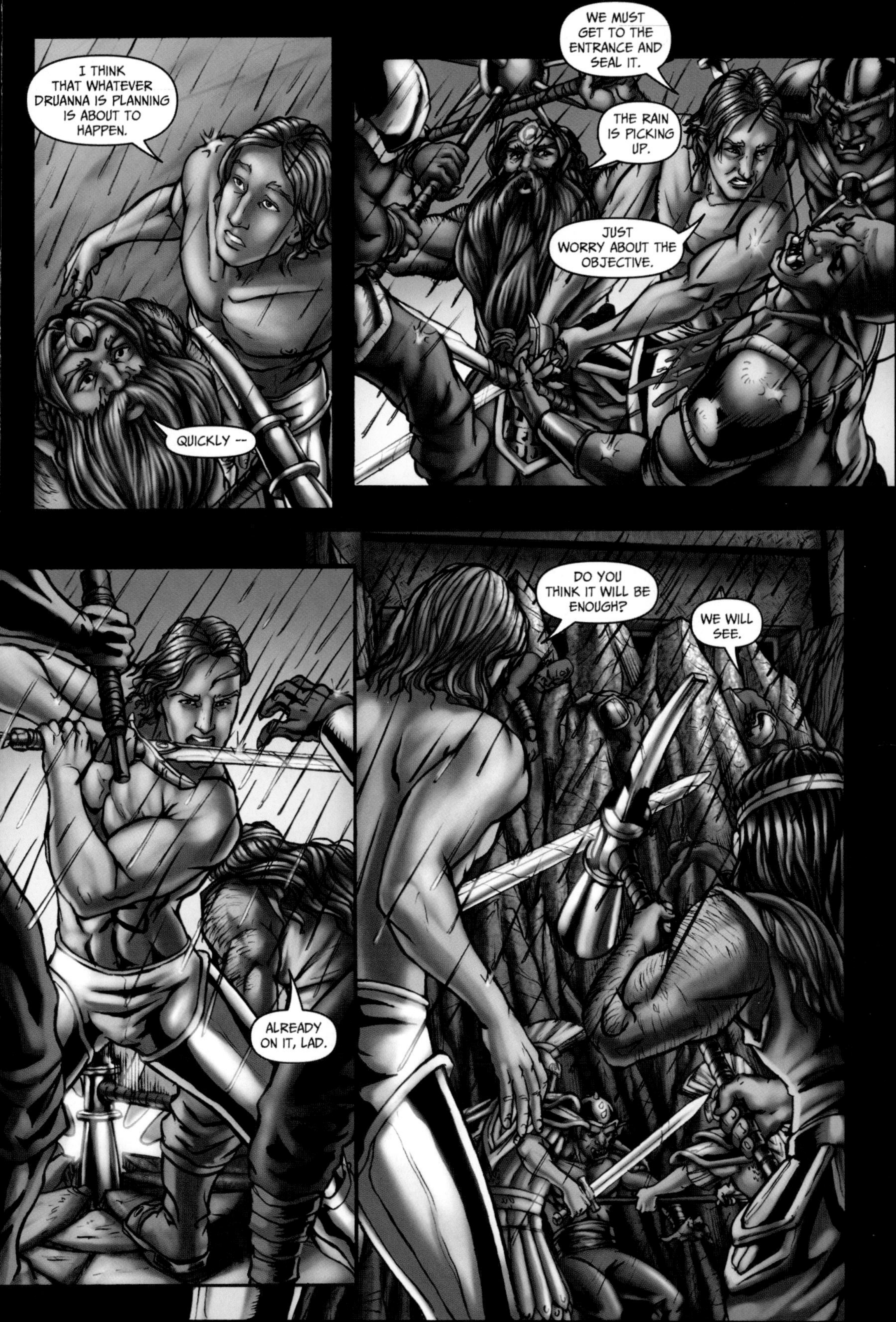

I THINK THAT WHATEVER DRUANNA IS PLANNING IS ABOUT TO HAPPEN.
QUICKLY --
WE MUST GET TO THE ENTRANCE AND SEAL IT.
THE RAIN IS PICKING UP.
JUST WORRY ABOUT THE OBJECTIVE.
ALREADY ON IT, LAD.
DO YOU THINK IT WILL BE ENOUGH?
WE WILL SEE.

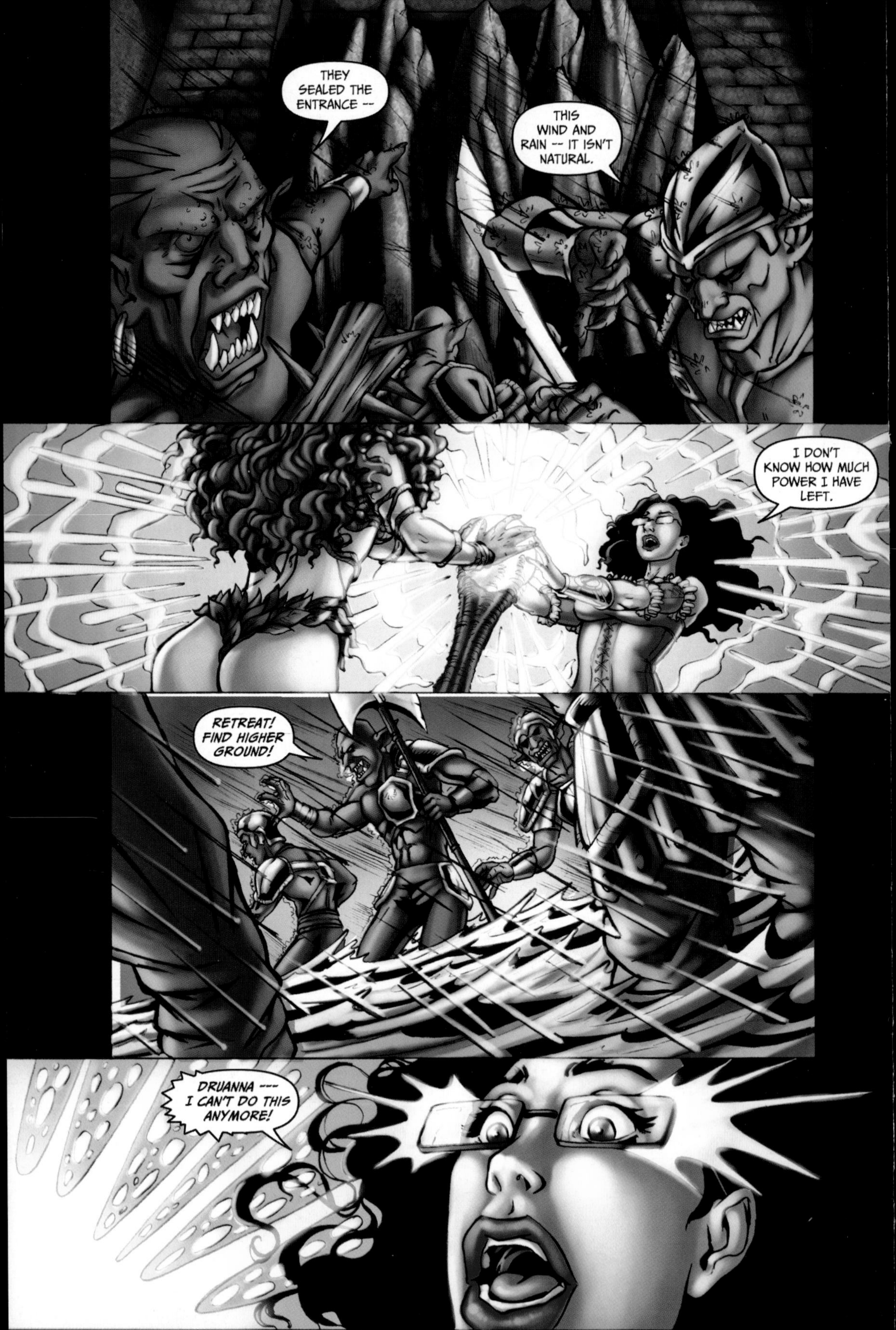
THEY SEALED THE ENTRANCE --
THIS WIND AND RAIN -- IT ISN'T NATURAL.
I DON'T KNOW HOW MUCH POWER I HAVE LEFT.
RETREAT! FIND HIGHER GROUND!
DRUANNA --- I CAN'T DO THIS ANYMORE!

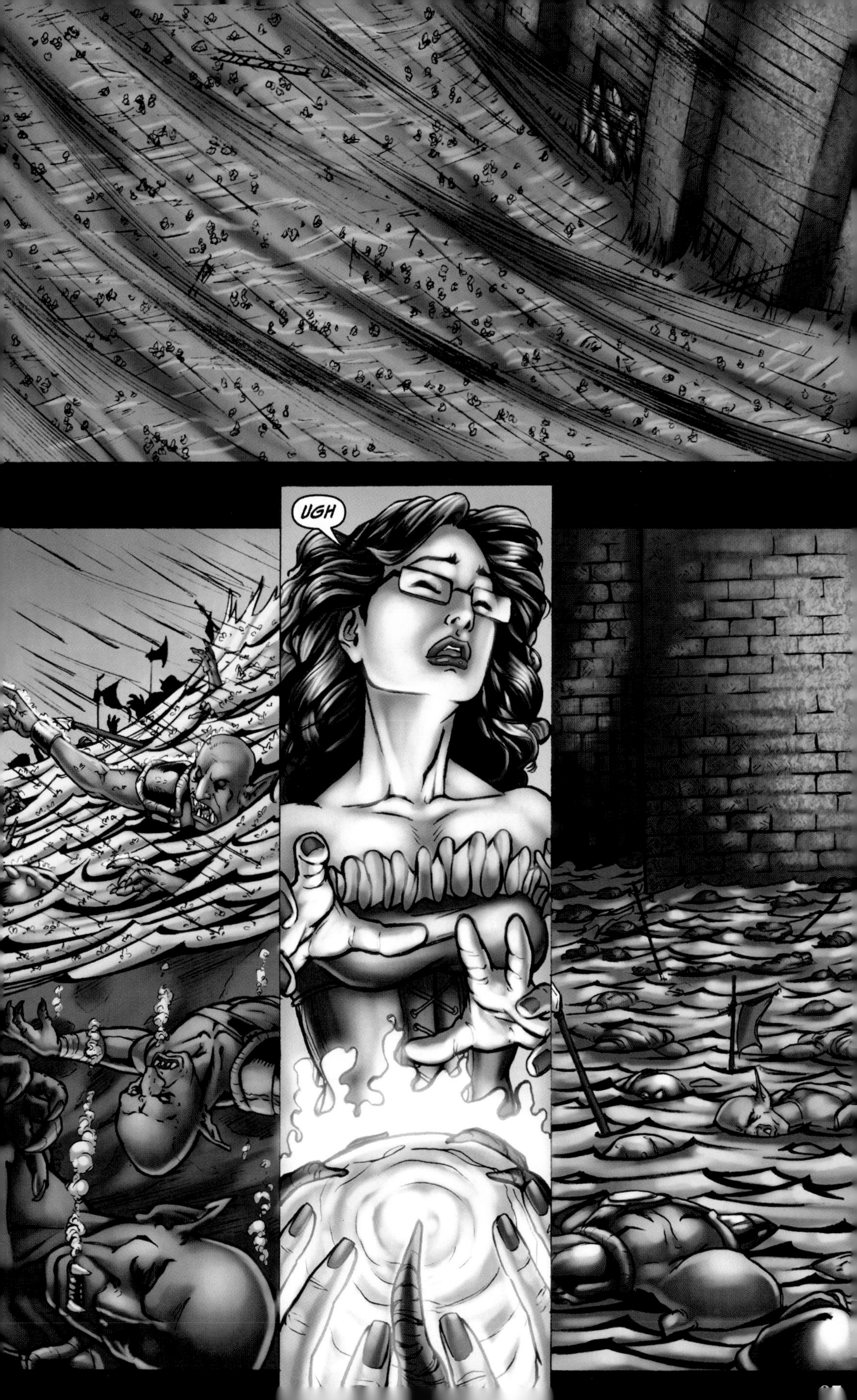
UGH

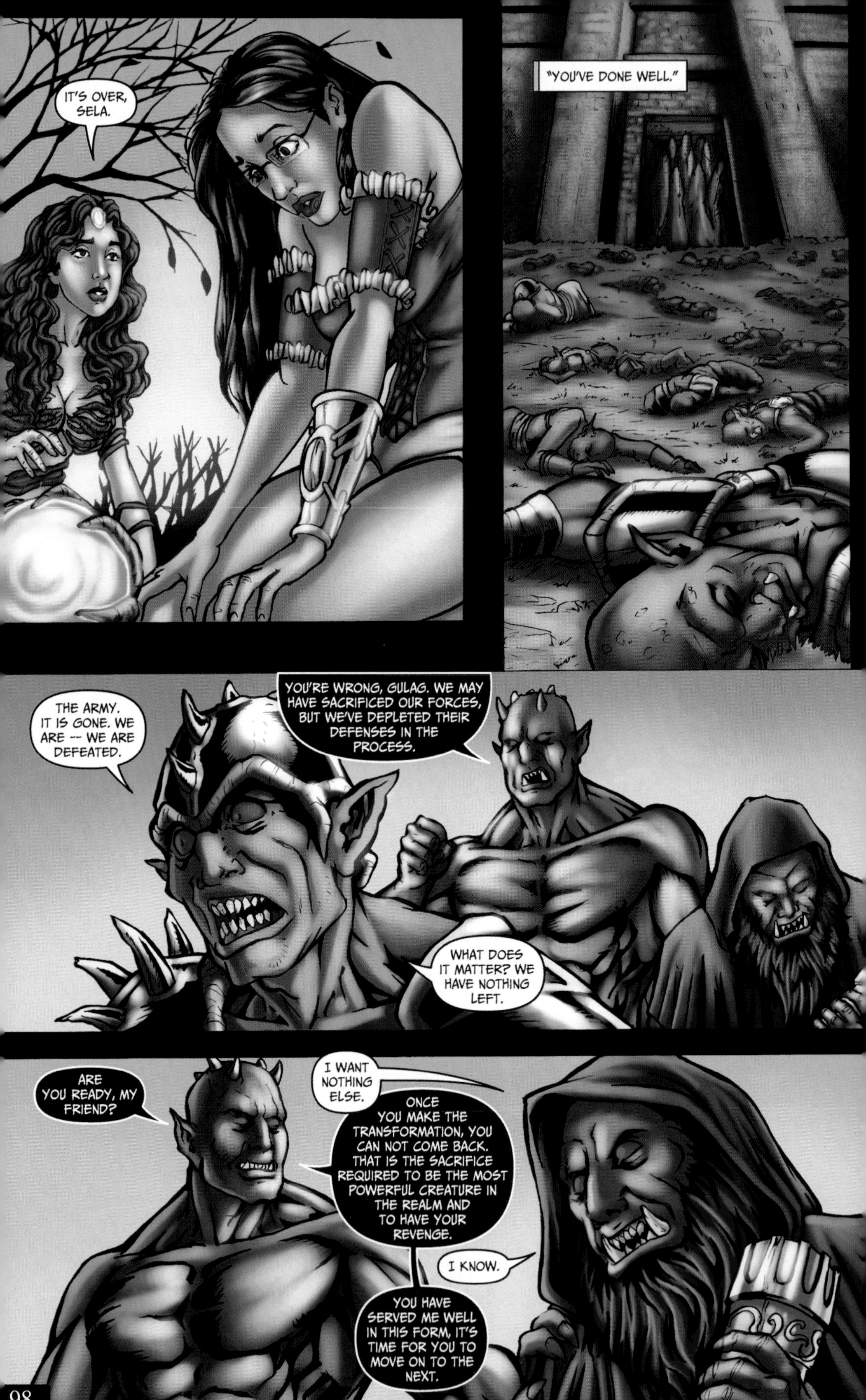
IT'S OVER, SELA.
"YOU'VE DONE WELL."
THE ARMY. IT IS GONE. WE ARE -- WE ARE DEFEATED.
YOU'RE WRONG, GULAG. WE MAY HAVE SACRIFICED OUR FORCES, BUT WE'VE DEPLETED THEIR DEFENSES IN THE PROCESS.
WHAT DOES IT MATTER? WE HAVE NOTHING LEFT.
ARE YOU READY, MY FRIEND?
I WANT NOTHING ELSE.
ONCE YOU MAKE THE TRANSFORMATION, YOU CAN NOT COME BACK. THAT IS THE SACRIFICE REQUIRED TO BE THE MOST POWERFUL CREATURE IN THE REALM AND TO HAVE YOUR REVENGE.
I KNOW.
YOU HAVE SERVED ME WELL IN THIS FORM, IT'S TIME FOR YOU TO MOVE ON TO THE NEXT.

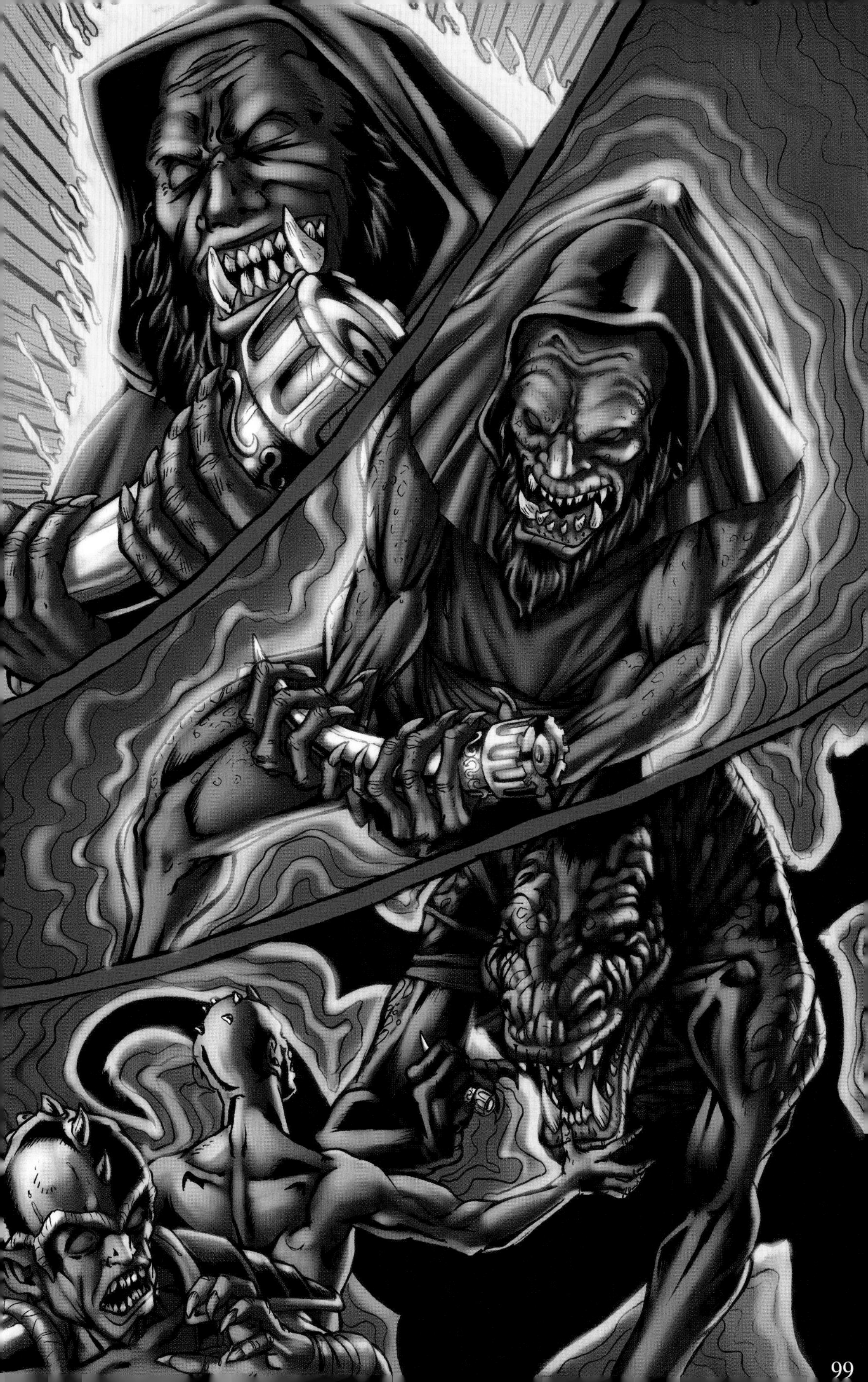

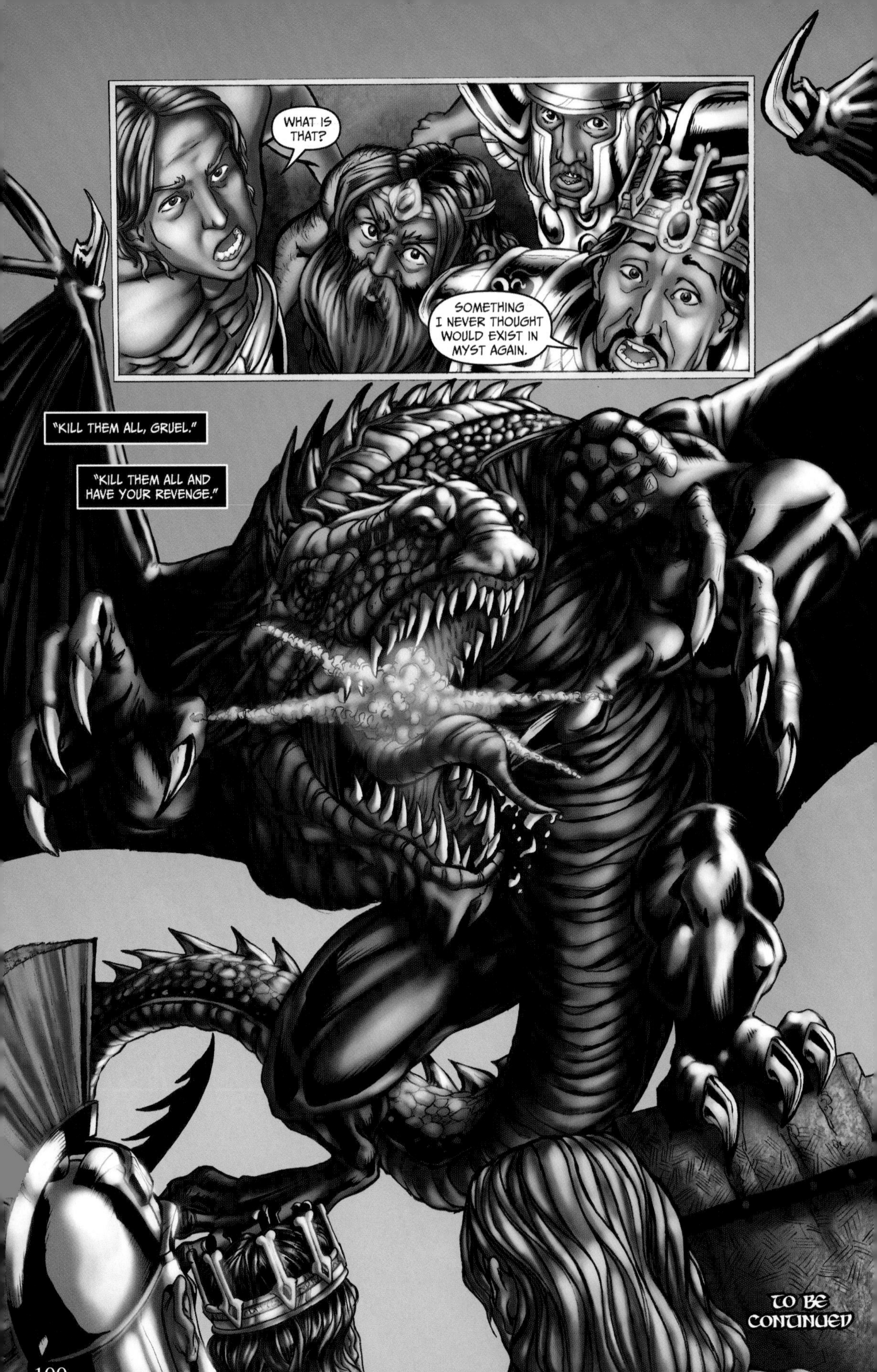
WHAT IS THAT?
SOMETHING I NEVER THOUGHT WOULD EXIST IN MYST AGAIN.
"KILL THEM ALL, GRUEL."
"KILL THEM ALL AND HAVE YOUR REVENGE."
TO BE CONTINUED

Grimm Fairy Tales

Volume 10

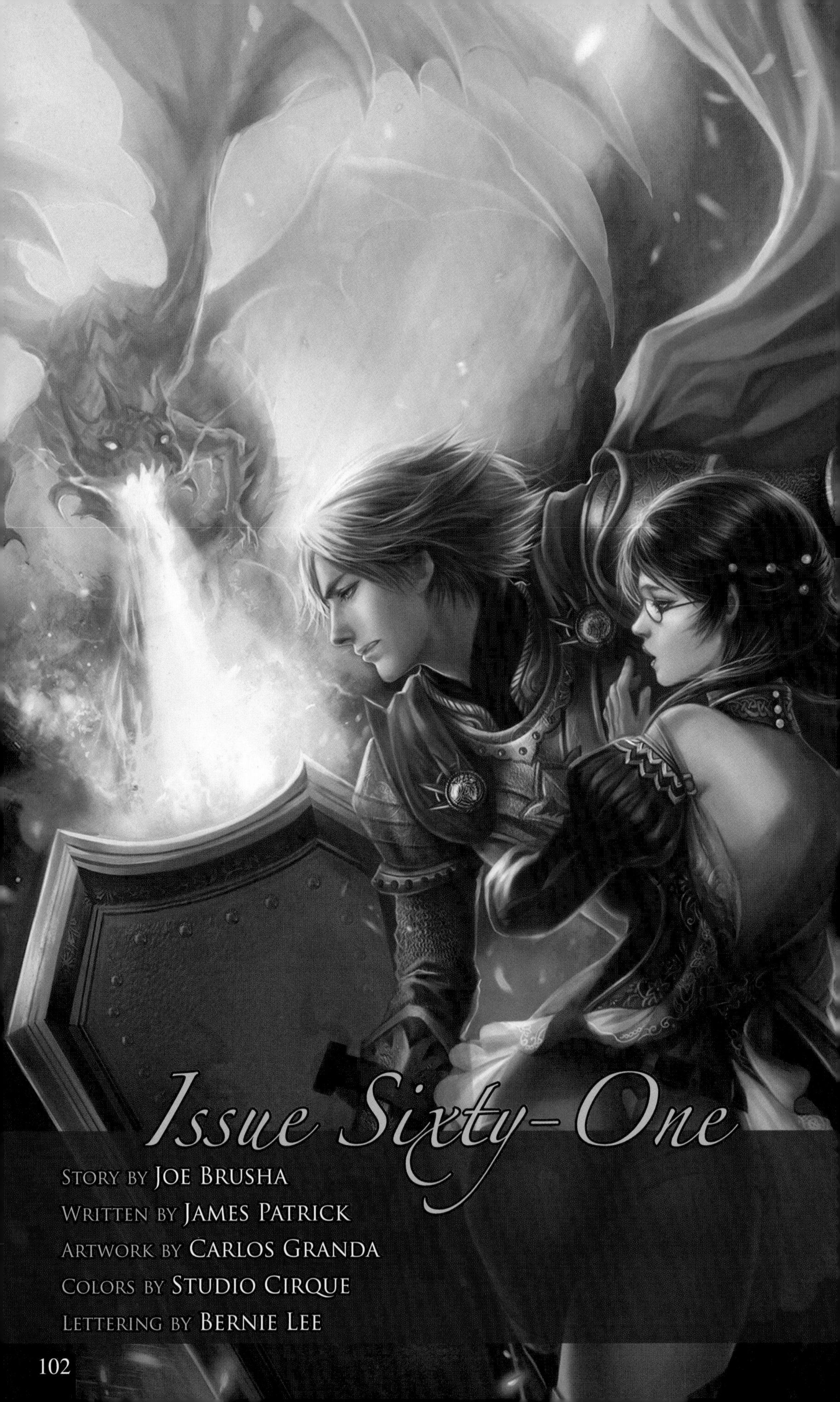

Issue Sixty-One

Story by Joe Brusha
Written by James Patrick
Artwork by Carlos Granda
Colors by Studio Cirque
Lettering by Bernie Lee

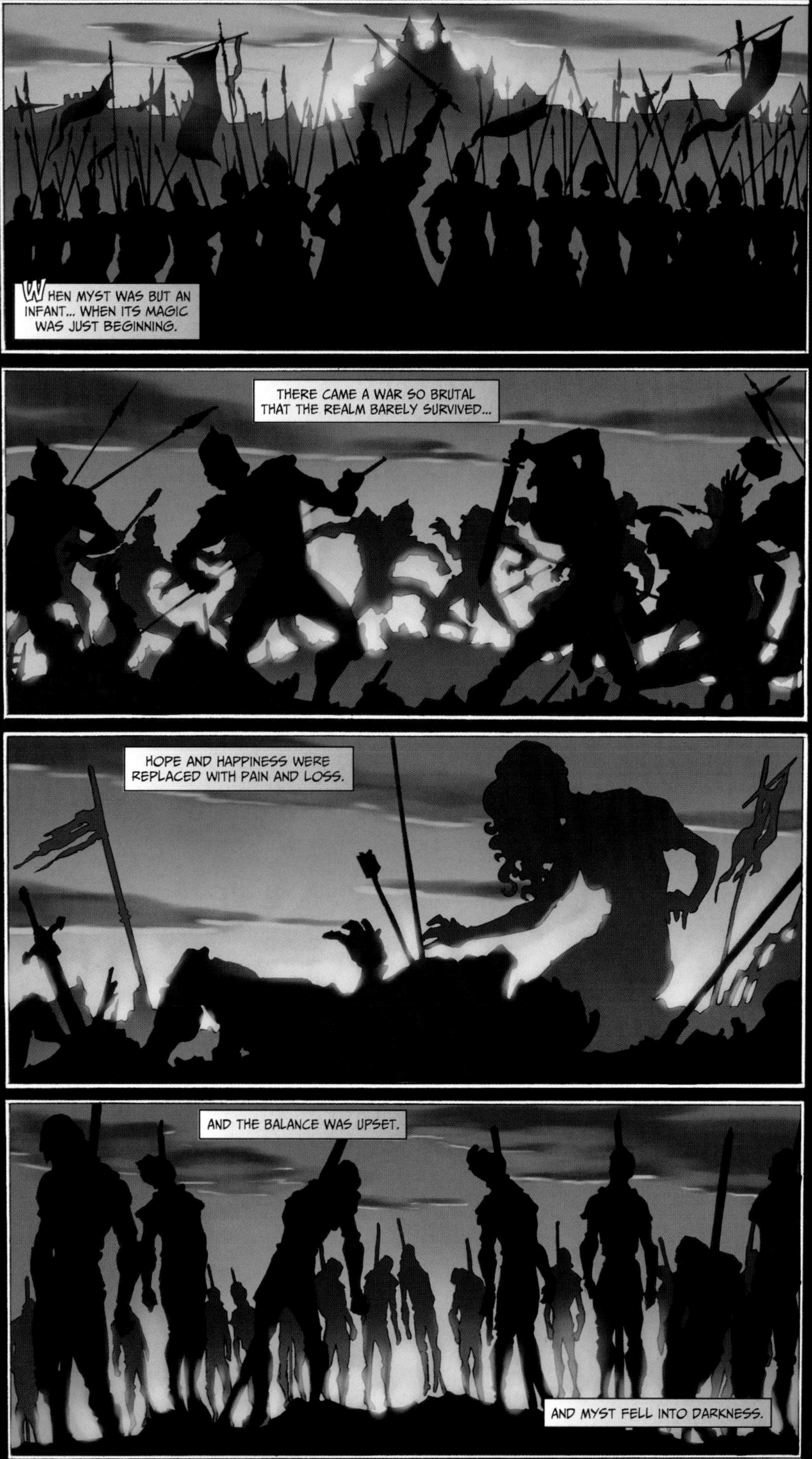
WHEN MYST WAS BUT AN INFANT... WHEN ITS MAGIC WAS JUST BEGINNING.
THERE CAME A WAR SO BRUTAL THAT THE REALM BARELY SURVIVED...
HOPE AND HAPPINESS WERE REPLACED WITH PAIN AND LOSS.
AND THE BALANCE WAS UPSET.
AND MYST FELL INTO DARKNESS.

FROM THAT DARKNESS ROSE THE MOST DANGEROUS AND BRUTAL OF MYST'S CREATURES.

AND THE SHADOW DRAGON BEGAN ITS REIGN.

THE OTHER DRAGONS WERE THE FIRST TO BE DESTROYED, NEARLY EXTINGUISHED FROM ALL BUT MEMORY BY THE SHADOW DRAGONS.

THE DARKNESS GREW DEEPER.

NEXT TO FALL WERE MEN AND ORCS...

AND SOON ALL LIVING THINGS FELL TO THEIR RULE.

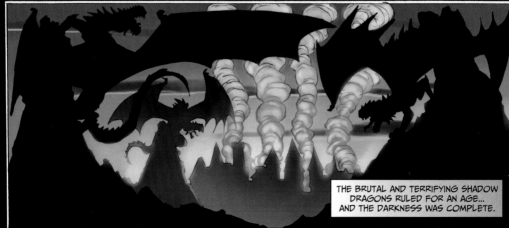

THE BRUTAL AND TERRIFYING SHADOW DRAGONS RULED FOR AN AGE... AND THE DARKNESS WAS COMPLETE.

SELFLESSNESS BROUGHT BACK A SMALL BEAM OF LIGHT.

LIGHT THAT SPREAD LIKE WILDFIRE ACROSS THE REALM AS MORE SUCH ACTS OCCURRED.

A LIGHT THAT BROUGHT HOPE... HOPE THAT BEGAN TO RESTORE MYST'S BALANCE.

BUT THE DRAGONS STILL COULD NOT BE SLAIN. THEY WERE STILL TOO POWERFUL.

THEIR HEARTS GREW EVEN MORE BRUTAL...

AND THEY DESTROYED THEMSELVES.

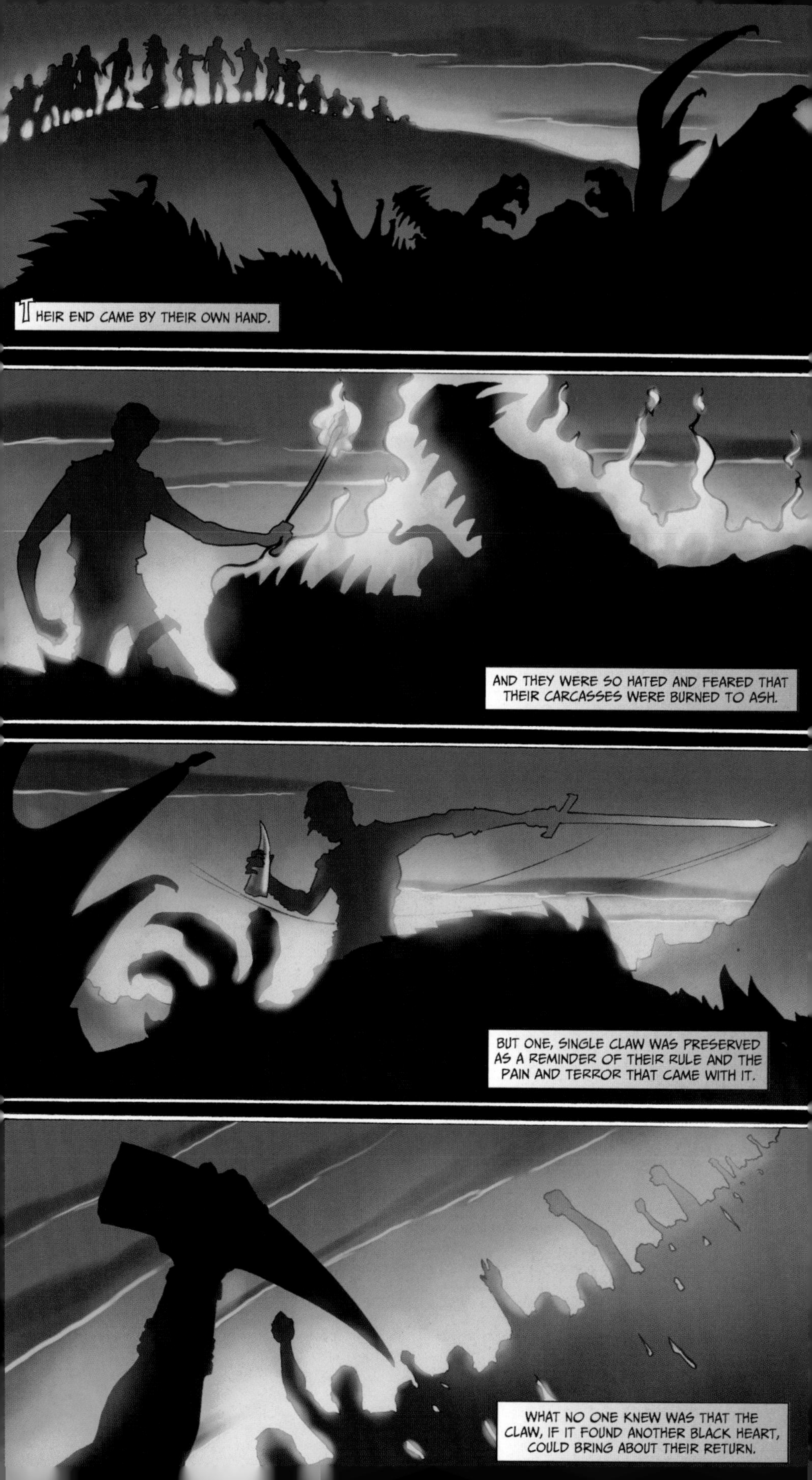
THEIR END CAME BY THEIR OWN HAND.
AND THEY WERE SO HATED AND FEARED THAT THEIR CARCASSES WERE BURNED TO ASH.
BUT ONE, SINGLE CLAW WAS PRESERVED AS A REMINDER OF THEIR RULE AND THE PAIN AND TERROR THAT CAME WITH IT.
WHAT NO ONE KNEW WAS THAT THE CLAW, IF IT FOUND ANOTHER BLACK HEART, COULD BRING ABOUT THEIR RETURN.

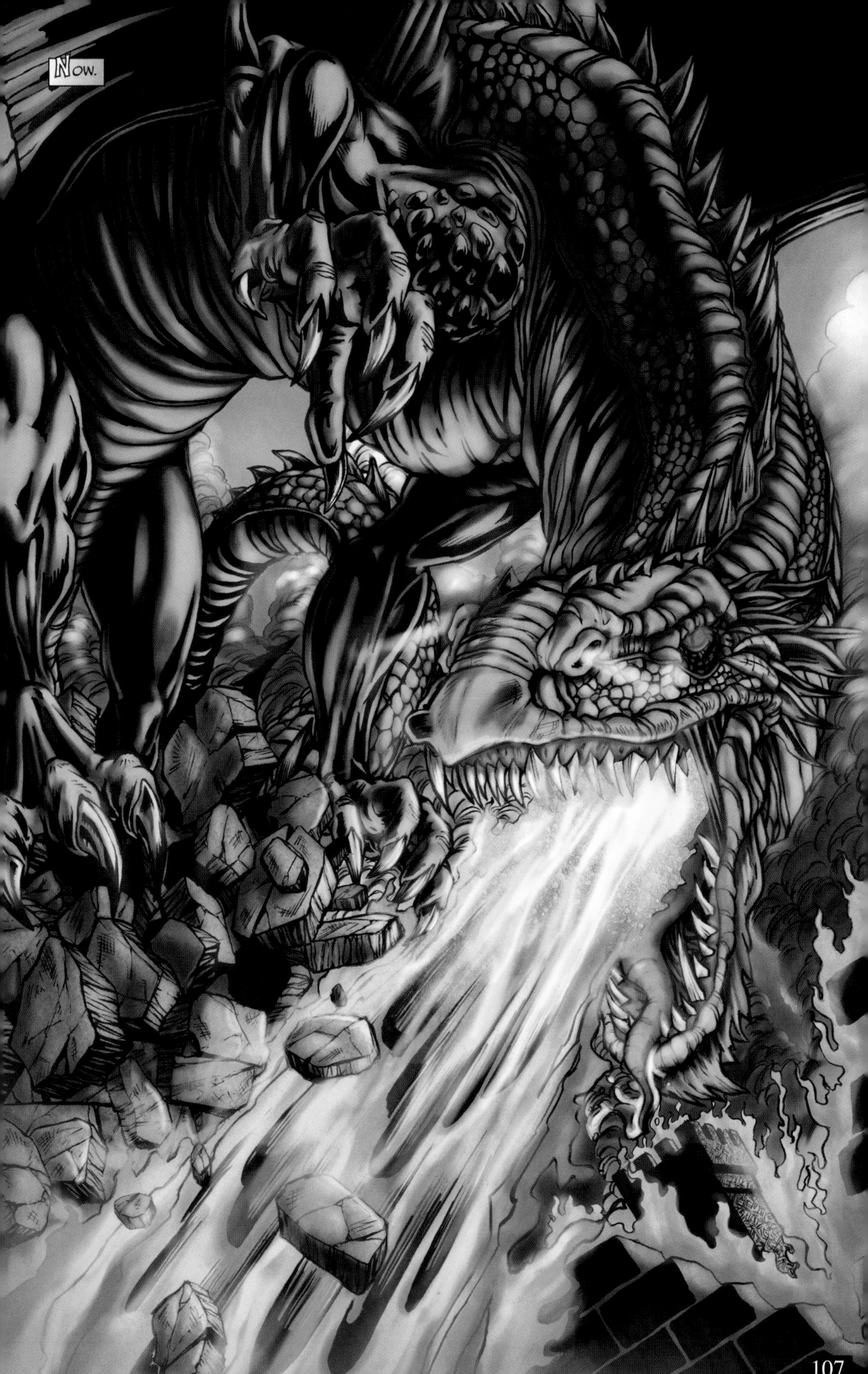
Now.

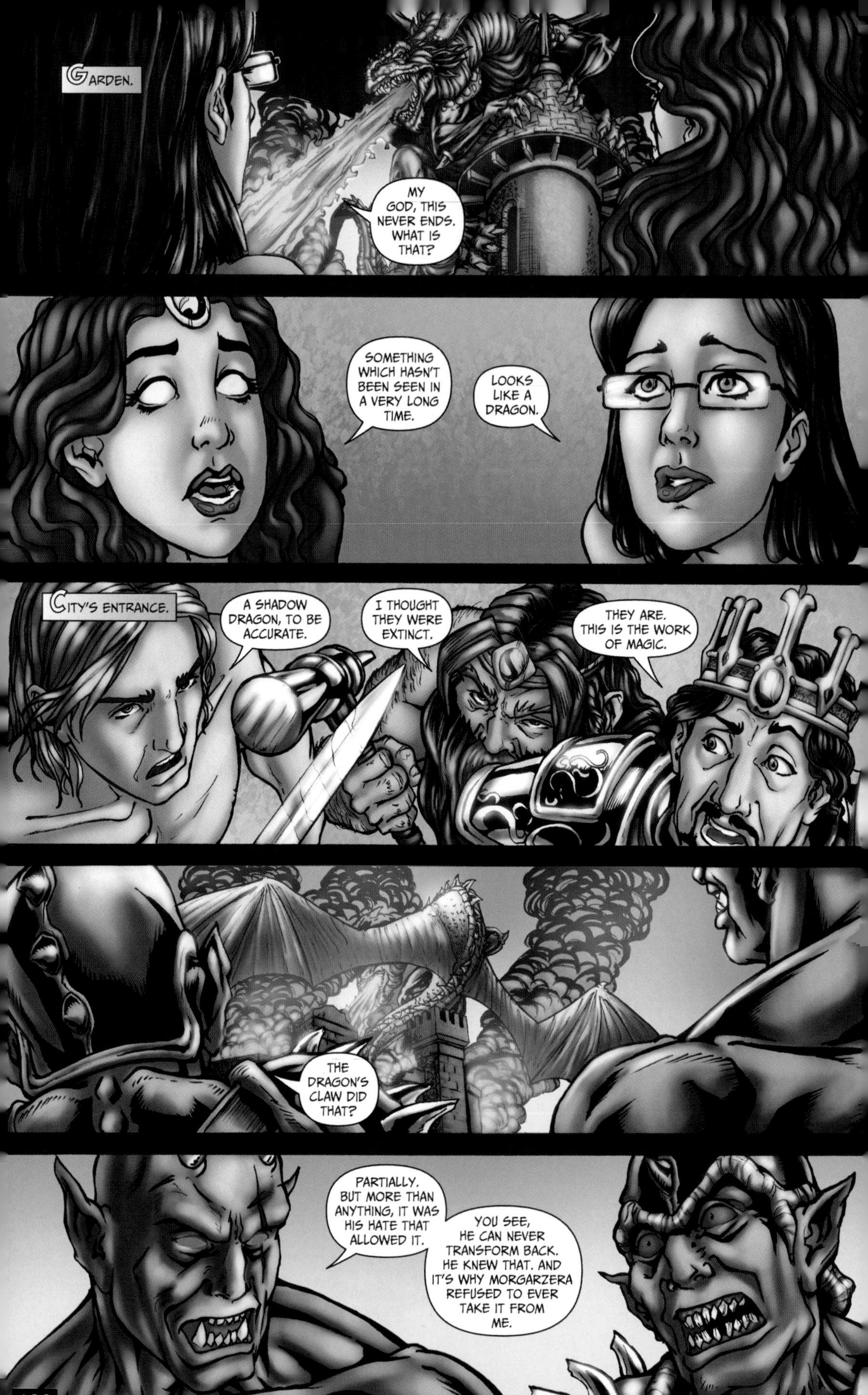
GARDEN.
MY GOD, THIS NEVER ENDS. WHAT IS THAT?
SOMETHING WHICH HASN'T BEEN SEEN IN A VERY LONG TIME.
LOOKS LIKE A DRAGON.
CITY'S ENTRANCE.
A SHADOW DRAGON, TO BE ACCURATE.
I THOUGHT THEY WERE EXTINCT.
THEY ARE. THIS IS THE WORK OF MAGIC.
THE DRAGON'S CLAW DID THAT?
PARTIALLY. BUT MORE THAN ANYTHING, IT WAS HIS HATE THAT ALLOWED IT.
YOU SEE, HE CAN NEVER TRANSFORM BACK. HE KNEW THAT. AND IT'S WHY MORGARZERA REFUSED TO EVER TAKE IT FROM ME.

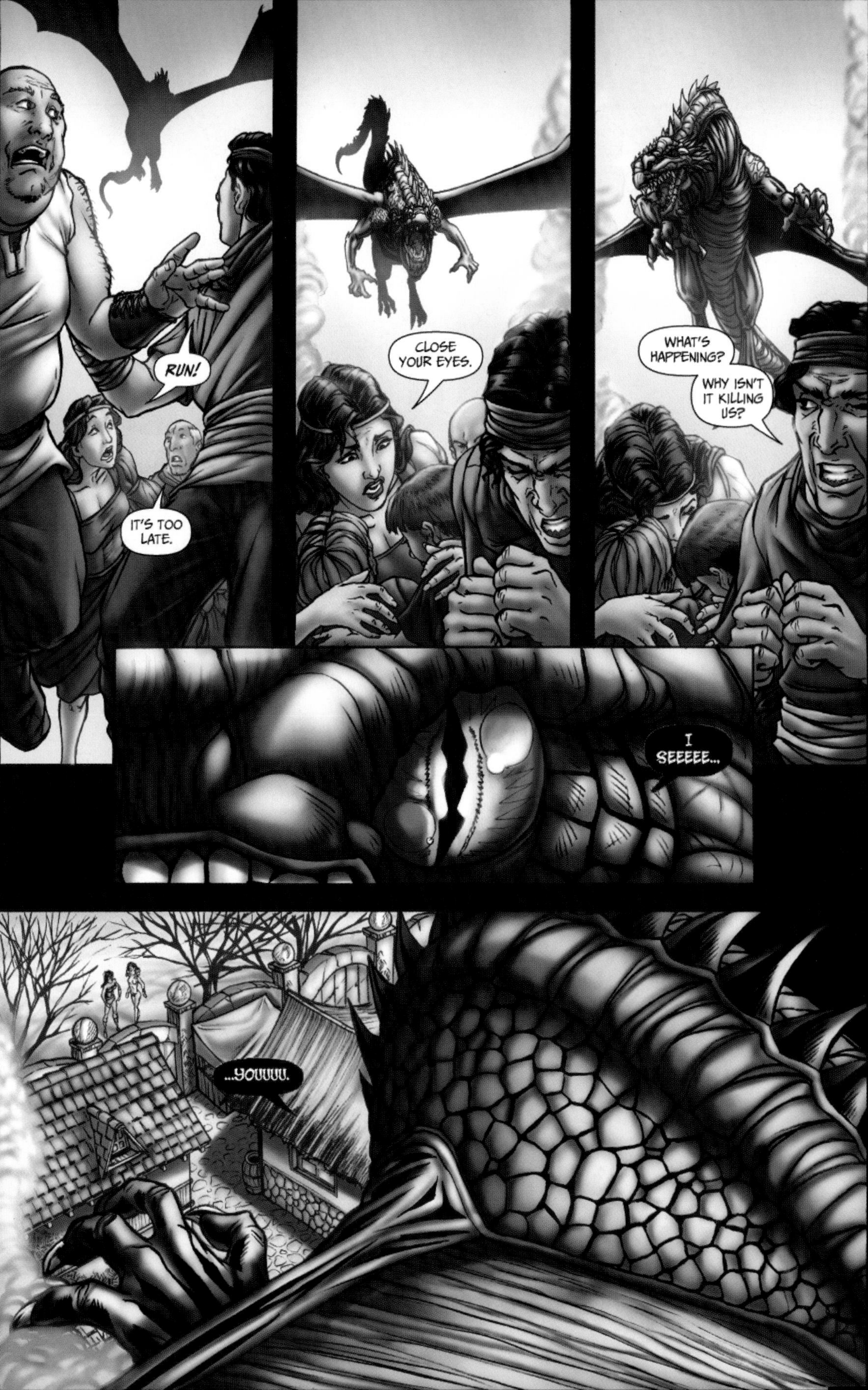
RUN!
IT'S TOO LATE.
CLOSE YOUR EYES.
WHAT'S HAPPENING?
WHY ISN'T IT KILLING US?
I SEEEEE...
...YOUUUU.

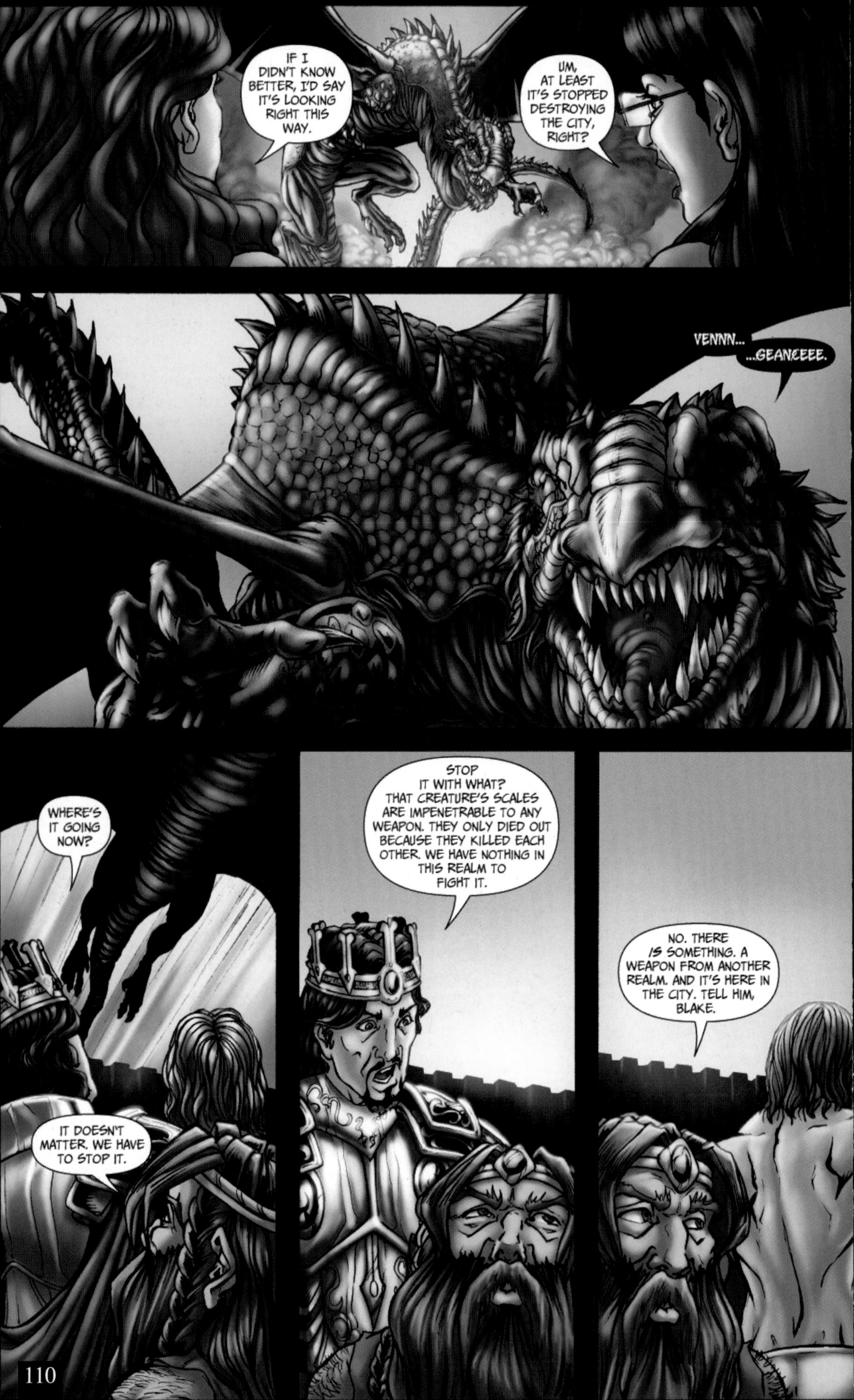
IF I DIDN'T KNOW BETTER, I'D SAY IT'S LOOKING RIGHT THIS WAY.
UM, AT LEAST IT'S STOPPED DESTROYING THE CITY, RIGHT?
VENNN...
...GEANCEEE.
WHERE'S IT GOING NOW?
IT DOESN'T MATTER. WE HAVE TO STOP IT.
STOP IT WITH WHAT? THAT CREATURE'S SCALES ARE IMPENETRABLE TO ANY WEAPON. THEY ONLY DIED OUT BECAUSE THEY KILLED EACH OTHER. WE HAVE NOTHING IN THIS REALM TO FIGHT IT.
NO. THERE IS SOMETHING. A WEAPON FROM ANOTHER REALM. AND IT'S HERE IN THE CITY. TELL HIM, BLAKE.

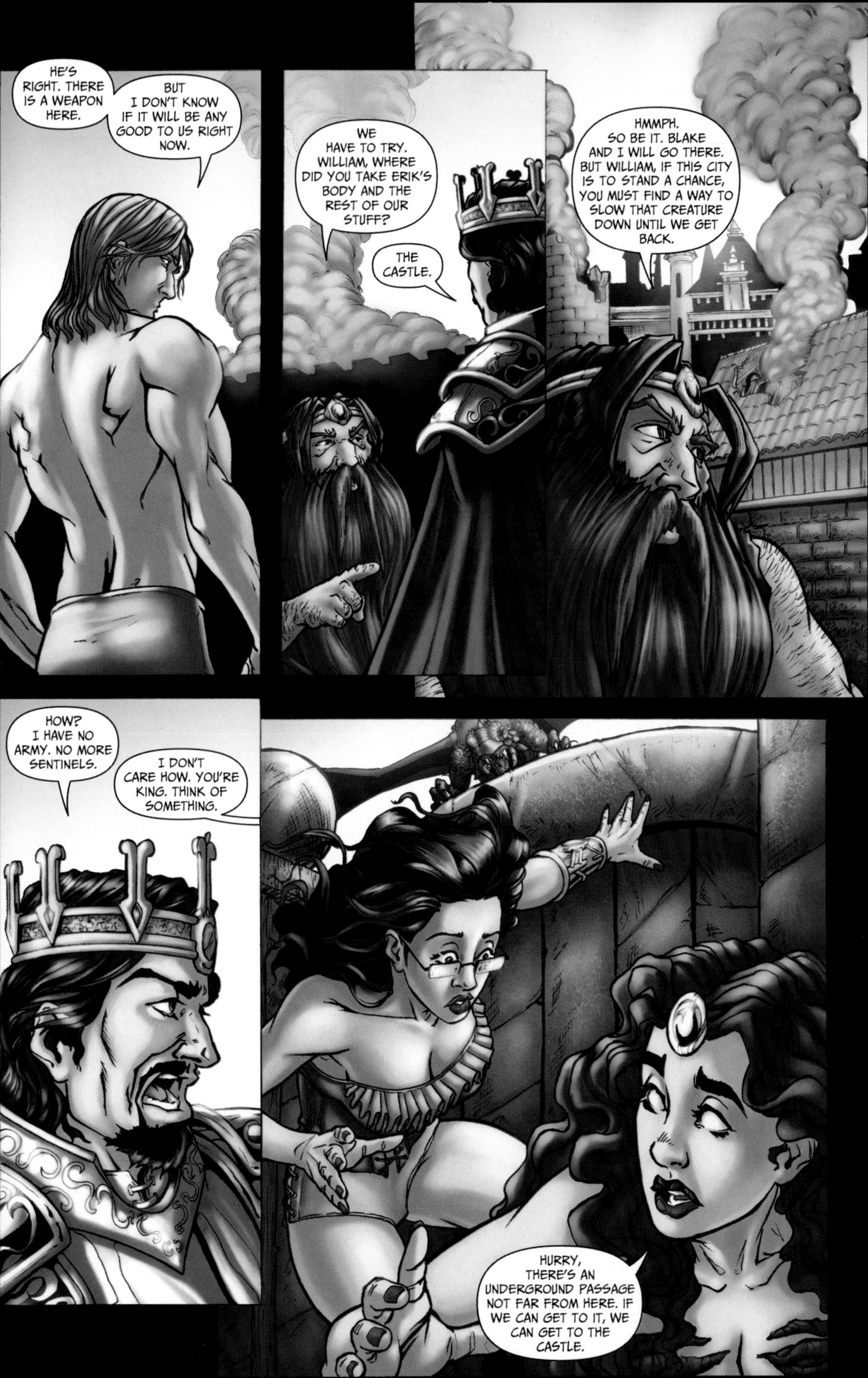

HE'S RIGHT. THERE IS A WEAPON HERE.
BUT I DON'T KNOW IF IT WILL BE ANY GOOD TO US RIGHT NOW.
WE HAVE TO TRY. WILLIAM, WHERE DID YOU TAKE ERIK'S BODY AND THE REST OF OUR STUFF?
THE CASTLE.
HMMPH. SO BE IT. BLAKE AND I WILL GO THERE. BUT WILLIAM, IF THIS CITY IS TO STAND A CHANCE, YOU MUST FIND A WAY TO SLOW THAT CREATURE DOWN UNTIL WE GET BACK.
HOW? I HAVE NO ARMY. NO MORE SENTINELS.
I DON'T CARE HOW. YOU'RE KING. THINK OF SOMETHING.
HURRY, THERE'S AN UNDERGROUND PASSAGE NOT FAR FROM HERE. IF WE CAN GET TO IT, WE CAN GET TO THE CASTLE.

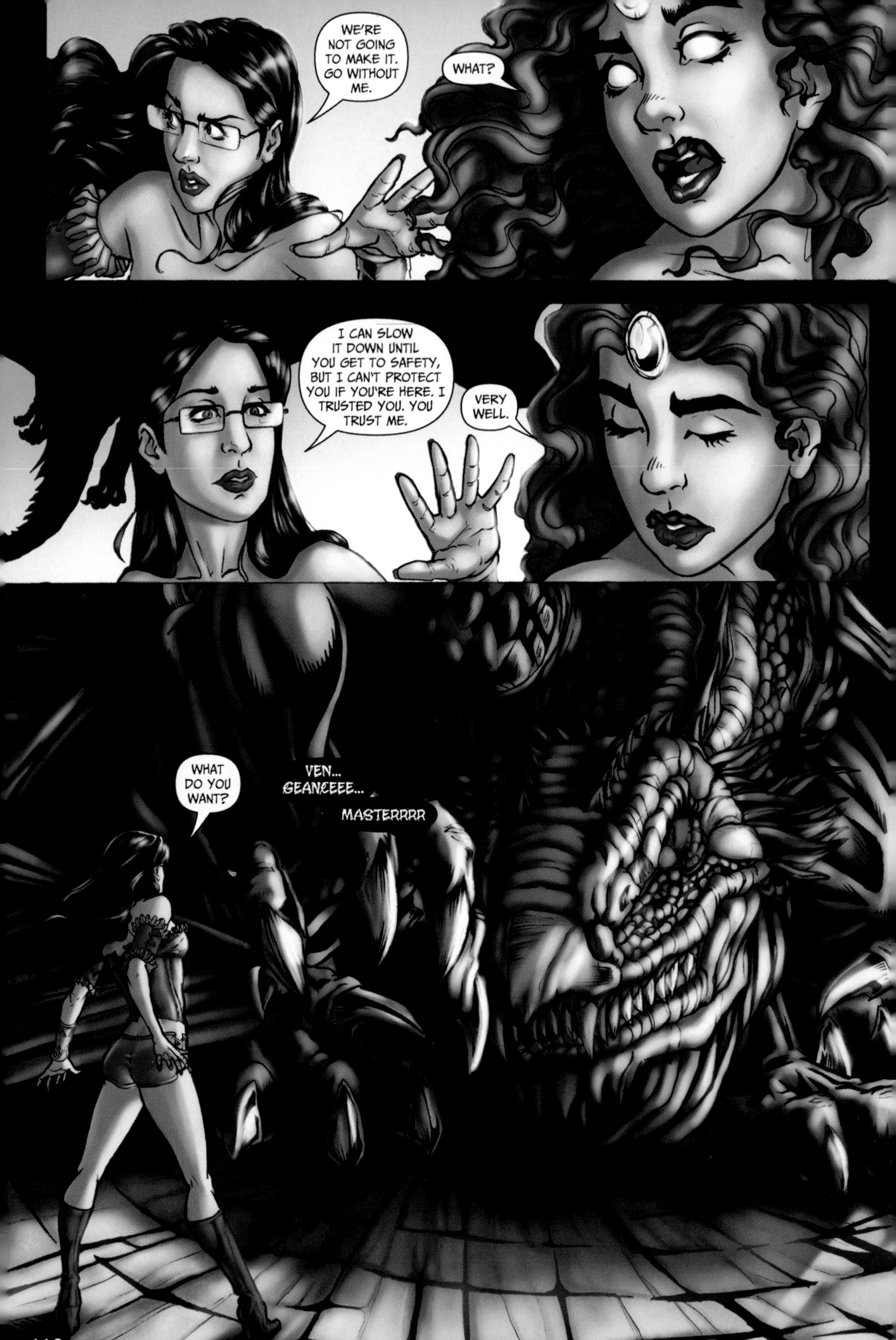
WE'RE NOT GOING TO MAKE IT. GO WITHOUT ME.
WHAT?
I CAN SLOW IT DOWN UNTIL YOU GET TO SAFETY, BUT I CAN'T PROTECT YOU IF YOU'RE HERE. I TRUSTED YOU. YOU TRUST ME.
VERY WELL.
WHAT DO YOU WANT?
VEN... GEANCEEE...
MASTERRRR

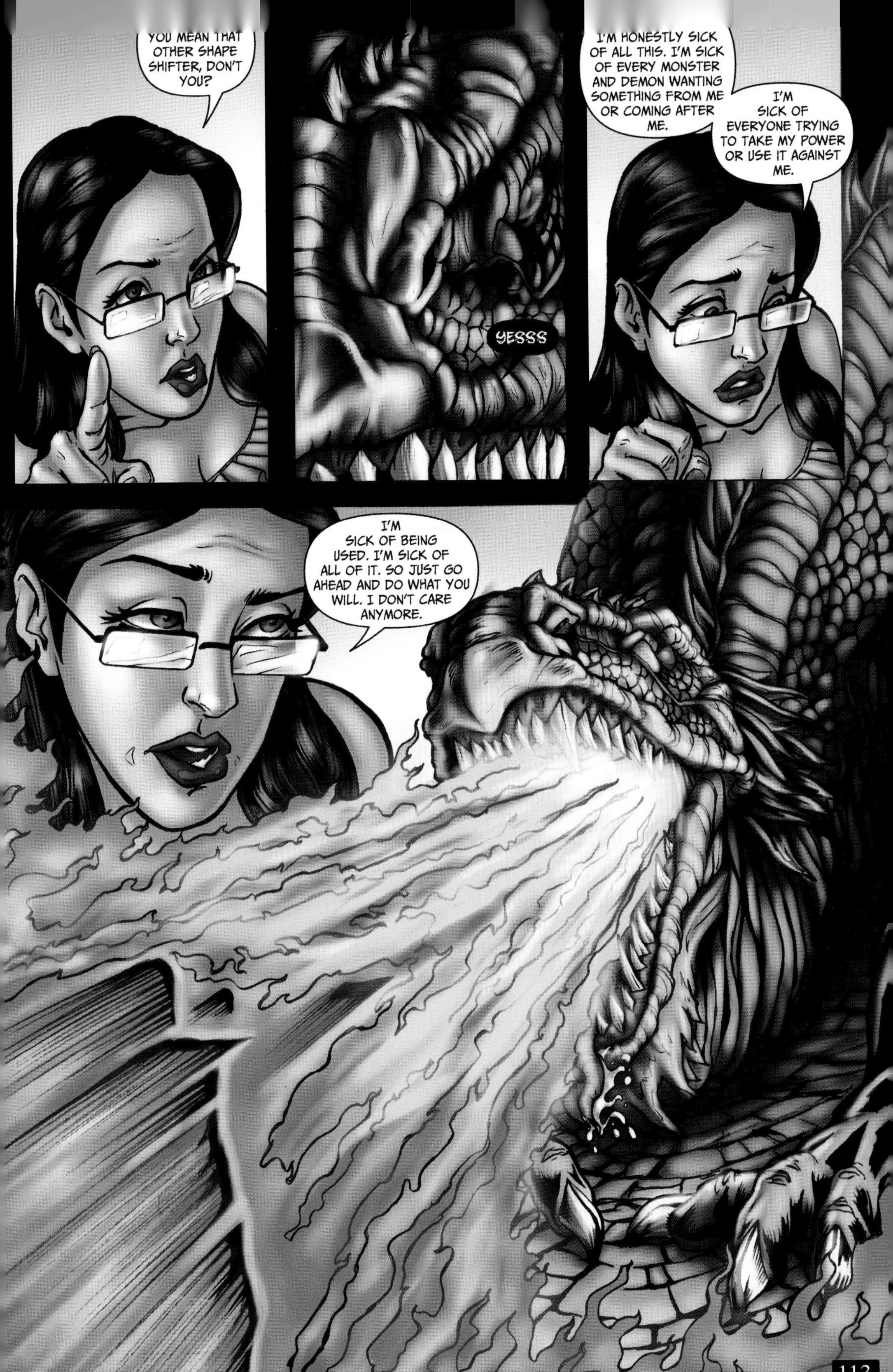
YOU MEAN THAT OTHER SHAPE SHIFTER, DON'T YOU?
YESSS
I'M HONESTLY SICK OF ALL THIS. I'M SICK OF EVERY MONSTER AND DEMON WANTING SOMETHING FROM ME OR COMING AFTER ME.
I'M SICK OF EVERYONE TRYING TO TAKE MY POWER OR USE IT AGAINST ME.
I'M SICK OF BEING USED. I'M SICK OF ALL OF IT. SO JUST GO AHEAD AND DO WHAT YOU WILL. I DON'T CARE ANYMORE.

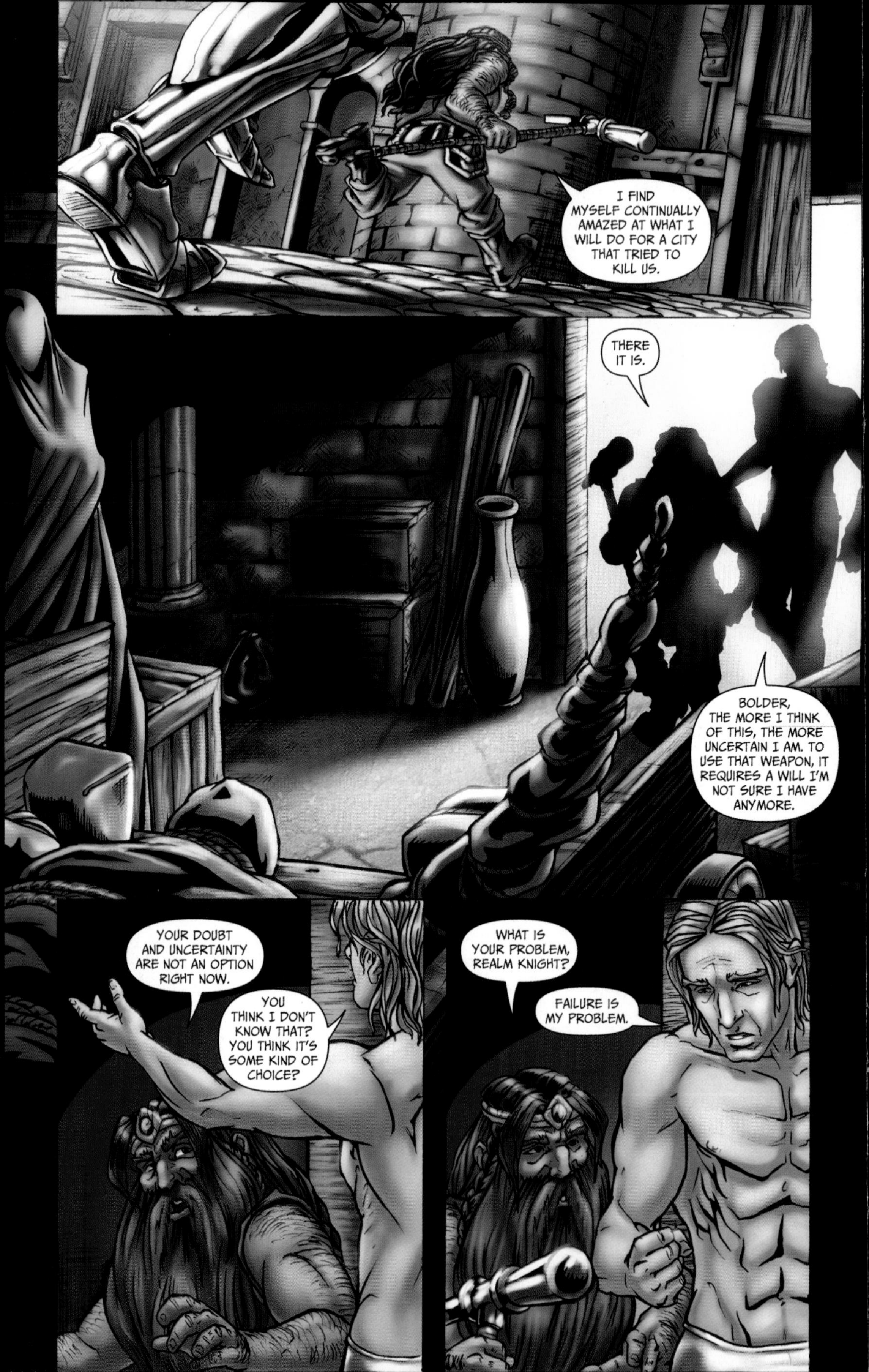
I FIND MYSELF CONTINUALLY AMAZED AT WHAT I WILL DO FOR A CITY THAT TRIED TO KILL US.
THERE IT IS.
BOLDER, THE MORE I THINK OF THIS, THE MORE UNCERTAIN I AM. TO USE THAT WEAPON, IT REQUIRES A WILL I'M NOT SURE I HAVE ANYMORE.
YOUR DOUBT AND UNCERTAINTY ARE NOT AN OPTION RIGHT NOW.
YOU THINK I DON'T KNOW THAT? YOU THINK IT'S SOME KIND OF CHOICE?
WHAT IS YOUR PROBLEM, REALM KNIGHT?
FAILURE IS MY PROBLEM.

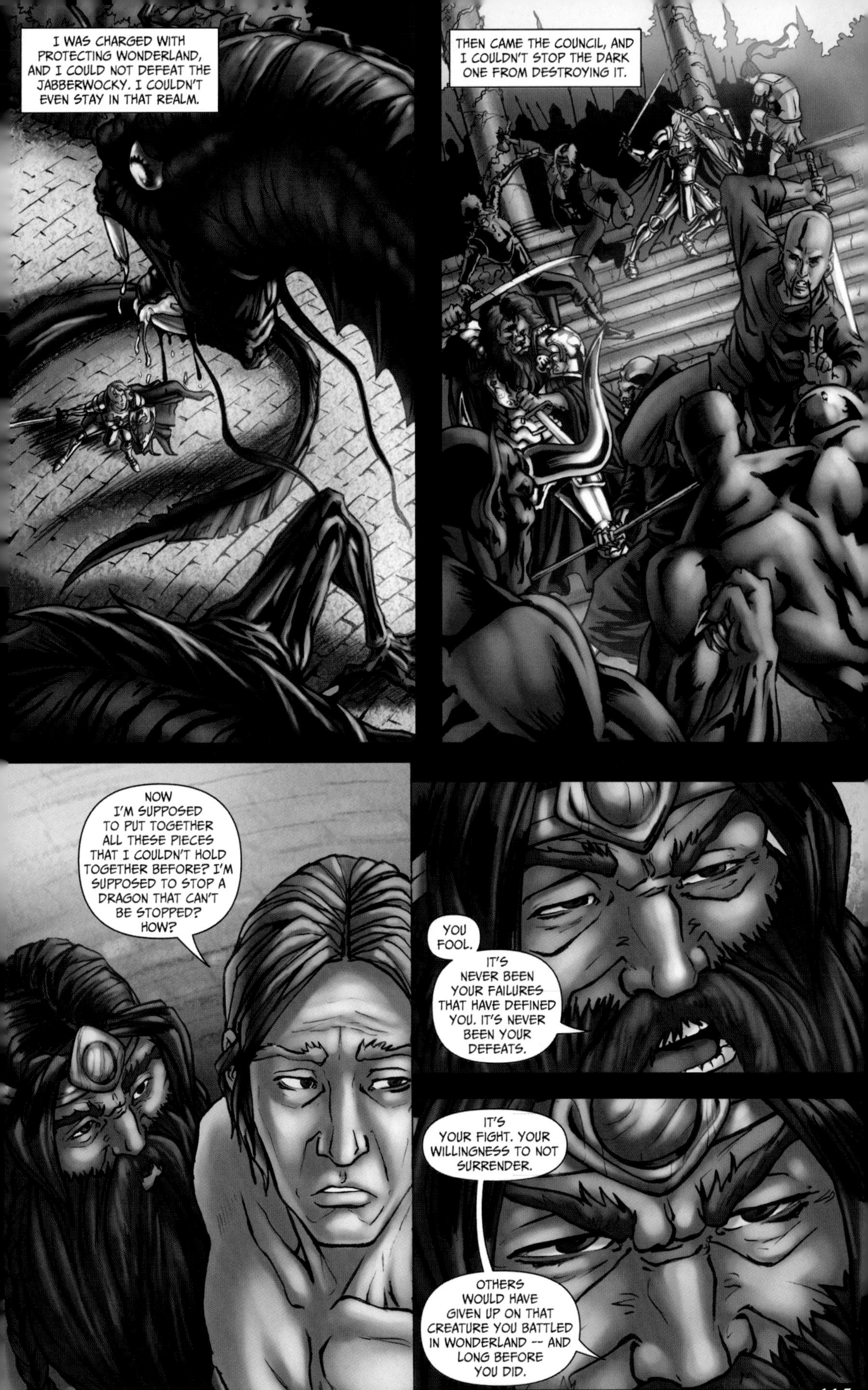

I WAS CHARGED WITH PROTECTING WONDERLAND, AND I COULD NOT DEFEAT THE JABBERWOCKY. I COULDN'T EVEN STAY IN THAT REALM.
THEN CAME THE COUNCIL, AND I COULDN'T STOP THE DARK ONE FROM DESTROYING IT.
NOW I'M SUPPOSED TO PUT TOGETHER ALL THESE PIECES THAT I COULDN'T HOLD TOGETHER BEFORE? I'M SUPPOSED TO STOP A DRAGON THAT CAN'T BE STOPPED? HOW?
YOU FOOL.
IT'S NEVER BEEN YOUR FAILURES THAT HAVE DEFINED YOU. IT'S NEVER BEEN YOUR DEFEATS.
IT'S YOUR FIGHT. YOUR WILLINGNESS TO NOT SURRENDER.
OTHERS WOULD HAVE GIVEN UP ON THAT CREATURE YOU BATTLED IN WONDERLAND -- AND LONG BEFORE YOU DID.

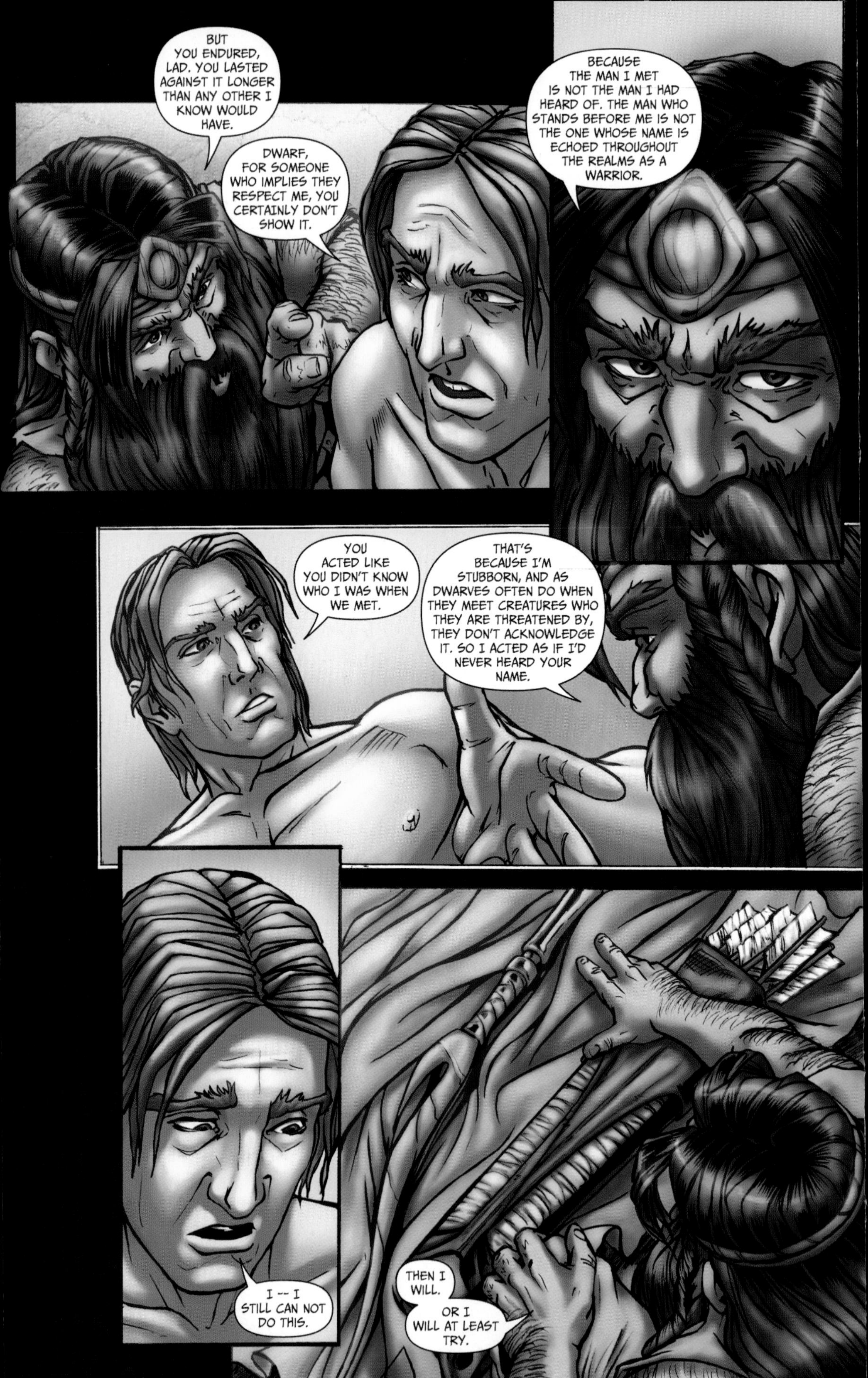
BUT YOU ENDURED, LAD. YOU LASTED AGAINST IT LONGER THAN ANY OTHER I KNOW WOULD HAVE.
DWARF, FOR SOMEONE WHO IMPLIES THEY RESPECT ME, YOU CERTAINLY DON'T SHOW IT.
BECAUSE THE MAN I MET IS NOT THE MAN I HAD HEARD OF. THE MAN WHO STANDS BEFORE ME IS NOT THE ONE WHOSE NAME IS ECHOED THROUGHOUT THE REALMS AS A WARRIOR.
YOU ACTED LIKE YOU DIDN'T KNOW WHO I WAS WHEN WE MET.
THAT'S BECAUSE I'M STUBBORN, AND AS DWARVES OFTEN DO WHEN THEY MEET CREATURES WHO THEY ARE THREATENED BY, THEY DON'T ACKNOWLEDGE IT. SO I ACTED AS IF I'D NEVER HEARD YOUR NAME.
I -- I STILL CAN NOT DO THIS.
THEN I WILL.
OR I WILL AT LEAST TRY.

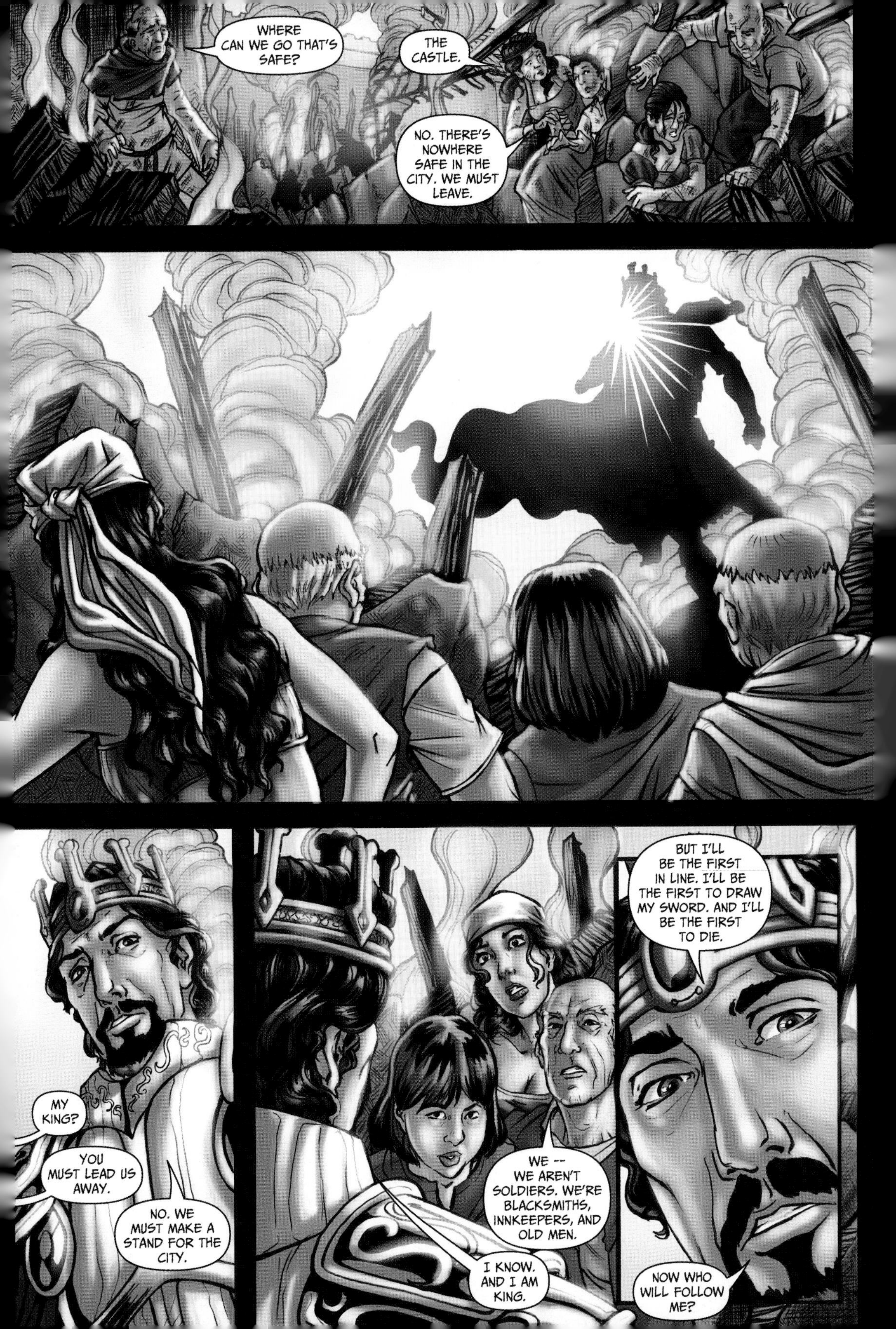
WHERE CAN WE GO THAT'S SAFE?
THE CASTLE.
NO. THERE'S NOWHERE SAFE IN THE CITY. WE MUST LEAVE.
MY KING?
YOU MUST LEAD US AWAY.
NO. WE MUST MAKE A STAND FOR THE CITY.
WE -- WE AREN'T SOLDIERS. WE'RE BLACKSMITHS, INNKEEPERS, AND OLD MEN.
I KNOW. AND I AM KING.
BUT I'LL BE THE FIRST IN LINE. I'LL BE THE FIRST TO DRAW MY SWORD. AND I'LL BE THE FIRST TO DIE.
NOW WHO WILL FOLLOW ME?

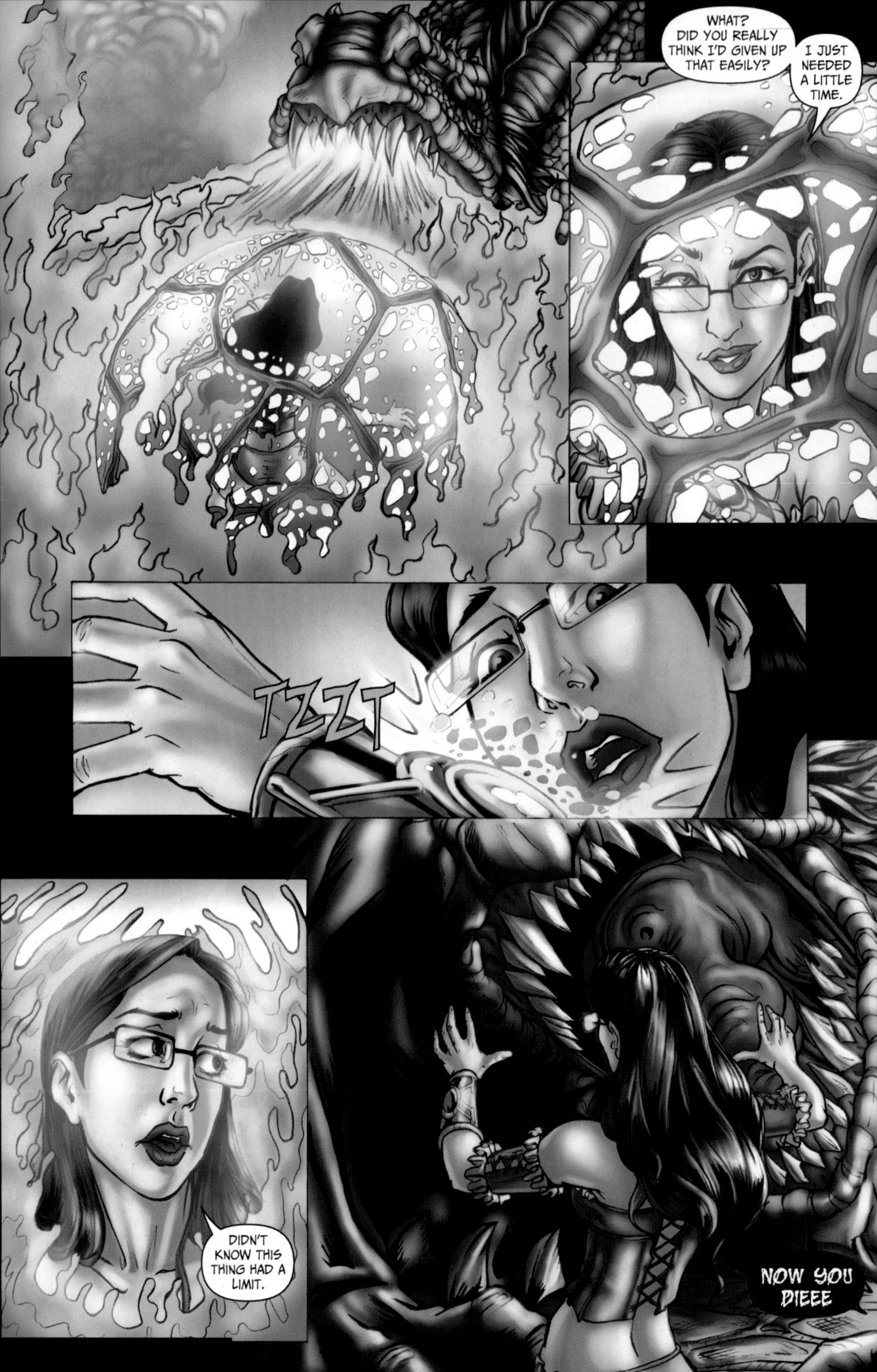
WHAT? DID YOU REALLY THINK I'D GIVEN UP THAT EASILY?
I JUST NEEDED A LITTLE TIME.
TZZT
DIDN'T KNOW THIS THING HAD A LIMIT.
NOW YOU DIEEE

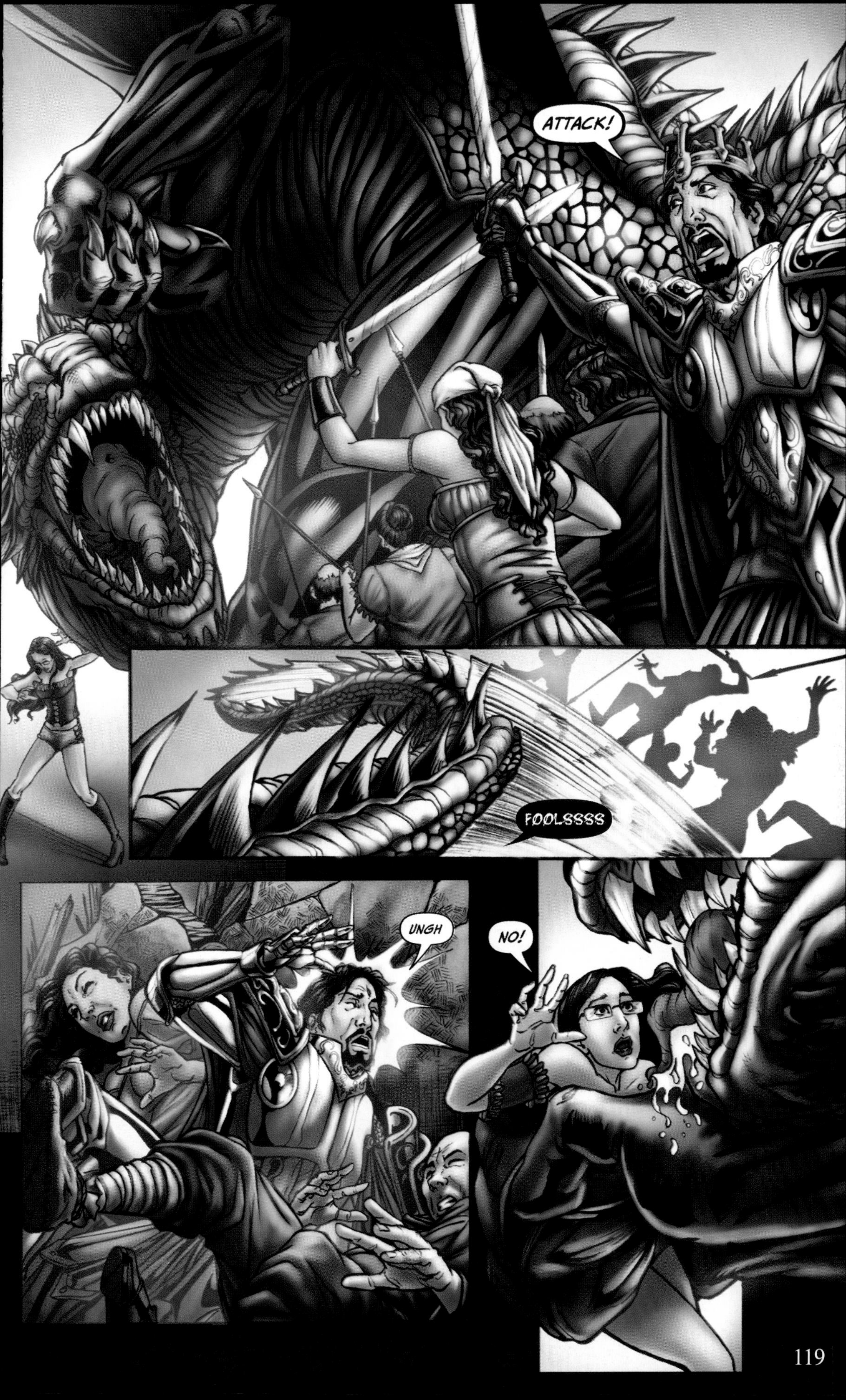

ATTACK!
FOOLSSSS
UNGH
NO!

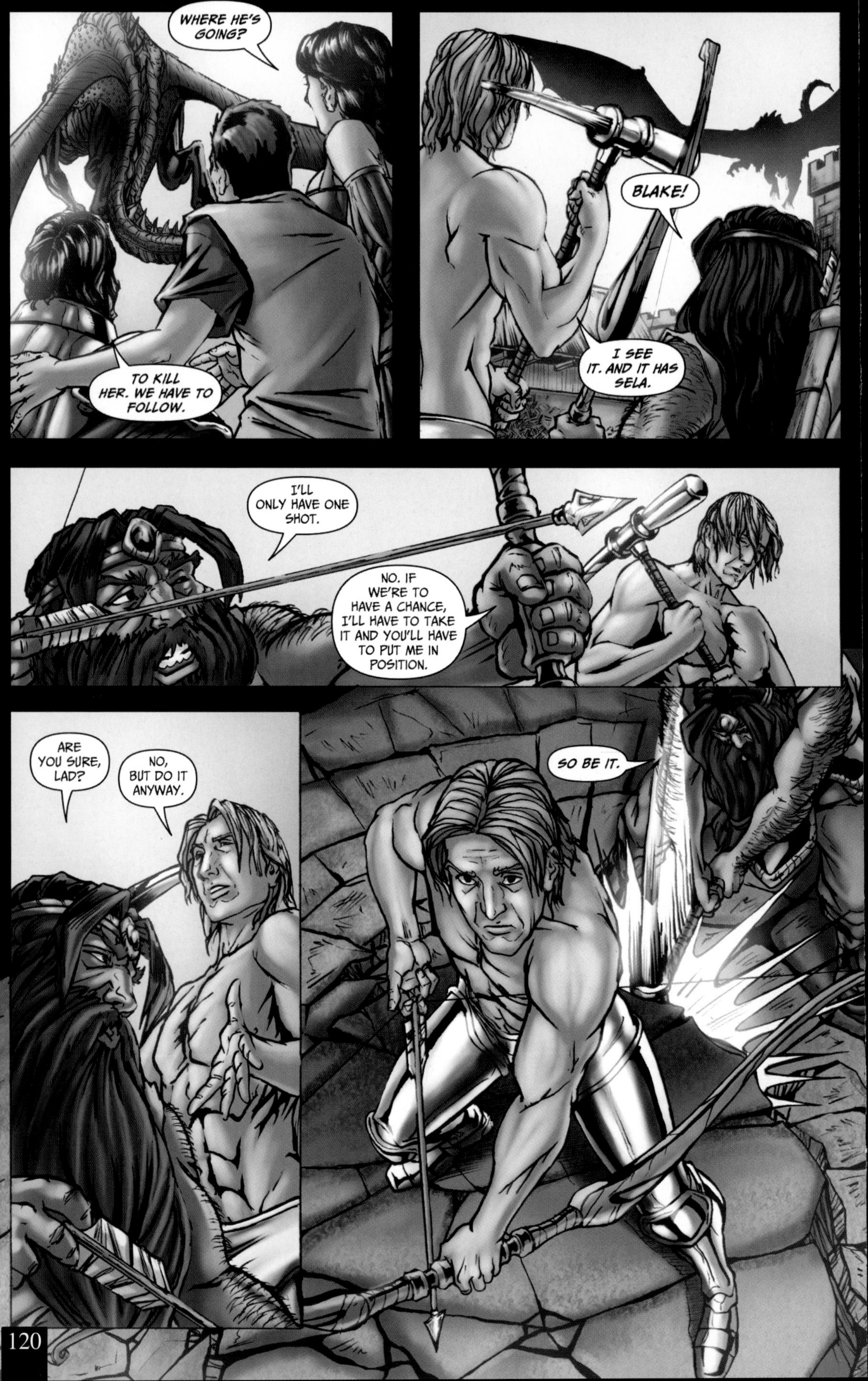
WHERE HE'S GOING?
TO KILL HER. WE HAVE TO FOLLOW.
BLAKE!
I SEE IT. AND IT HAS SELA.
I'LL ONLY HAVE ONE SHOT.
NO. IF WE'RE TO HAVE A CHANCE, I'LL HAVE TO TAKE IT AND YOU'LL HAVE TO PUT ME IN POSITION.
ARE YOU SURE, LAD?
NO, BUT DO IT ANYWAY.
SO BE IT.

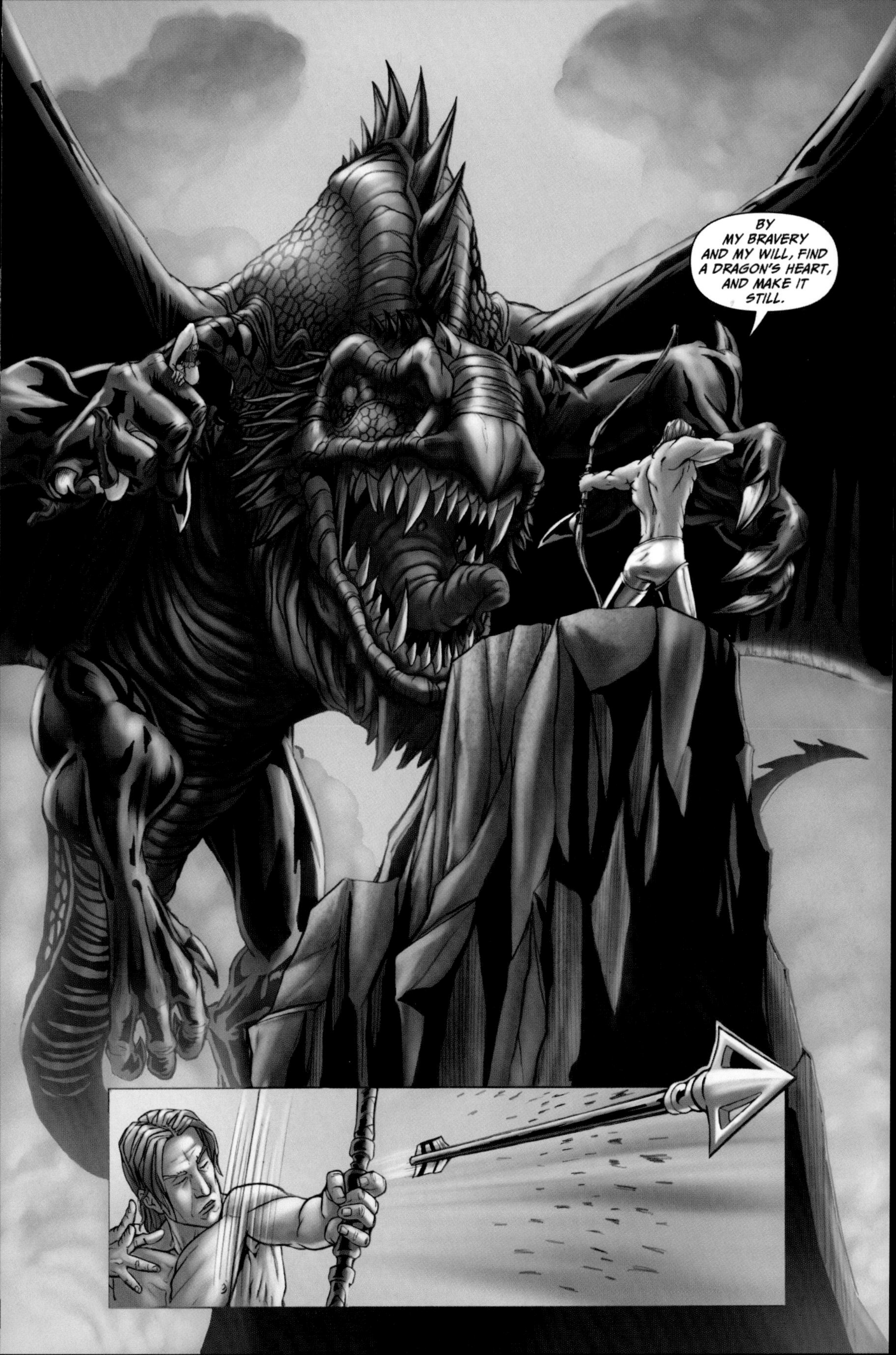
BY MY BRAVERY AND MY WILL, FIND A DRAGON'S HEART, AND MAKE IT STILL.

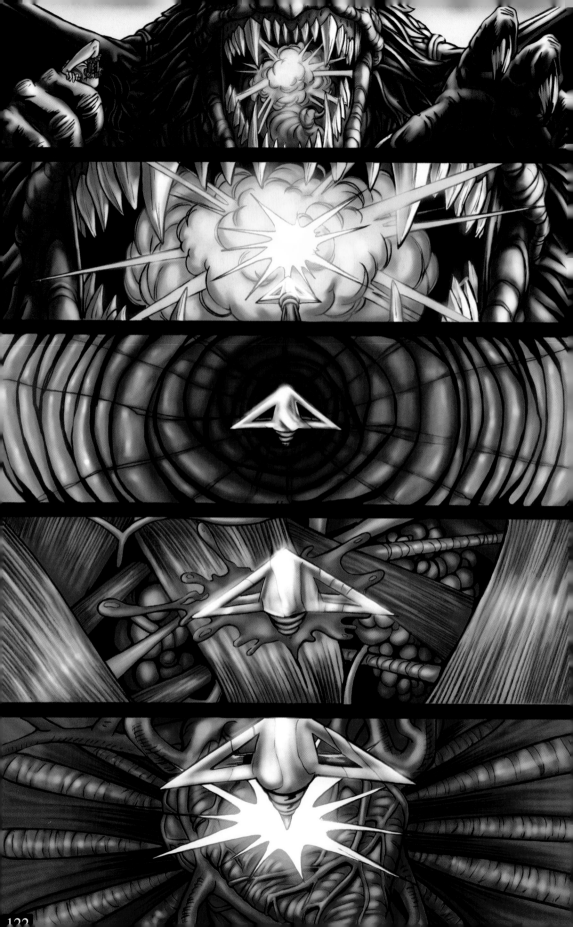

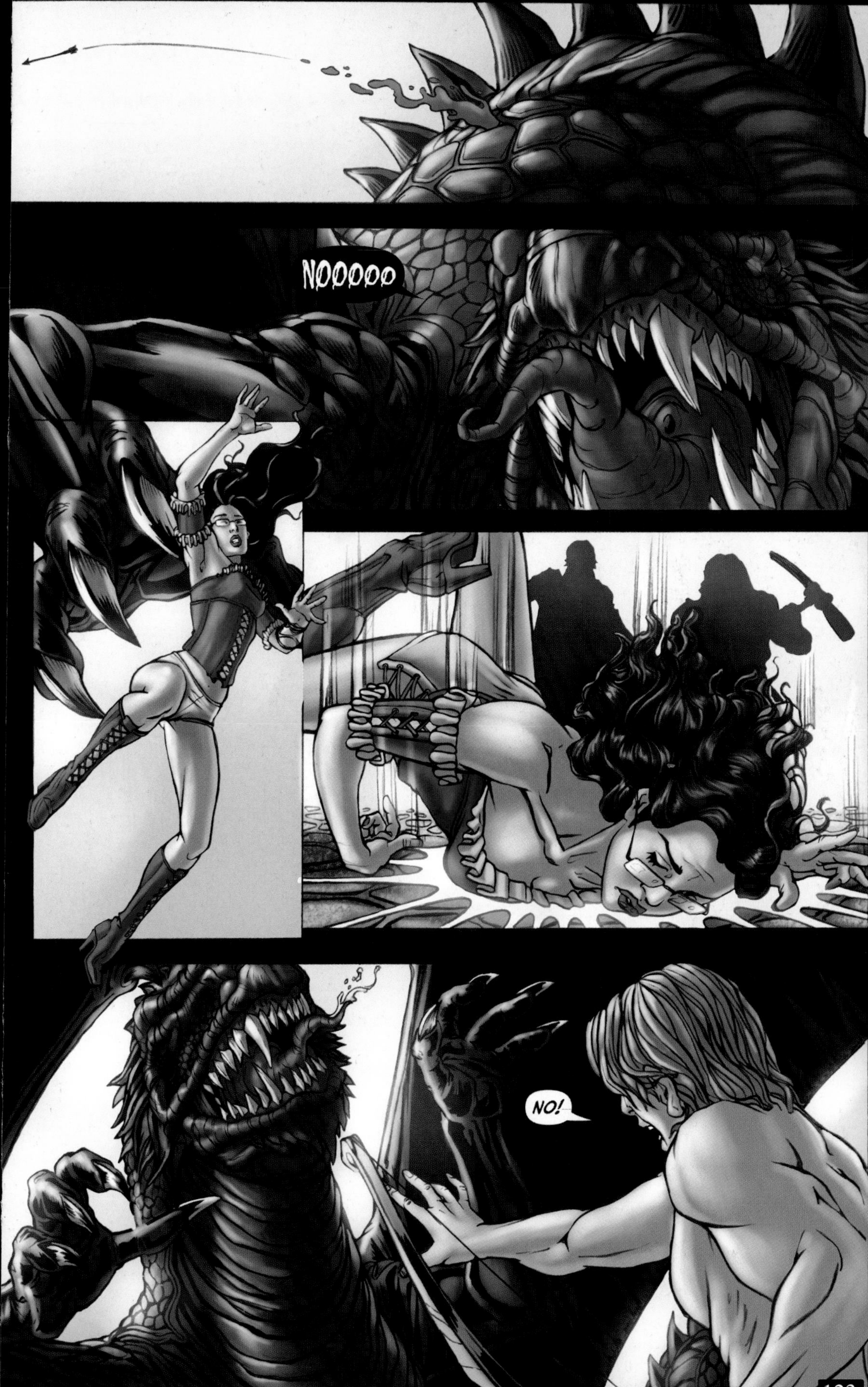
NOOOOO
NO!

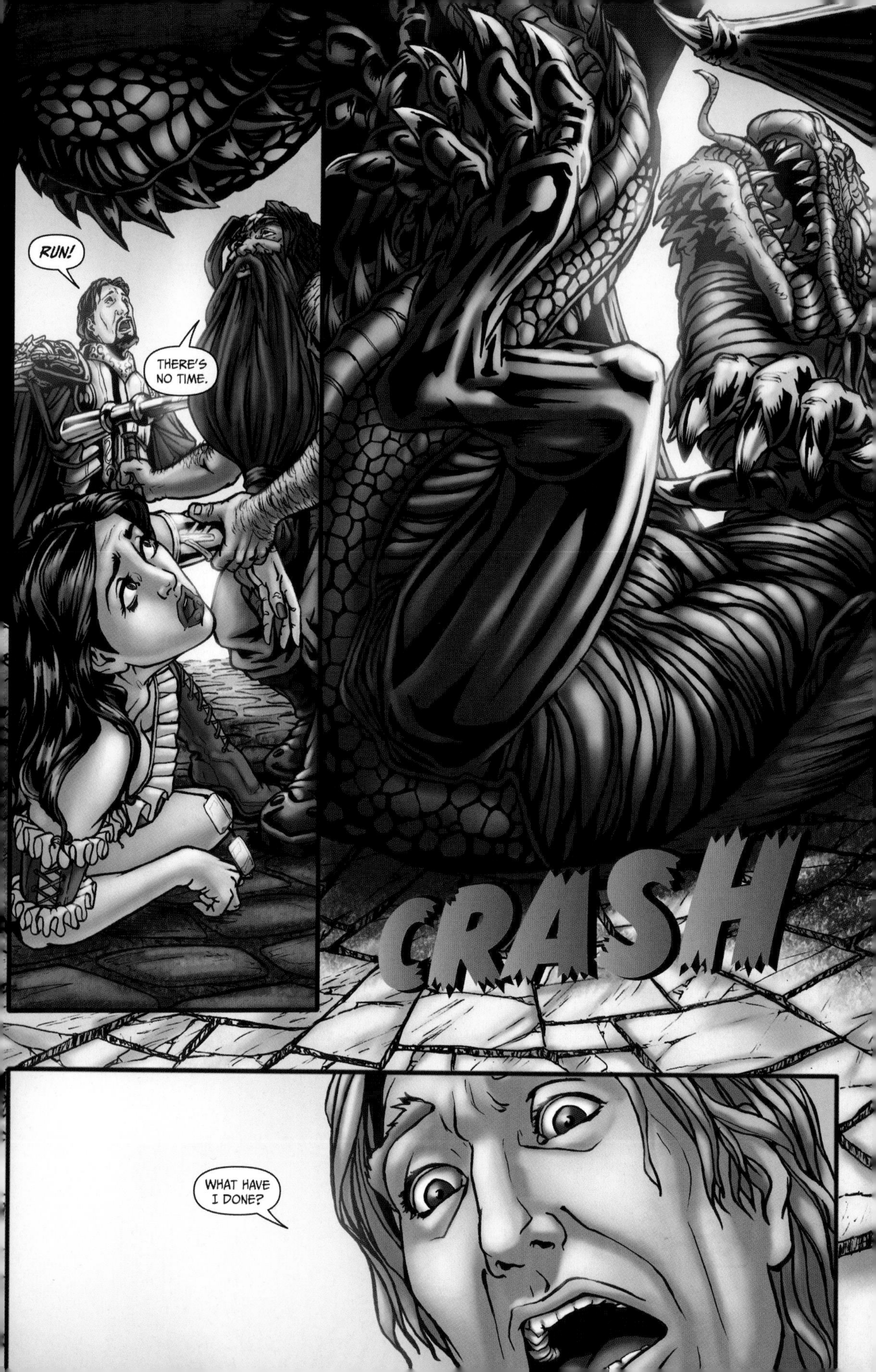
RUN!
THERE'S NO TIME.
CRASH
WHAT HAVE I DONE?

Grimm Fairy Tales
Volume 10

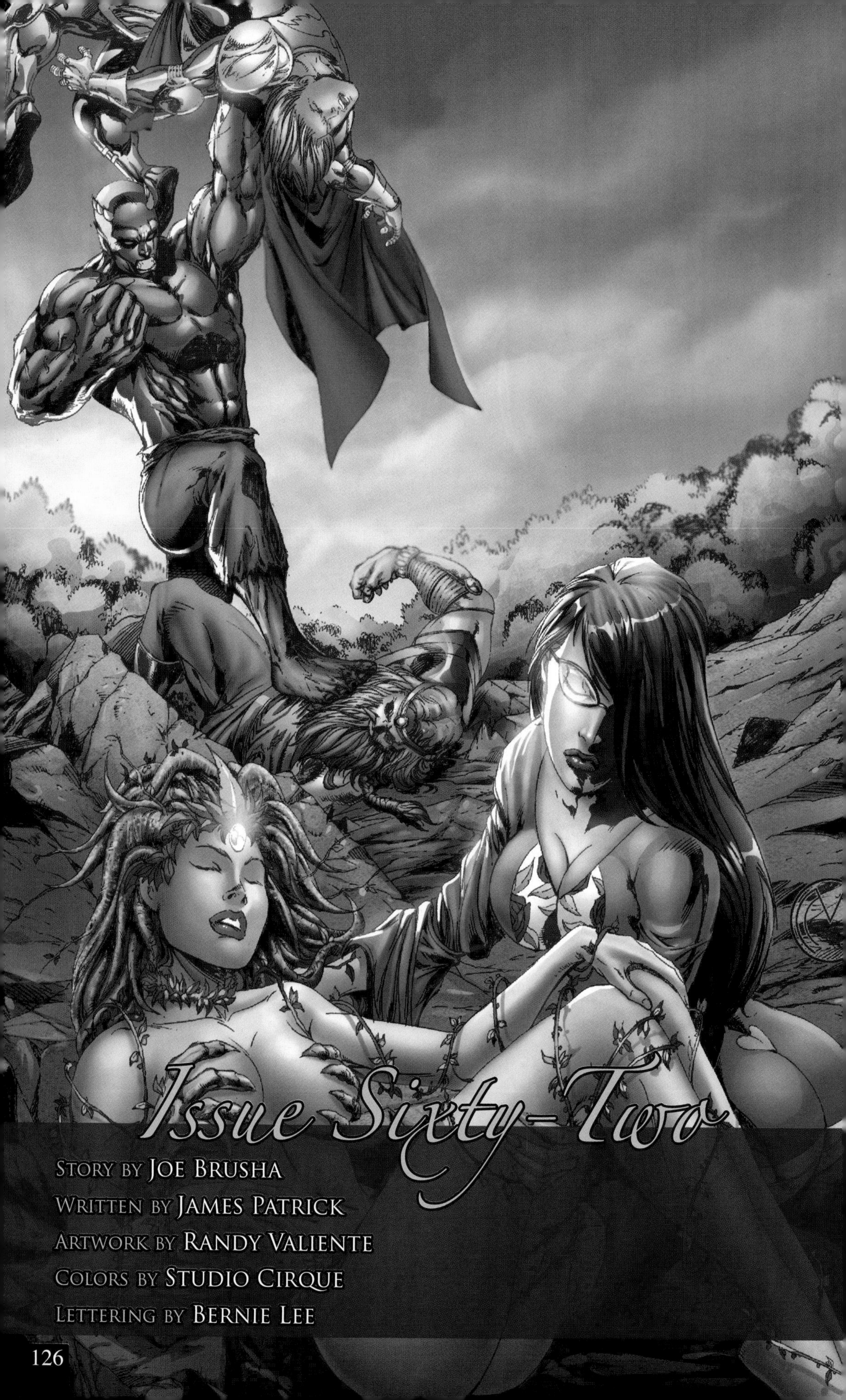

Issue Sixty-Two

Story by Joe Brusha
Written by James Patrick
Artwork by Randy Valiente
Colors by Studio Cirque
Lettering by Bernie Lee

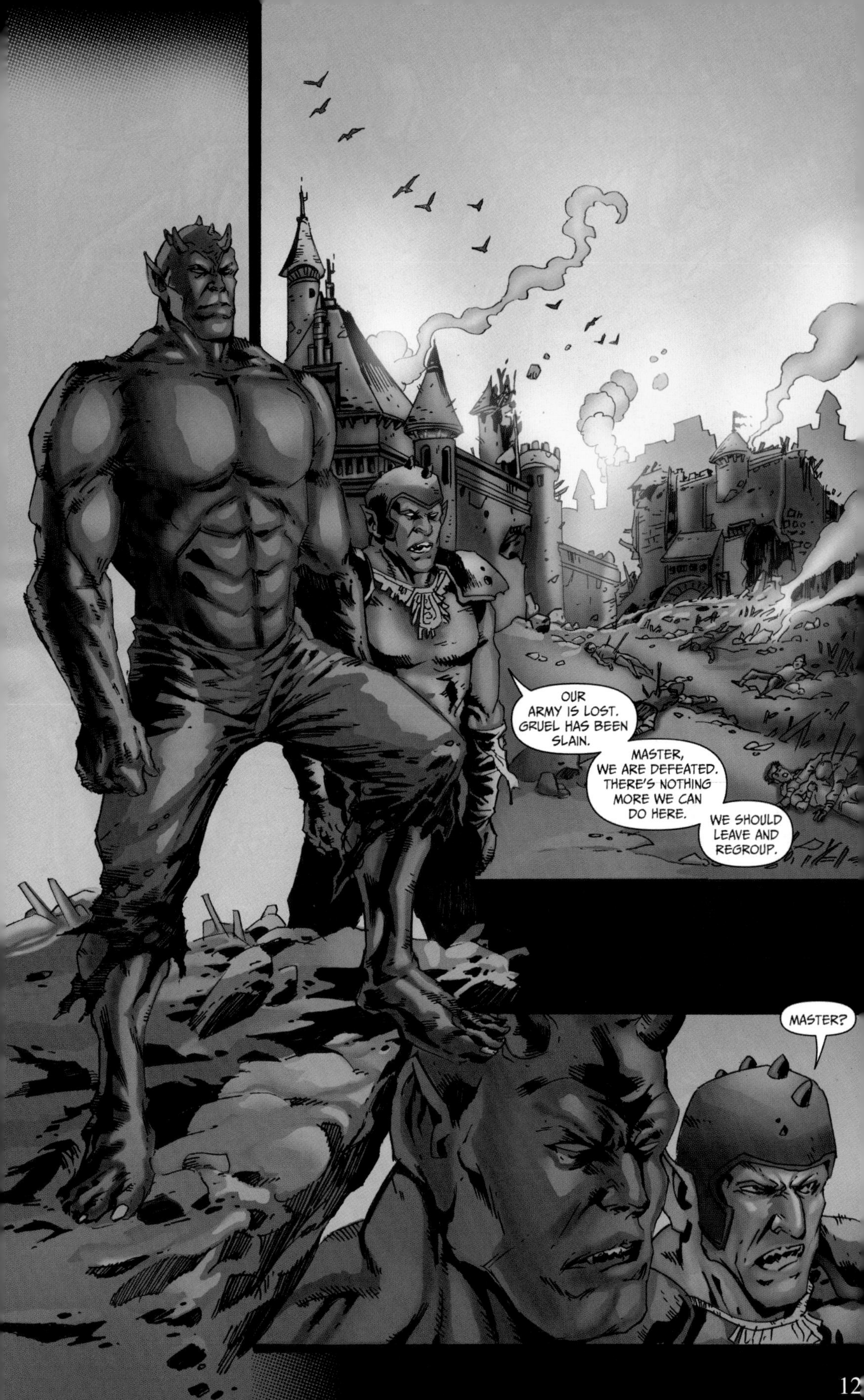
OUR ARMY IS LOST. GRUEL HAS BEEN SLAIN.
MASTER, WE ARE DEFEATED. THERE'S NOTHING MORE WE CAN DO HERE.
WE SHOULD LEAVE AND REGROUP.
MASTER?

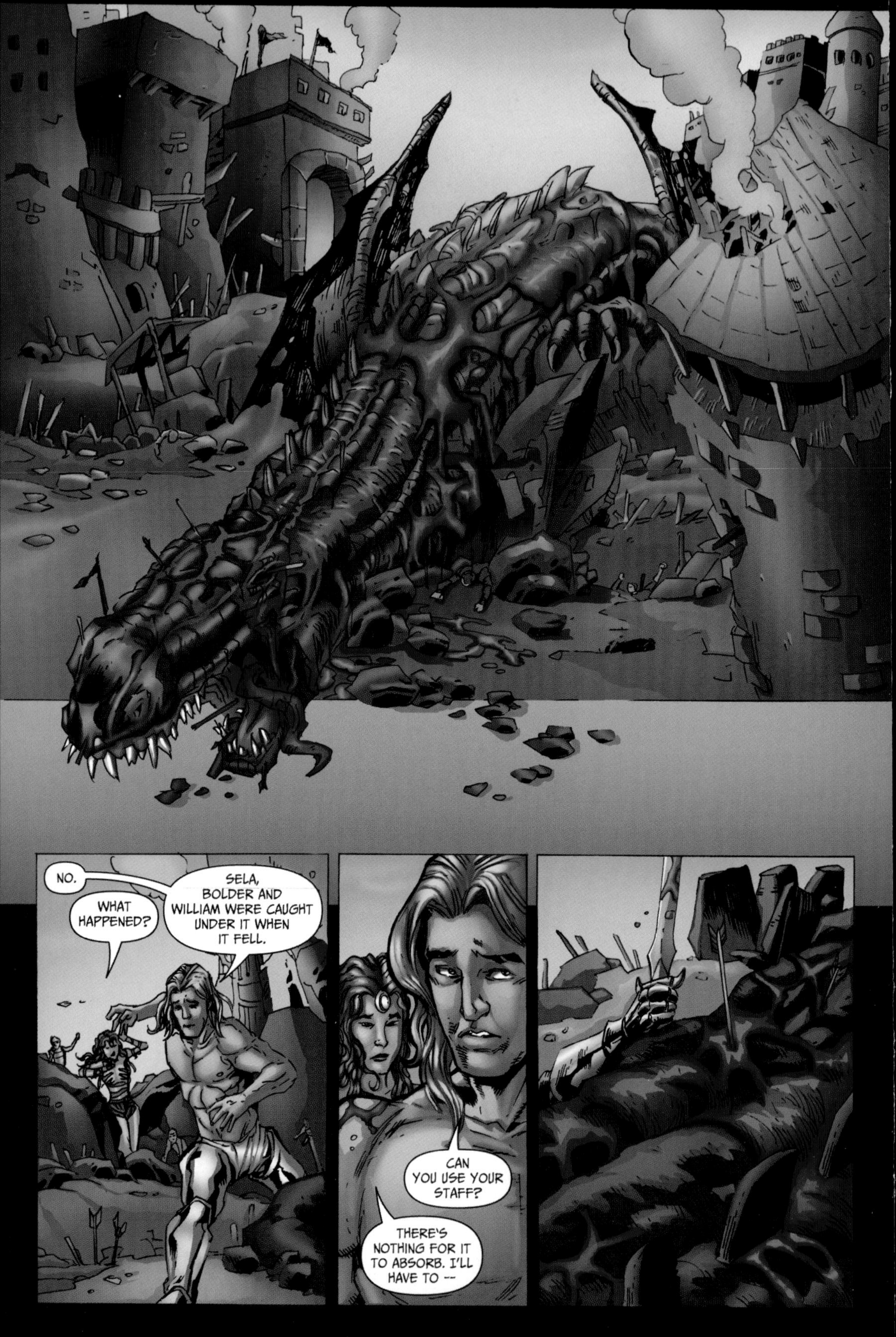
NO.
WHAT HAPPENED?
SELA, BOLDER AND WILLIAM WERE CAUGHT UNDER IT WHEN IT FELL.
CAN YOU USE YOUR STAFF?
THERE'S NOTHING FOR IT TO ABSORB. I'LL HAVE TO --

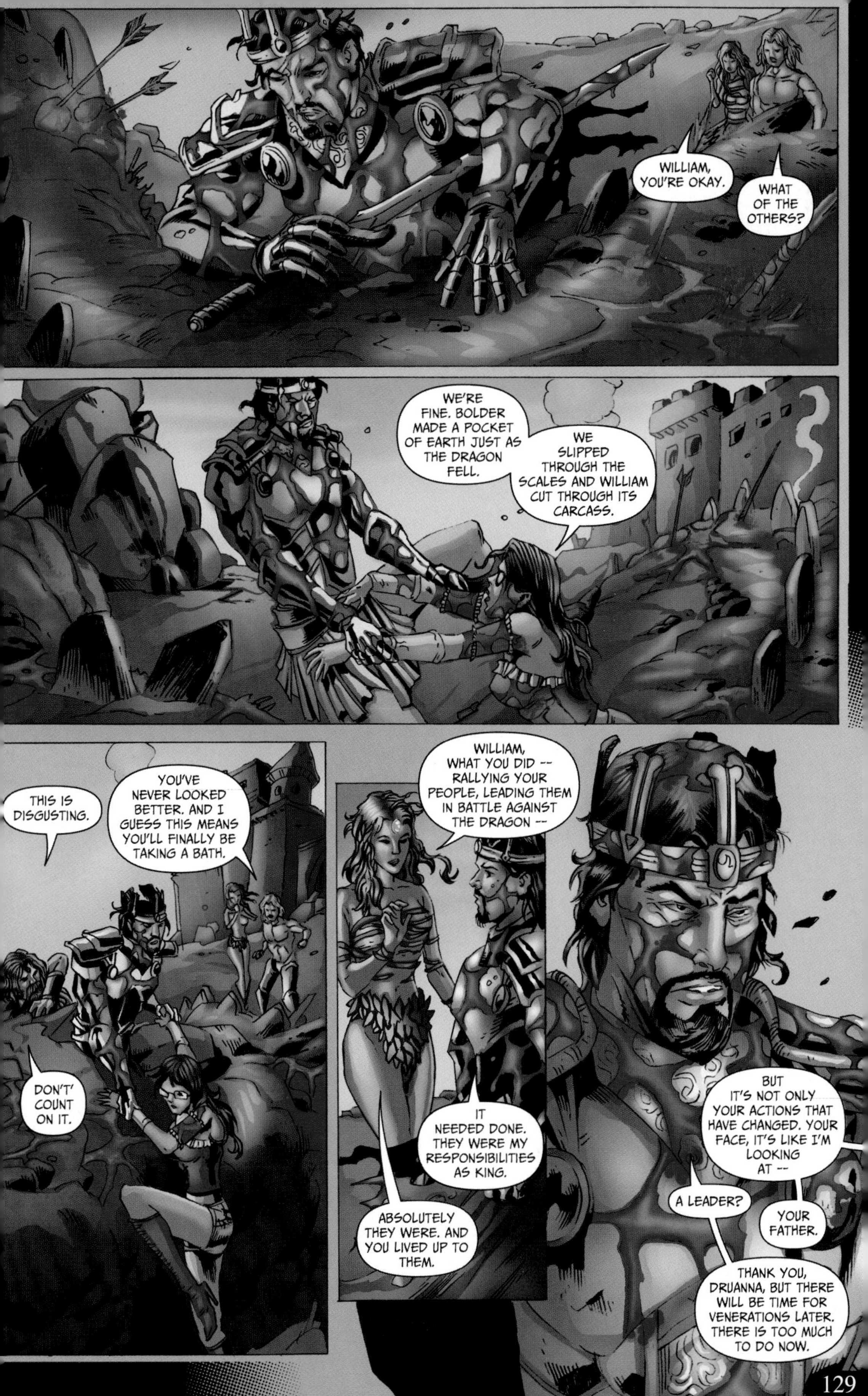
WILLIAM, YOU'RE OKAY.
WHAT OF THE OTHERS?
WE'RE FINE. BOLDER MADE A POCKET OF EARTH JUST AS THE DRAGON FELL.
WE SLIPPED THROUGH THE SCALES AND WILLIAM CUT THROUGH ITS CARCASS.
THIS IS DISGUSTING.
YOU'VE NEVER LOOKED BETTER. AND I GUESS THIS MEANS YOU'LL FINALLY BE TAKING A BATH.
DON'T' COUNT ON IT.
WILLIAM, WHAT YOU DID -- RALLYING YOUR PEOPLE, LEADING THEM IN BATTLE AGAINST THE DRAGON --
IT NEEDED DONE. THEY WERE MY RESPONSIBILITIES AS KING.
ABSOLUTELY THEY WERE. AND YOU LIVED UP TO THEM.
BUT IT'S NOT ONLY YOUR ACTIONS THAT HAVE CHANGED. YOUR FACE, IT'S LIKE I'M LOOKING AT --
A LEADER?
YOUR FATHER.
THANK YOU, DRUANNA, BUT THERE WILL BE TIME FOR VENERATIONS LATER. THERE IS TOO MUCH TO DO NOW.

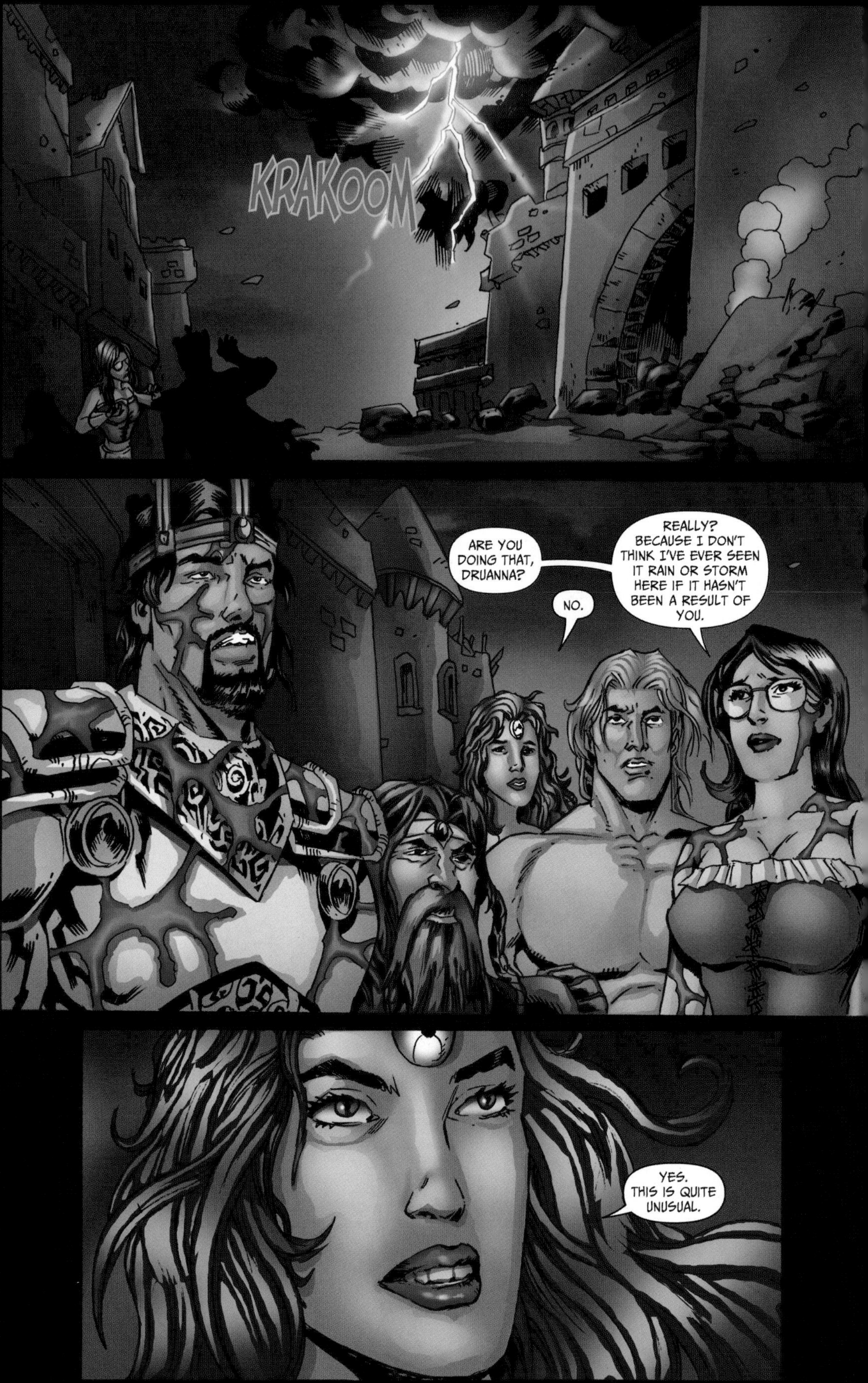
KRAKOOM
ARE YOU DOING THAT, DRUANNA?
NO.
REALLY? BECAUSE I DON'T THINK I'VE EVER SEEN IT RAIN OR STORM HERE IF IT HASN'T BEEN A RESULT OF YOU.
YES. THIS IS QUITE UNUSUAL.

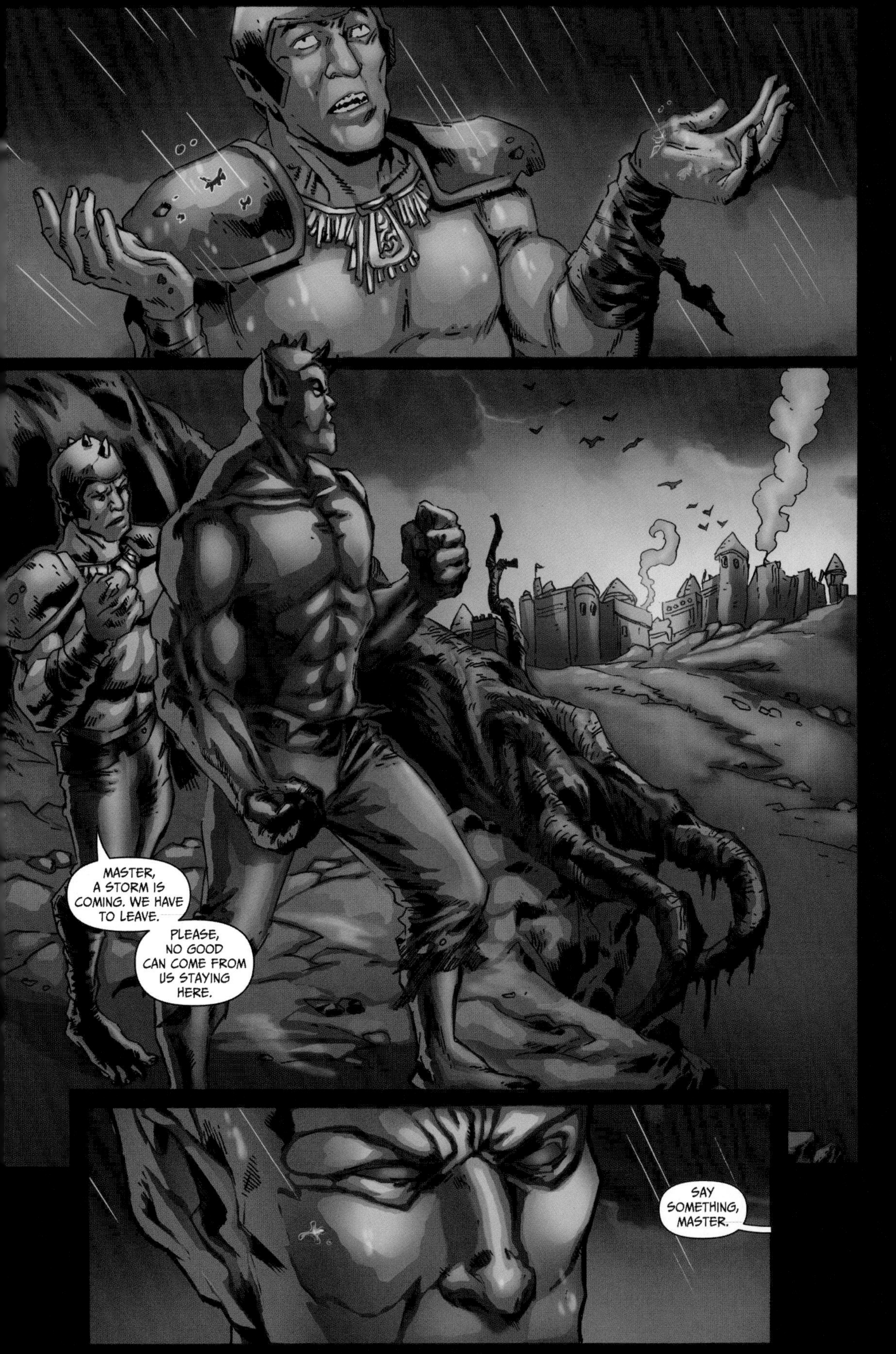
MASTER, A STORM IS COMING. WE HAVE TO LEAVE.
PLEASE, NO GOOD CAN COME FROM US STAYING HERE.
SAY SOMETHING, MASTER.

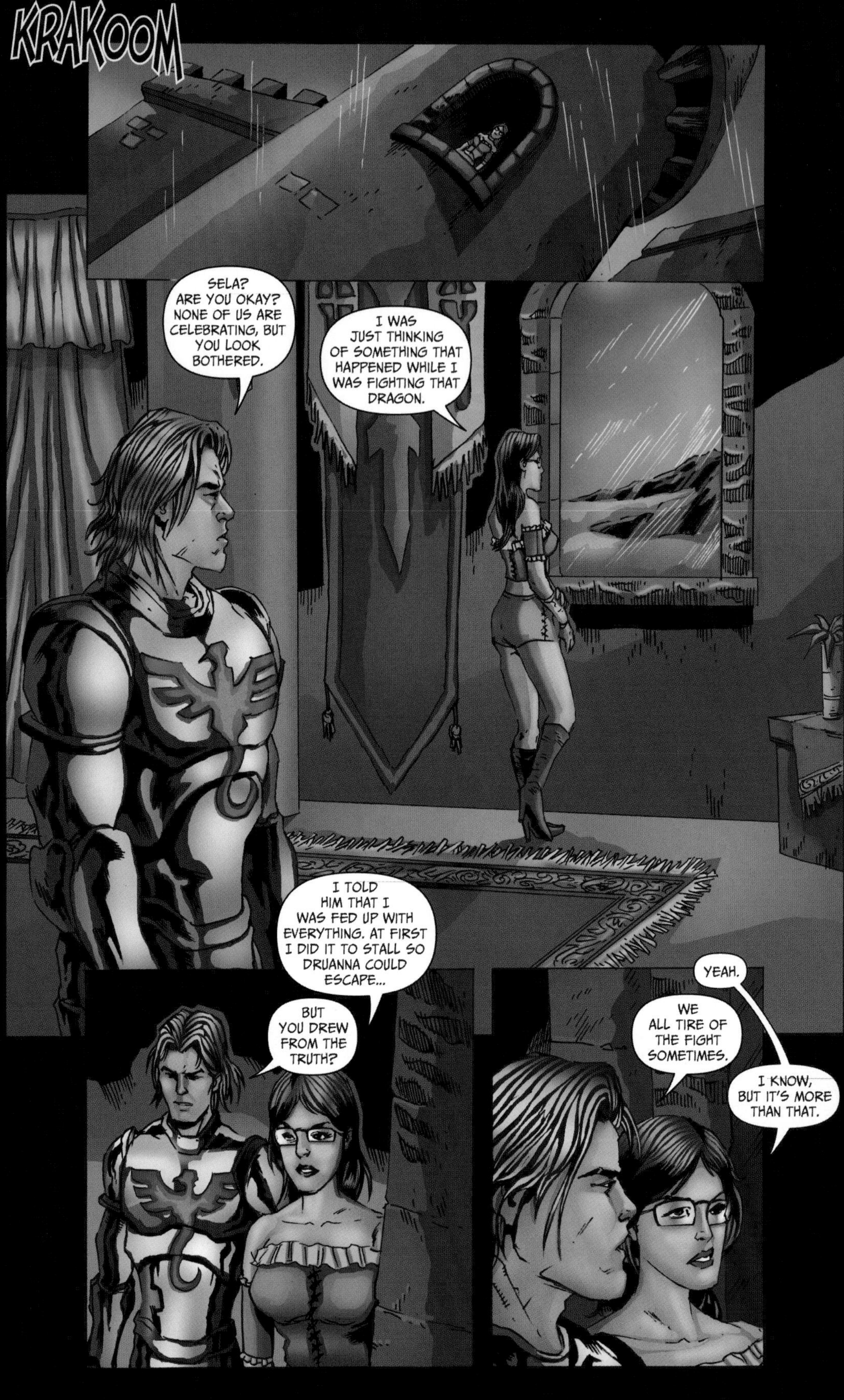
KRAKOOM
SELA? ARE YOU OKAY? NONE OF US ARE CELEBRATING, BUT YOU LOOK BOTHERED.
I WAS JUST THINKING OF SOMETHING THAT HAPPENED WHILE I WAS FIGHTING THAT DRAGON.
I TOLD HIM THAT I WAS FED UP WITH EVERYTHING. AT FIRST I DID IT TO STALL SO DRUANNA COULD ESCAPE...
BUT YOU DREW FROM THE TRUTH?
YEAH.
WE ALL TIRE OF THE FIGHT SOMETIMES.
I KNOW, BUT IT'S MORE THAN THAT.

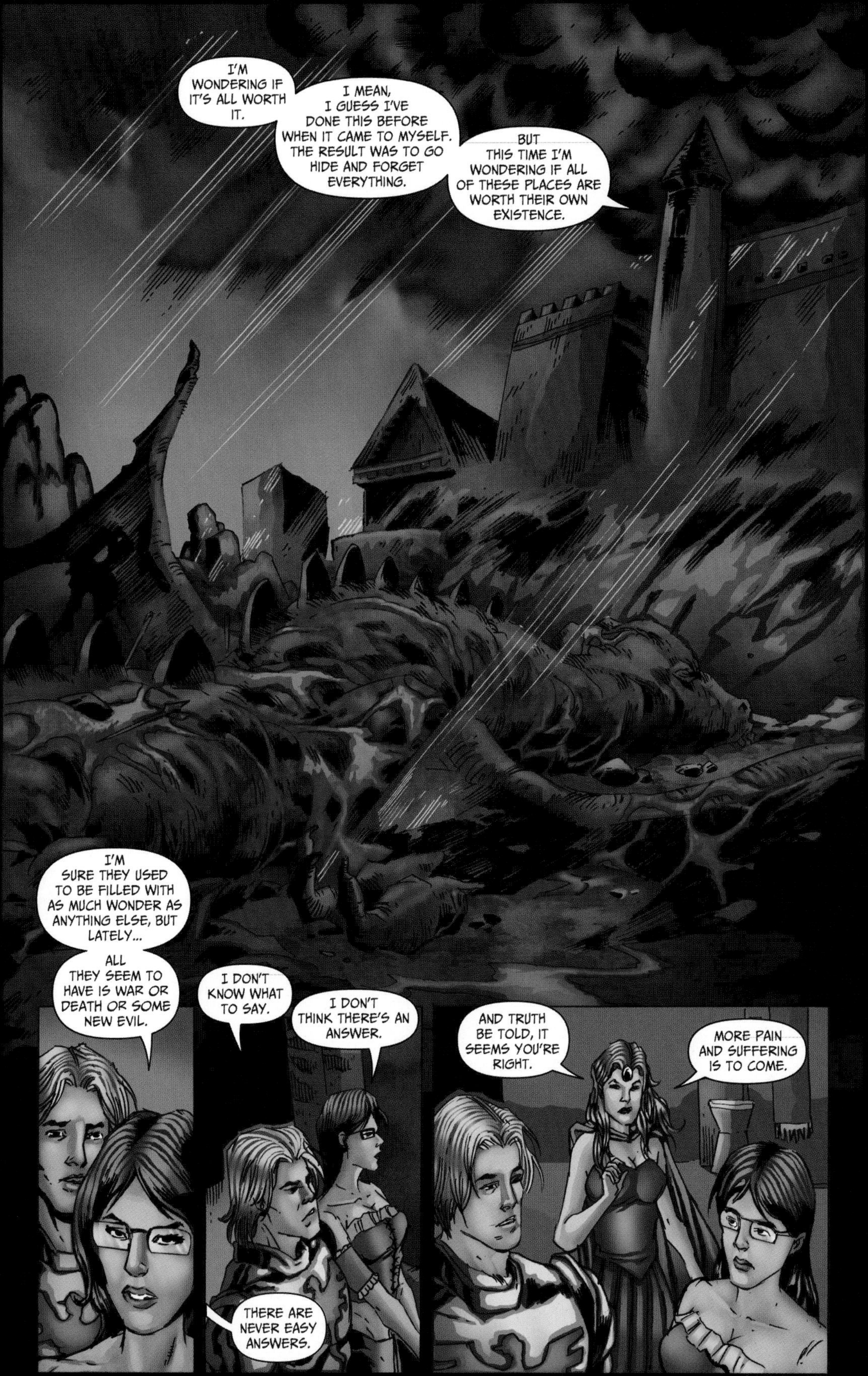
I'M WONDERING IF IT'S ALL WORTH IT.
I MEAN, I GUESS I'VE DONE THIS BEFORE WHEN IT CAME TO MYSELF. THE RESULT WAS TO GO HIDE AND FORGET EVERYTHING.
BUT THIS TIME I'M WONDERING IF ALL OF THESE PLACES ARE WORTH THEIR OWN EXISTENCE.
I'M SURE THEY USED TO BE FILLED WITH AS MUCH WONDER AS ANYTHING ELSE, BUT LATELY...
ALL THEY SEEM TO HAVE IS WAR OR DEATH OR SOME NEW EVIL.
I DON'T KNOW WHAT TO SAY.
I DON'T THINK THERE'S AN ANSWER.
THERE ARE NEVER EASY ANSWERS.
AND TRUTH BE TOLD, IT SEEMS YOU'RE RIGHT.
MORE PAIN AND SUFFERING IS TO COME.

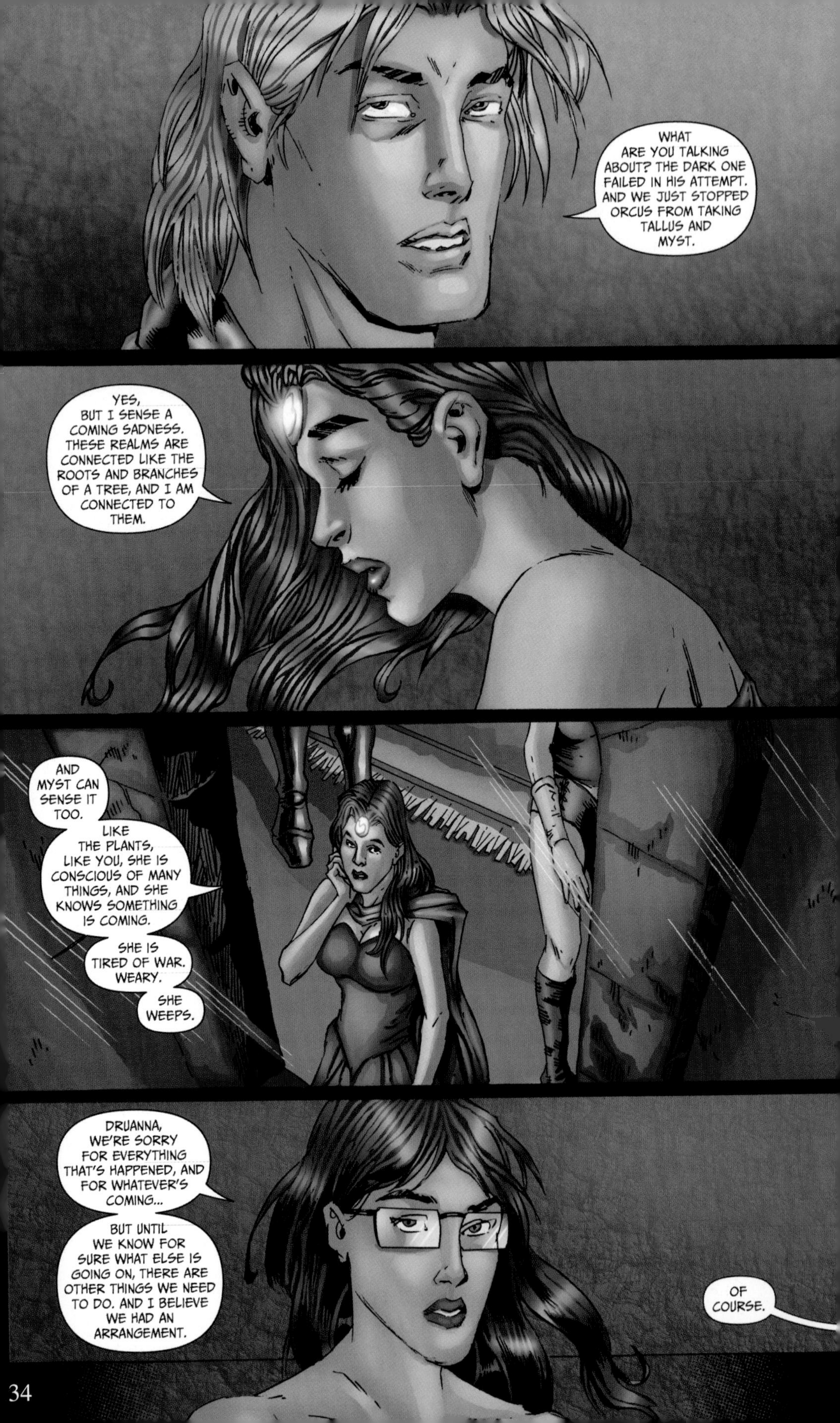
WHAT ARE YOU TALKING ABOUT? THE DARK ONE FAILED IN HIS ATTEMPT. AND WE JUST STOPPED ORCUS FROM TAKING TALLUS AND MYST.
YES, BUT I SENSE A COMING SADNESS. THESE REALMS ARE CONNECTED LIKE THE ROOTS AND BRANCHES OF A TREE, AND I AM CONNECTED TO THEM.
AND MYST CAN SENSE IT TOO.
LIKE THE PLANTS, LIKE YOU, SHE IS CONSCIOUS OF MANY THINGS, AND SHE KNOWS SOMETHING IS COMING.
SHE IS TIRED OF WAR. WEARY.
SHE WEEPS.
DRUANNA, WE'RE SORRY FOR EVERYTHING THAT'S HAPPENED, AND FOR WHATEVER'S COMING...
BUT UNTIL WE KNOW FOR SURE WHAT ELSE IS GOING ON, THERE ARE OTHER THINGS WE NEED TO DO. AND I BELIEVE WE HAD AN ARRANGEMENT.
OF COURSE.

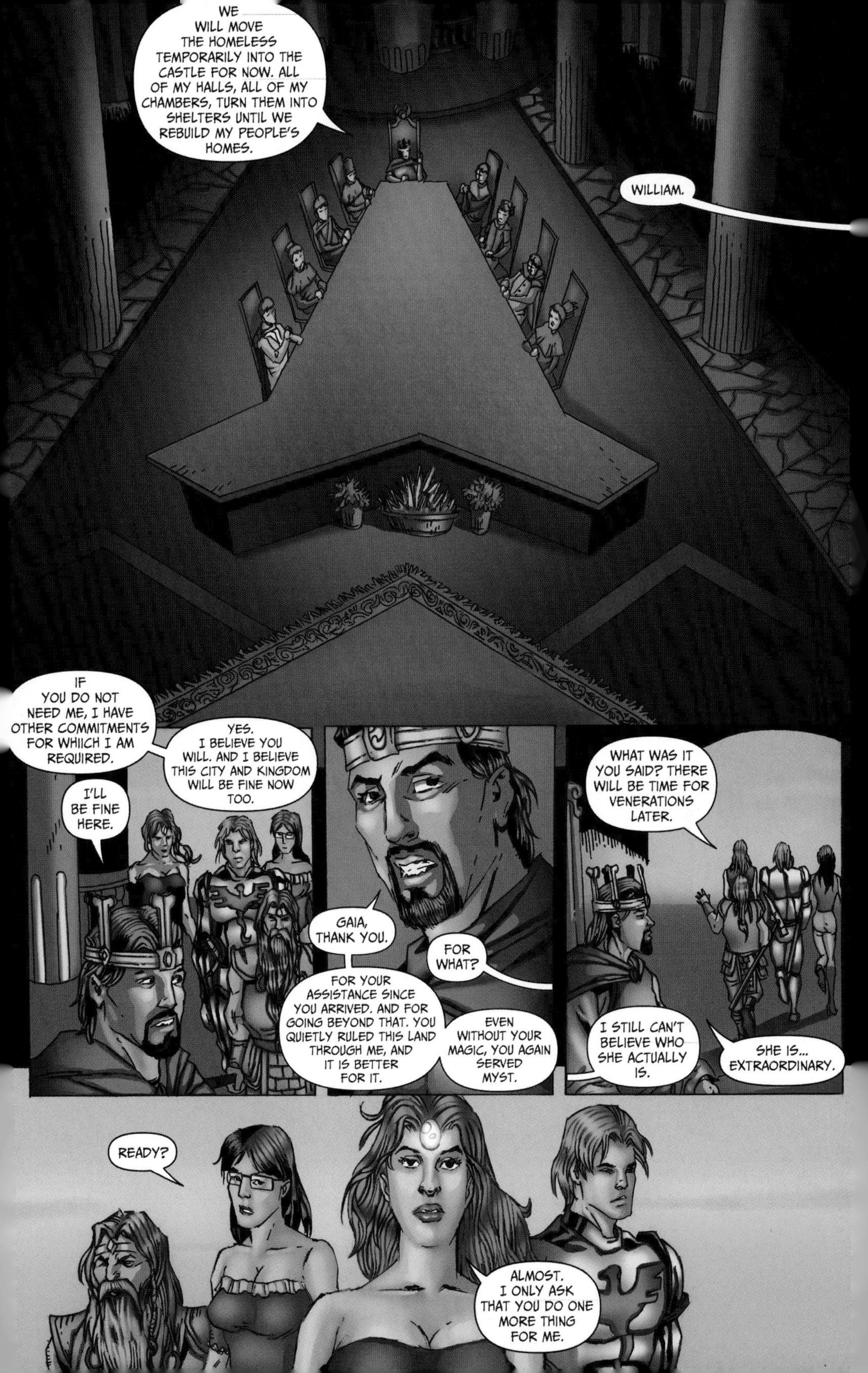
WE WILL MOVE THE HOMELESS TEMPORARILY INTO THE CASTLE FOR NOW. ALL OF MY HALLS, ALL OF MY CHAMBERS, TURN THEM INTO SHELTERS UNTIL WE REBUILD MY PEOPLE'S HOMES.
WILLIAM.
IF YOU DO NOT NEED ME, I HAVE OTHER COMMITMENTS FOR WHIICH I AM REQUIRED.
I'LL BE FINE HERE.
YES. I BELIEVE YOU WILL. AND I BELIEVE THIS CITY AND KINGDOM WILL BE FINE NOW TOO.
GAIA, THANK YOU.
FOR WHAT?
FOR YOUR ASSISTANCE SINCE YOU ARRIVED. AND FOR GOING BEYOND THAT. YOU QUIETLY RULED THIS LAND THROUGH ME, AND IT IS BETTER FOR IT.
EVEN WITHOUT YOUR MAGIC, YOU AGAIN SERVED MYST.
WHAT WAS IT YOU SAID? THERE WILL BE TIME FOR VENERATIONS LATER.
I STILL CAN'T BELIEVE WHO SHE ACTUALLY IS.
SHE IS... EXTRAORDINARY.
READY?
ALMOST. I ONLY ASK THAT YOU DO ONE MORE THING FOR ME.

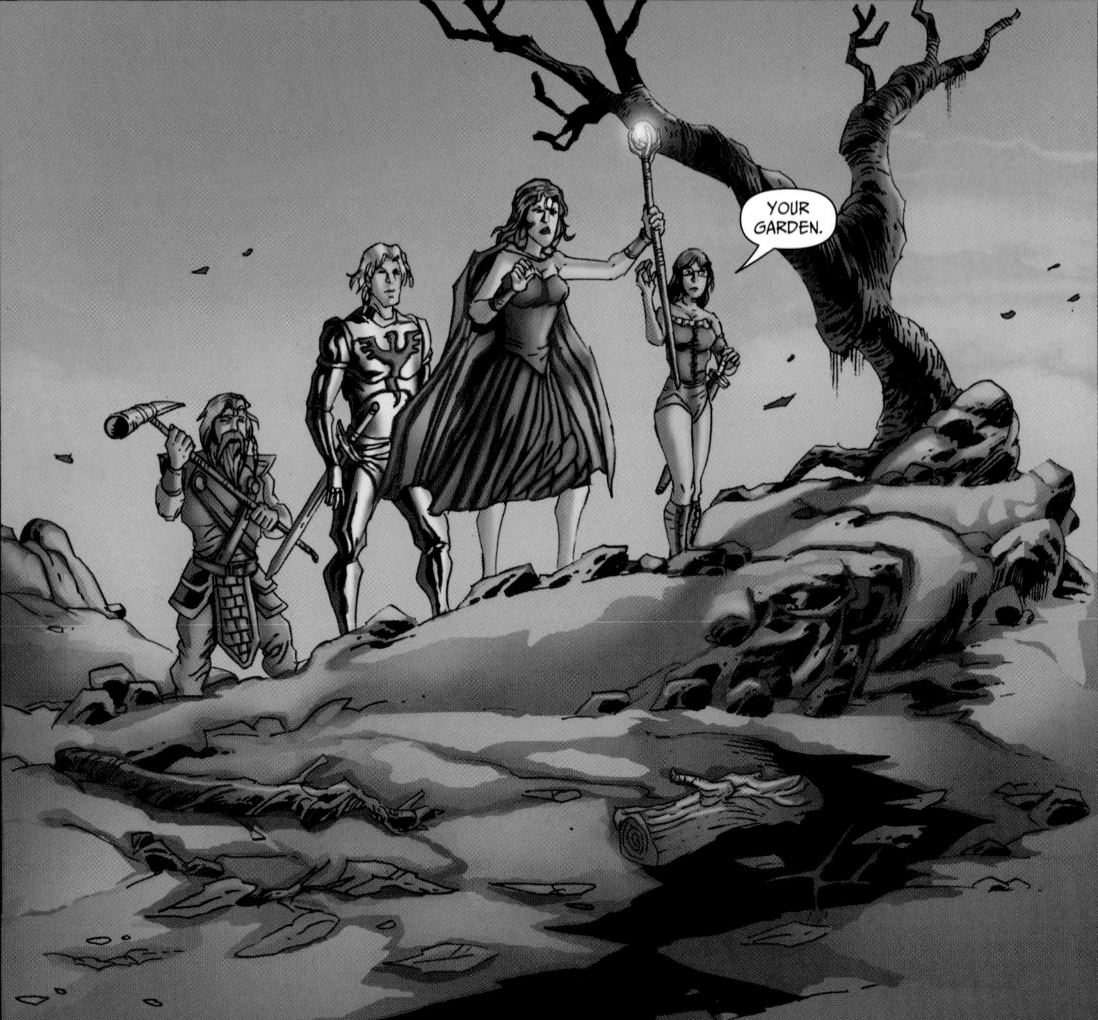
YOUR GARDEN.

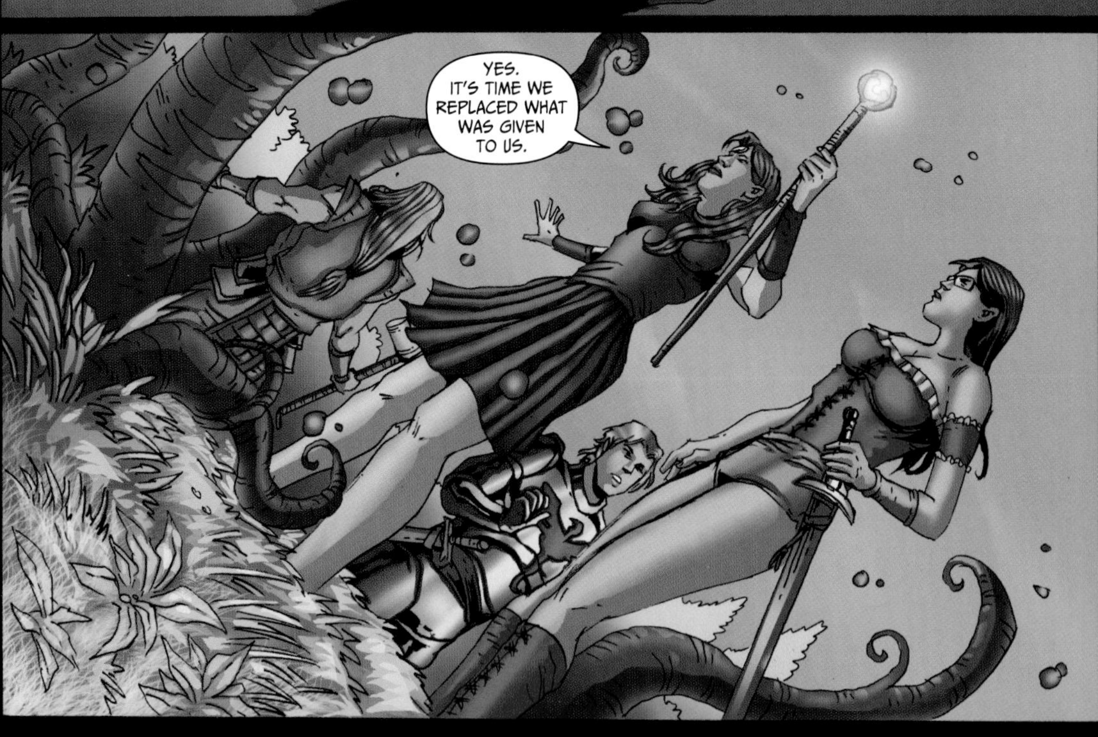
YES. IT'S TIME WE REPLACED WHAT WAS GIVEN TO US.

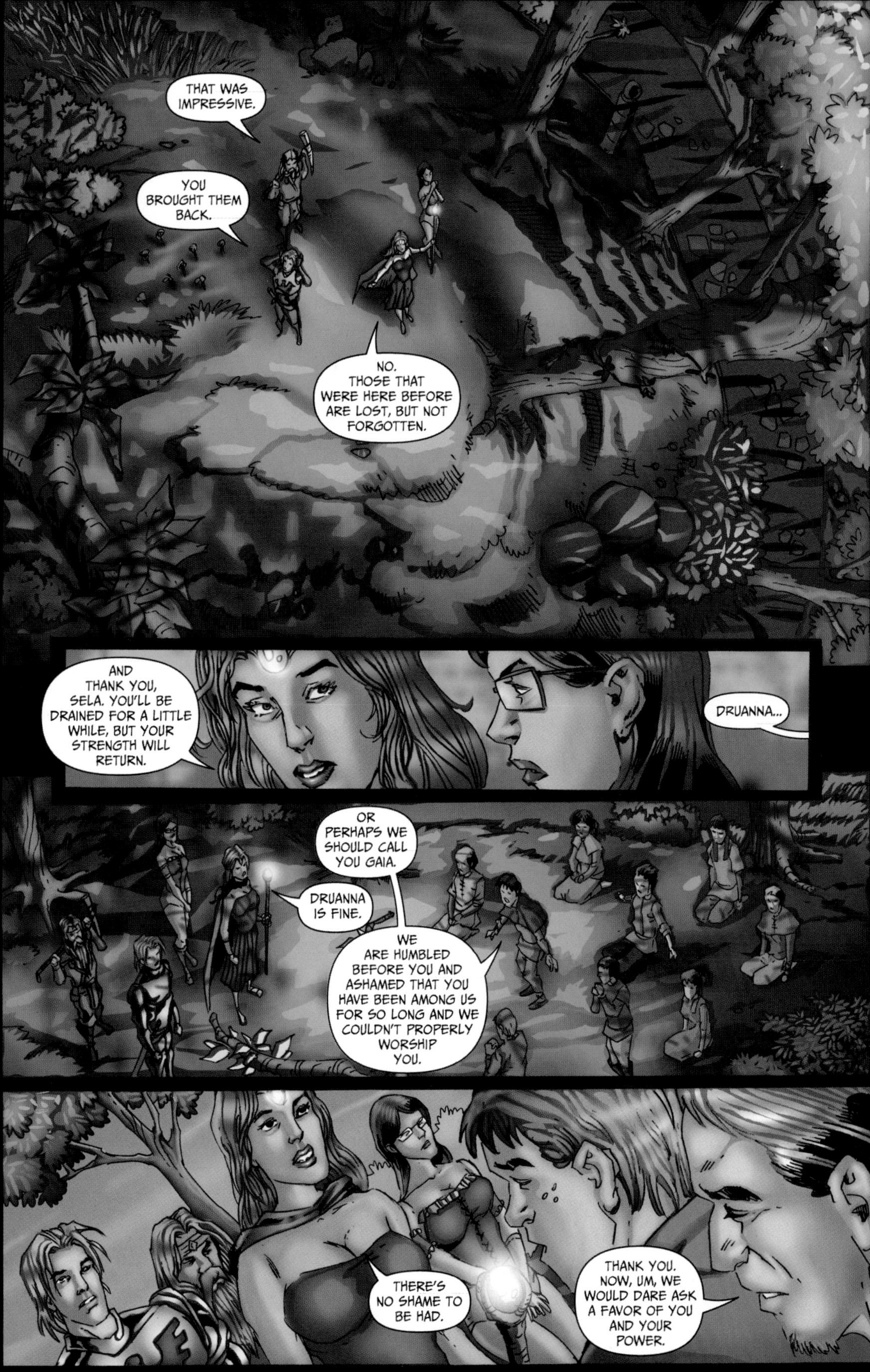
THAT WAS IMPRESSIVE.
YOU BROUGHT THEM BACK.
NO. THOSE THAT WERE HERE BEFORE ARE LOST, BUT NOT FORGOTTEN.
AND THANK YOU, SELA. YOU'LL BE DRAINED FOR A LITTLE WHILE, BUT YOUR STRENGTH WILL RETURN.
DRUANNA...
OR PERHAPS WE SHOULD CALL YOU GAIA.
DRUANNA IS FINE.
WE ARE HUMBLED BEFORE YOU AND ASHAMED THAT YOU HAVE BEEN AMONG US FOR SO LONG AND WE COULDN'T PROPERLY WORSHIP YOU.
THERE'S NO SHAME TO BE HAD.
THANK YOU. NOW, UM, WE WOULD DARE ASK A FAVOR OF YOU AND YOUR POWER.

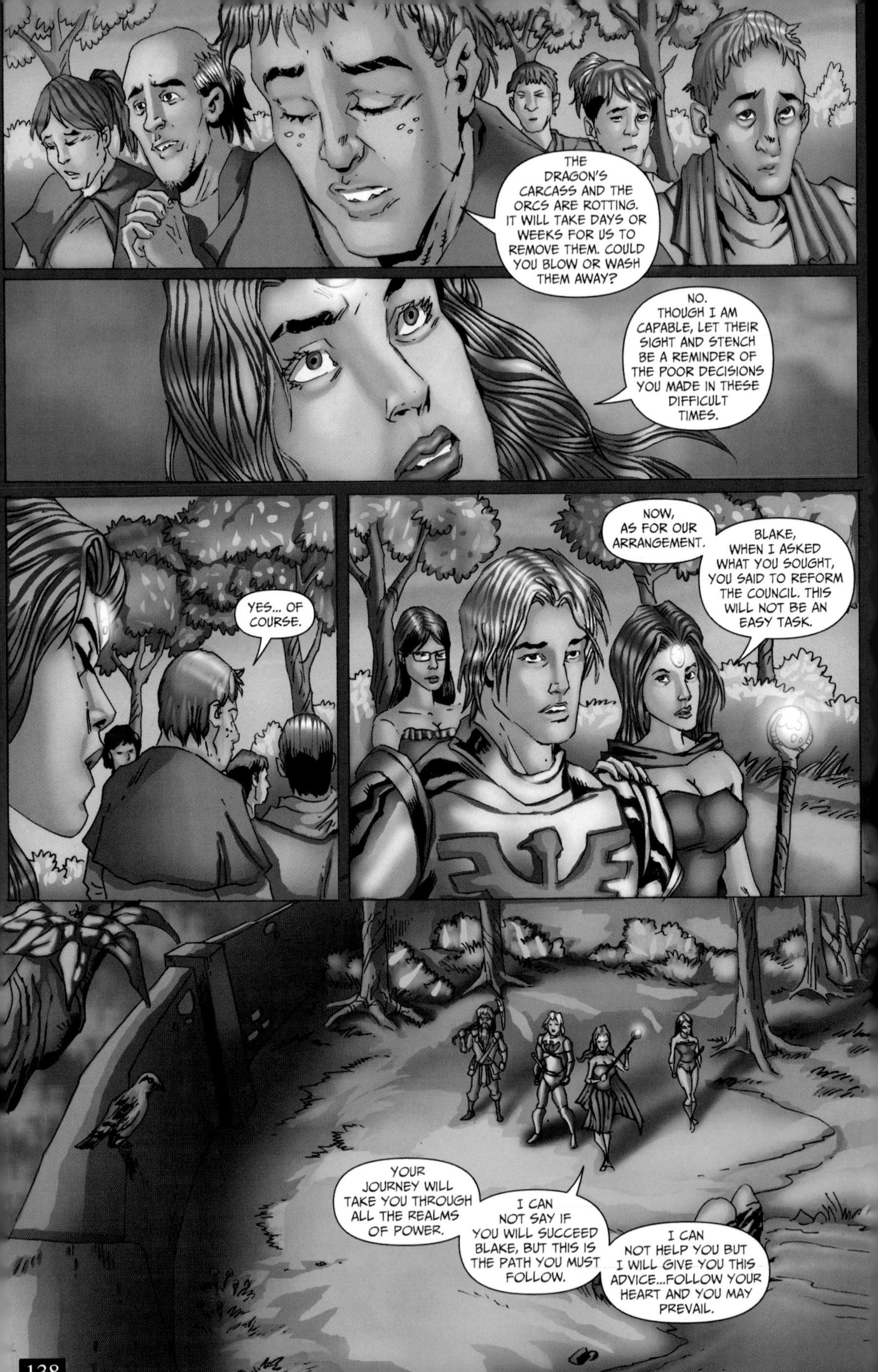
THE DRAGON'S CARCASS AND THE ORCS ARE ROTTING. IT WILL TAKE DAYS OR WEEKS FOR US TO REMOVE THEM. COULD YOU BLOW OR WASH THEM AWAY?
NO. THOUGH I AM CAPABLE, LET THEIR SIGHT AND STENCH BE A REMINDER OF THE POOR DECISIONS YOU MADE IN THESE DIFFICULT TIMES.
YES... OF COURSE.
NOW, AS FOR OUR ARRANGEMENT.
BLAKE, WHEN I ASKED WHAT YOU SOUGHT, YOU SAID TO REFORM THE COUNCIL. THIS WILL NOT BE AN EASY TASK.
YOUR JOURNEY WILL TAKE YOU THROUGH ALL THE REALMS OF POWER.
I CAN NOT SAY IF YOU WILL SUCCEED BLAKE, BUT THIS IS THE PATH YOU MUST FOLLOW.
I CAN NOT HELP YOU BUT I WILL GIVE YOU THIS ADVICE...FOLLOW YOUR HEART AND YOU MAY PREVAIL.

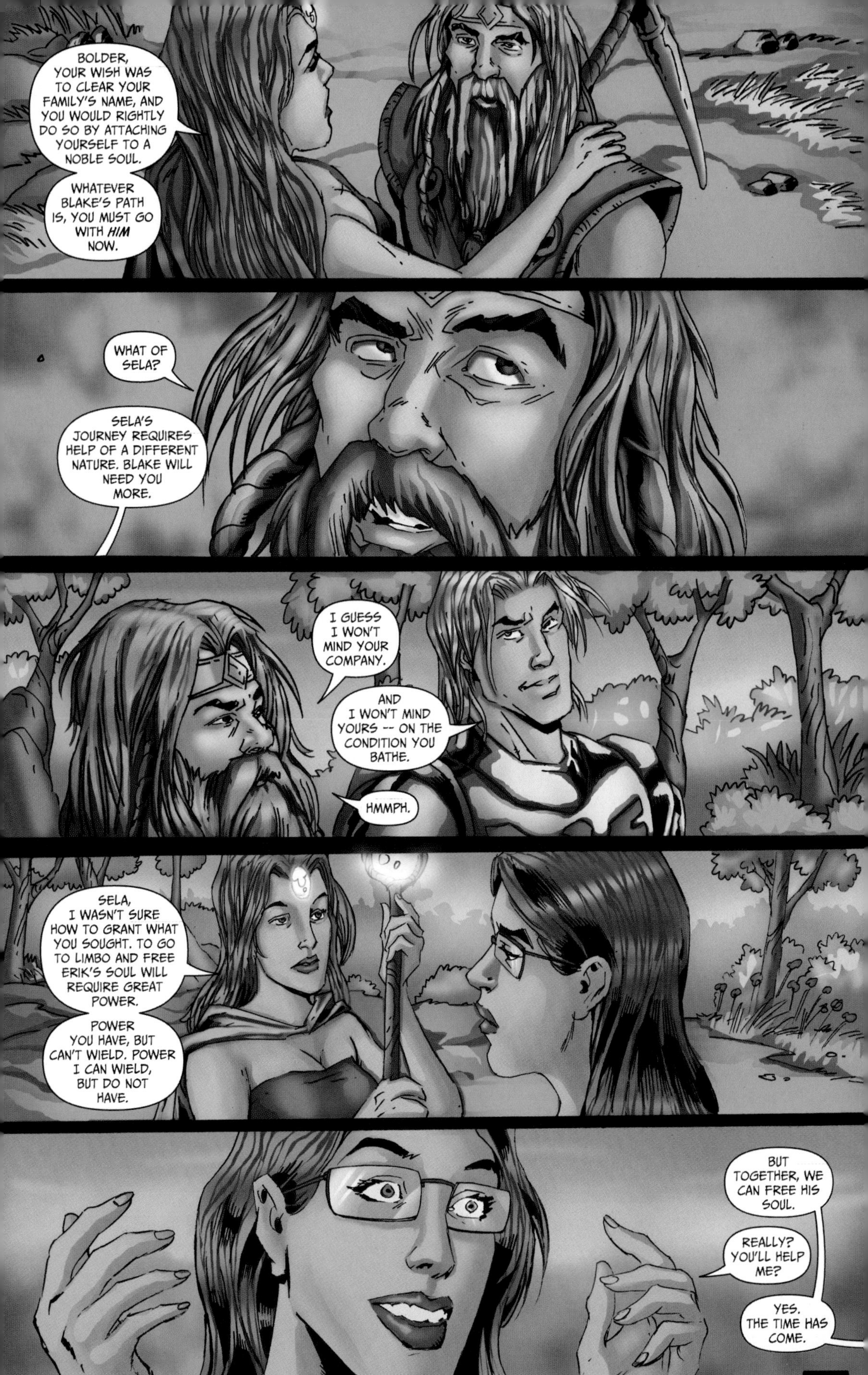
BOLDER, YOUR WISH WAS TO CLEAR YOUR FAMILY'S NAME, AND YOU WOULD RIGHTLY DO SO BY ATTACHING YOURSELF TO A NOBLE SOUL.
WHATEVER BLAKE'S PATH IS, YOU MUST GO WITH *HIM* NOW.
WHAT OF SELA?
SELA'S JOURNEY REQUIRES HELP OF A DIFFERENT NATURE. BLAKE WILL NEED YOU MORE.
I GUESS I WON'T MIND YOUR COMPANY.
AND I WON'T MIND YOURS -- ON THE CONDITION YOU BATHE.
HMMPH.
SELA, I WASN'T SURE HOW TO GRANT WHAT YOU SOUGHT. TO GO TO LIMBO AND FREE ERIK'S SOUL WILL REQUIRE GREAT POWER.
POWER YOU HAVE, BUT CAN'T WIELD. POWER I CAN WIELD, BUT DO NOT HAVE.
BUT TOGETHER, WE CAN FREE HIS SOUL.
REALLY? YOU'LL HELP ME?
YES. THE TIME HAS COME.

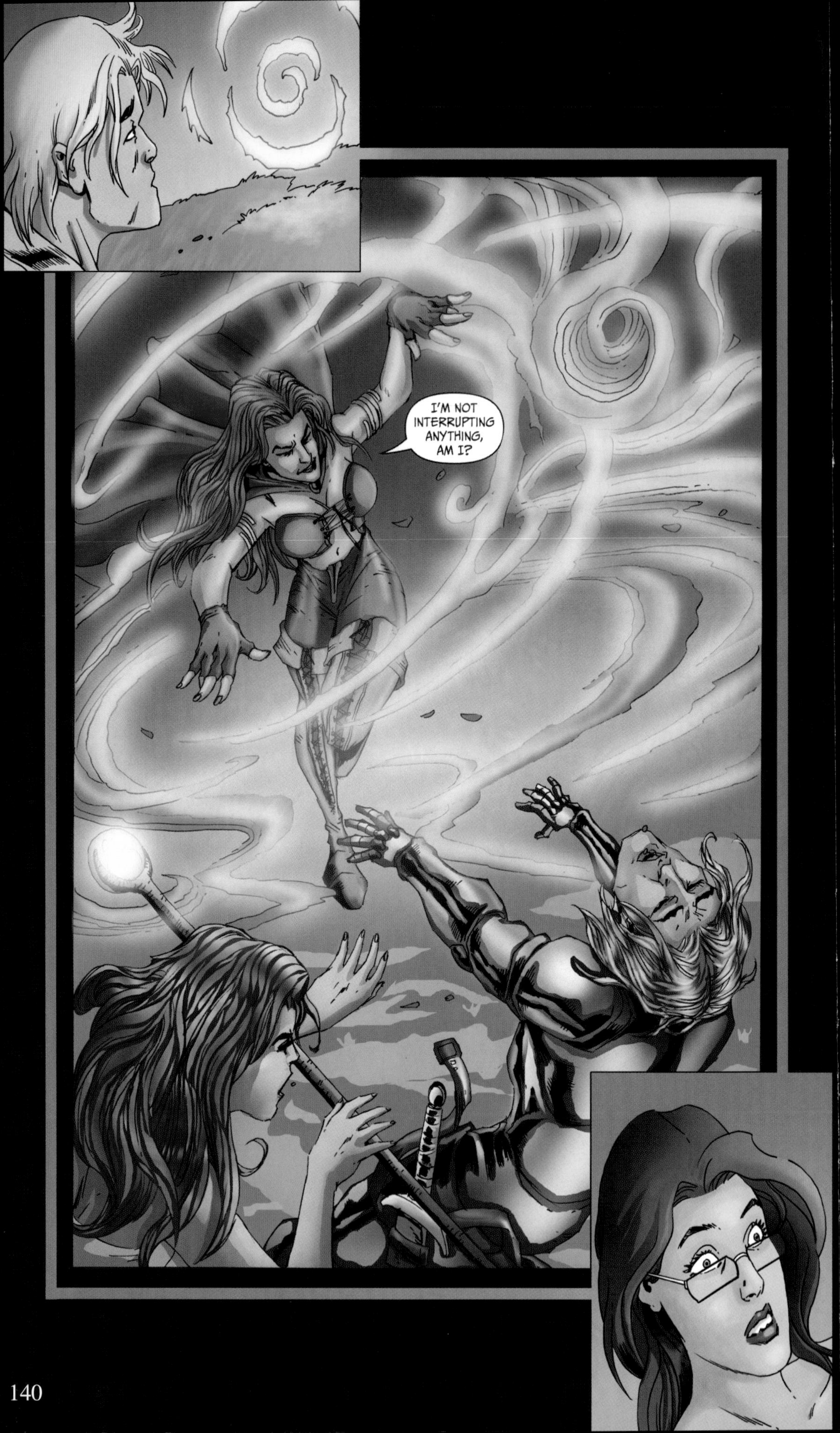
I'M NOT INTERRUPTING ANYTHING, AM I?

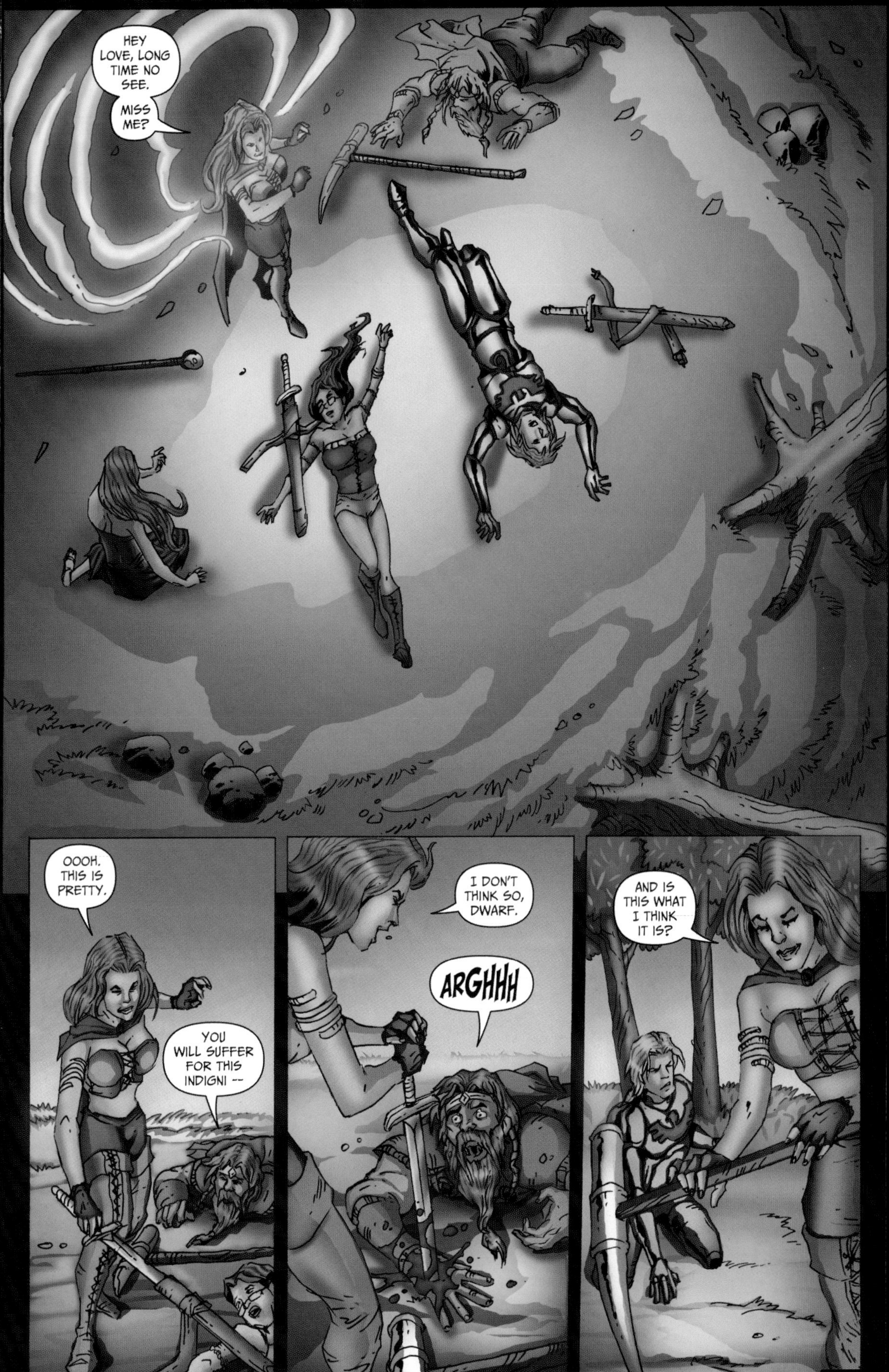
HEY LOVE, LONG TIME NO SEE.
MISS ME?
OOOH. THIS IS PRETTY.
YOU WILL SUFFER FOR THIS INDIGNI --
I DON'T THINK SO, DWARF.
ARGHHH
AND IS THIS WHAT I THINK IT IS?

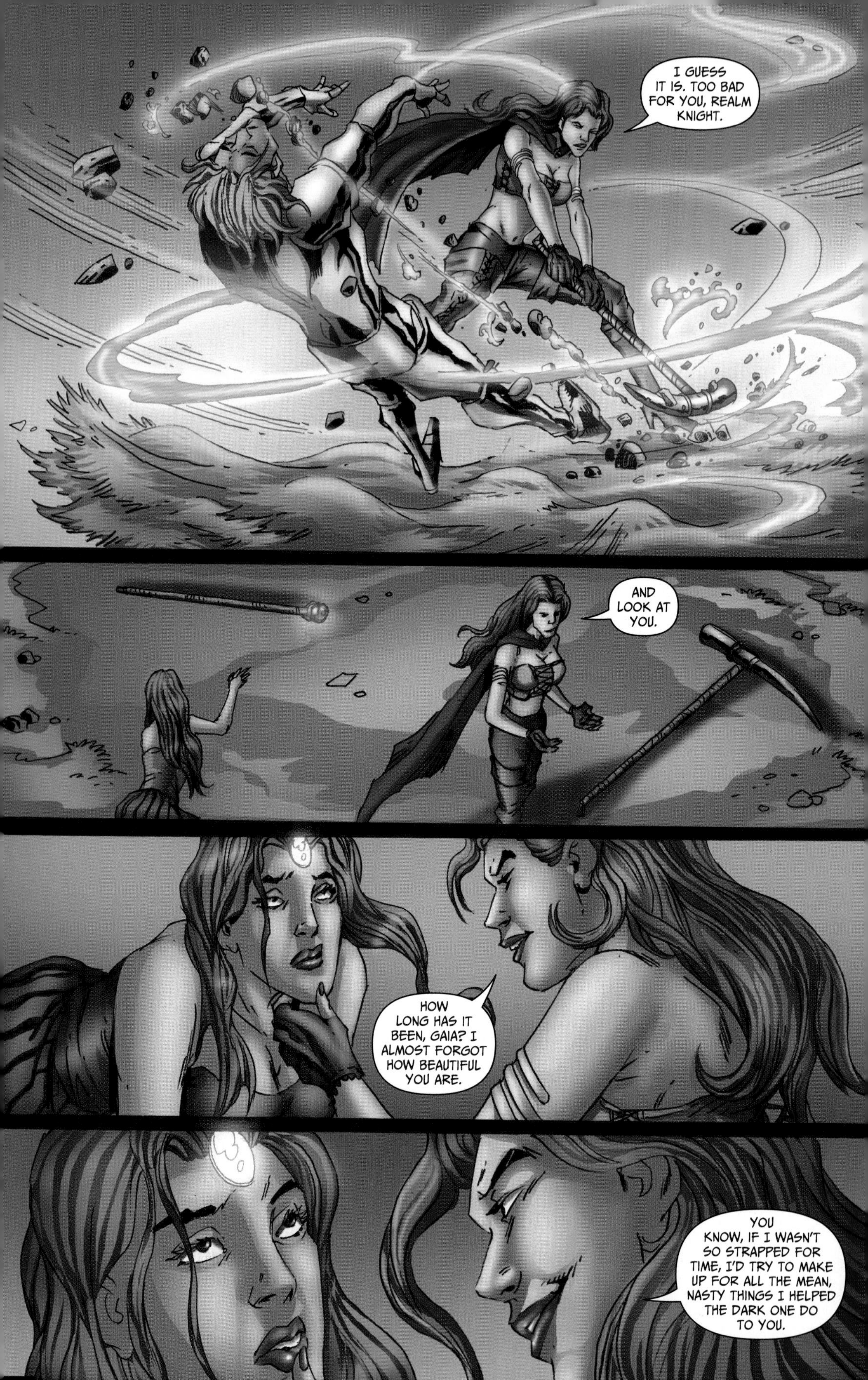
I GUESS IT IS. TOO BAD FOR YOU, REALM KNIGHT.
AND LOOK AT YOU.
HOW LONG HAS IT BEEN, GAIA? I ALMOST FORGOT HOW BEAUTIFUL YOU ARE.
YOU KNOW, IF I WASN'T SO STRAPPED FOR TIME, I'D TRY TO MAKE UP FOR ALL THE MEAN, NASTY THINGS I HELPED THE DARK ONE DO TO YOU.

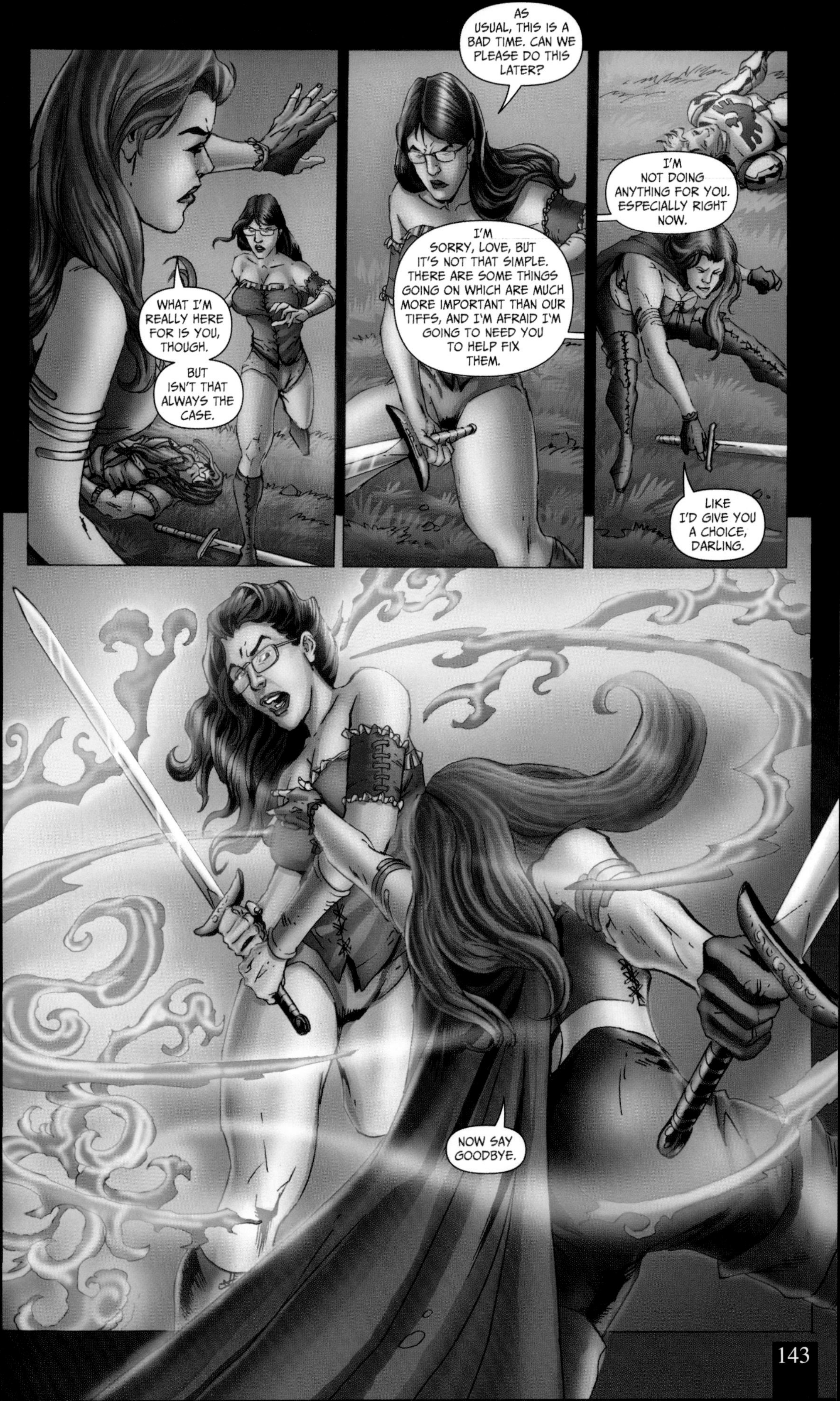

WHAT I'M REALLY HERE FOR IS YOU, THOUGH.
BUT ISN'T THAT ALWAYS THE CASE.
AS USUAL, THIS IS A BAD TIME. CAN WE PLEASE DO THIS LATER?
I'M SORRY, LOVE, BUT IT'S NOT THAT SIMPLE. THERE ARE SOME THINGS GOING ON WHICH ARE MUCH MORE IMPORTANT THAN OUR TIFFS, AND I'M AFRAID I'M GOING TO NEED YOU TO HELP FIX THEM.
I'M NOT DOING ANYTHING FOR YOU. ESPECIALLY RIGHT NOW.
LIKE I'D GIVE YOU A CHOICE, DARLING.
NOW SAY GOODBYE.

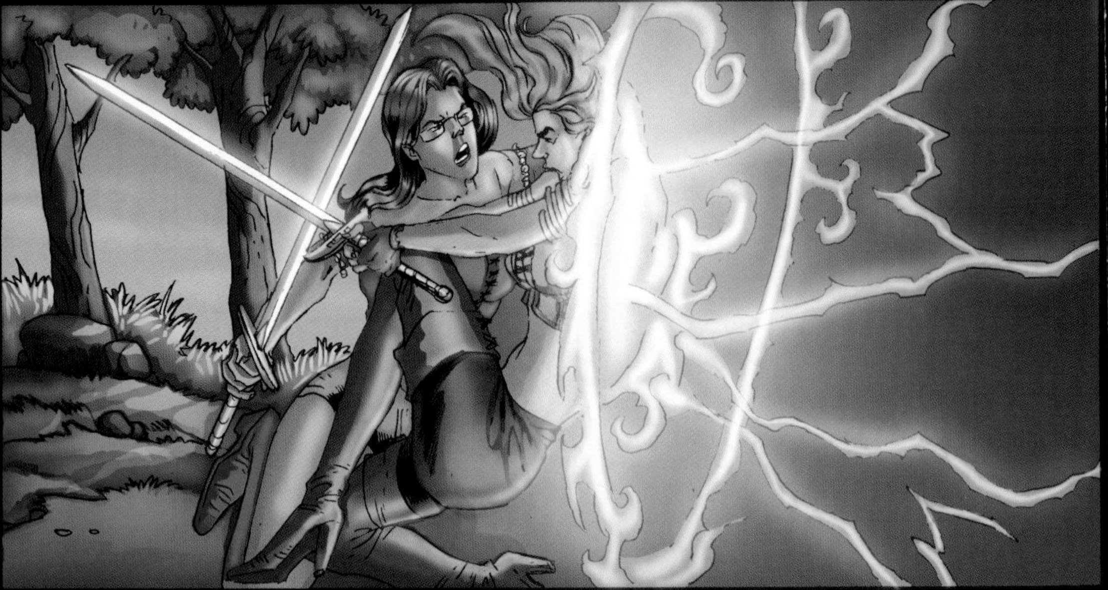

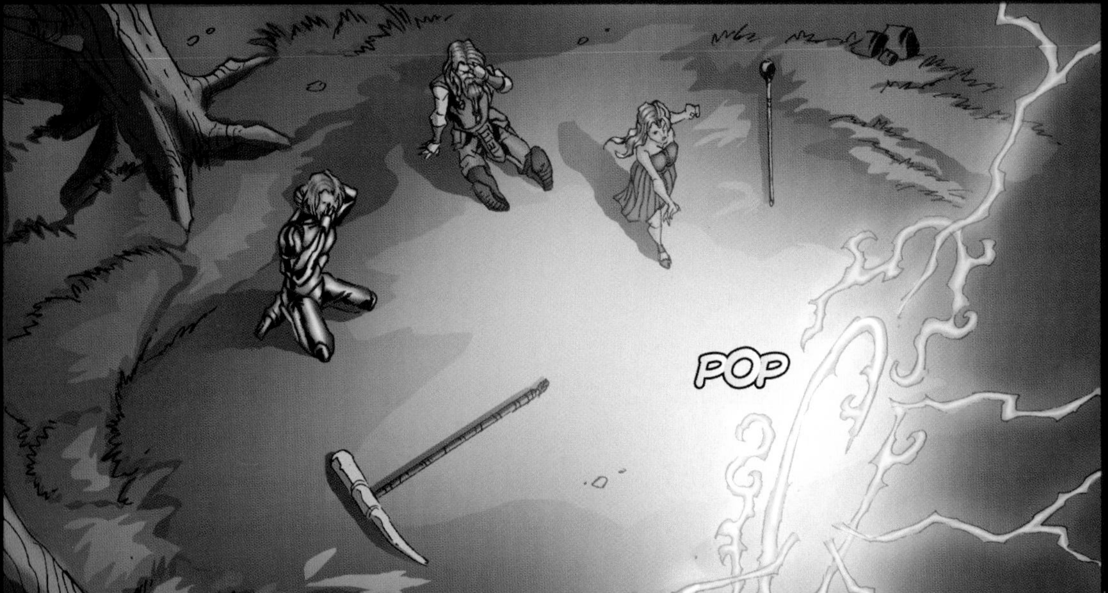
POP

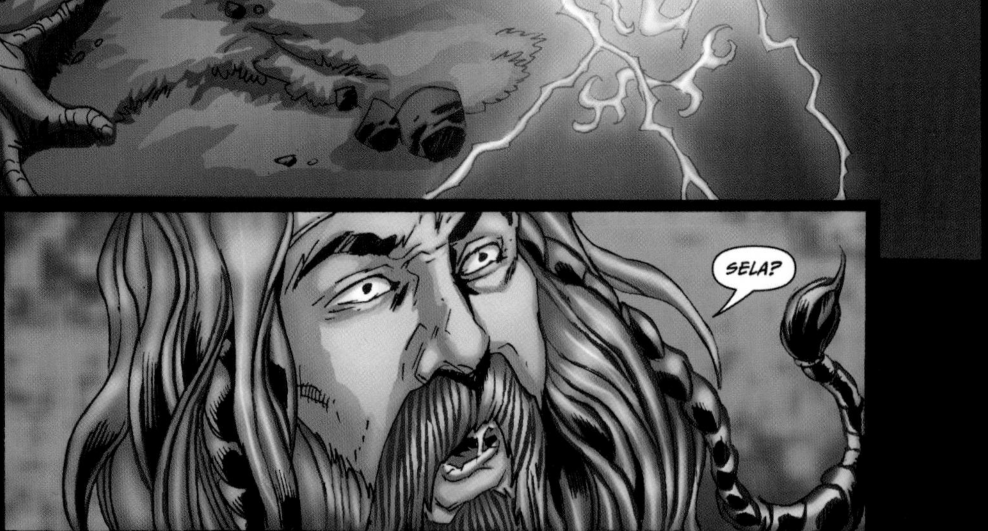
SELA?

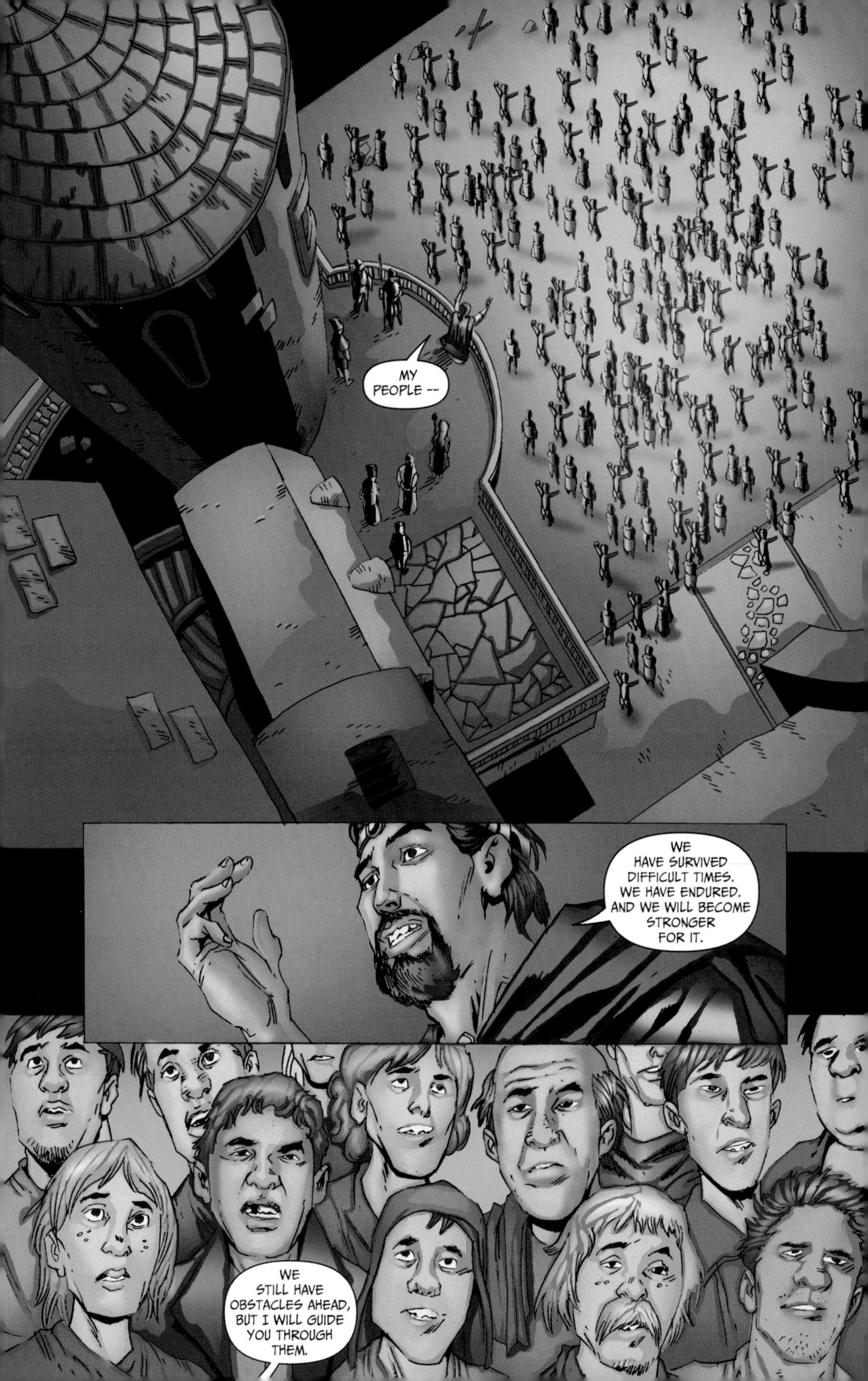
MY PEOPLE --
WE HAVE SURVIVED DIFFICULT TIMES. WE HAVE ENDURED. AND WE WILL BECOME STRONGER FOR IT.
WE STILL HAVE OBSTACLES AHEAD, BUT I WILL GUIDE YOU THROUGH THEM.

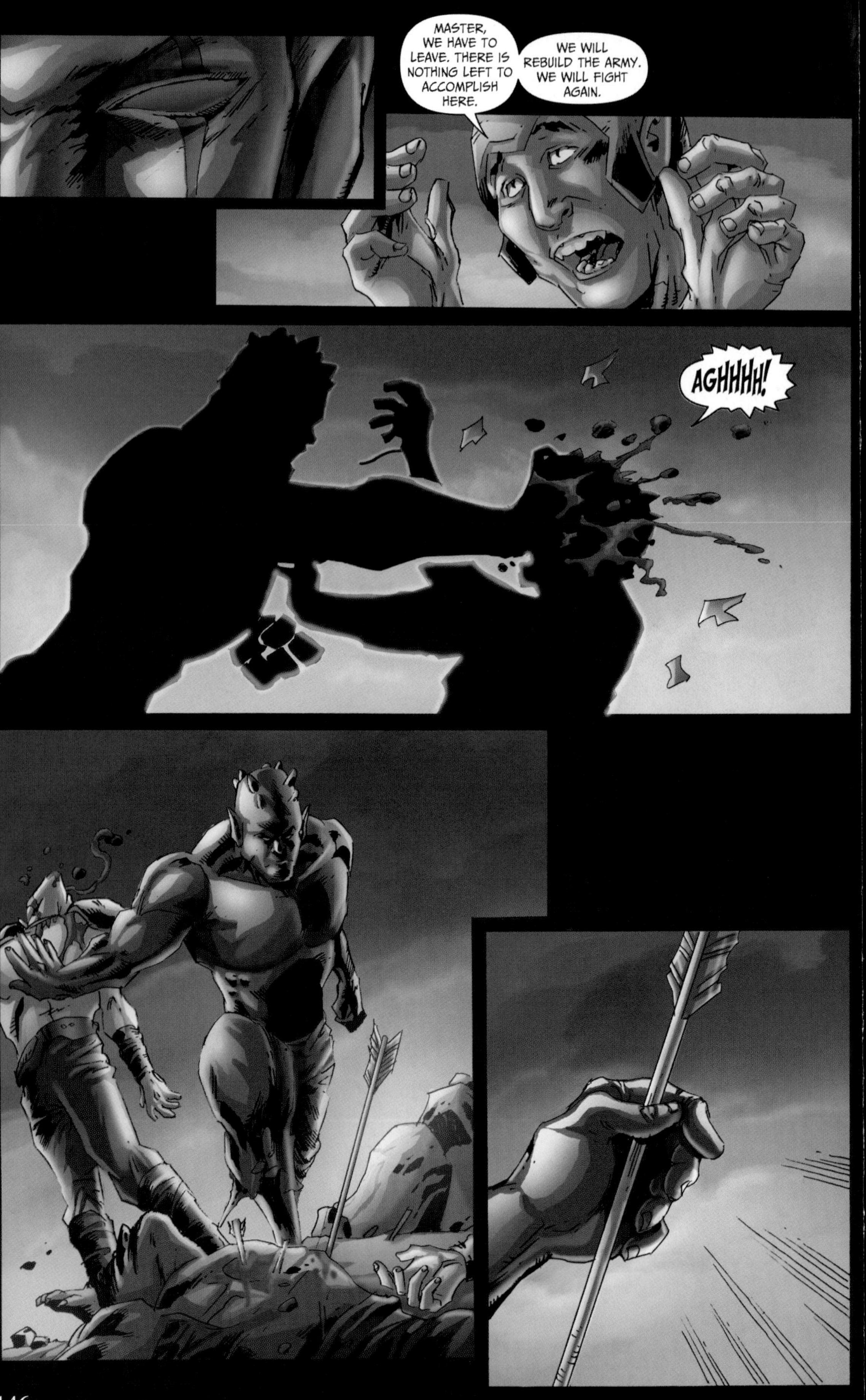
MASTER, WE HAVE TO LEAVE. THERE IS NOTHING LEFT TO ACCOMPLISH HERE.
WE WILL REBUILD THE ARMY. WE WILL FIGHT AGAIN.
AGHHHH!

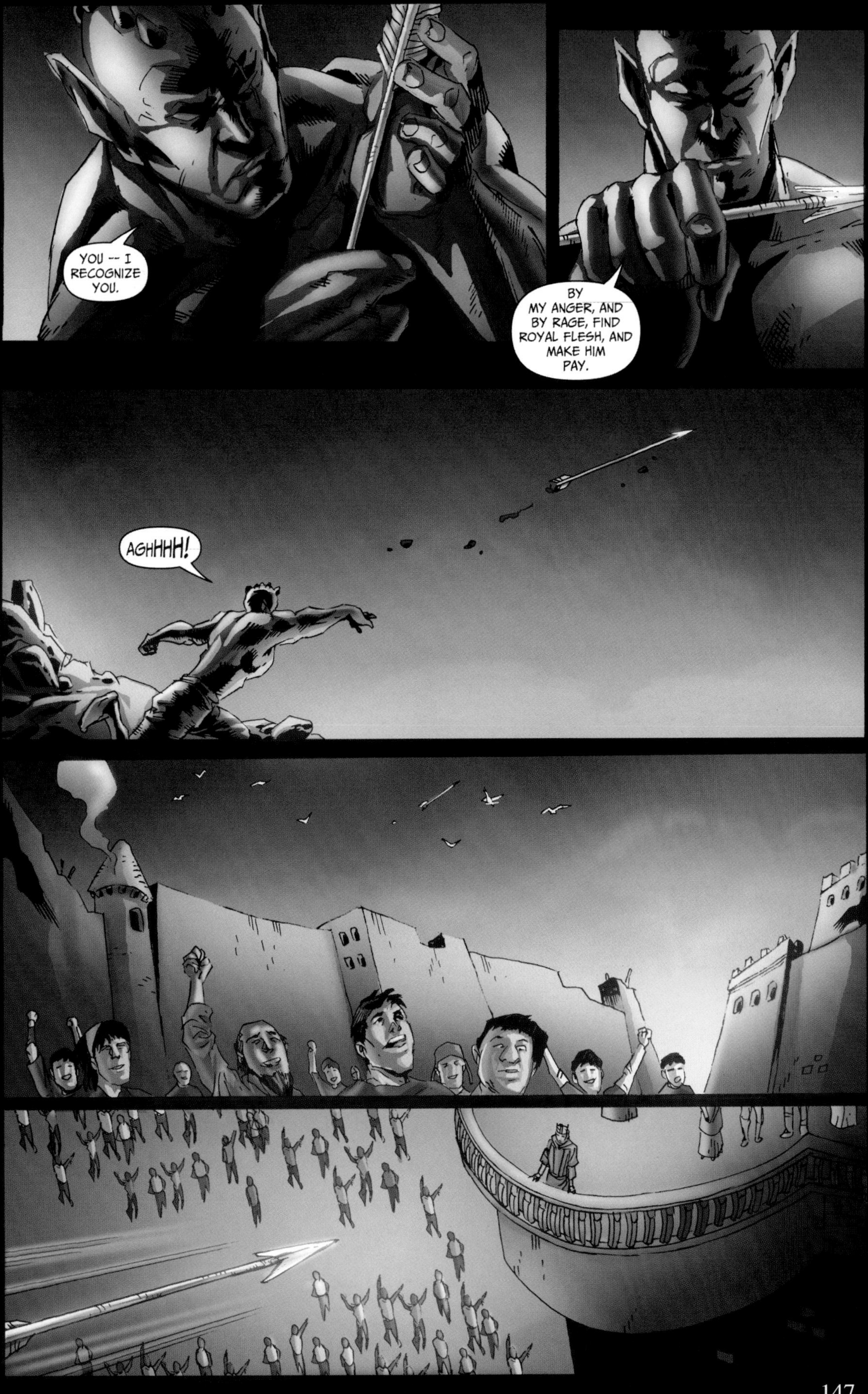
YOU -- I RECOGNIZE YOU.
BY MY ANGER, AND BY RAGE, FIND ROYAL FLESH, AND MAKE HIM PAY.
AGHHHH!

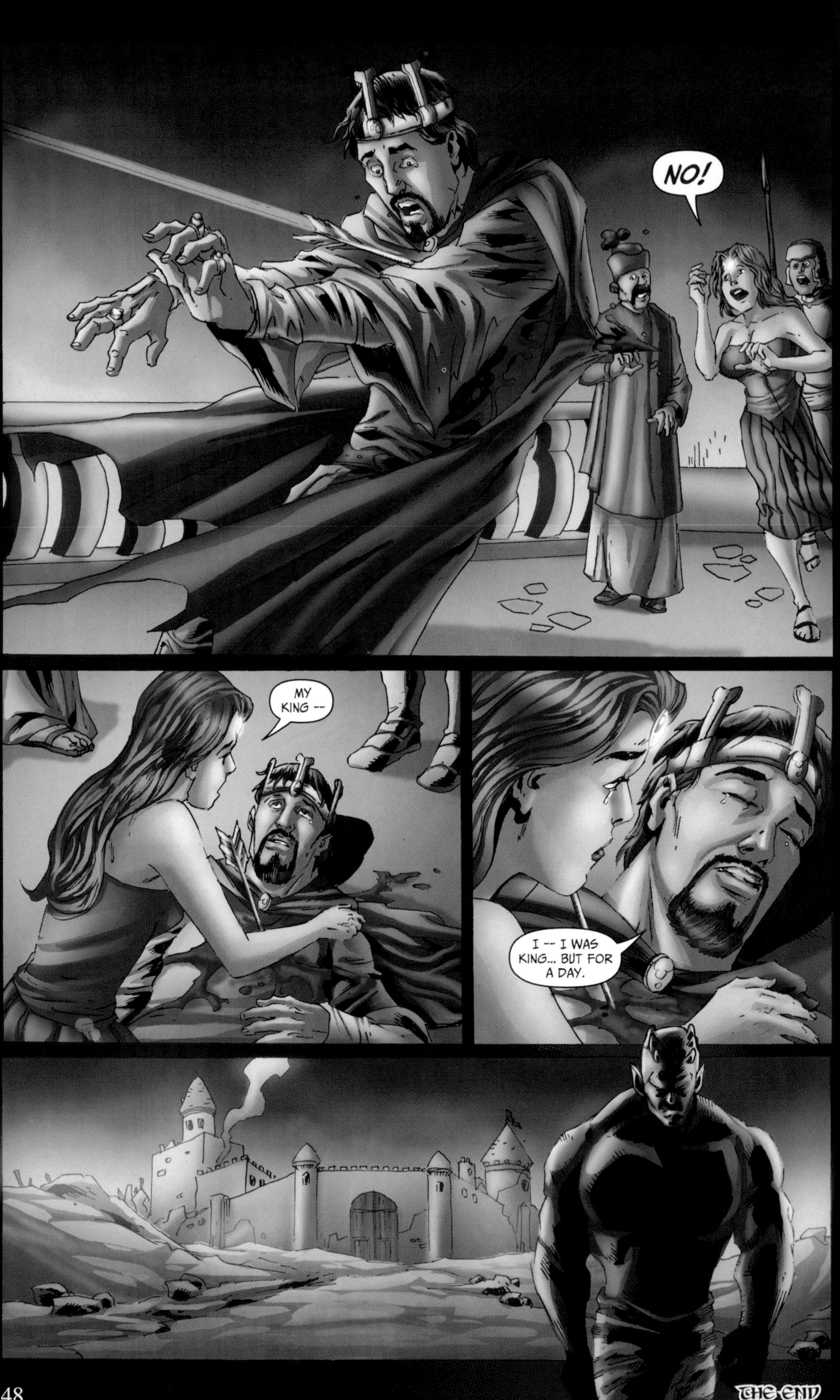
NO!
MY KING --
I -- I WAS KING... BUT FOR A DAY.
THE END

Grimm Fairy Tales

Volume 10

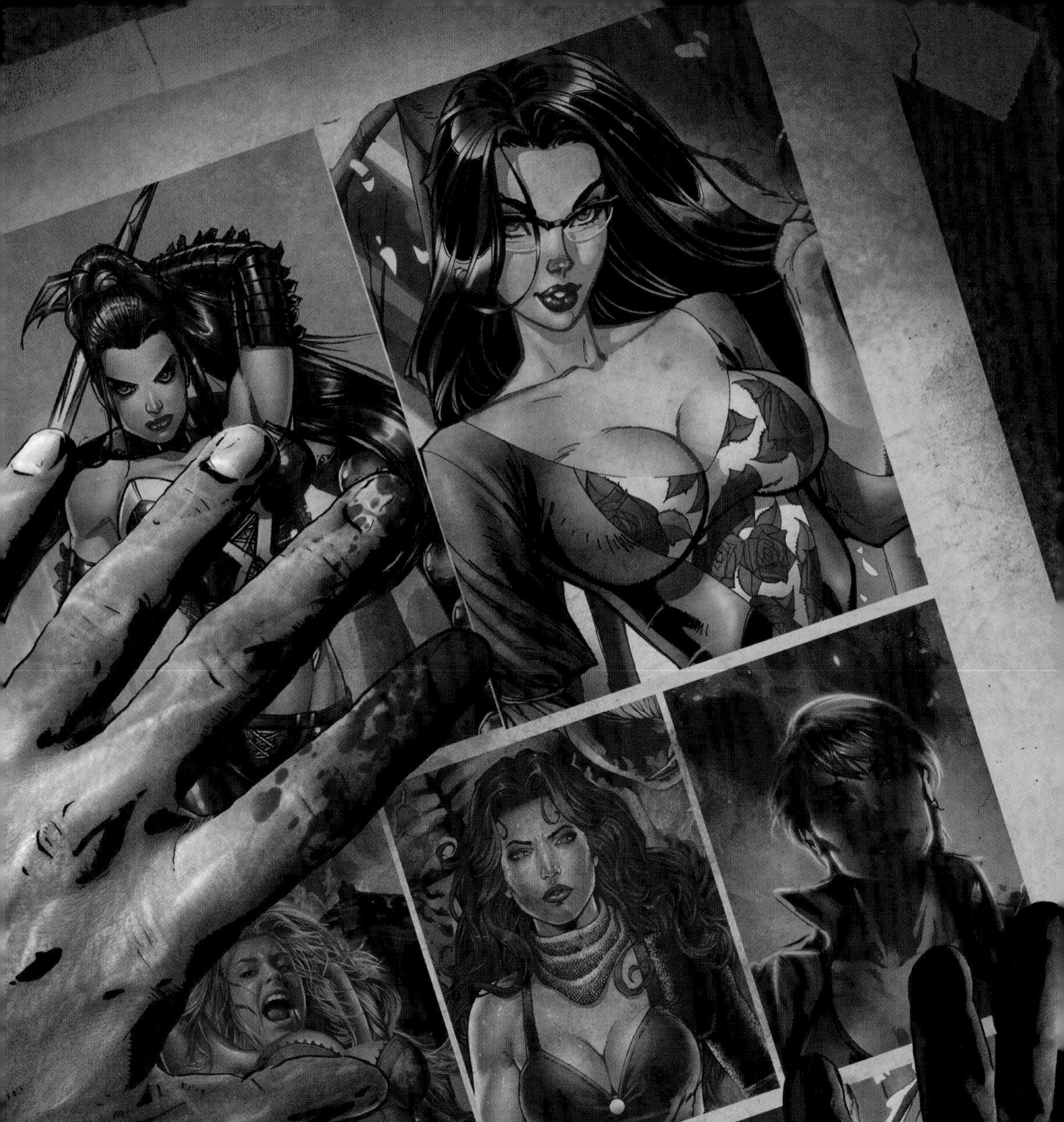

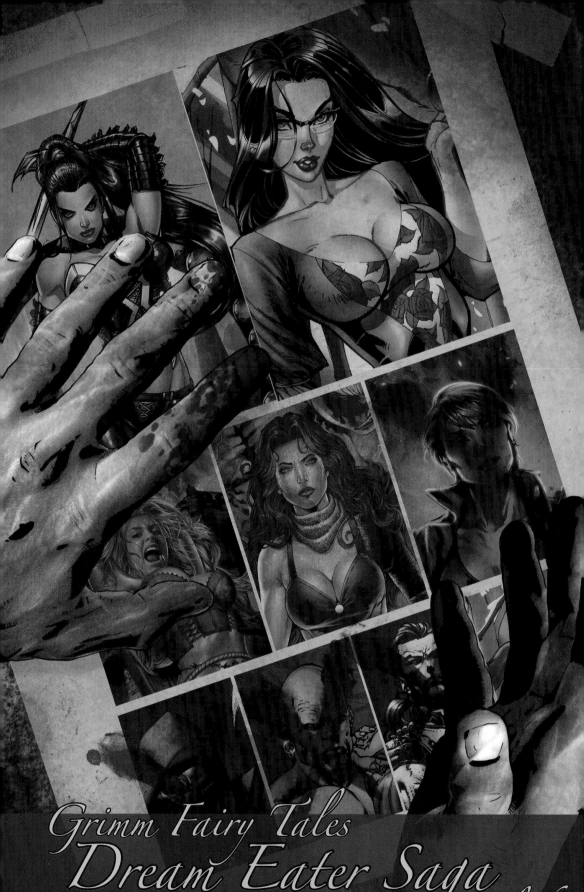

Grimm Fairy Tales Dream Eater Saga Prelude

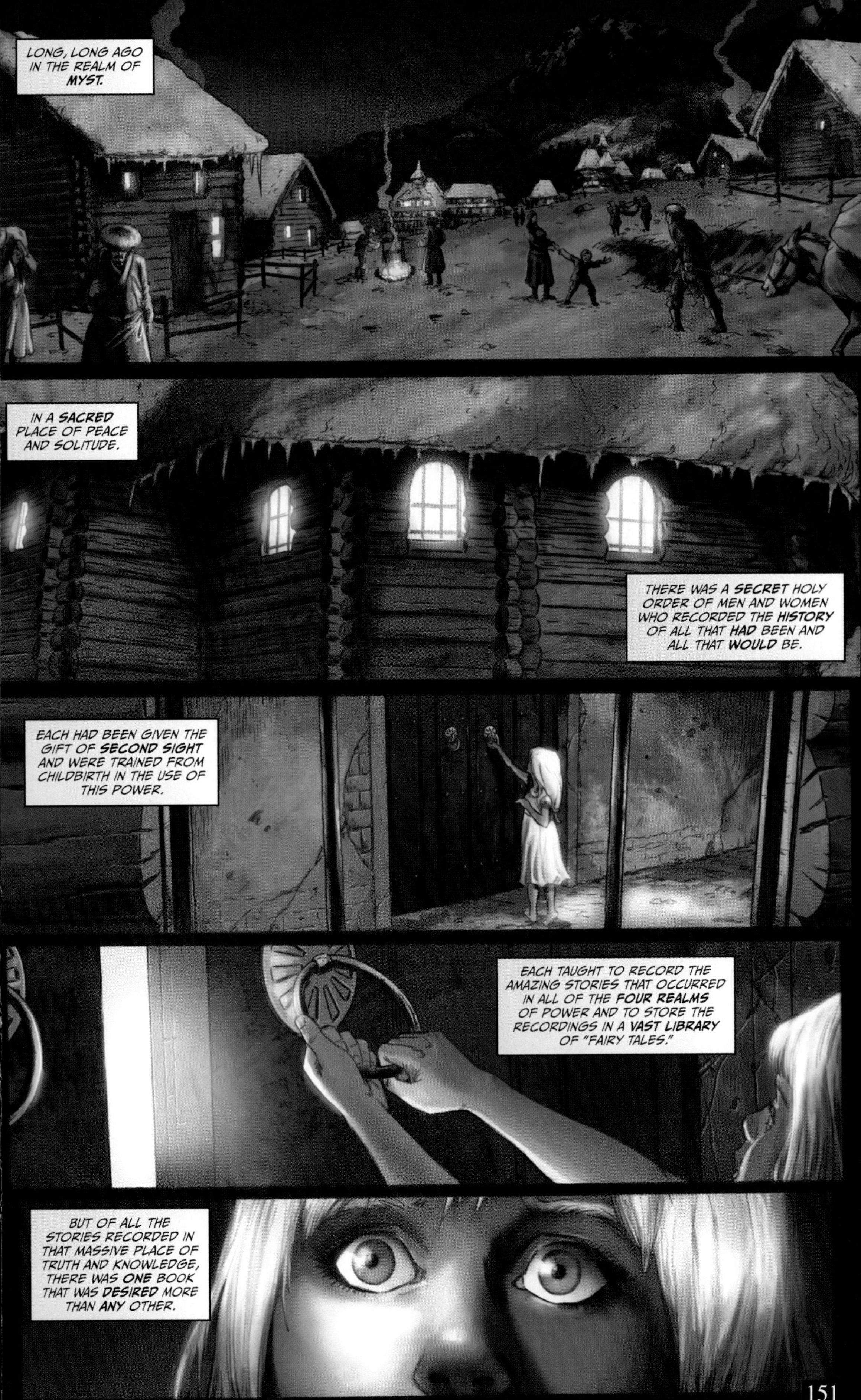
LONG, LONG AGO IN THE REALM OF **MYST.**
IN A **SACRED** PLACE OF PEACE AND SOLITUDE.
THERE WAS A **SECRET** HOLY ORDER OF MEN AND WOMEN WHO RECORDED THE **HISTORY** OF ALL THAT **HAD** BEEN AND ALL THAT **WOULD** BE.
EACH HAD BEEN GIVEN THE GIFT OF **SECOND SIGHT** AND WERE TRAINED FROM CHILDBIRTH IN THE USE OF THIS POWER.
EACH TAUGHT TO RECORD THE AMAZING STORIES THAT OCCURRED IN ALL OF THE **FOUR REALMS** OF POWER AND TO STORE THE RECORDINGS IN A **VAST LIBRARY** OF "FAIRY TALES."
BUT OF ALL THE STORIES RECORDED IN THAT MASSIVE PLACE OF TRUTH AND KNOWLEDGE, THERE WAS **ONE** BOOK THAT WAS **DESIRED** MORE THAN **ANY** OTHER.

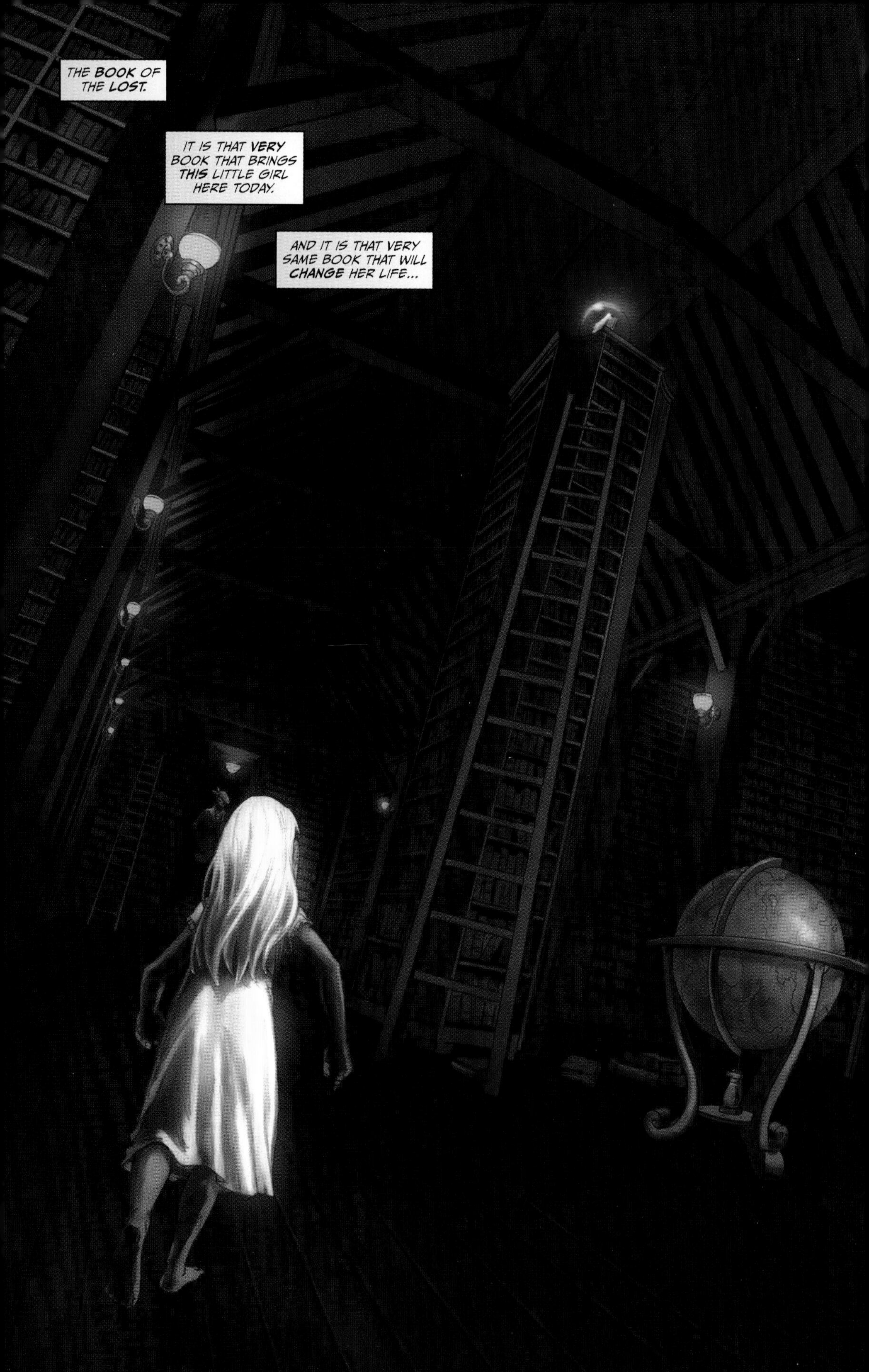
THE BOOK OF THE LOST.
IT IS THAT VERY BOOK THAT BRINGS THIS LITTLE GIRL HERE TODAY.
AND IT IS THAT VERY SAME BOOK THAT WILL CHANGE HER LIFE...

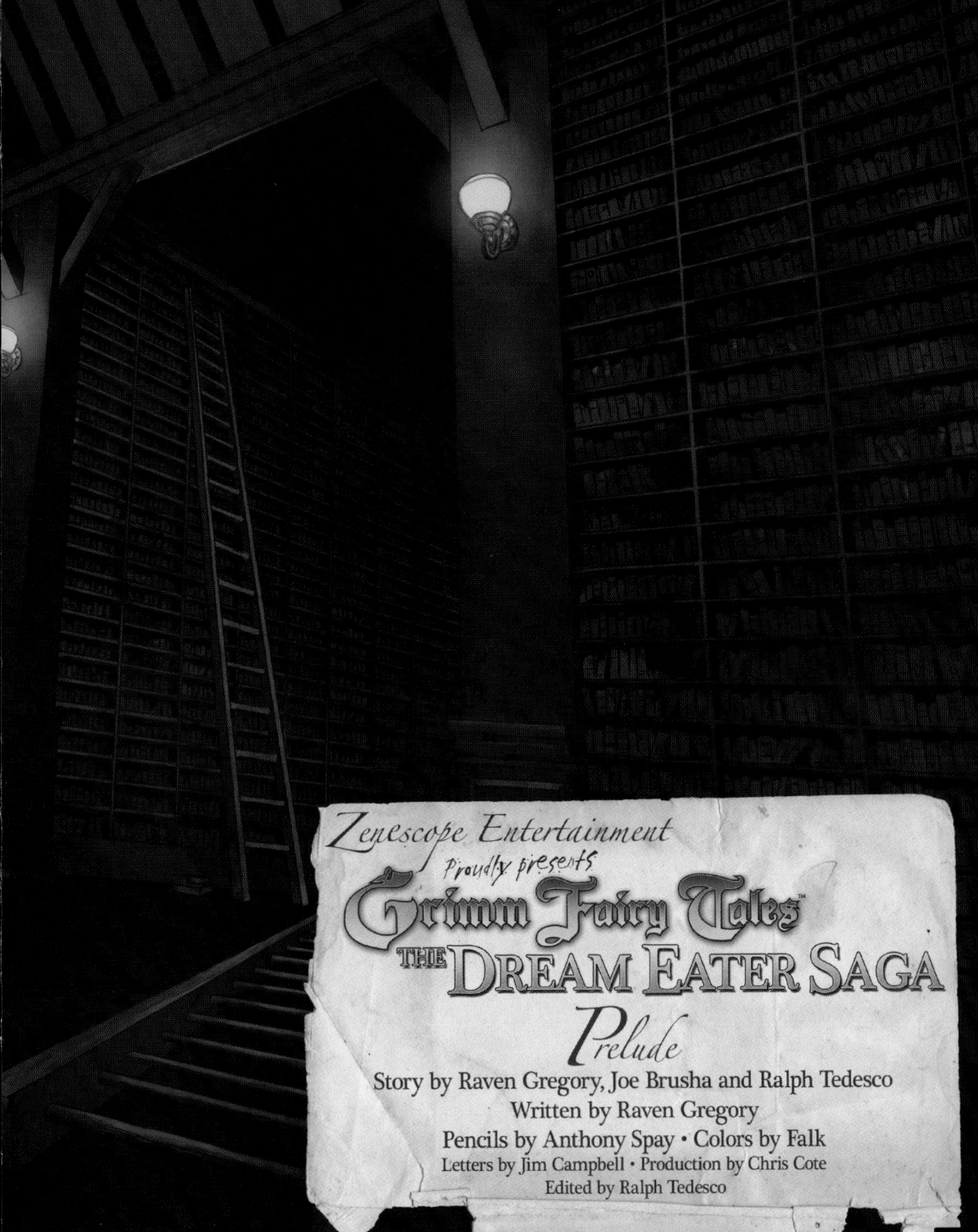
Zenescope Entertainment
Proudly presents
Grimm Fairy Tales™
THE DREAM EATER SAGA
Prelude
Story by Raven Gregory, Joe Brusha and Ralph Tedesco
Written by Raven Gregory
Pencils by Anthony Spay • Colors by Falk
Letters by Jim Campbell • Production by Chris Cote
Edited by Ralph Tedesco

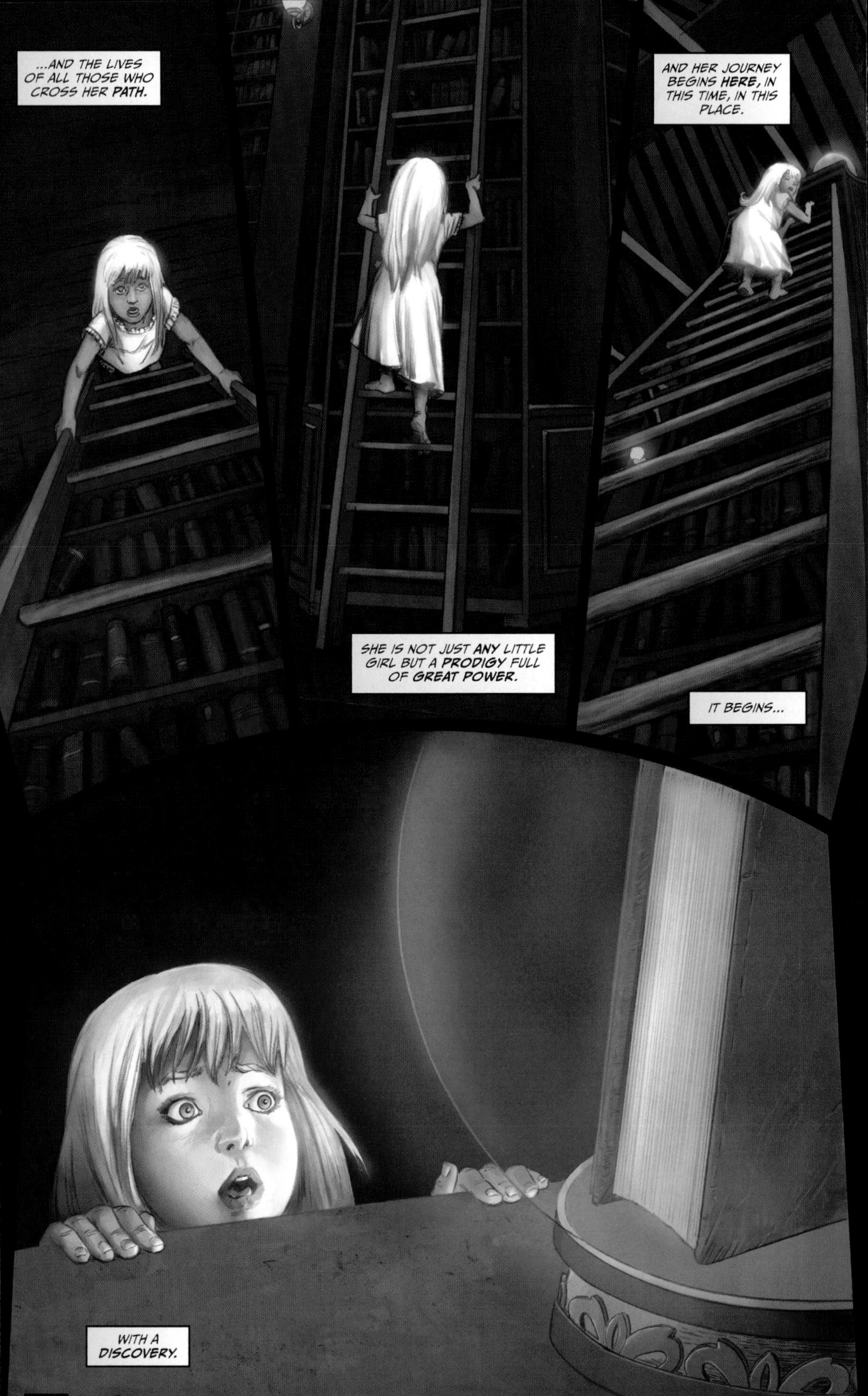
...AND THE LIVES OF ALL THOSE WHO CROSS HER PATH.
AND HER JOURNEY BEGINS HERE, IN THIS TIME, IN THIS PLACE.
SHE IS NOT JUST ANY LITTLE GIRL BUT A PRODIGY FULL OF GREAT POWER.
IT BEGINS...
WITH A DISCOVERY.

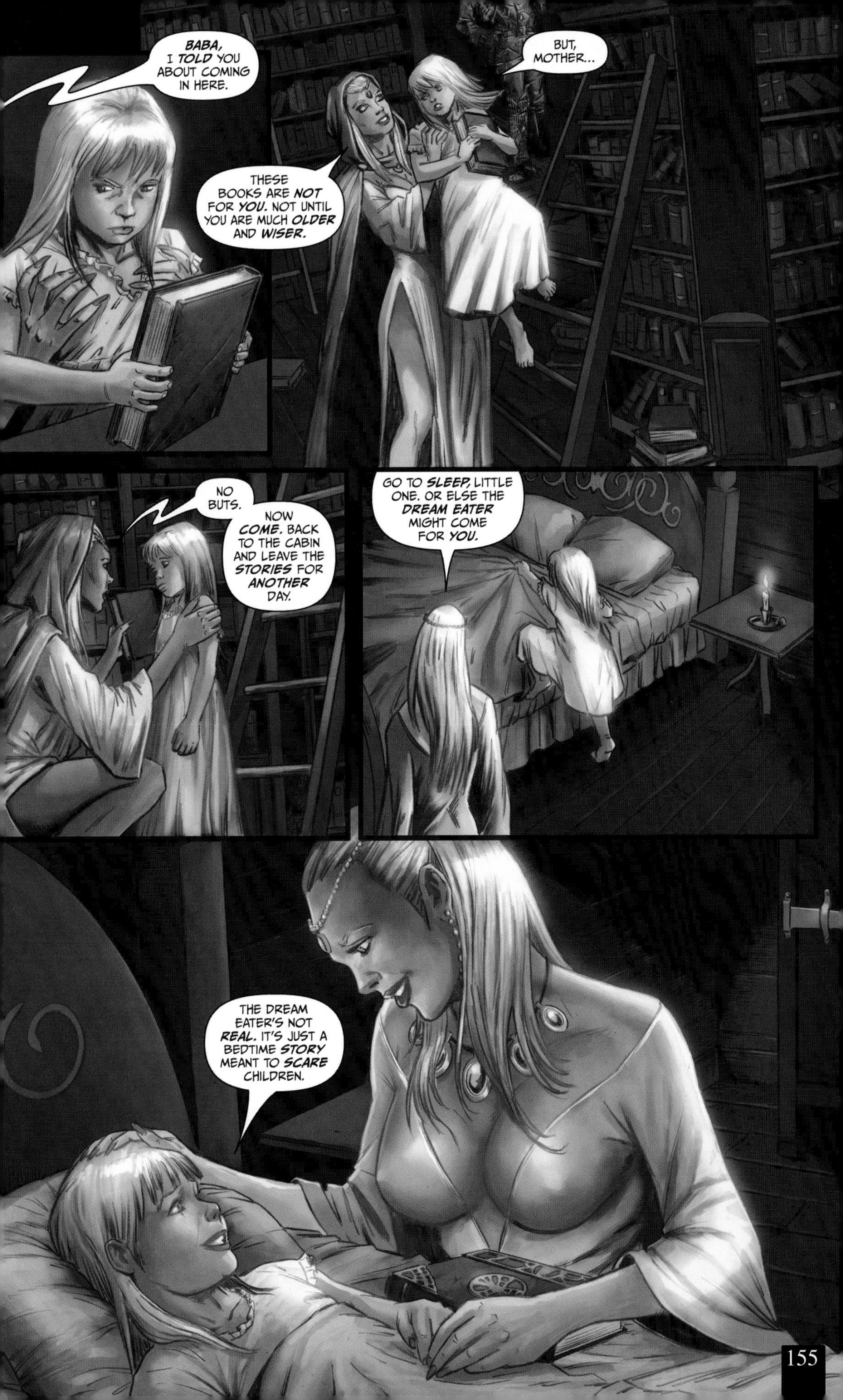
BABA, I TOLD YOU ABOUT COMING IN HERE.
BUT, MOTHER...
THESE BOOKS ARE NOT FOR YOU. NOT UNTIL YOU ARE MUCH OLDER AND WISER.
NO BUTS.
NOW COME. BACK TO THE CABIN AND LEAVE THE STORIES FOR ANOTHER DAY.
GO TO SLEEP, LITTLE ONE. OR ELSE THE DREAM EATER MIGHT COME FOR YOU.
THE DREAM EATER'S NOT REAL. IT'S JUST A BEDTIME STORY MEANT TO SCARE CHILDREN.

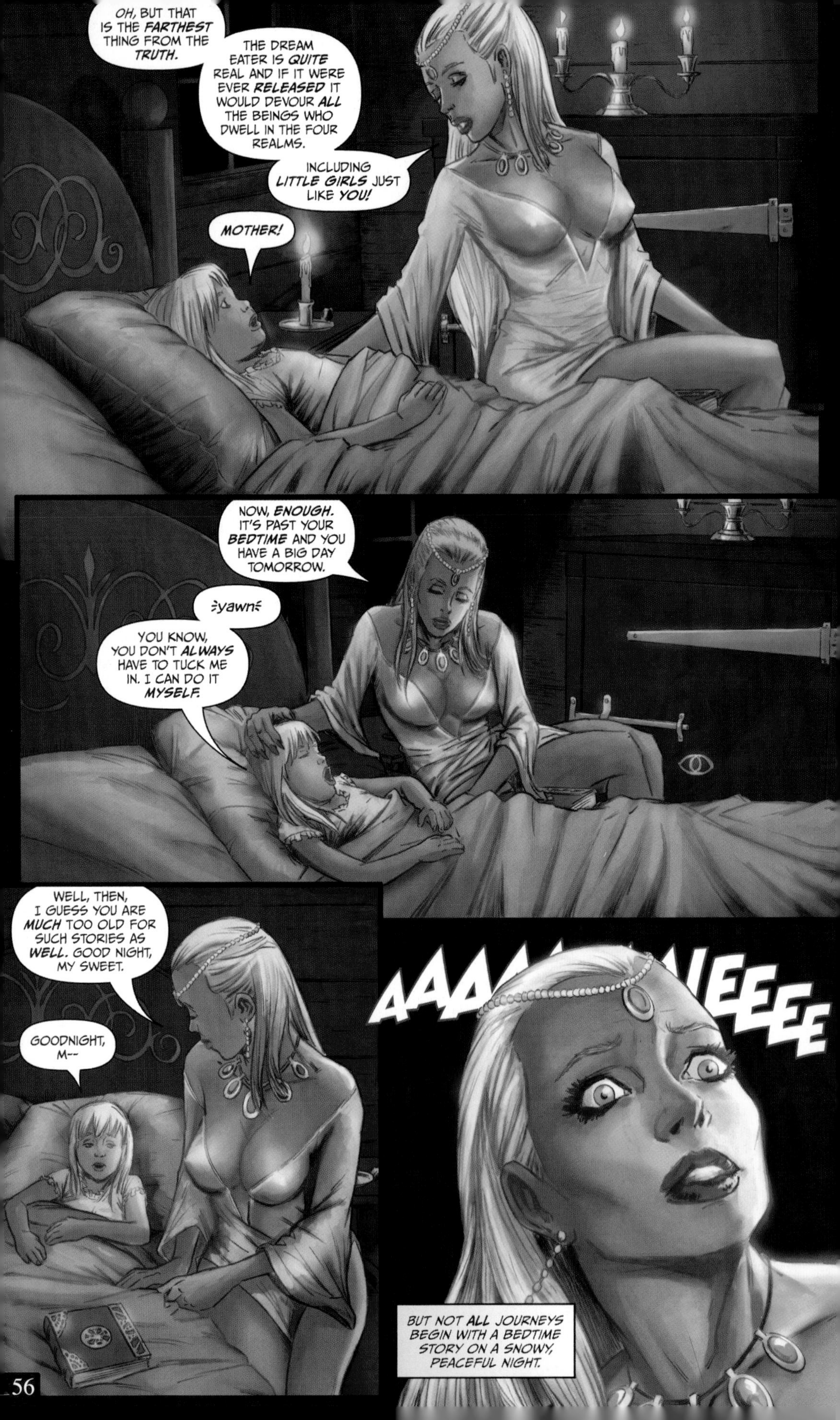
OH, BUT THAT IS THE *FARTHEST* THING FROM THE *TRUTH.*
THE DREAM EATER IS *QUITE* REAL AND IF IT WERE EVER *RELEASED* IT WOULD DEVOUR *ALL* THE BEINGS WHO DWELL IN THE FOUR REALMS.
INCLUDING *LITTLE GIRLS* JUST LIKE *YOU!*
MOTHER!
NOW, *ENOUGH.* IT'S PAST YOUR *BEDTIME* AND YOU HAVE A BIG DAY TOMORROW.
yawn
YOU KNOW, YOU DON'T *ALWAYS* HAVE TO TUCK ME IN. I CAN DO IT *MYSELF.*
WELL, THEN, I GUESS YOU ARE *MUCH* TOO OLD FOR SUCH STORIES AS *WELL.* GOOD NIGHT, MY SWEET.
GOODNIGHT, M--
AAAA IEEEE
BUT NOT *ALL* JOURNEYS BEGIN WITH A BEDTIME STORY ON A SNOWY, PEACEFUL NIGHT.

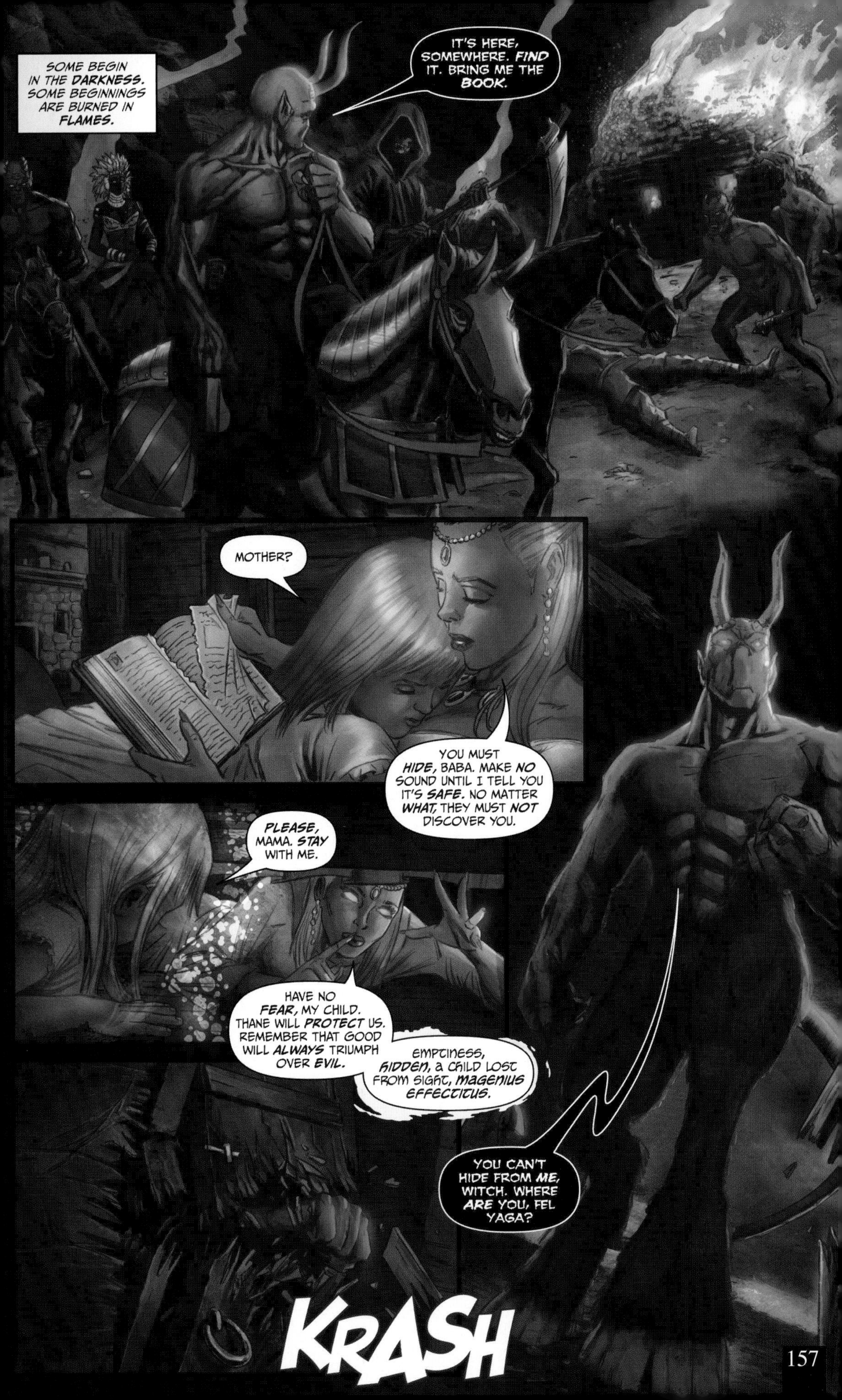
SOME BEGIN IN THE DARKNESS. SOME BEGINNINGS ARE BURNED IN FLAMES.
IT'S HERE, SOMEWHERE. FIND IT. BRING ME THE BOOK.
MOTHER?
YOU MUST HIDE, BABA. MAKE NO SOUND UNTIL I TELL YOU IT'S SAFE. NO MATTER WHAT, THEY MUST NOT DISCOVER YOU.
PLEASE, MAMA. STAY WITH ME.
HAVE NO FEAR, MY CHILD. THANE WILL PROTECT US. REMEMBER THAT GOOD WILL ALWAYS TRIUMPH OVER EVIL.
EMPTINESS, HIDDEN, A CHILD LOST FROM SIGHT, MAGENIUS EFFECTITUS.
YOU CAN'T HIDE FROM ME, WITCH. WHERE ARE YOU, FEL YAGA?
KRASH

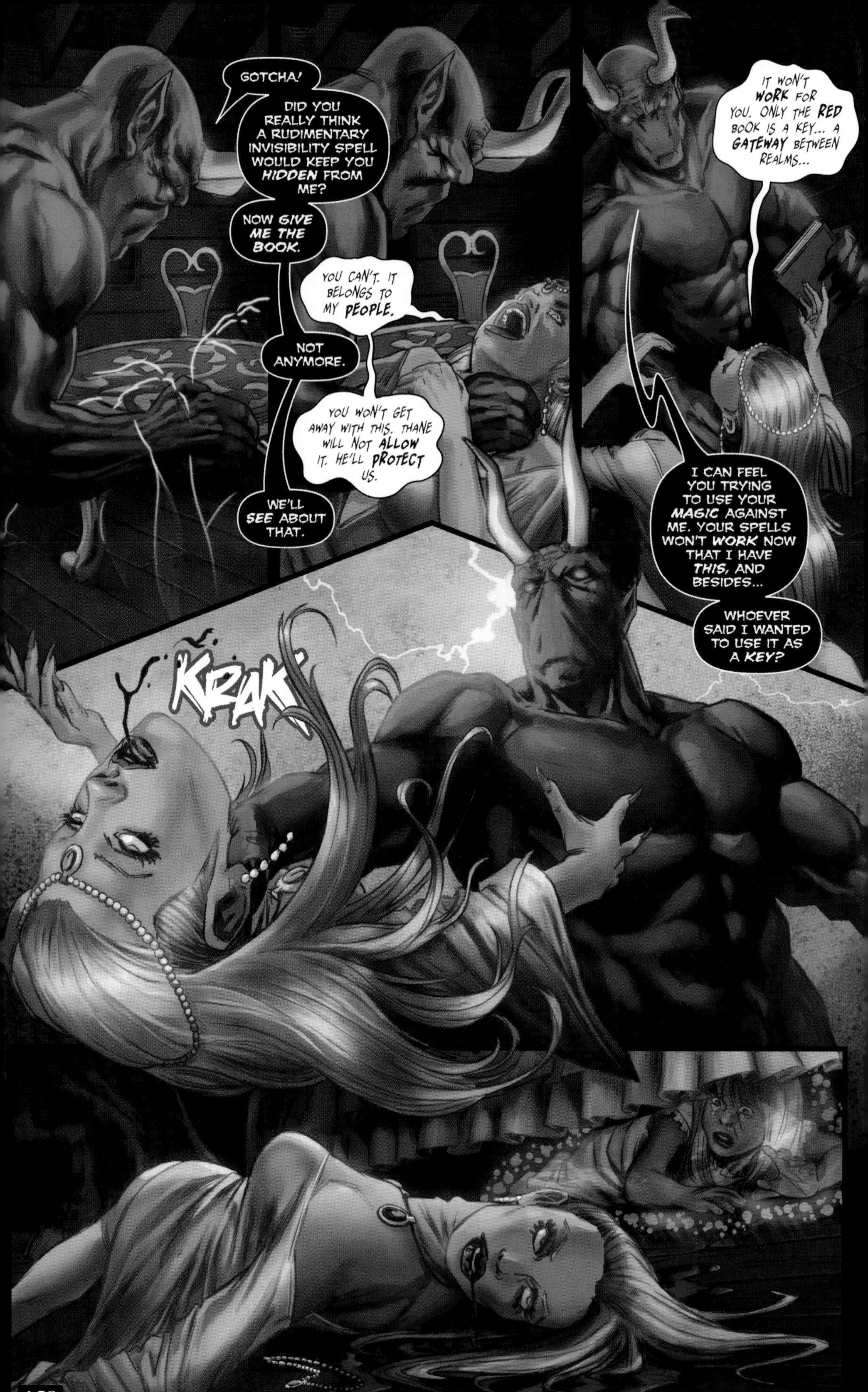
GOTCHA!
DID YOU REALLY THINK A RUDIMENTARY INVISIBILITY SPELL WOULD KEEP YOU HIDDEN FROM ME?
NOW GIVE ME THE BOOK.
YOU CAN'T. IT BELONGS TO MY PEOPLE.
NOT ANYMORE.
YOU WON'T GET AWAY WITH THIS. THANE WILL NOT ALLOW IT. HE'LL PROTECT US.
WE'LL SEE ABOUT THAT.
IT WON'T WORK FOR YOU. ONLY THE RED BOOK IS A KEY... A GATEWAY BETWEEN REALMS...
I CAN FEEL YOU TRYING TO USE YOUR MAGIC AGAINST ME. YOUR SPELLS WON'T WORK NOW THAT I HAVE THIS, AND BESIDES...
WHOEVER SAID I WANTED TO USE IT AS A KEY?
KRAK

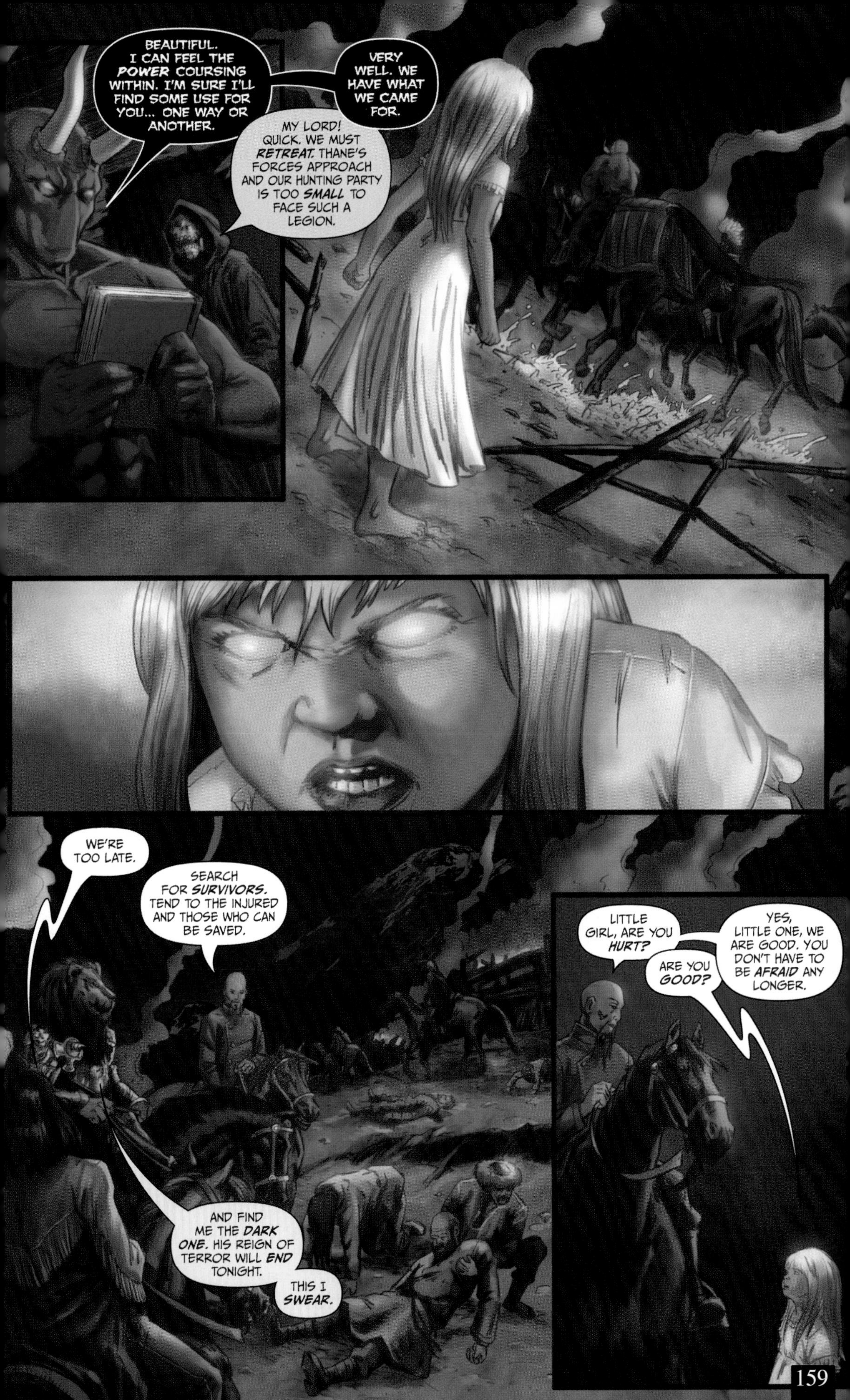

BEAUTIFUL. I CAN FEEL THE POWER COURSING WITHIN. I'M SURE I'LL FIND SOME USE FOR YOU... ONE WAY OR ANOTHER.
VERY WELL. WE HAVE WHAT WE CAME FOR.
MY LORD! QUICK. WE MUST RETREAT. THANE'S FORCES APPROACH AND OUR HUNTING PARTY IS TOO SMALL TO FACE SUCH A LEGION.
WE'RE TOO LATE.
SEARCH FOR SURVIVORS. TEND TO THE INJURED AND THOSE WHO CAN BE SAVED.
AND FIND ME THE DARK ONE. HIS REIGN OF TERROR WILL END TONIGHT.
THIS I SWEAR.
LITTLE GIRL, ARE YOU HURT?
ARE YOU GOOD?
YES, LITTLE ONE, WE ARE GOOD. YOU DON'T HAVE TO BE AFRAID ANY LONGER.

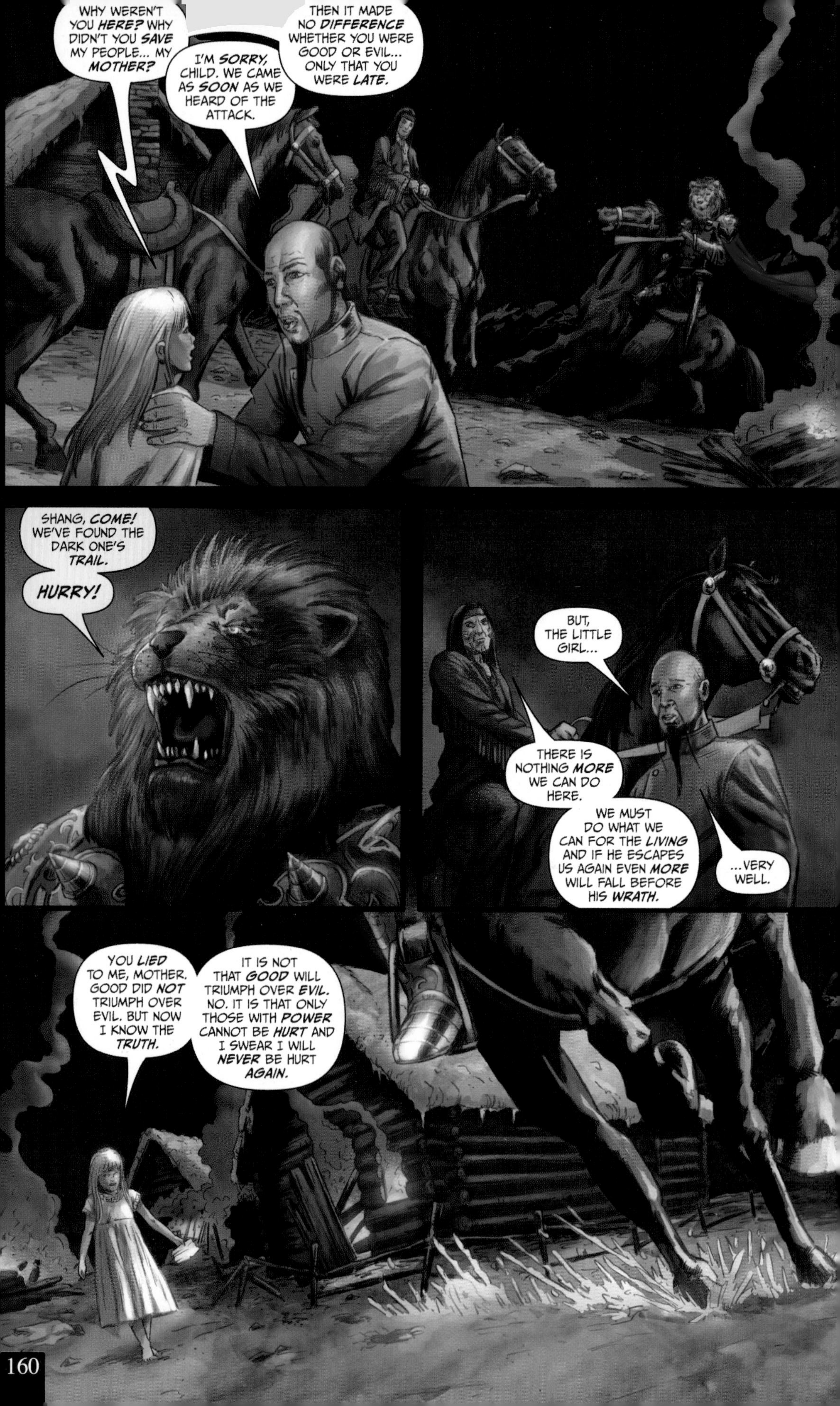
WHY WEREN'T YOU HERE? WHY DIDN'T YOU SAVE MY PEOPLE... MY MOTHER?
I'M SORRY, CHILD. WE CAME AS SOON AS WE HEARD OF THE ATTACK.
THEN IT MADE NO DIFFERENCE WHETHER YOU WERE GOOD OR EVIL... ONLY THAT YOU WERE LATE.
SHANG, COME! WE'VE FOUND THE DARK ONE'S TRAIL.
HURRY!
BUT, THE LITTLE GIRL...
THERE IS NOTHING MORE WE CAN DO HERE.
WE MUST DO WHAT WE CAN FOR THE LIVING AND IF HE ESCAPES US AGAIN EVEN MORE WILL FALL BEFORE HIS WRATH.
...VERY WELL.
YOU LIED TO ME, MOTHER. GOOD DID NOT TRIUMPH OVER EVIL. BUT NOW I KNOW THE TRUTH.
IT IS NOT THAT GOOD WILL TRIUMPH OVER EVIL. NO. IT IS THAT ONLY THOSE WITH POWER CANNOT BE HURT AND I SWEAR I WILL NEVER BE HURT AGAIN.

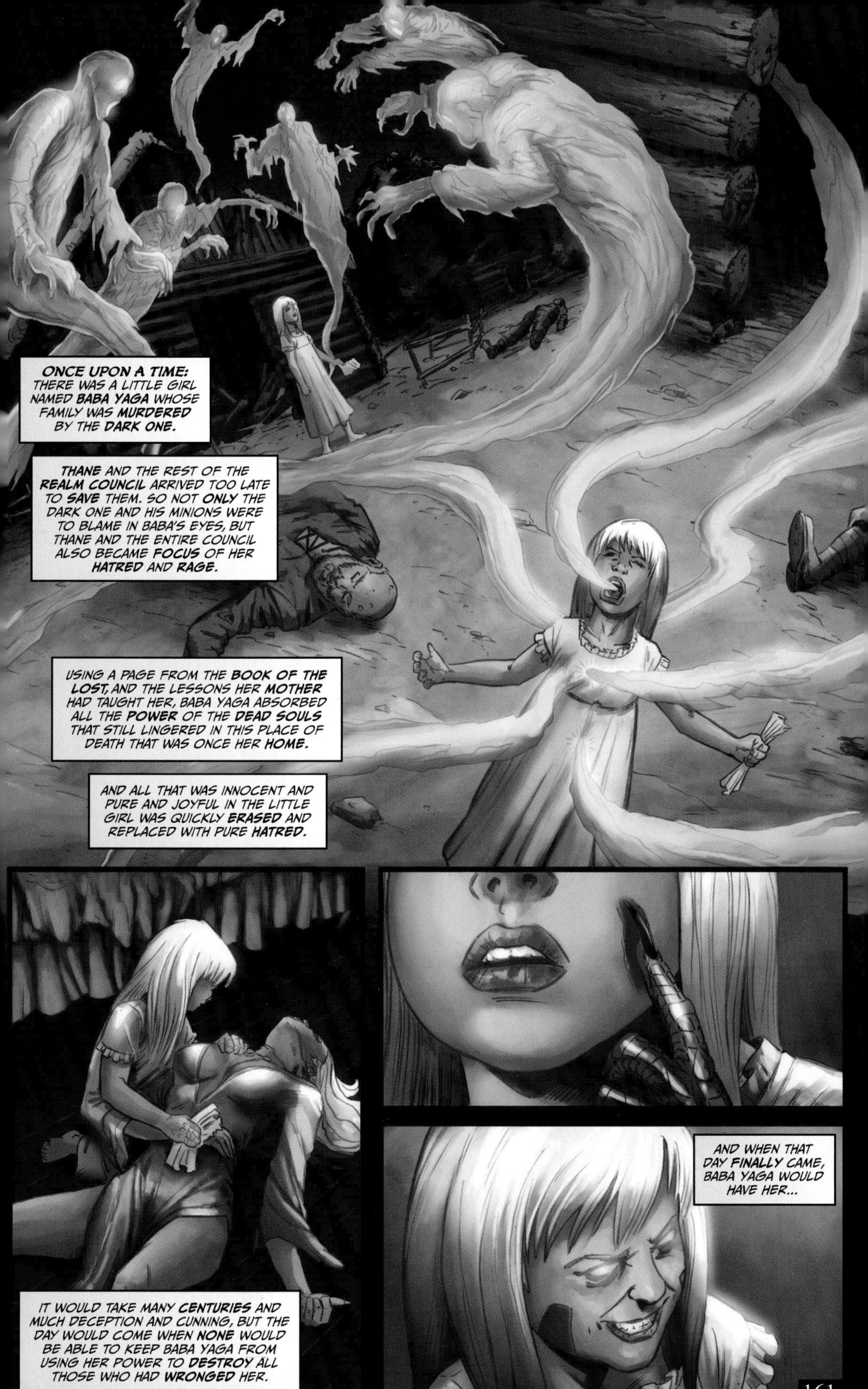
ONCE UPON A TIME: THERE WAS A LITTLE GIRL NAMED BABA YAGA WHOSE FAMILY WAS MURDERED BY THE DARK ONE.
THANE AND THE REST OF THE REALM COUNCIL ARRIVED TOO LATE TO SAVE THEM. SO NOT ONLY THE DARK ONE AND HIS MINIONS WERE TO BLAME IN BABA'S EYES, BUT THANE AND THE ENTIRE COUNCIL ALSO BECAME FOCUS OF HER HATRED AND RAGE.
USING A PAGE FROM THE BOOK OF THE LOST, AND THE LESSONS HER MOTHER HAD TAUGHT HER, BABA YAGA ABSORBED ALL THE POWER OF THE DEAD SOULS THAT STILL LINGERED IN THIS PLACE OF DEATH THAT WAS ONCE HER HOME.
AND ALL THAT WAS INNOCENT AND PURE AND JOYFUL IN THE LITTLE GIRL WAS QUICKLY ERASED AND REPLACED WITH PURE HATRED.
IT WOULD TAKE MANY CENTURIES AND MUCH DECEPTION AND CUNNING, BUT THE DAY WOULD COME WHEN NONE WOULD BE ABLE TO KEEP BABA YAGA FROM USING HER POWER TO DESTROY ALL THOSE WHO HAD WRONGED HER.
AND WHEN THAT DAY FINALLY CAME, BABA YAGA WOULD HAVE HER...

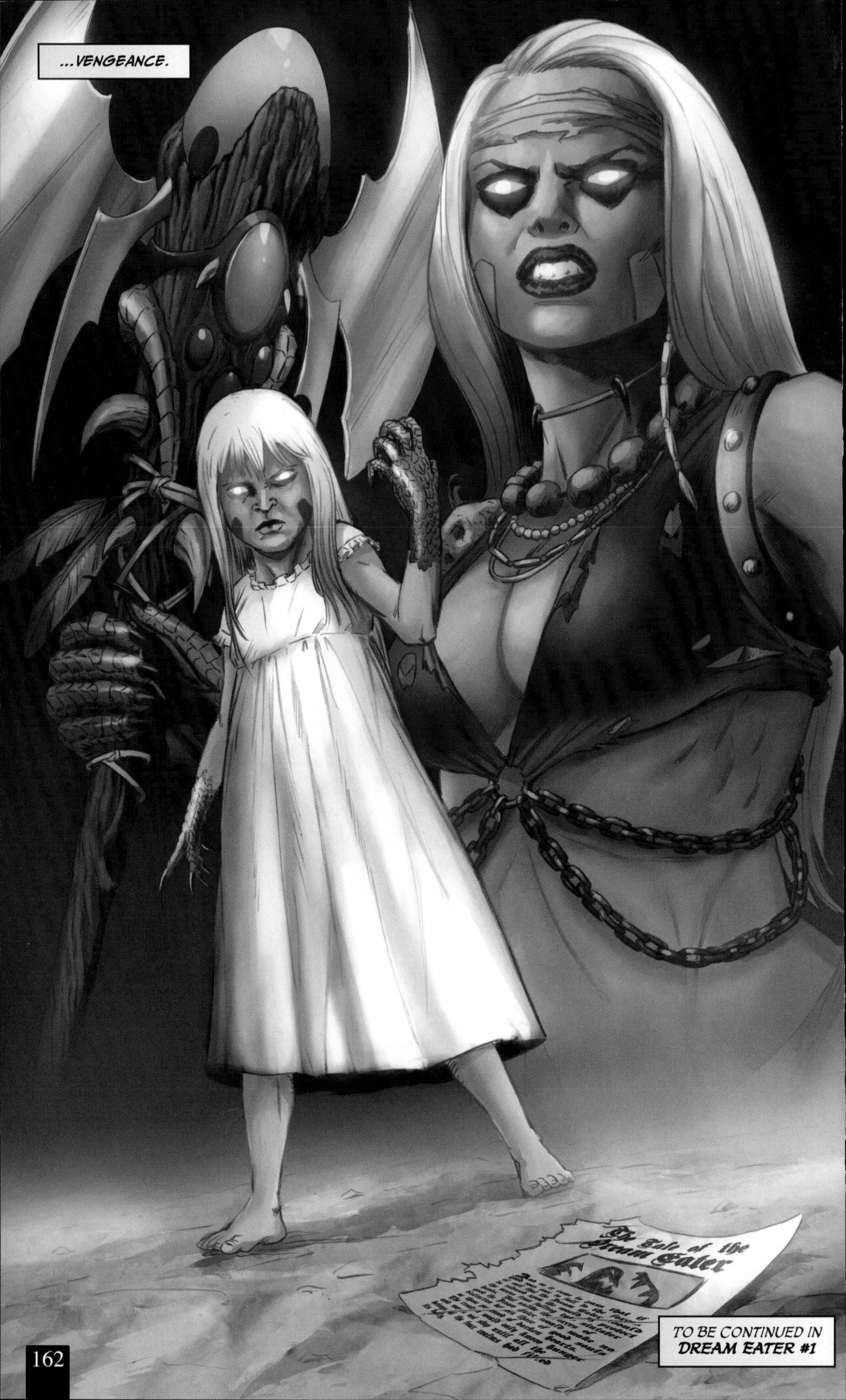
...VENGEANCE.
The Tale of the Dream Eater
TO BE CONTINUED IN
DREAM EATER #1

Grimm Fairy Tales

Volume 10

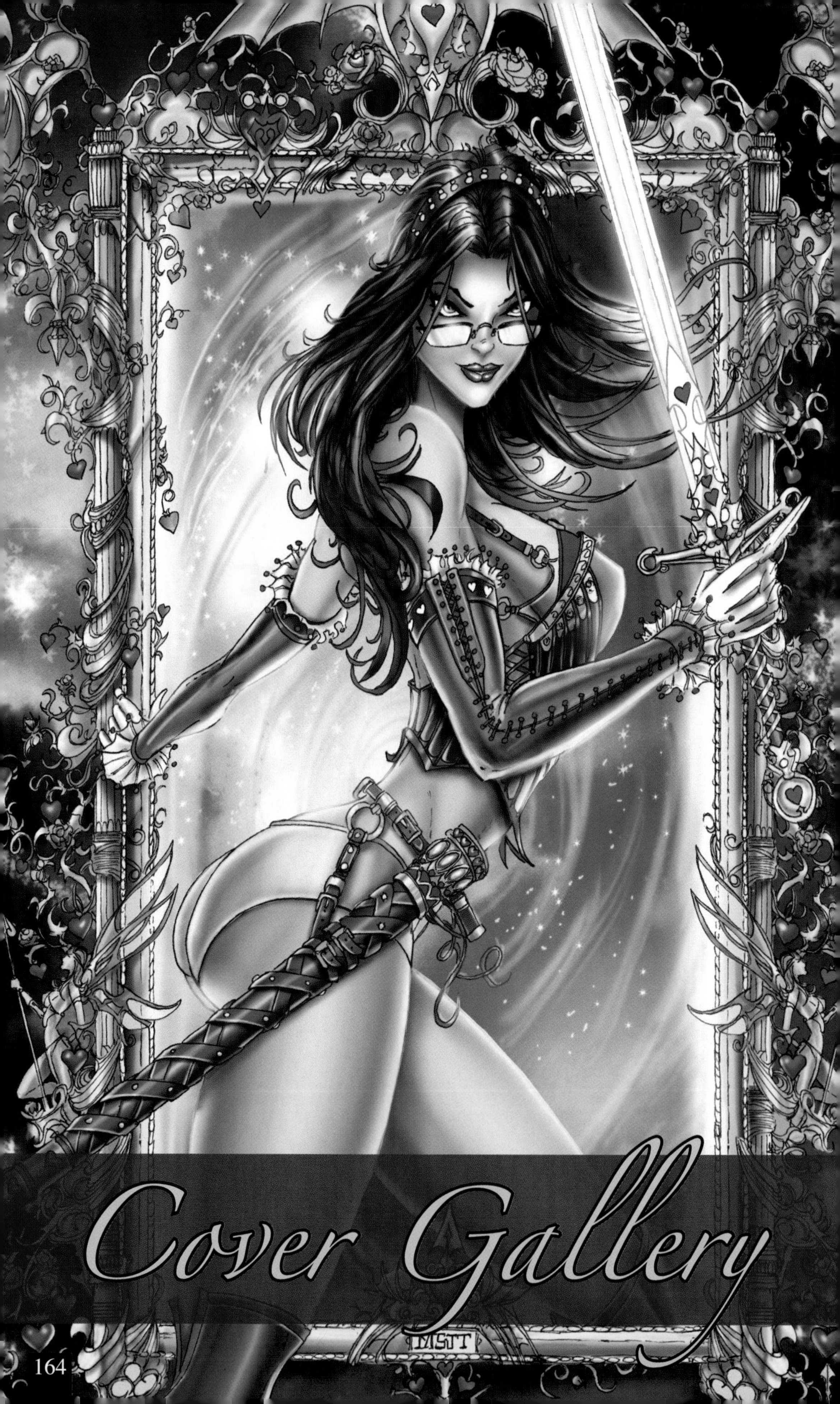

Cover Gallery

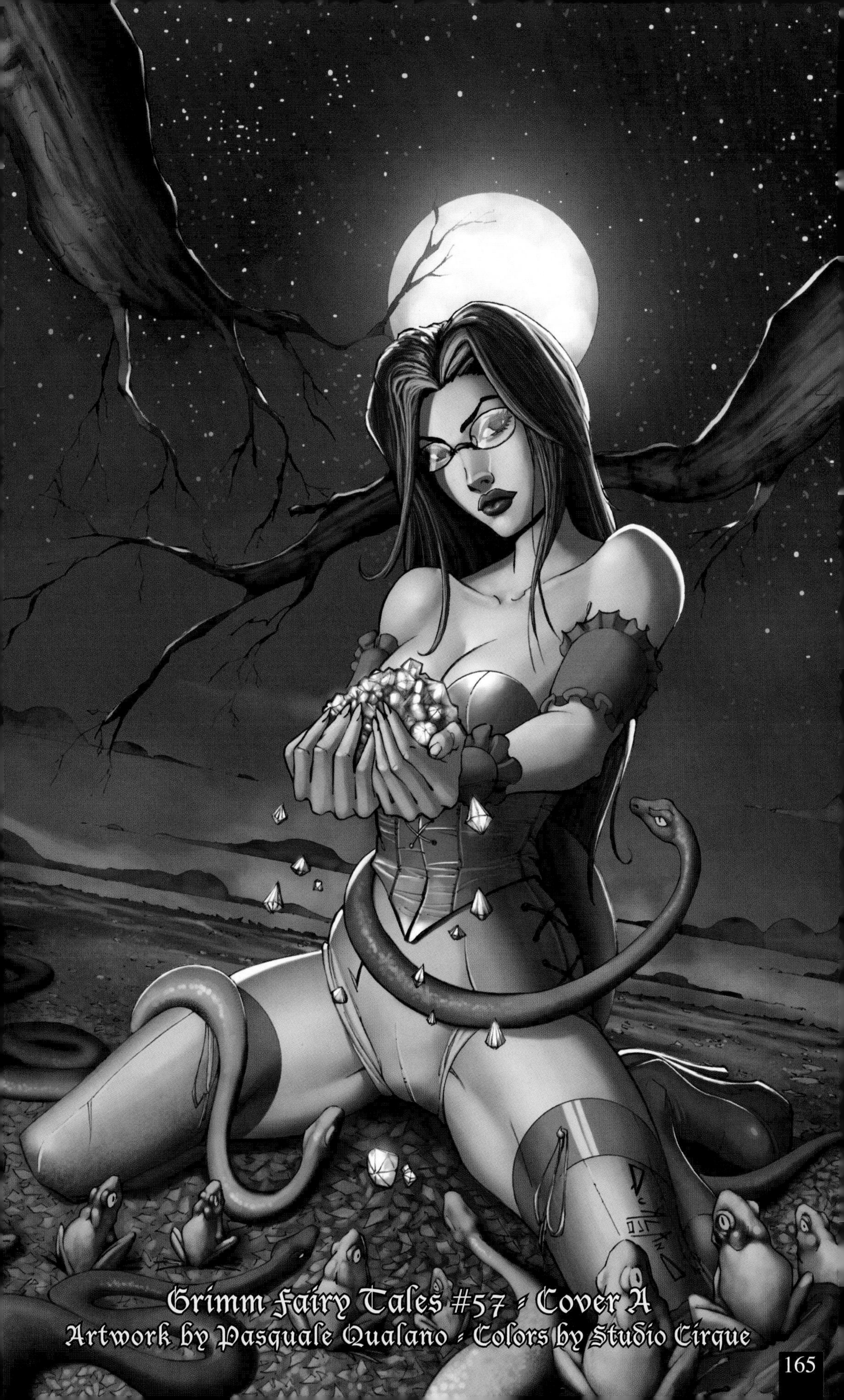

Grimm Fairy Tales #57 - Cover A
Artwork by Pasquale Qualano - Colors by Studio Cirque

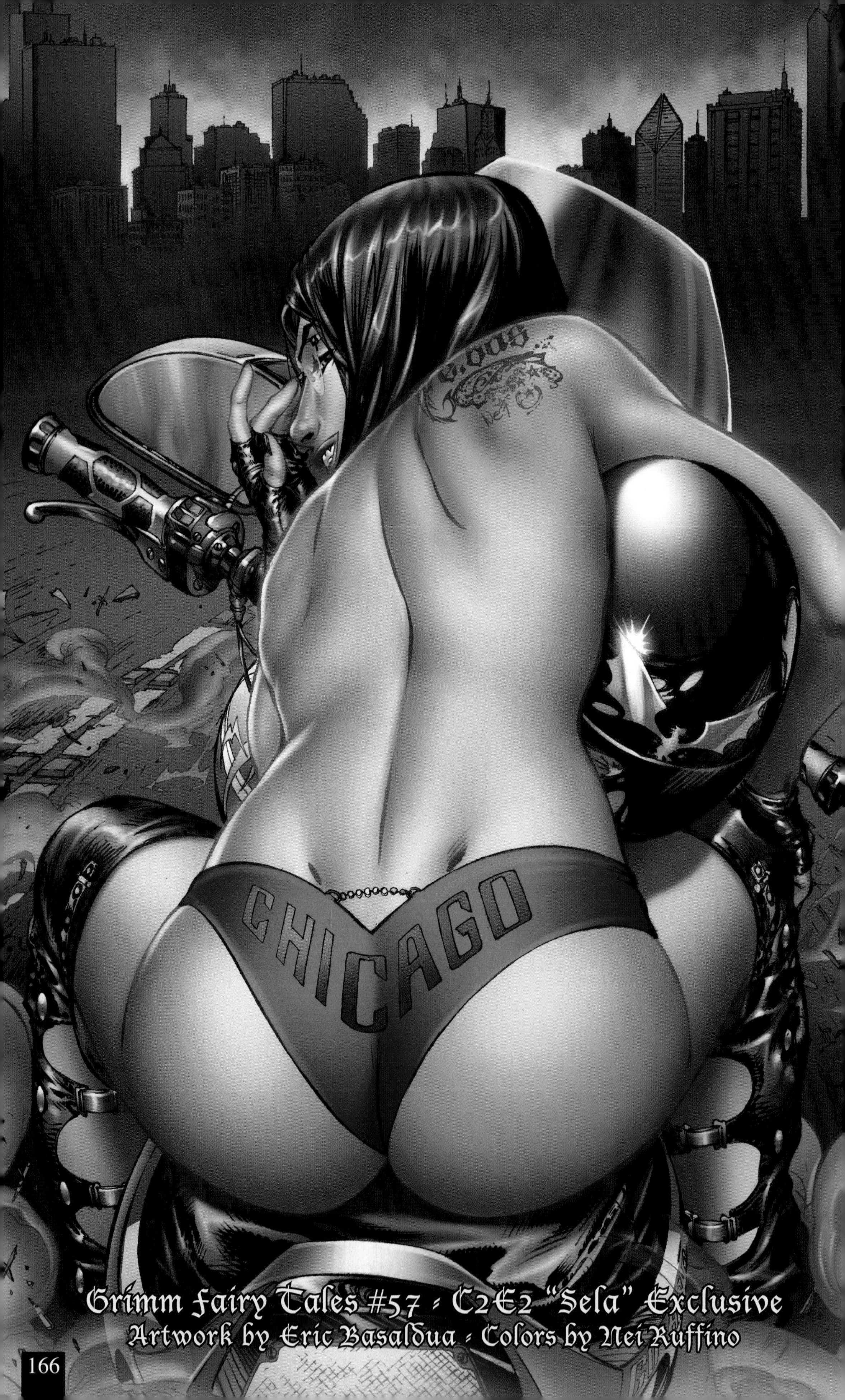
CHICAGO

Grimm Fairy Tales #57 - C2E2 "Sela" Exclusive
Artwork by Eric Basaldua - Colors by Nei Ruffino

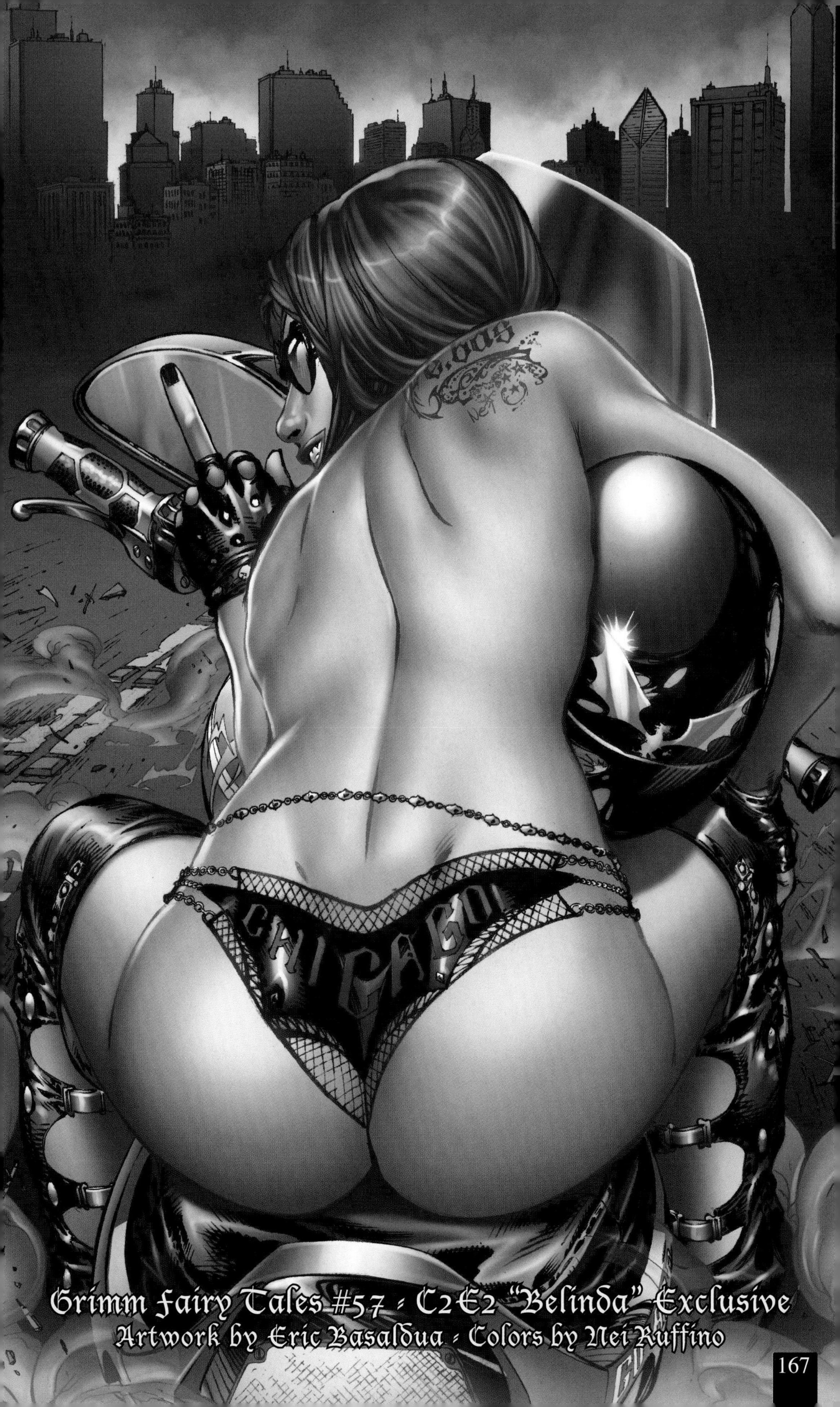

Grimm Fairy Tales #57 - C2E2 "Belinda" Exclusive
Artwork by Eric Basaldua - Colors by Nei Ruffino

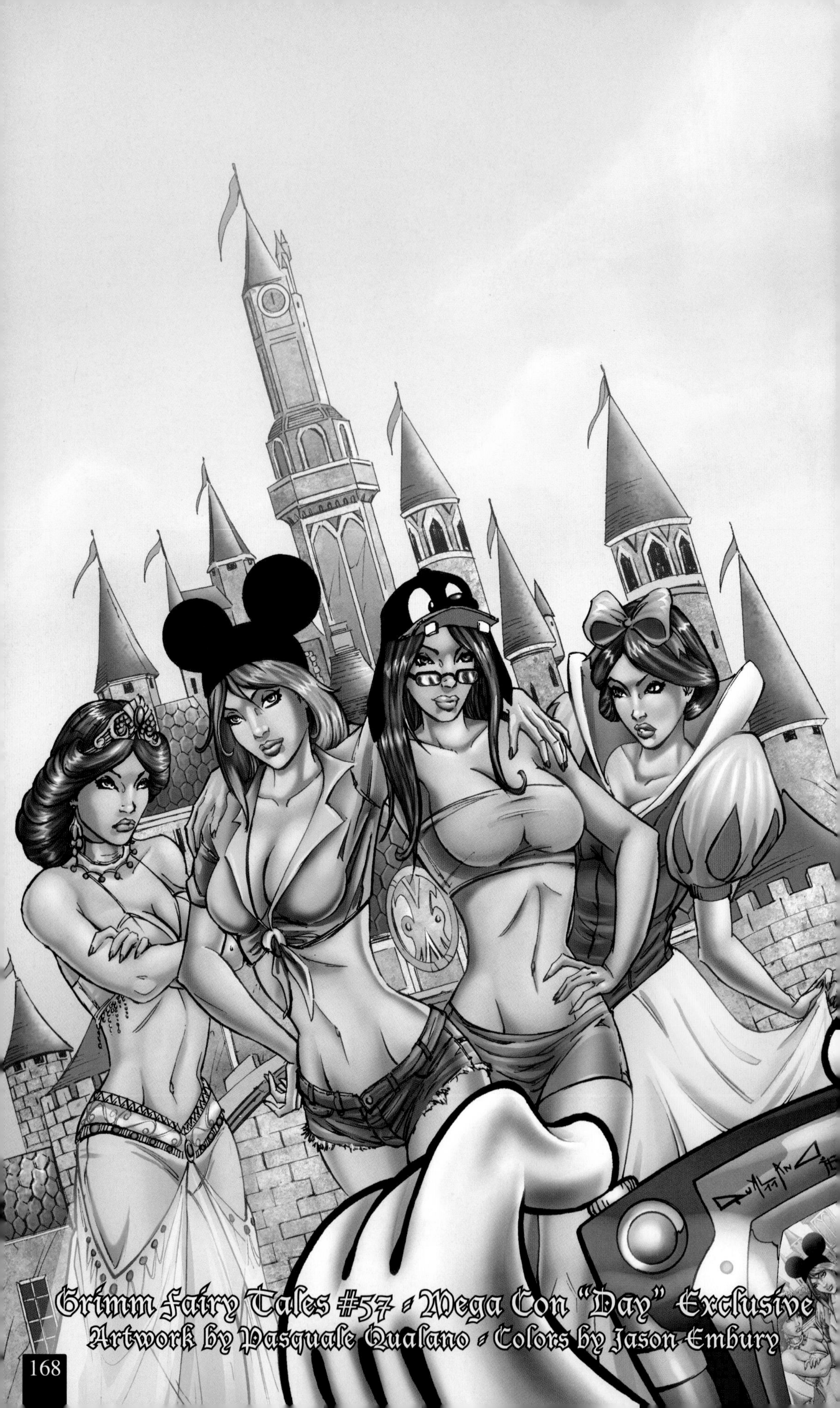

Grimm Fairy Tales #57 - Mega Con "Day" Exclusive
Artwork by Pasquale Qualano - Colors by Jason Embury

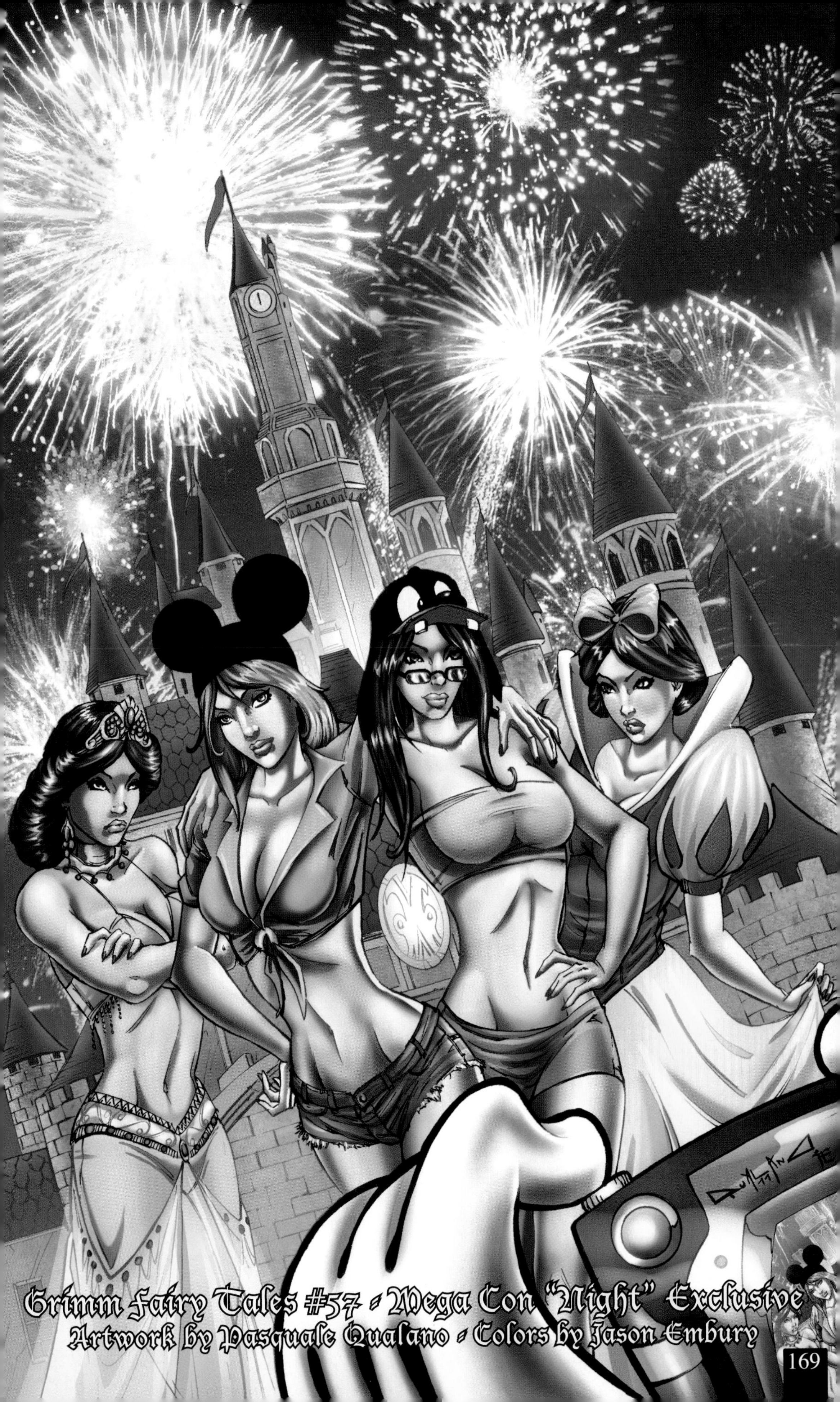

Grimm Fairy Tales #57 - Mega Con "Night" Exclusive
Artwork by Pasquale Qualano - Colors by Jason Embury

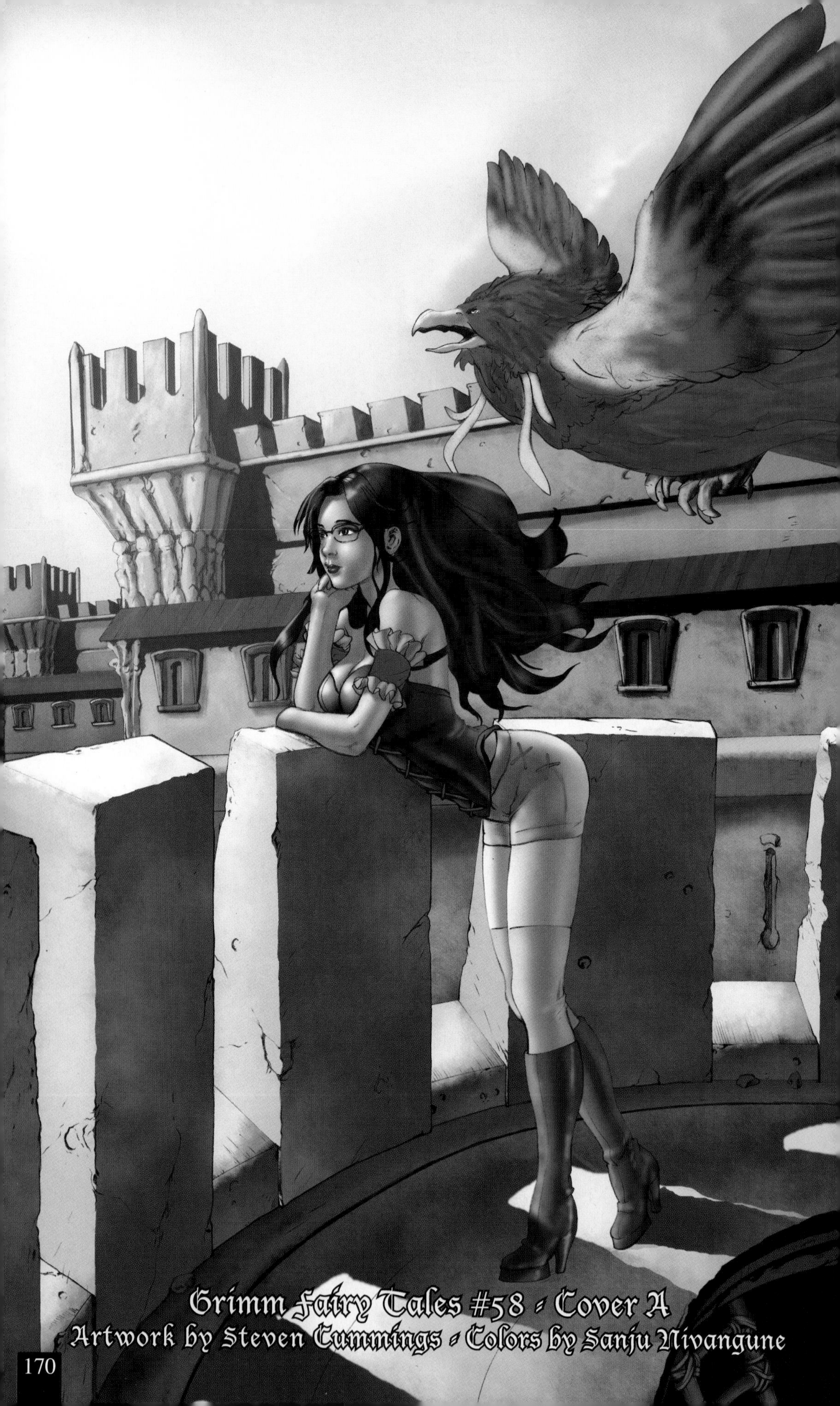

Grimm Fairy Tales #58 - Cover A
Artwork by Steven Cummings - Colors by Sanju Nivangune

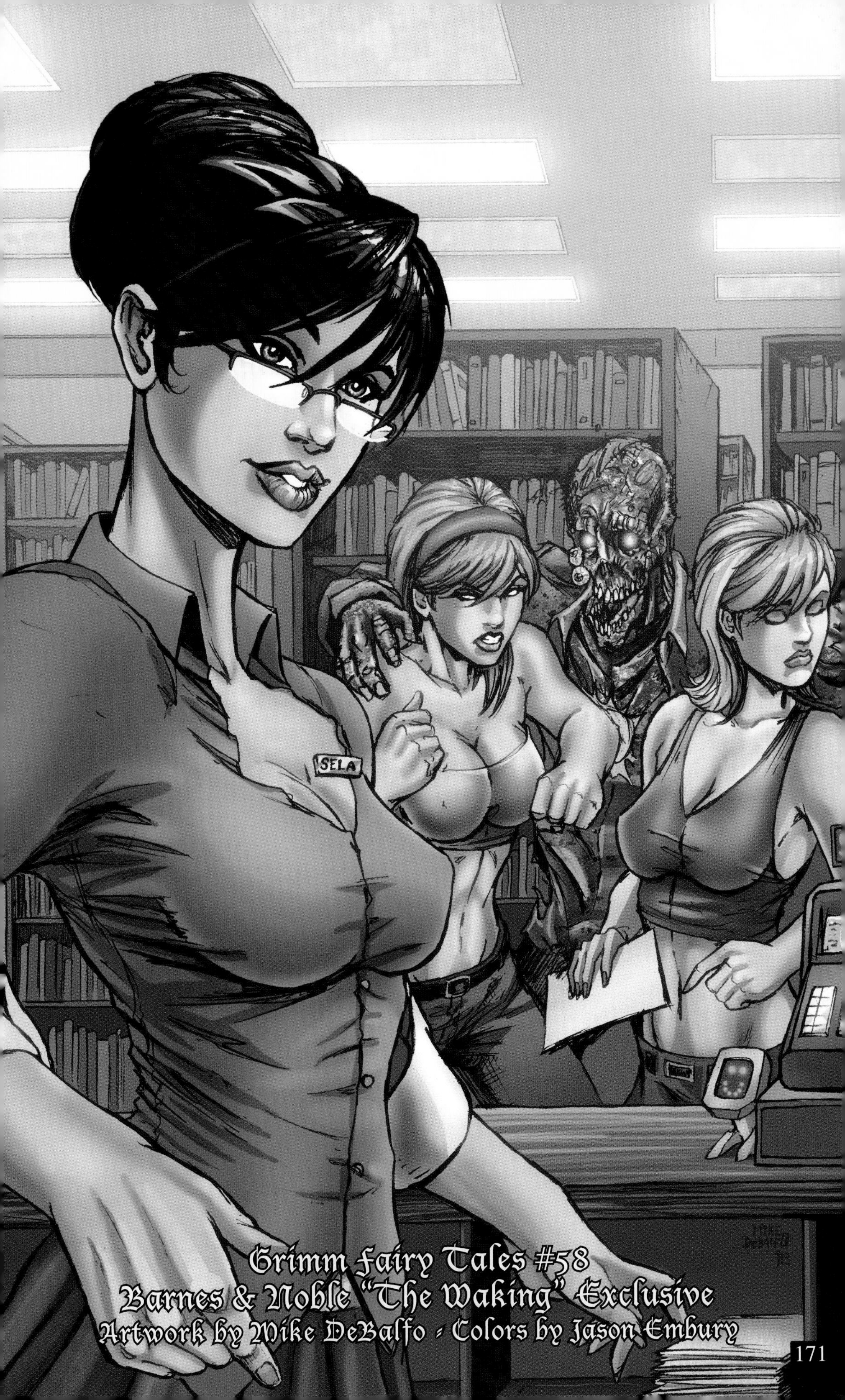
SELA

Grimm Fairy Tales #58
Barnes & Noble "The Waking" Exclusive
Artwork by Mike DeBalfo - Colors by Jason Embury

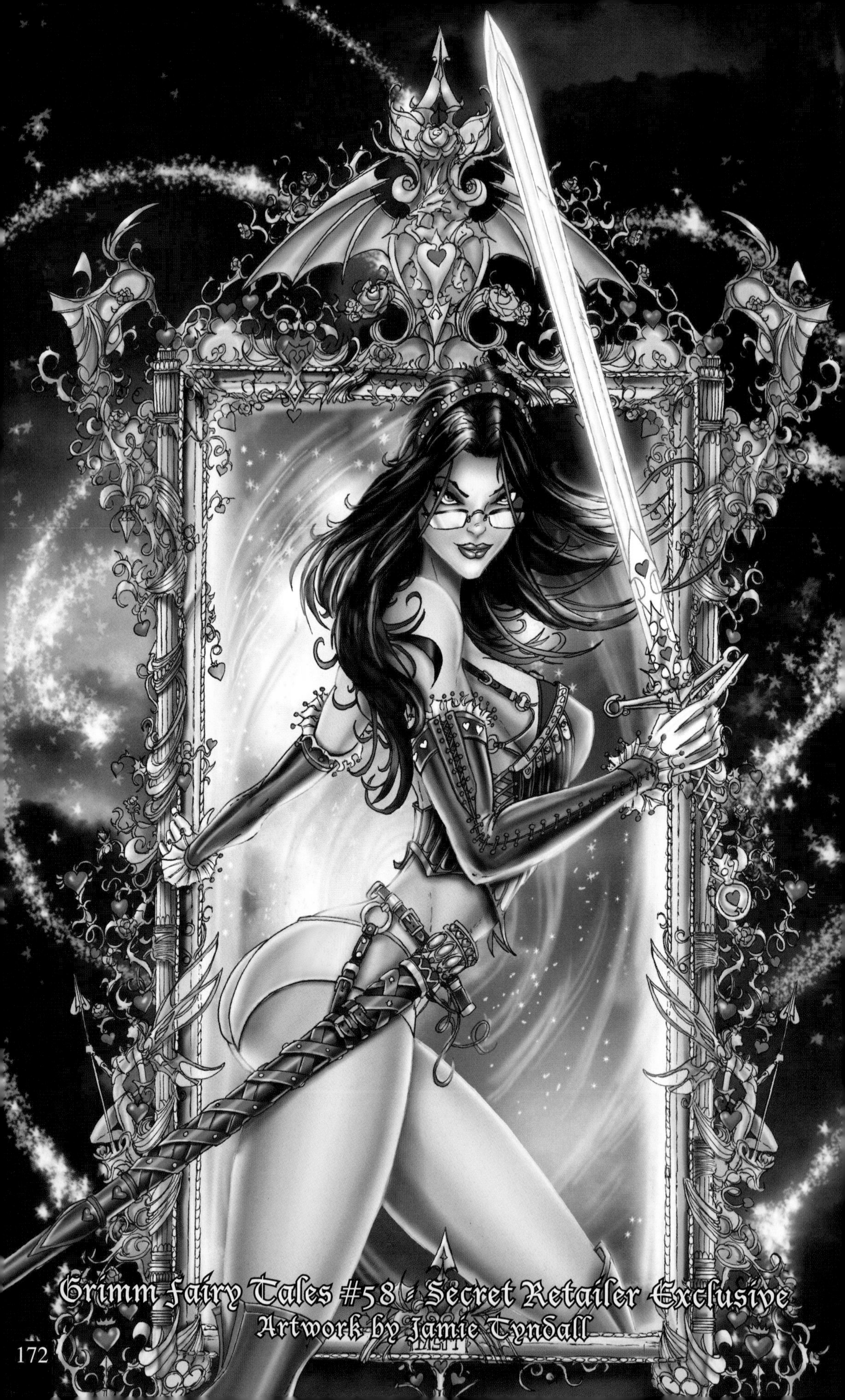

Grimm Fairy Tales #58 - Secret Retailer Exclusive
Artwork by Jamie Tyndall

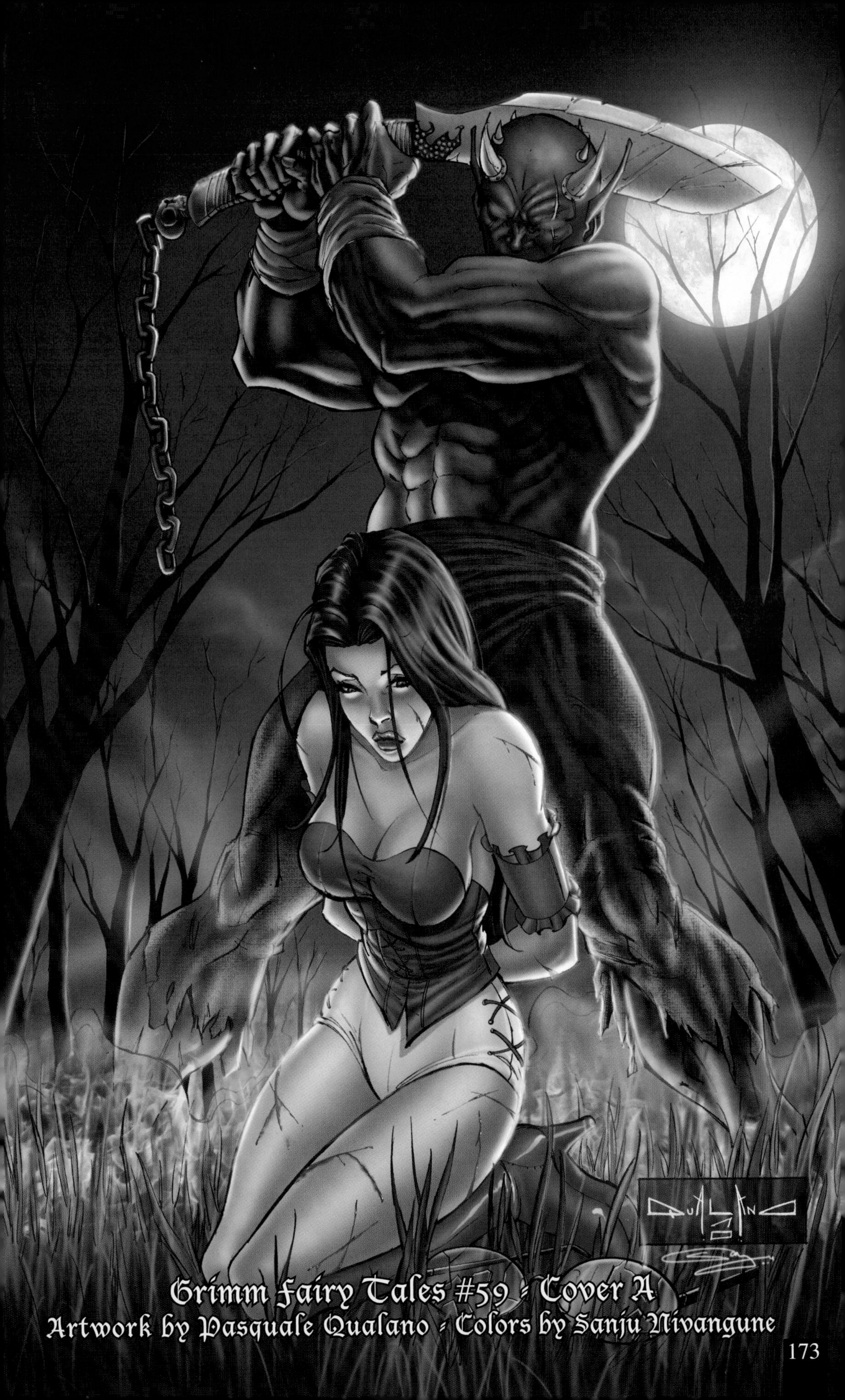

Grimm Fairy Tales #59 - Cover A
Artwork by Pasquale Qualano - Colors by Sanju Nivangune

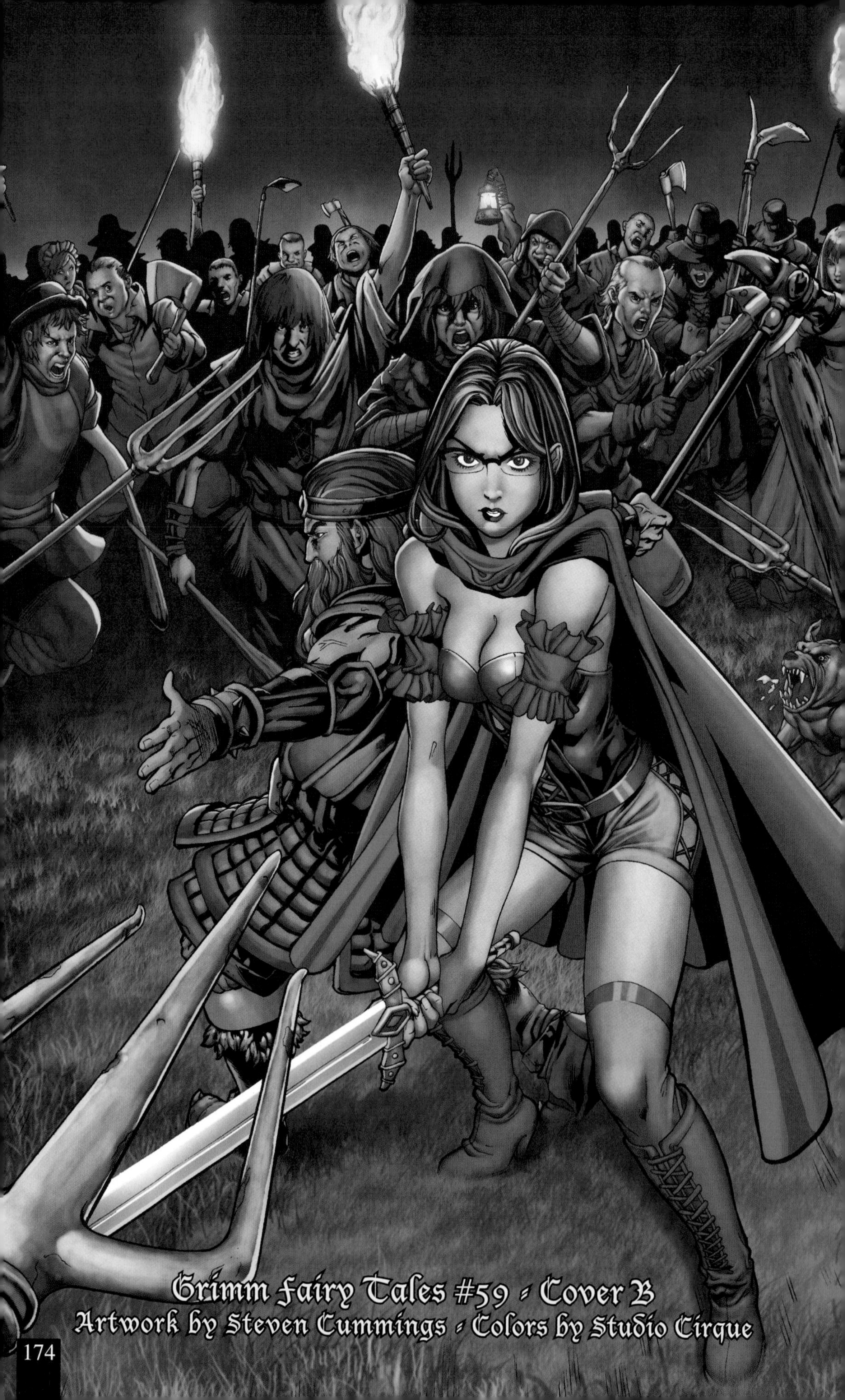

Grimm Fairy Tales #59 - Cover B
Artwork by Steven Cummings - Colors by Studio Cirque

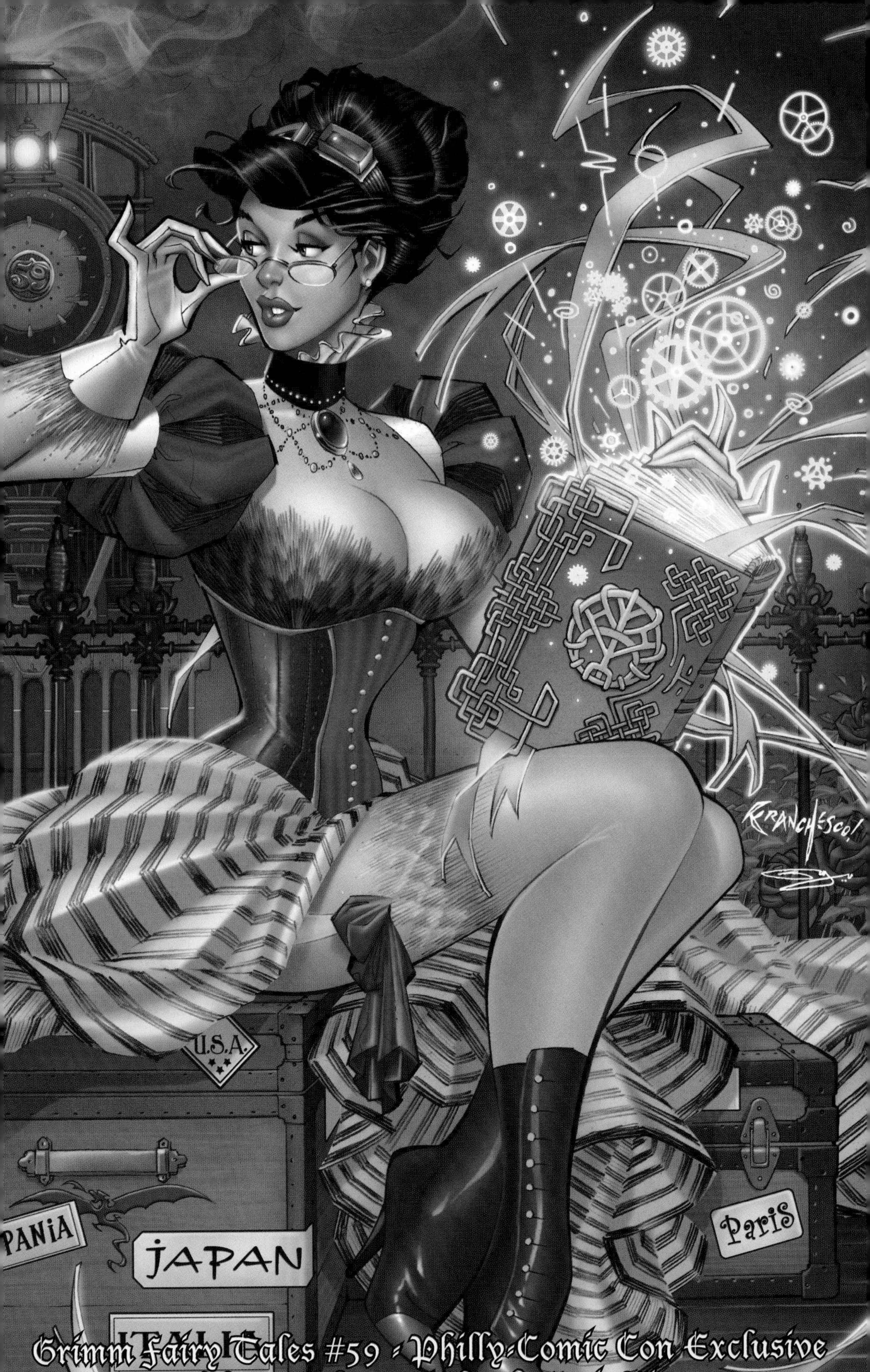
U.S.A.
PANIA
JAPAN
Paris
FRANCHESCO!

Grimm Fairy Tales #59 - Philly Comic Con Exclusive
Artwork by Franchesco - Colors by Sanju Nivangune

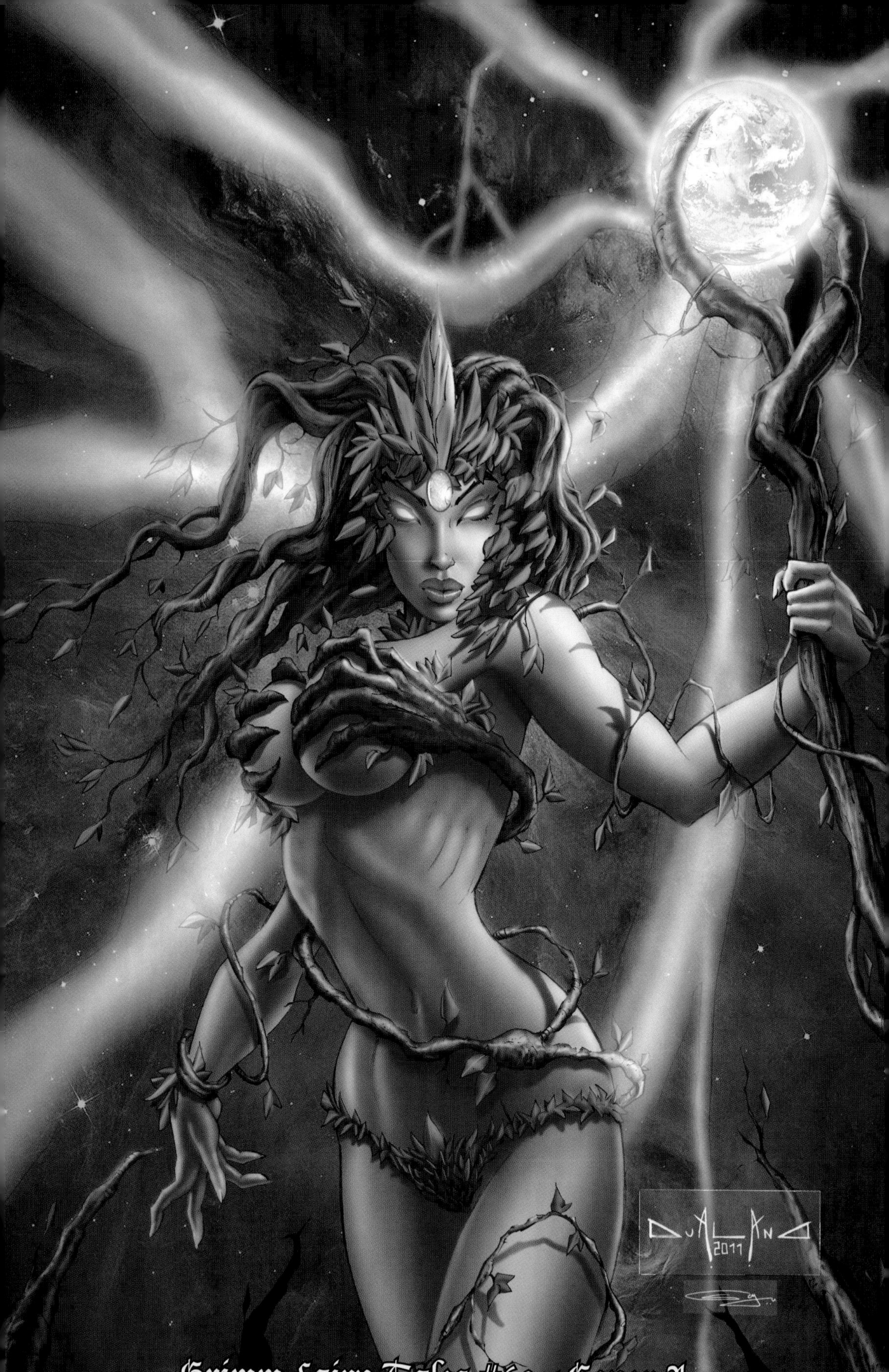

Grimm Fairy Tales #60 - Cover A
Artwork by Pasquale Qualano - Colors by Sanju Nivangune

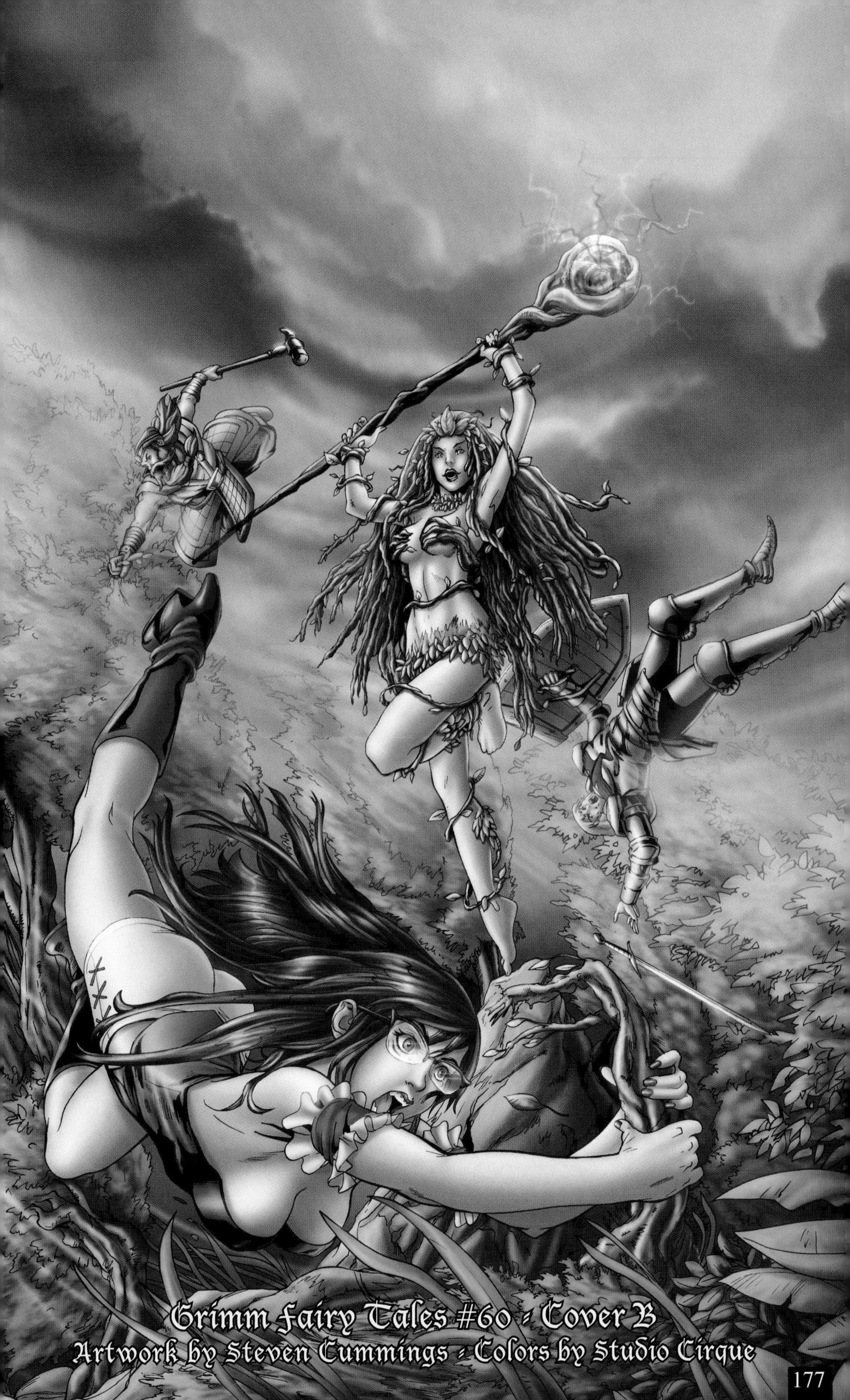

Grimm Fairy Tales #60 - Cover B
Artwork by Steven Cummings - Colors by Studio Cirque

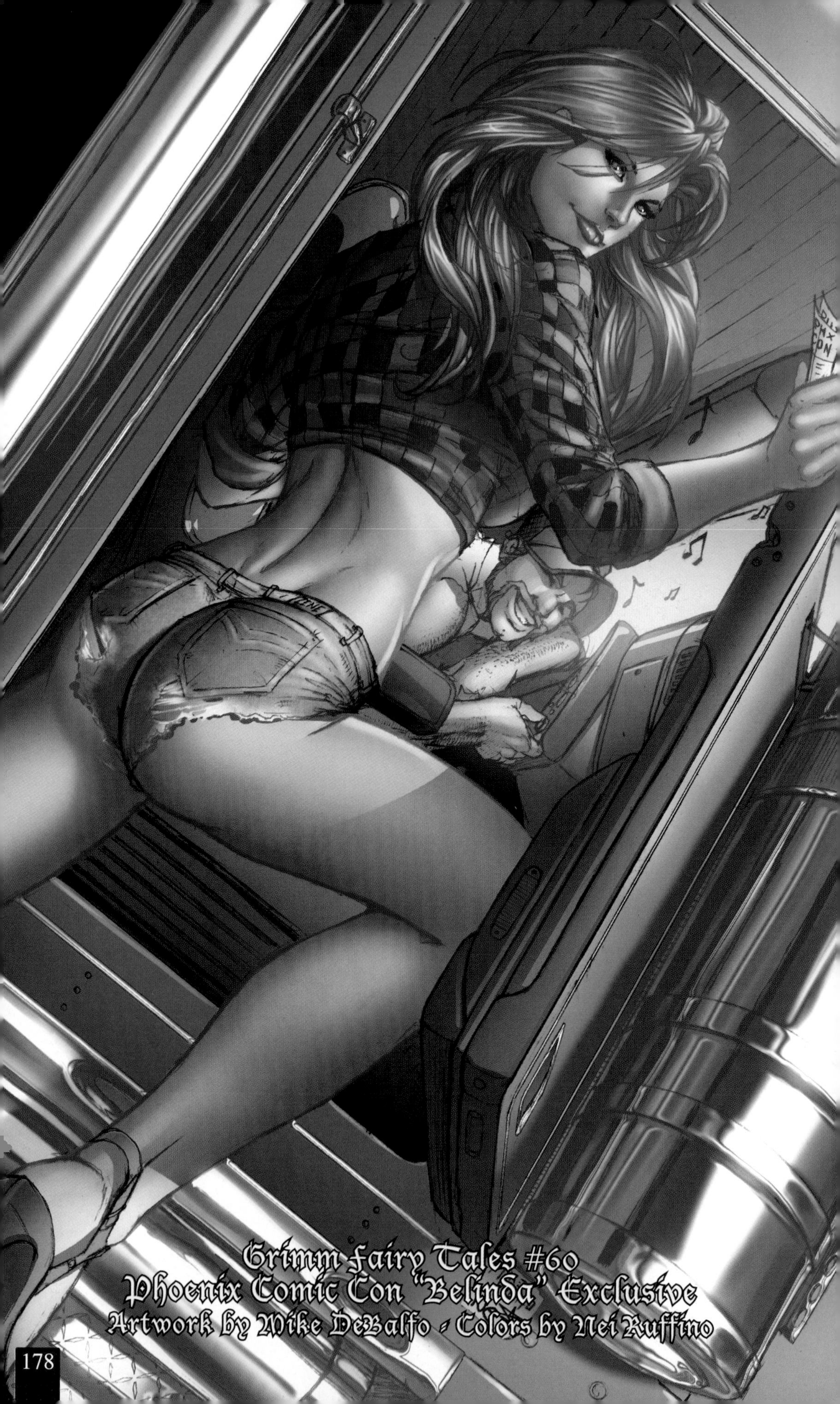

Grimm Fairy Tales #60
Phoenix Comic Con "Belinda" Exclusive
Artwork by Mike DeBalfo - Colors by Nei Ruffino

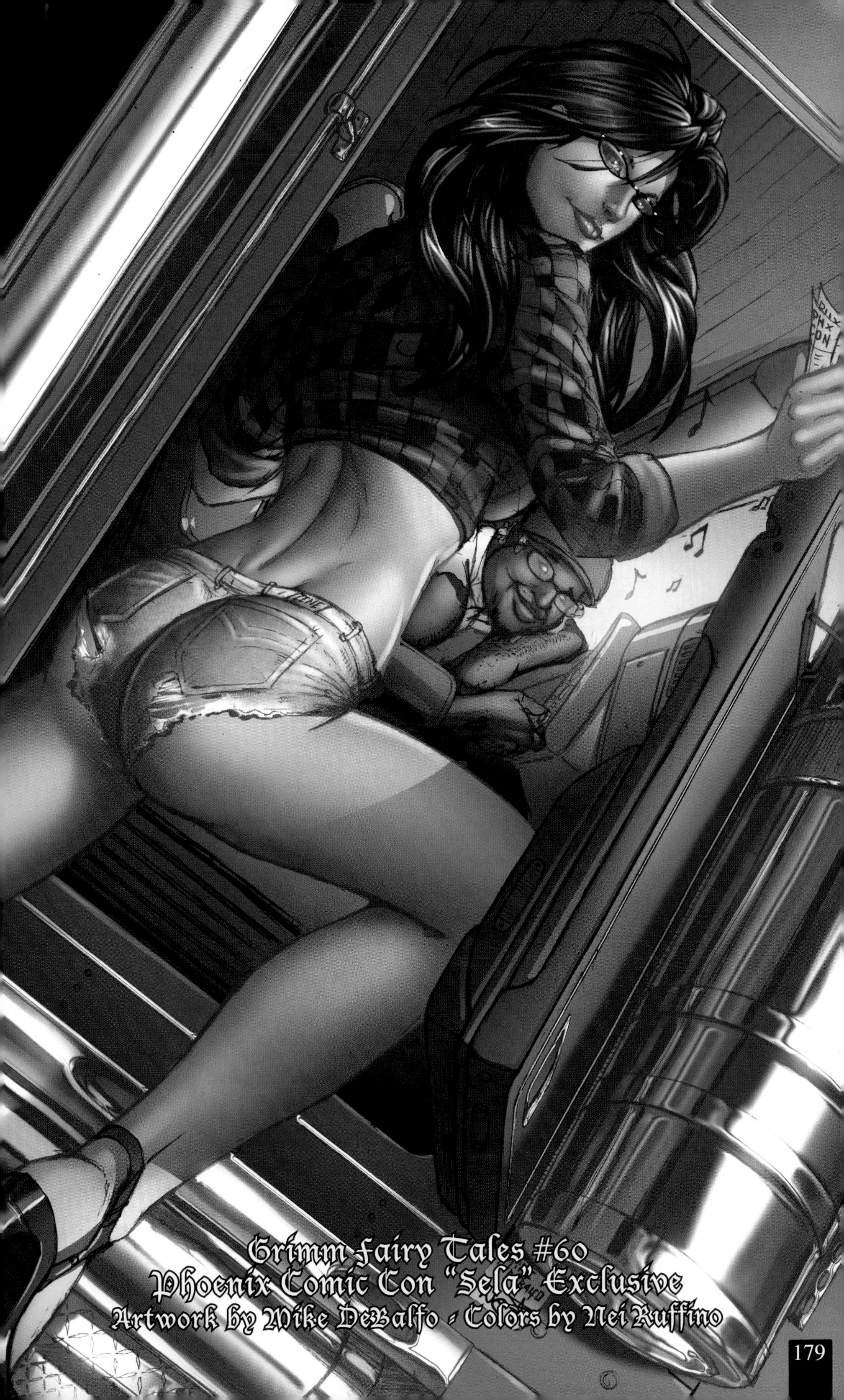

Grimm Fairy Tales #60
Phoenix Comic Con "Sela" Exclusive
Artwork by Mike DeBalfo - Colors by Nei Ruffino

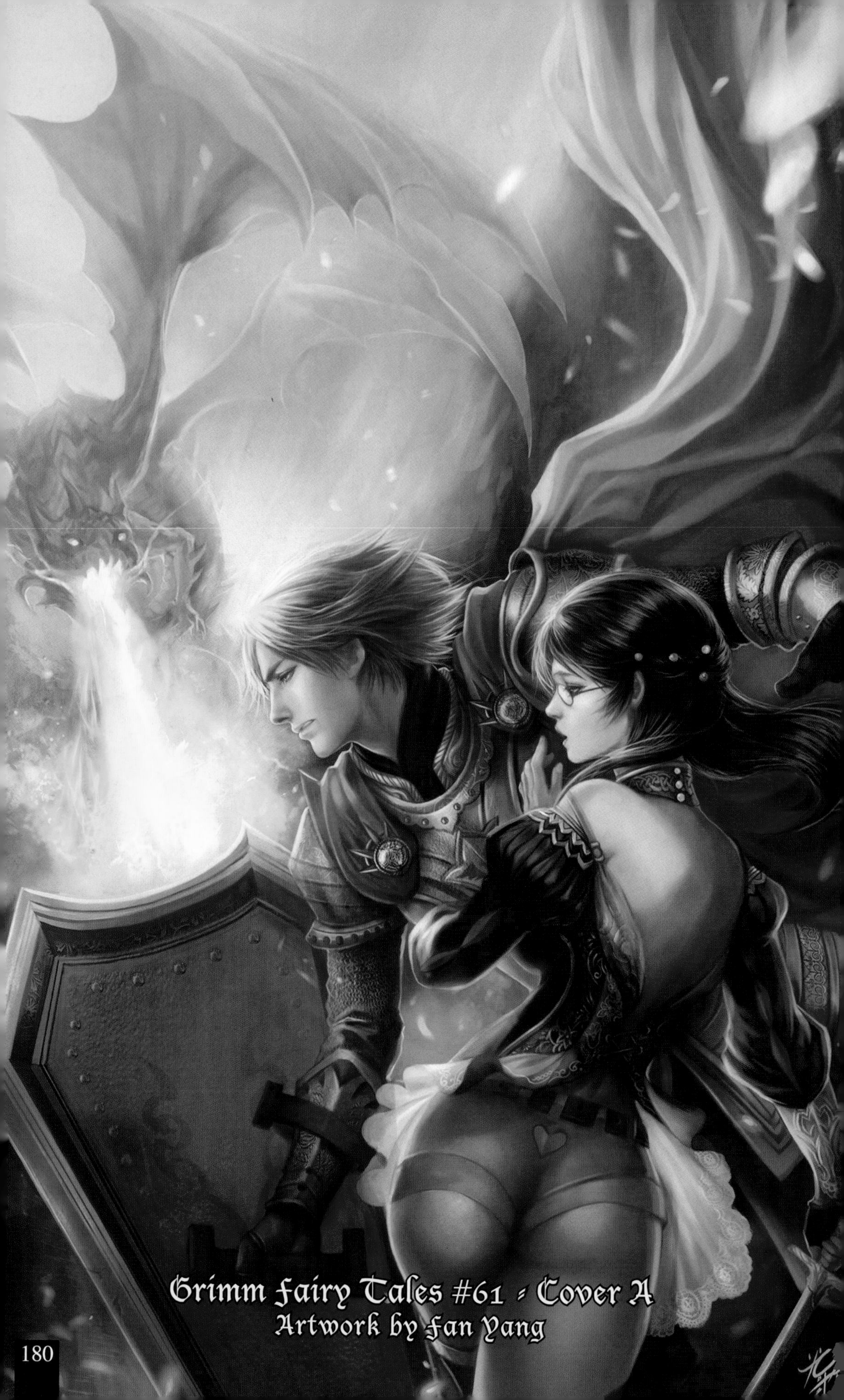

Grimm Fairy Tales #61 - Cover A
Artwork by Fan Yang

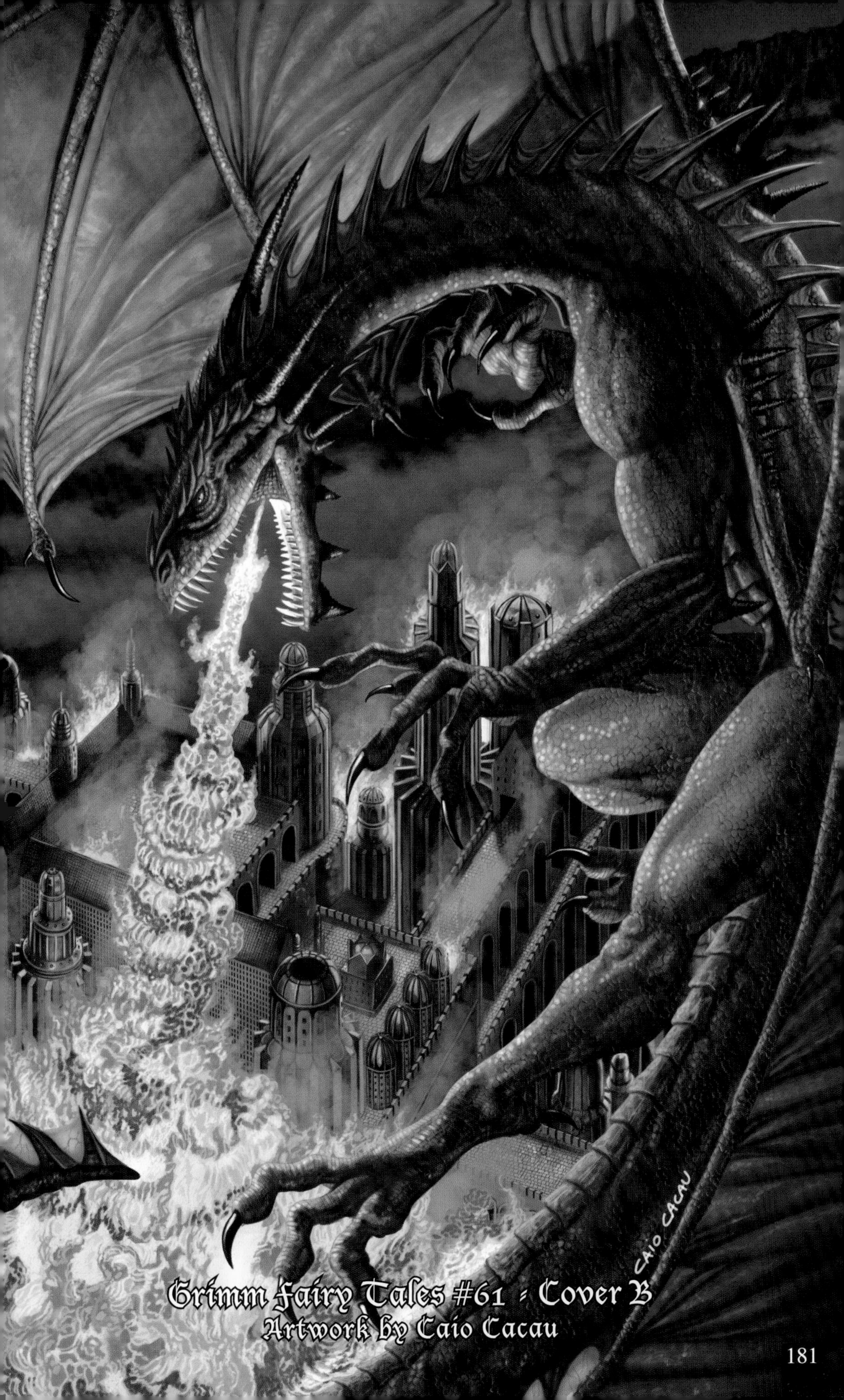
CAIO CACAU

Grimm Fairy Tales #61 - Cover B
Artwork by Caio Cacau

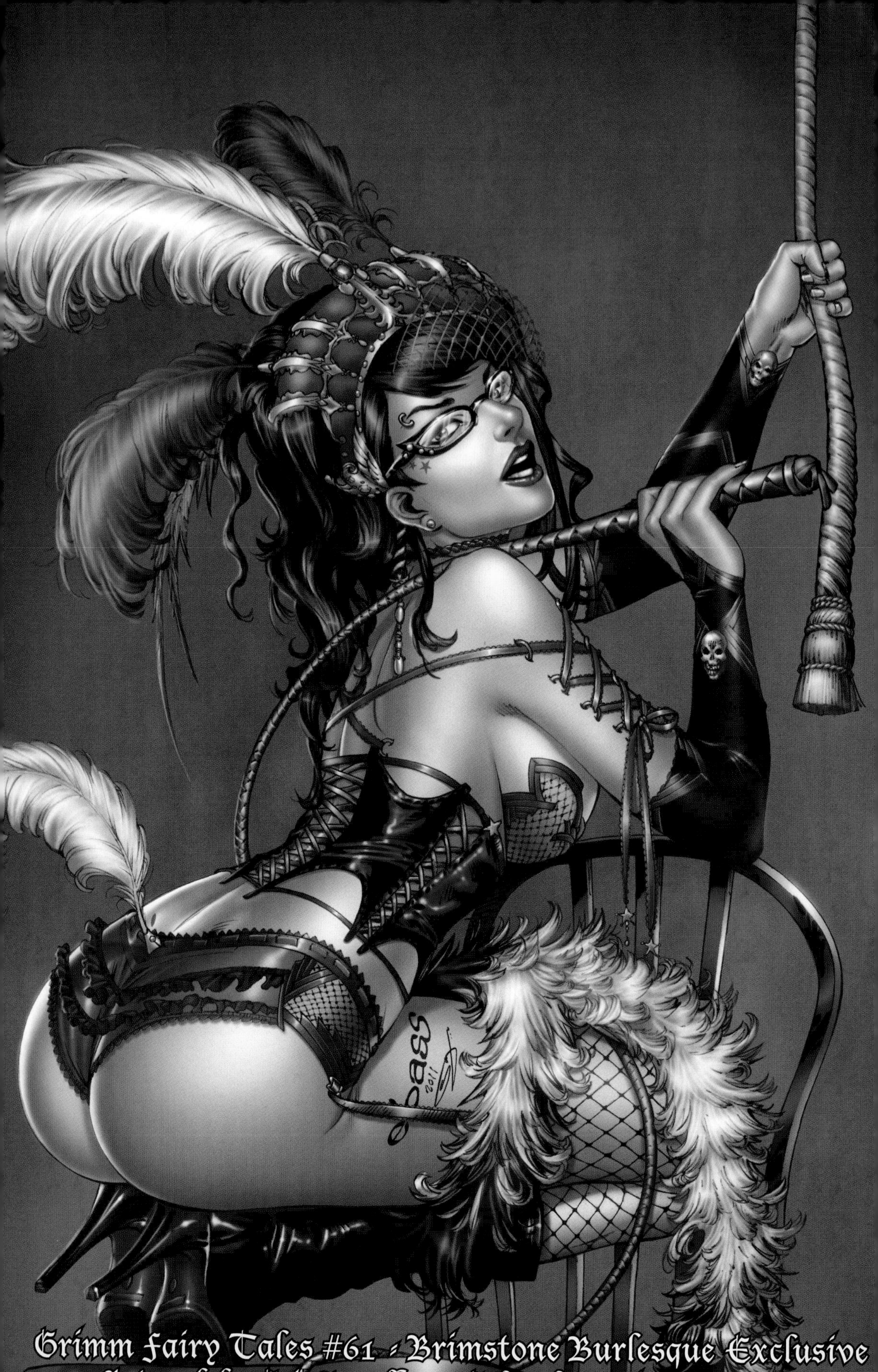

Grimm Fairy Tales #61 - Brimstone Burlesque Exclusive
Artwork by Eric Basaldua - Colors by Sanju Nivangune

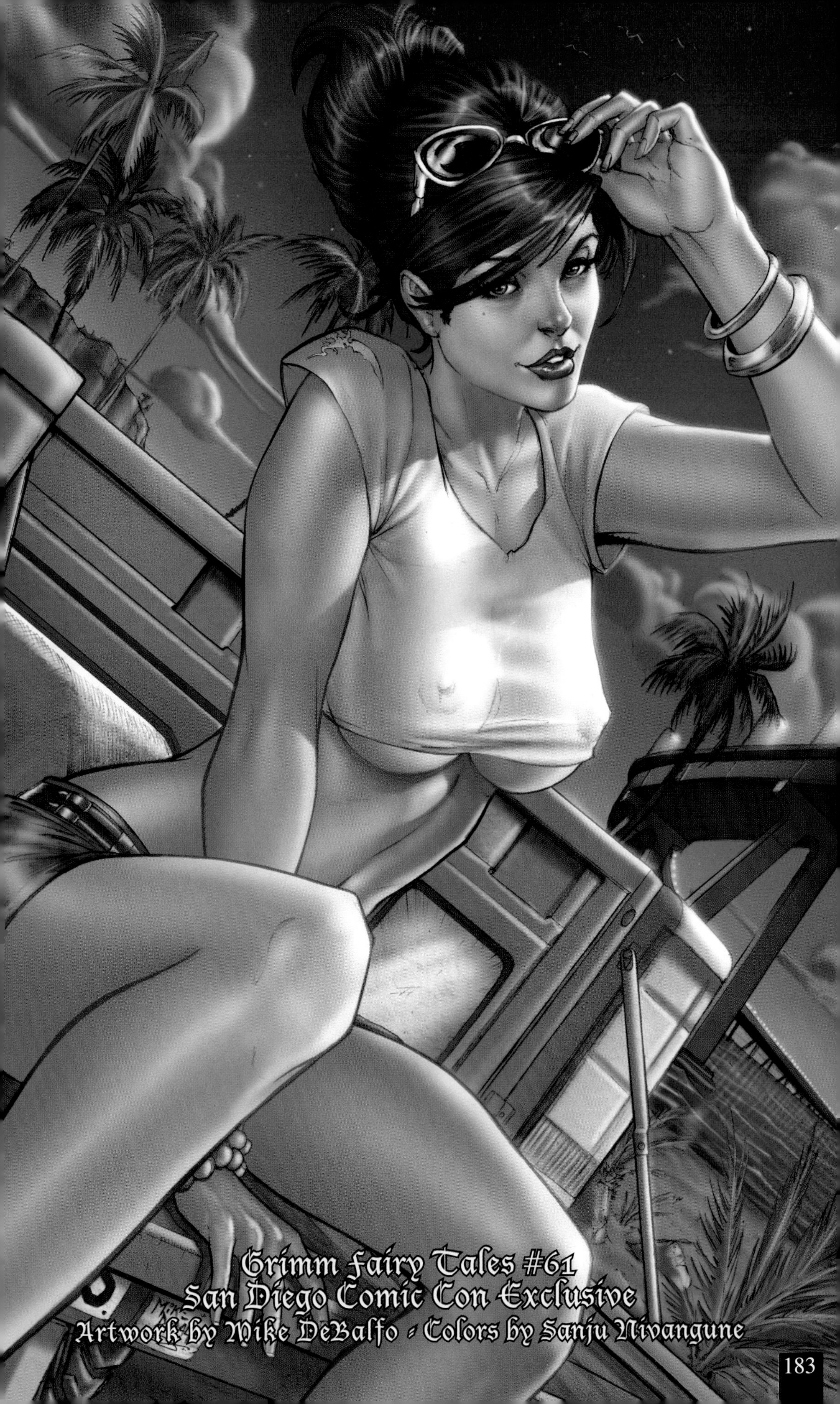

Grimm Fairy Tales #61
San Diego Comic Con Exclusive
Artwork by Mike DeBalfo - Colors by Sanju Nivangune

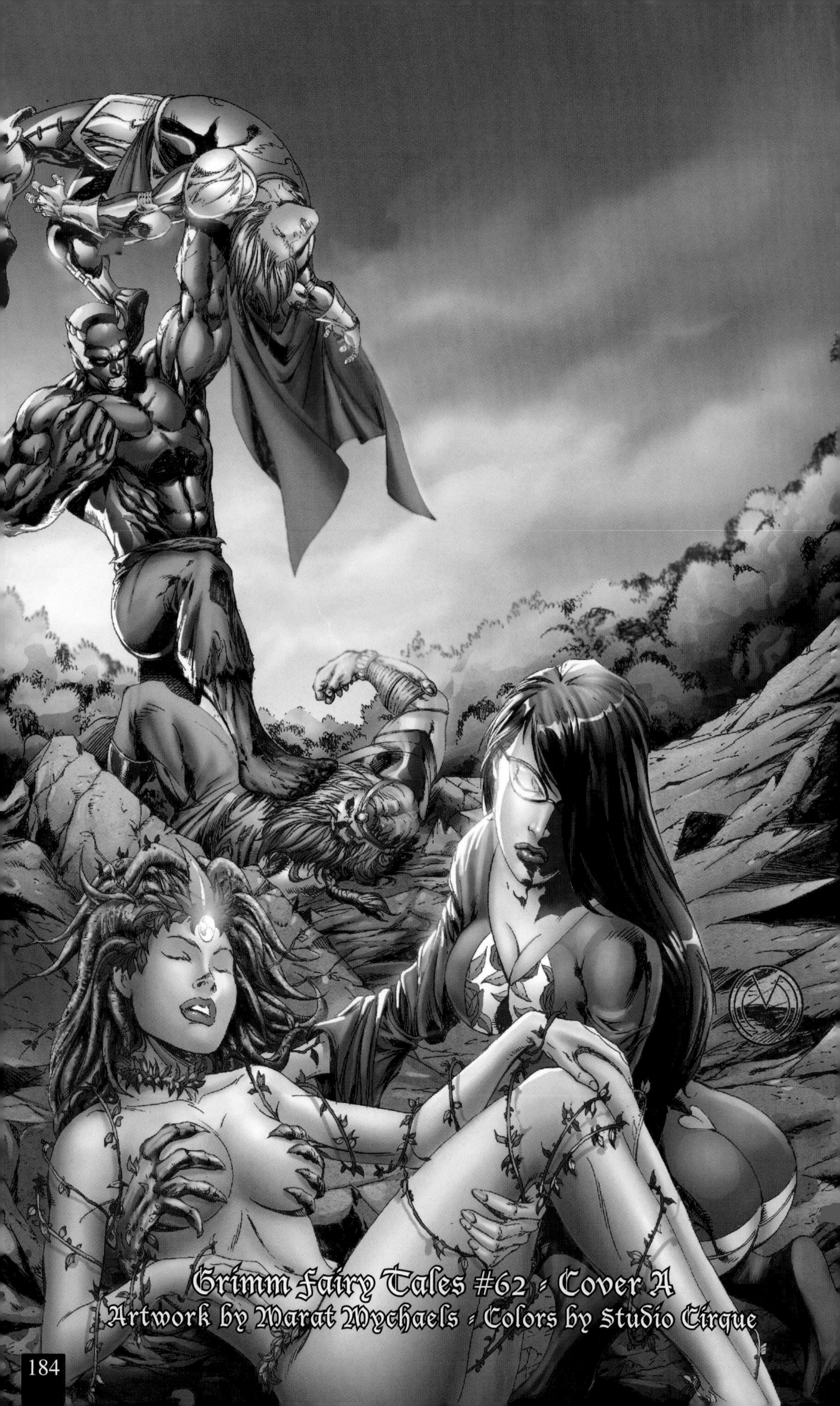

Grimm Fairy Tales #62 - Cover A
Artwork by Marat Mychaels - Colors by Studio Cirque

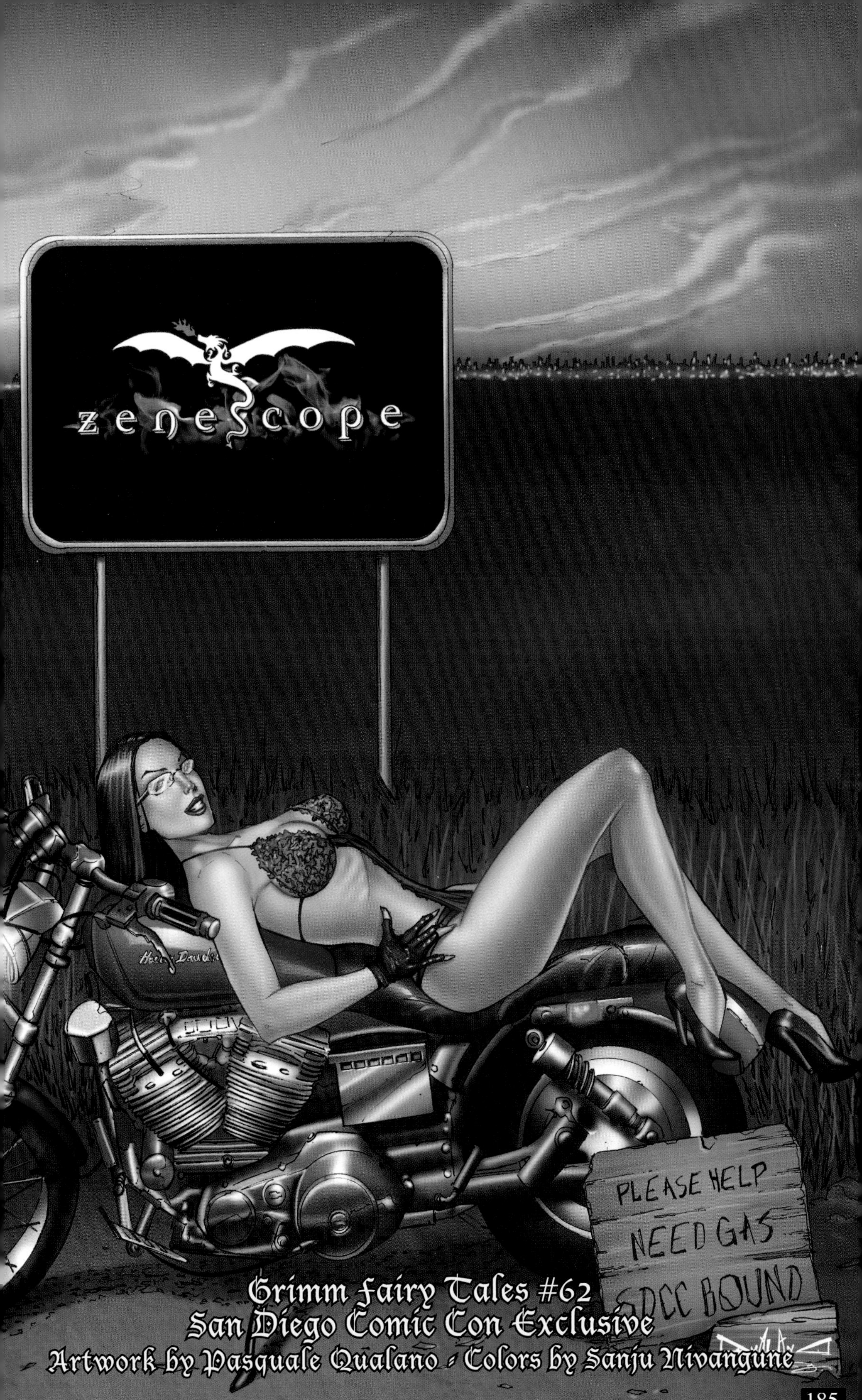
zenescope
PLEASE HELP
NEED GAS
SDCC BOUND

Grimm Fairy Tales #62
San Diego Comic Con Exclusive
Artwork by Pasquale Qualano - Colors by Sanju Nivangune

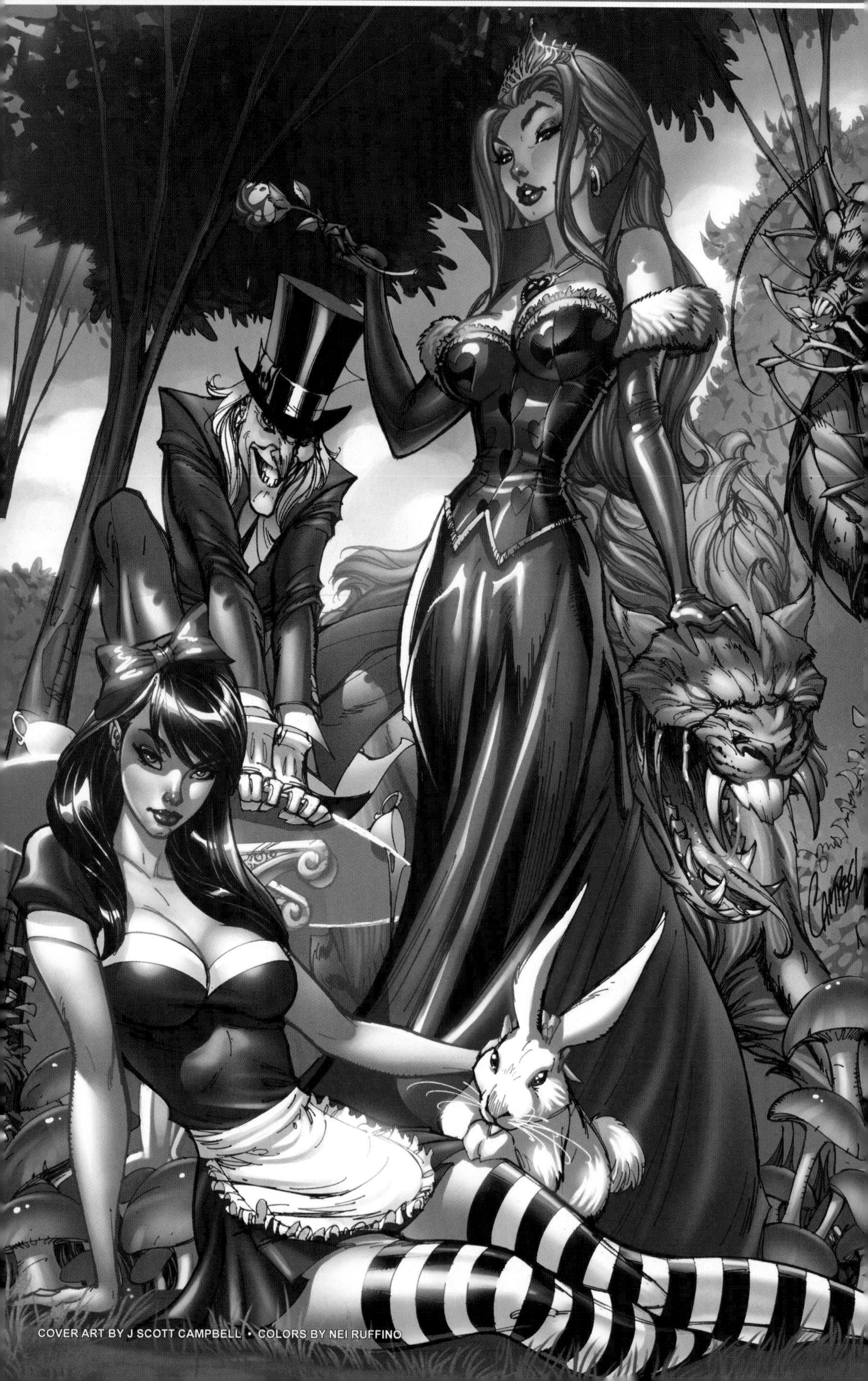

COVER ART BY J SCOTT CAMPBELL • COLORS BY NEI RUFFINO

Wonderland

WONDERLAND IS A PRESENT DAY, HORROR-FILLED REINVENTION OF THE CLASSIC ALICE'S ADVENTURES IN WONDERLAND; A CLASSIC STORY RETOLD FOR A NEW GENERATION OF READER. ALICE IS NO LONGER THE LITTLE GIRL YOU ONCE KNEW. YEARS HAVE PASSED SINCE SHE TOOK HER TRIP DOWN THE MYSTERIOUS RABBIT HOLE. A GROWN WOMAN NOW, WITH A HUSBAND AND KIDS OF HER OWN, ALICE HAS EVERYTHING A PERSON COULD WANT...ASIDE FROM HER SANITY. NOW ALICE'S DAUGHTER, CALIE, WILL BE FORCED TO TAKE THE SAME JOURNEY AS HER MOTHER DID YEARS BEFORE. IT'S A JOURNEY INTO A PLACE FULL OF HORROR WHERE THE ADVENTURES OF ALICE WERE ONLY THE BEGINNING.

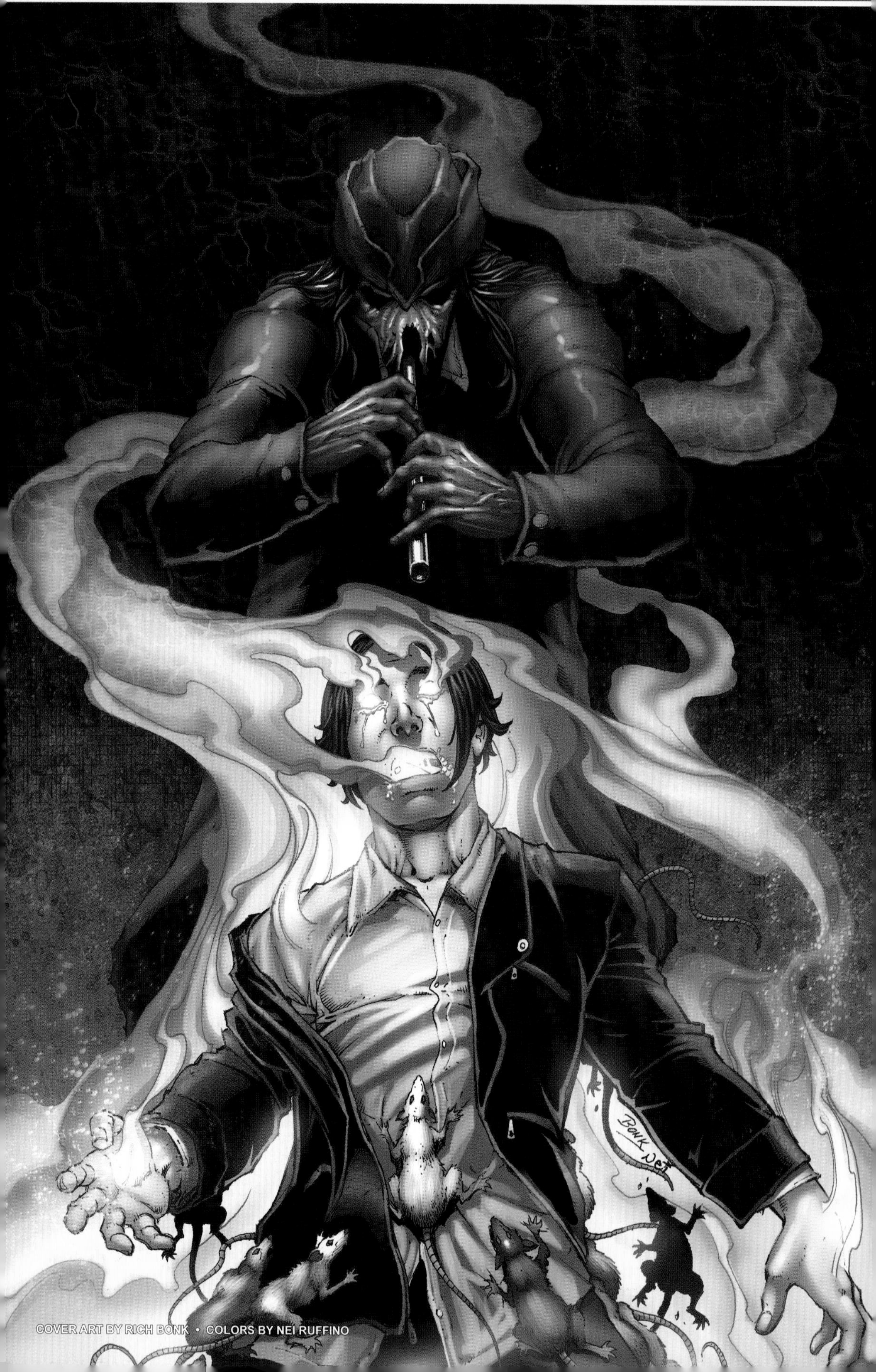
BONK NEI

COVER ART BY RICH BONK • COLORS BY NEI RUFFINO

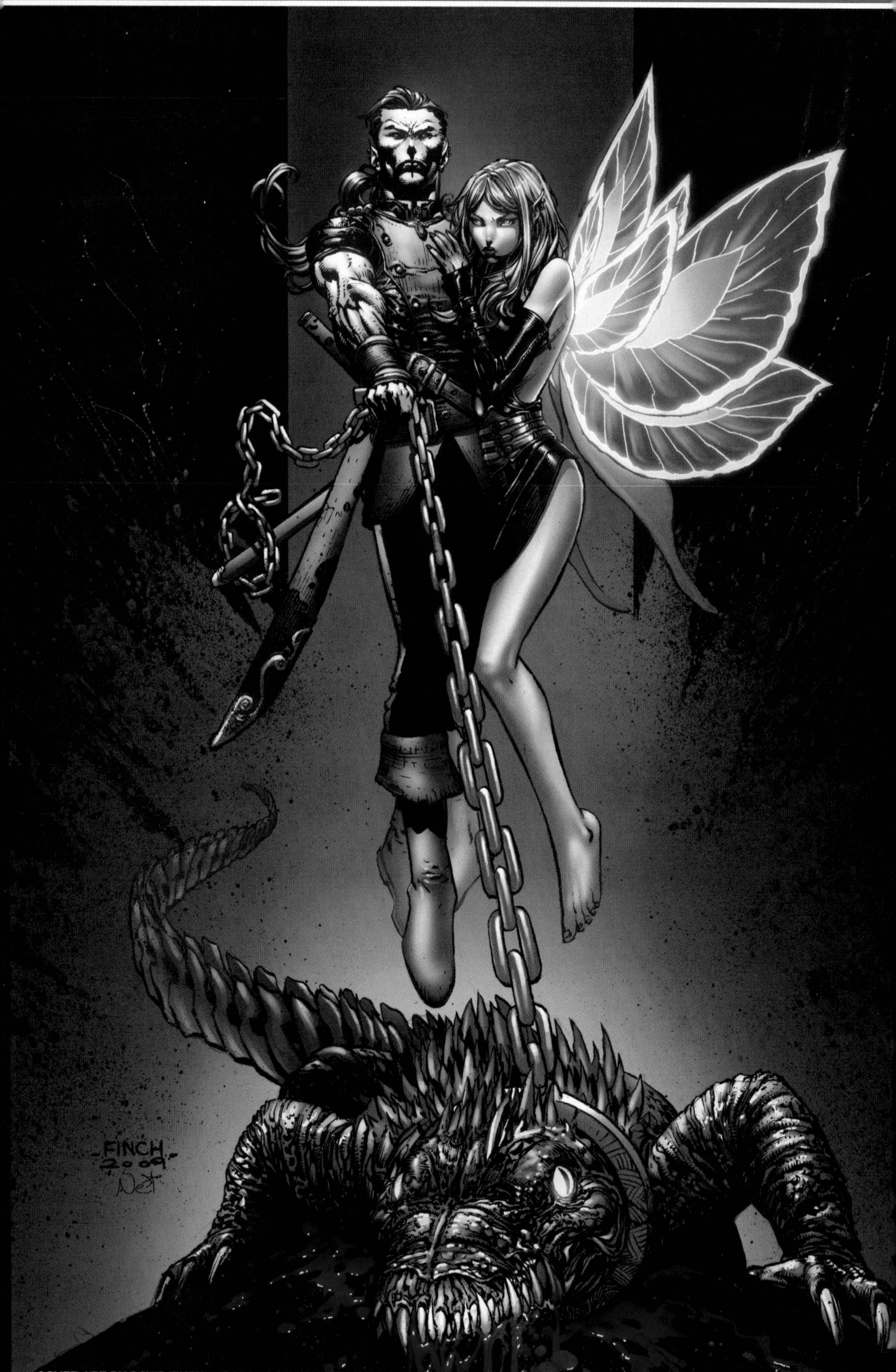
FINCH 2009

COVER ART BY DAVID FINCH • COLORS BY NEI RUFFINO